Ferdinand Lundberg

THE COMING WORLD TRANSFORMATION

Books by Ferdinand Lundberg

IMPERIAL HEARST: A Social Biography

AMERICA'S 60 FAMILIES

MODERN WOMAN: The Lost Sex
(with M. L. F. Farnham)

TREASON OF THE PEOPLE

THE COMING WORLD TRANSFORMATION

THE COMING
WORLD
TRANSFORMATION

Ferdinand Lundberg

DOUBLEDAY & COMPANY, INC.

Garden City, New York

1963

Grateful acknowledgment is made to the following publishers for permission to include copyrighted excerpts which appear in this volume:

Basic Books, Inc., for an excerpt from *The Logic of Scientific Discovery* by Karl Popper.

Engineering and Mining Journal (July 17, 1926) for an adaptation of the chart on iron ore reserves.

Harcourt, Brace & World, Inc., for selections from *The Structure of Science* by Ernest Nagel.

J. B. Lippincott Company for excerpts adapted from Deasy et al.: *The World's Nations,* 1958, by J. B. Lippincott Company by permission of the publisher.

The Noonday Press for material from Condorcet's *Progress of the Human Mind,* translated by June Barracloush, and by permission of Weidenfeld & Nicolson Limited.

We none of us can help hoping that when anyone undertakes to prophesy the future, the facts will prove him wrong.

—SIR CHARLES DARWIN

When all the logical consequences of an innovation are presented simultaneously, the shock to habits is so great that men tend to reject the whole, whereas, if they had been invited to take one step every ten or twenty years, they could have been coaxed along the path of progress without much resistance.

—BERTRAND RUSSELL

CONTENTS

FOREWORD

The primary purpose of this book is practical: to predict on a systematic and theoretically justifiable basis future developments of basic and general importance. Europe and North America occupy the foreground, with South America, Asia, and Africa coming in for supporting attention. No claim is suggested that the whole of the future, or even the whole of the future within a certain limited period, is being predicted. But it is indeed claimed that the skeletal outline of a large segment of that part of the future people in general are most concerned about—the cultural, social, political, and economic—is being predicted within limits of sufficient preciseness to be significant and to merit considered attention.

The maximum time range of most of the predictions ventured is 150 years, or about five conventional generations. Here and there some predictions of longer range are ventured. But the fact that approximately 150 years is the limit for most of my predictions does not mean that the world must wait for precisely 150 years to see all of them wholly or partially realized. Many should be fulfilled wholly or partially in shorter, although precisely undetermined, intervals of time.

But though the central purpose of this book is practical, as I have remarked, the very nature of the project inevitably raises important theoretical questions, particularly of a logical, psychological, and cultural nature. Man, we know, has an insatiable desire to see into the future, to read as much of his fate as seems possible. But this desire, as the mythic past shows, is in itself no guarantee that he can do so.

Is it at all possible to predict the future or any part of it? If it is possible, what means are available with which to predict? Again, is there any method or point of view to guide our predicting? If there is, what is this method? And does the method, whatever it may be, apply to an unlimited or to a restricted range of subject matter? If restricted, what are the restrictions?

Such formidable questions and related ones are raised in the body of the book and in appendices, although most effort, as I have said, is given to making specific predictions. And such specific predictions will themselves throw light on the methods used.

                                                                    F. L.

THE COMING WORLD TRANSFORMATION

CHAPTER I

HORIZONS AND PERSPECTIVES

Man's world, according to a mass of suggestive evidence, hesitates uncertainly today on the threshold of some of the most spectacular changes ever seen. Root-and-branch changes that can be foreseen as highly probable will take place within an interval of 150 years, or five generations, at most. The beginnings of many of these changes will be clearly visible within from twenty-five to fifty years. Some are coming into view even now.

The changes to come, I contend, will make those witnessed in the momentous historical periods 1500–1650, 1650–1800 and 1800–1950 appear by contrast far less remarkable. Many changes to come, it may be granted, will be no more than the further effects and extensions of changes and innovations in these earlier eventful periods. For the changes to come, representing an accumulation and intricate complication of influences, will be a transforming climax to what has happened between 1500 and the present.

Already the time under consideration has been given its peculiarly appropriate name: the Atomic Age. But noting this should not be taken to suggest that the nuclear and thermonuclear developments of physics uniquely provide the key to understanding the time of transformation that is coming—that time, indeed, that is already here. For in the period into whose nearer reaches we have already slipped many necessary decisions deferred and evaded in the past must finally be made. It is far from the case that the advent of nuclear power is the only new development, or even the central development, that must be reckoned with in the future period with which we are concerned.

One tremendous development of significance to everybody, a development that closely links the periods 1650–1800 and 1800–1950, is commonly known as the Industrial Revolution. In the long run it will no doubt be fully as consequential as the Agricultural Revolution of some 10,000–12,000 years ago that took man out of the grazing and hunting stages and made possible the prized phenomenon known as civilization. Perhaps the Industrial Revolution will be even more crucial for man's ultimate fate. It has by no means yet run its world-wide course nor, apparently, has it yet attained its full technical range. Perhaps the Industrial Revolution, in the long run, will provide at least the basis for a civilization unmarred by the many atavisms and asymmetries of our own. If it does—that, I take it, will be genuine progress.

But very probably the advent of printing, not widely practiced in Europe until 1500, was a much more fundamental influence for change than was the steam-driven engine, which became the prime tool of the Industrial Revolution and the forerunner of the Technical Revolution of 1800–1950. It was printing that disseminated the ideas, new and old, that nurtured the kind of concentrated ingenuity that made possible the Industrial Revolution. Printing made generally available not only the ancient learning but also the hitherto scattered reports on the newest emerging techniques in various fields of endeavor. It stimulated men to develop their ideas with a view to communicating them to readers unknown. Printing, in other words, was itself an incitement to creation and made possible for the first time the increasingly effective socialization of intelligence.[1]

But while the full human effects of the Agricultural Revolution have no doubt now all revealed themselves, only some effects have been disclosed of the profound Cultural Revolution fostered by printing, the subsequent Scientific Revolution, and the more familiar Industrial and Technical Revolutions. Most such effects, contrary to common belief, are yet to come into view. As far as changes in the world of the industrial era are concerned, the surface has hardly been scratched. And it is with these as yet unrealized, pending changes that we are mainly concerned in this book.

It was with the very late advent of civilization in man's career on earth that change became most rapid. Progressively the process of change has been accelerating, thus periodically upsetting a creature of settled habit such as man. If by way of illustration we take each hour on a standard clock face as equal to 100,000 years of estimated human history, then the 8000-odd years assigned to civilized man occupies only the last five minutes of a twelve-hour circuit. Except for speech, rudimentary agriculture, fire, the stone hammer, the lever, the spear, and cooking, almost all notable human inventions belong in this five-minute period—the wheel, domestication of animals, irrigation, cities, writing, literature, ships, trade, religion, computation, philosophy, machinery, and science.

And while slowly accelerating change has continually been a marked feature of civilization, the most extraordinary change has been seen in the past 450 years—or in the last twenty seconds of the twelve-hour clock circuit representing man's time on earth. For in this latter, kaleidoscopic period have occurred the spread of printing with movable type; the creation of nearly all of mathematics; the establishment and swift growth of physical science and power technology; the rise of mechanized industry and the proliferation of large cities; the emergence of huge nation-states; the development of global trade; the perfection of advanced metallurgy; the use in profusion of fuels such as coal, petroleum, and uranium; the wholesale production of electricity, vast, suicidal, mechanized wars, and the fantastic multiplication of the once scarce human species through the placing of medical technology on a scientific basis.

With reference to our clock model, then, predicting for the next 150 years amounts only to foretelling what is to happen in the next seven seconds of man's twelve-hour career. Owing to the fact of acceleration, however, these seven seconds (150 years) promise to produce far more social and cultural change than did the preceding twenty seconds (450 years).

The ultimate impotence of traditionalism, or refusal to recognize the inevitability and inexorability of change, is emphasized by the acceleration of change as shown by the clock model. Ineffective in the past except by intensifying difficulties attendant upon change, traditionalism will be equally ineffective, although perhaps just as troublesome, in the looming future. For traditionalism, despite naïve attempts at justifying itself philosophically, reduces to little more than an attitude of frozen, terrified rigidity in fluid situations that rationally require attitudes of flexibility and adaptability.

No doubt it is the sensing by many people of tremendous impending changes that lends special interest at this time to the whole subject of the future and has led to a wide readership for a host of books and magazine articles in this century dealing with aspects, mainly technological, of the future. But the technological aspects, it can easily be shown, are at this stage the least novel and actually serve to distract attention from the prospective changes of most profound interest.

What we are primarily concerned about in *The Coming World*

Transformation are those deeper and, humanly speaking, more affecting aspects of the future that will be part of the immediate daily experience of what is variously referred to as the man in the street, the plain man, and the ordinary person. Very few people in the next 150 years are going to travel about through space, work for space-travel enterprises, or live at missile-launching stations. Our area of central interest extends far beyond technological changes to social and cultural changes—that is, to changes of an economic, political, governmental or regulatory, educational, familial, recreational, scientific, religious, and ideological character. It extends, in other words, to the spheres wherein people in general are said to *live*. Also considered in these pages are changes in relation to what are regarded as social problems, which involve more or less individual and social disorganization and deterioration. Will such problems be solved? If they are, what forms will the solutions probably assume?

Expected Technical Developments

Confidently scheduled technological developments, commonplaces now to attentive newspaper readers, include the following:

1. The gradual emergence in the advanced economies of an industrial network of automatic and semiautomatic offices and factories— that is, automation. A substantial beginning toward this development has already taken place in a number of industries. The heavily manned factory is, it would seem, a historically transitory phenomenon. Factory workers, indeed, may become almost as rare as blacksmiths and millers. By reason of the same causes the proportion of office workers will also be severely reduced.

2. The harnessing of sun power, or solar radiation, adding greatly to the energy sources of the earth.

3. The harnessing also of the process of thermonuclear fusion, making available truly unlimited energy and providing the basis for a much higher world standard of consumption.

4. The large-scale purification of sea water with the abundant new energy, itself perhaps derived in large part from water, thereby permitting the irrigation and cultivation of many present desert areas.

5. The development of an electric storage battery of much greater voltage than is now possible, allowing the operation of high-powered vehicles and tractors by means of batteries and electric motors rather

than internal combustion engines, for which fuel will in some 100 years be scarce.

6. The development through chemistry of hundreds of new useful compounds out of cheap and abundant common raw materials.

7. Greatly advanced methods of food production, including the far more efficient extraction of foods and non-food chemicals from the oceans. As far as the oceans are concerned, man is still largely in the hunting stage. He must still get around to *cultivating* the oceans, a step that may well lie beyond our 150-year range. But someday the oceans will no doubt be systematically cultivated and mined, like the land, if advanced or scientific man remains in being. A latter-day extension is possible, then, to the Agricultural Revolution, through the aid of the Technical and the Scientific Revolutions.

8. The development of an effective, low-cost contraceptive pill without side effects.

9. Some extensive influence over the weather, short of controlling it, by means of special techniques.

On the basis of already known scientific principles a mechanism or electronic device can right now be constructed for almost any terrestrial purpose short of providing perpetual motion or the achievement of immortality. It is no longer a question of thinking of some particular device. Special situations suggest the device in every case, and after the suggestion has been noted it becomes at once merely a question of feasibility. Inventions the public never heard about exist in profusion. They are found particularly in medical appliances, often a special invention for a single person. Mechanical and electronic inventions, indeed, can now be produced on order. In fact, no sooner does the idea occur to the inventor—like the idea of a typewriter that takes oral dictation and transcribes what is said into writing—than he actualizes it. In the words of Alfred North Whitehead, "The greatest invention of the Nineteenth Century was the art of inventing."

It is not difficult, applying known principles, to think up hundreds of new inventions. It would be tedious, however, to list technically possible new inventions, for all such inventions make use of principles already known. But although one cannot say that it is possible to develop telepathic devices, it would be a rash person who would assert that such devices are impossible. For before the invention of the telescope and the microscope the possibility of such power-conferring instruments had not been dreamed of.

So, although technical advance and invention need to be considered in probing the future, they are by no means the whole story. And factors other than the technical are involved—many factors, as will appear.

In passing, something to be noticed about men's tools and mechanisms—and man, in the words of Benjamin Franklin, is the "tool-making animal"—is that they are all extensions of his primordial capabilities and natural endowments. His mechanisms mirror and project man on a greatly magnified scale.

All tools and mechanisms for manufacturing (which literally means hand-making), molding, shaping, connecting, and lifting are extensions of the hand. Those for carrying or transportation are extensions of the feet and hands, although in the airplane man has also given himself wings. The intercontinental ballistics missile is obviously but a latter-day extension of the hand-propelled slingshot, a symbol of man's transformation from pygmy to giant.

The microscope, camera, stellar telescope, eyeglasses, searchlight, radarscope, X ray, electronscope, and television are obvious extensions of the eye. Writing, printing, the telegraph, telephone, and radio are extensions of both the voice and sense of hearing. Extensions of physical taste, touch, and smell are alone lacking in this seemingly inexorable process of development, although taste and smell are unquestionably supplemented by chemical analysis to detect poisonous and noxious substances. However, the range of things pleasant to taste and smell has been enormously increased through man's creative prowess.

Now the extension of the brain, of intelligence, is at hand in high-speed electronic computing, data-processing apparatus. Such apparatus performs the work of intelligence by the combinatory evaluation in a short time of a great many tiny bits of information. The apparatus, in fact, is able to assimilate, retain, combine, and rapidly evaluate far more information than can hundreds of trained men working over a period of many years.

And such equipment is now being constructed so as to be able to apply its conclusions instantly to the feedback control of elaborate networks of manufacturing and operating mechanisms. We thus have thrown open to us the possibility of automatic or self-operated versions, in whole or in part, of the whole range of pre-existing tools and mechanisms. Entire factories, in brief, can be constructed and are indeed being constructed to carry on the process of manufacture with a minimum utilization of human hands and moment-to-moment human decisions.

While the new computers and control devices add enormously to the facility and speed with which complicated operations can be carried out, in basic principle they are not new, extending as they do back to low-speed gear mechanisms developed in the seventeenth century by Pascal and Leibnitz. It is in speed and great number of factors that can be handled that today's electronic computers excel. But other devices also exist that extend and enhance human brain power. Memory, for example, has been reinforced by the phonograph, electronic tape, camera, and other visual and auditory recording devices. Enormous "memory" files can now be developed in combination with the computing machines.

Man's functional environment has also been greatly expanded. Daylight has been brought into the night by means of the electric lamp, thus greatly increasing man's effective day and, with it, actually his life. While fire and heating have long modified cold climates in man's favor, temperature modification with air-cooling apparatus may now be extended to hot climates.

So we see modern man as both a titan and, in many ways, a magician whose discretionary intelligence is not always immediately equal to the responsibilities inexorably created by his many mechanisms. He can stride a continent or an ocean in a very few hours. In his office or home is a device that will in his absence record any incoming oral messages. He can be reached for a conversation in a few minutes while he is far away. He can talk to his home at any minute from almost any part of the earth. Soon he will no doubt be able to see whomever he is talking to and he can then hold a face-to-face conversation with anybody in any part of the world. An extensive range of traditional human diseases and ailments is now curable, often quickly and cheaply, and more will unquestionably become curable. Although many human terrors remain, many have been removed. Man's worst remaining enemy is undeniably himself. For in his never long absent irrational rages and moods of collective fright he now possesses the power to destroy not only entire civilizations but also all representatives of his own species.

Preliminary Conspectus of Changes to Come

But now, leaving until later the theoretical basis on which our predictions are made, it seems advisable to sketch in a preliminary way some of the changes that seem likely to take place in man's sociocultural future. The changes predicted, it may be said, depend upon a period of relative peace in the world. All our calculations would be upset, it is evident, by the advent of a general thermonuclear war. Localized wars would probably not distort them by much. In view of the lively apprehensions of precisely such a thermonuclear war, it may seem to some readers that we have introduced a big exception. As to this it may be said that it is perfectly scientific to stipulate the conditions under which a prediction holds. Again, if the fact that a thermonuclear war will invalidate our predictions is taken as making them irrelevant, then all enterprises of contemporary man that require tranquil times are equally irrelevant. If there is to be a general thermonuclear war, there is surely nothing more misguided than building skyscrapers, power dams, hospitals, and new cities as in the Soviet Union and the United States.

As to whether there will be a thermonuclear war—what prediction can be made in this connection? An absolutely certain conditional prediction can be made (and such are the predictions of science), namely: if rational counsels prevail in the major governments, there will be no thermonuclear war. But *will* rational counsels prevail? As to this question, obviously, no sound prediction can be made. This, however, can be said: governments in the past have usually at least *tried* to behave rationally, to make decisions in the light of their understanding of the evidence. Where they have usually gone wrong is in their interpretation of the evidence. What the thermonuclear scientists have done is to force upon governments a new, highly volatile factor for rational consideration. But just how governments will interpret this factor under varying conditions can clearly not be foretold. All one can do is to surmise, keeping in mind that after experiments with it in World War I the leading governments never again resorted to gas warfare. Not even the demented Adolf Hitler waged gas warfare, deterred no doubt by the fact that he knew there would be reprisals in kind, as there were reprisals in kind to his ruthless bombings of cities.

So our predictions are ventured on the assumption that there will not be thermonuclear missile warfare, at least not on a large scale.

Sociocultural change down through history has most often—though not solely—been indicated first in the economic sphere. And for this reason we will first consider the economic sphere. It is possible, however, for local change at least first to be political, as the example of Soviet Russia itself shows, contrary to the Marxist doctrine it purports to be guided by. But although Marx was clearly wrong in stipulating that *local* change first shows itself in an alteration of local economic affairs in every case, he read history correctly in that *general* sociocultural change is preceded by economic change. Even in Soviet Russia, where much change has been wrought by purely political decision, it would have been impossible for the political managers to decide to industrialize the country if a large part of the world had not already been industrialized. Modern science and the technology developed around the steam engine were not brought into being by any political decision, nor was the system of trade known as the business system. Political decisions were in fact later forced into being by these developments. Where forced or politically induced industrialization has taken place, as in Russia and China, it has been resorted to in order to avoid increasing economic and political subservience to the industrialized parts of the world. So it is indeed a fact that economic and technical development in the outside world played a role in the decisions of Russia and China to industrialize. In other words the economic factor did, as Marx in fact held, precede and influence the political development, although not in the precise way he envisaged.

In any event, and whether Marx was right or wrong, we shall look at economic innovations first. Certainly technological changes as they are put into operation first affect the economic institution of society most perceptibly. Long before people's lives were altered by television, for example, laboratories and factories and staffs to man them first had to be established. The economic institution, of course, consists of the formal system of interrelationships and instruments in which men put forth their efforts to gain their livelihoods and to sustain customary standards of consumption.

Any accepted technological innovation affects the economic system at once as an item of producers' goods—that is, as something to be used in producing other goods—or as an item of consumers' goods, which directly induces satisfaction in its use. The development of new energy sources, such as nuclear power, argues for some persons that industrialization will soon spread over a very large area of the earth. Such an extension of the industrial system on a large scale is already under way in Soviet Russia and seems likely, in a widely shared view, to take place also in China, India, large sections of South America, and extensive parts of Africa. In brief, regions that until recently figured in the world's economic system solely as producers of raw materials now seem destined to produce manufactured goods for their own populations and for exchange on the world market. The kind of rapid development that has taken place in Japan in the past eighty-five years will, it is anticipated, take place pretty much throughout the world.

But, while industrialization will no doubt spread, the prospect that China, India, Africa, and South America will be industrial counterparts of Europe, including Russia, or the United States in 150 years seems to me extremely dim. For while industrialization makes progress in these regions, the industrial systems of Europe and the United States, according to all available evidence, will make further progress. One great difference between industrialization in Europe and the United States and industrialization of the kind that is now being pressed in Russia and China is that in Europe and the United States it developed spontaneously. In Russia, China, and elsewhere it must be imposed and forced by decision from above. That a political decision can be the prelude to industrialization the world has seen in the cases of Japan and of Russia. But many factors impede, if they do not entirely rule out, industrialization by decision imposed from above— shortages of raw materials, as in the case of Japan, more or less covert opposition by a superstitious peasant population, passive and defeatist attitudes toward the world held by the general population, as in Asia, natural barriers such as unfavorable climate, inconvenient terrain, and the like. What is often overlooked in considering the development of Europe and the United States is that they were aided by extremely favorable natural and historical conditions. Invasions seldom ran from Europe eastward but much more often from Asia into Europe. And although Africa was far nearer Europe than North or South America, Europeans did not migrate in any numbers to Africa. The reason for this is that conditions in Africa, as in Asia, by and large were relatively uninviting.

But probably the most important reason for believing that Russia will be the last large country to undergo successful *full* industrialization is that so much of the world's primitive materials in the form of fuels and metals has already been used up. Industrialization now involves more advanced techniques and special fuels that require highly complicated processes for utilization. Russia alone appears to have relatively large quantities of available prime materials left. This is not so true of China and India.

As Sir Charles Darwin points out, half of the coal burned in the history of the world was burned in the United States between 1920 and 1958; what is considered an optimistic estimate holds that the earth's coal at the present rate of consumption will be exhausted in 500 years—yet consumption is increasing. Petroleum is expected to be exhausted, at the rate of present usage, in a century. Half of all the metal mined in the history of the earth has been dug up in the forty-odd years since 1918, and available supplies of lead, tin, and copper, all necessary to an advanced technology, are so low that the outlook for laggards in industrialization is extremely bleak. "So I forecast," says Darwin, "that at the end of this century industrialization will not have spread very greatly over the less developed parts of the world."[2]

Nor is there any present evidence that the century from A.D. 2000 to 2100 will find the undeveloped countries more creative industrially. The excessive and superstitious populations of countries such as India and China are themselves barrier to sufficient capital formation, which can only come from surplus. And there can be little surplus where all effort must go to mere subsistence. So the backward nations will remain relatively backward.

Technical developments, it has been demonstrated, induce changes at first readily visible in their impact on the economic system. But although it is possible to anticipate changes, and extensive changes, that may be induced by specific technical developments such as automation and the harnessing of nuclear and thermonuclear reactions, what must not be overlooked is the general impact on the western nations of the *total* technical development of the past 450 years. These developments manifest themselves in the Occident as part of a slow-moving glacier that gains momentum with the passage of time. And it is because of the existence of this technical glacier, gradually gaining in momentum, that one is justified in making the general prediction that change will be much greater and more rapid in the next 150 years than in the past 150 years. The human scene in the year A.D. 2100, in other words, will differ from the human scene of 1950 far more than the scene of 1950 differs from A.D. 1800. To a citizen of

1950 the scene of the year A.D. 2100 would, in fact, be unrecognizable.

By way of a preliminary view of what the scene will be like in A.D. 2100 let us, then, first consider economic developments.

The Realm of Economics

Two kinds of property ownership, governmental and private, now prevail in the world and, with qualifications, seem likely to prevail for the next 150 years, the only issue being over how extensive a section of the world each kind of ownership will hold sway. What appears to be most likely, however, is a mixed form of ownership in each region. My prediction therefore is that, strange as it may seem, there will be private ownership in some degree restored in Soviet Russia and Soviet China if only in order to delegate more individual responsibility in some areas of the economy; and that there will be much more governmental ownership achieved than there is now in Europe and the United States. Western Europe, for example, at present has much more government ownership in the economic system than has the United States. The determining factor in deciding what sort of ownership shall be permitted in specific areas will be that of maximum utility.

But whether the ownership is defined as public or private, it will in nearly all cases be collective. Already collective ownership predominates in the American industrial economy, made necessary by the need for massive infusions of capital. There are, for example, reported to be some twelve to fifteen million stockholders in the United States; there are also many more individual owners of real estate, government and corporate bonds. Many of these owners are themselves institutions—educational and other endowments, investment trusts, banks and mutual and joint stock insurance companies. Including bank depositors and those in mutual insurance schemes (the latter predominating over joint stock insurance enterprises), ownership in the United States is diffused evidently among more than half the adult population. This is not to suggest that the ownership stake is even fairly equally shared, for ownership in many and perhaps most cases involves only a small stake and a relatively small number of owners (about 1 per cent of population) still possess a very large stake (about 28 per cent of assets). But ownership in the United

States is, for the most part, collective, and this collective ownership, through the medium of mutual insurance schemes, savings deposits, and the rapidly growing mutual investment funds, represents a stake for each participant in an extensive cross section of the economy.

Whether ownership is governmental or private in the future it will, in any event, be collective, and the collective stake even in private ownership, according to all evidence, will include a far larger section of the population than at present. As to very large individual owner-ship stakes in the long-range future of private ownership, these will unquestionably be ruled out by law. In brief, large private fortunes, it is my prediction, will be outlawed. Already in the United States and many European countries the tax laws are so drawn as to make increasingly difficult either the transfer of large fortunes through in-heritance or the accumulation of large fortunes out of dispropor-tionately large incomes or speculative windfalls. Loopholes no doubt exist in these laws, but they will from time to time be plugged.

Management control over these ownership stakes, however, will always, and necessarily, remain concentrated—in one central man-agement where government ownership prevails, in a number of sub-sidiary managements where private ownership is the rule.

Ownership apart, the world trend, including the trend in the United States, is obviously toward larger and larger productive units, both in agriculture and in industry. Concentration is taking place in function and management control as collectivization is in ownership. Although the United States has what are called anti-trust and anti-monopoly laws, what is of especial interest in this connection is the extent to which industrial concentration and collectivization have taken place despite these laws. As two authorities on this subject say, "The periodic laxity in antitrust-law enforcement, notably in the late 1890s and the 1920s, the virtual emasculation of the law as ap-plied to mergers under the judicially established rule of reason, the popular indifference to the aggrandizement of big business in the period of general apathy that followed World War I, and the com-plaisant attitude of Congress as shown in the grant of a long series of exemptions from antitrust prohibitions, all combined to concentrate economic power in an economy that had traditionally relied on de-centralized decision making for the protection of the public interest."[3]

Mergers in the United States, fewer in the 1930s and during World War II, again made themselves massively apparent after the second war had ended. The influences toward concentration were far more urgent and effective than the diffuse, halfhearted opposition to them. The anti-trust anti-monopoly ideology in the United States, although it may flare up from time to time, in the long run, it may be confidently predicted, will be ineffective in stemming the tide toward large, monopolistic industrial concentrations.

The results of historical processes are rarely symmetrical. Loose ends are continually left lying around. But in general in the United States and in Europe, as well as in Russia and elsewhere, single large units are going to constitute each industry in virtually all cases. For the sake of preserving some outmoded ideology, as in the United States, there may formally exist subunits with different nominal identities. But the direction will be centralized through tight agreements, as in many cases at present.

Just prior to World War II in the United States "in each of the following industries one corporation was either the sole seller or controlled the entire supply: virgin aluminum, shoe machinery, bottle machinery, optical glass, nickel, magnesium, and molybdenum. Four producers or less accounted for from 75 to 100 per cent, by value, of the product of industries producing one third, by value, of all manufactured products. Fifty-seven per cent of the value of all manufactured products was accounted for by industries in which the four largest producers, when there were that many, turned out half the total value."[4]

The number of producing units in an industry, economists are well aware, does not in itself reflect the degree of centralization. Industries with many producing units may be as effectively centralized as an industry under the monopoly control of a single unit. Such unity of policy in multiunit industries is achieved through trade-association agreements and trade-union contracts. The U.S. home-building industry, for example, although it has a few large materials suppliers at the top, is still centered on thousands of small contractors and workmen in the field. The contractors, however, through the existence of trade associations, present a national united front to home buyers as to quality within certain price ranges, styles of building, contractual provisions and the like. And behind the contractors stand the building-trades unions. The general effect of the combination is to maximize benefits for the sellers and to minimize benefits for the home buyers. It is, in brief, a winning game, economically, for the seller, a relatively losing game for the buyer.

In construction of private dwellings there have appeared since

World War II a number of large companies that construct prefabricated houses. An increasing large percentage of new construction is handled by these enterprises with consequent diminished demand on the small independent contractor. In trucking one views a similar panorama. Companies operating huge fleets of trucks are rapidly replacing the once numerous small operators of single vehicles.

In Europe, to be sure, there is hardly any anti-trust ideology at all and there is no strong sentiment against unification, concentration, and cartelization. In Russia each industry is governed by a central, governmentally-owned trust theoretically functioning in the public interest.

What of the future of this situation? No evidence whatever bears out the prospect that there will be any rollback, that many small business units making their own decisions will ever again be seen in this civilization. Nor is there any evidence to suggest that the situation will stabilize and remain as at present. For all parts of the economy must adjust to doing business as the dominant parts do. The prospect, then, is for concentration to continue to take place until the process is completed.

All industries in the future with which we are concerned will be subject to central guidance, either formally or informally and under either private or governmental auspices. Agriculture, still widely thought to be under the independent guidance of tens of thousands of private farmers, confronts us in fact with an industry that is subject increasingly to policy-making centralized, in the United States, in the national government. Farmers are directed in what they may plant and in how much of each commodity they may plant. They are also subsidized. In effect, each industry will in the future be subject to centralized guidance and control and in some cases, such as metallurgy, clusters of industries will most probably be under centralized guidance and control.

Turning now to another aspect, with the heavily manned factory or production unit becoming obsolete though increasing automation, what will happen to the millions of persons now employed in manufacturing? Will the work week be reduced to twenty hours or less in order to share the work, as some persons predict? Will the populace be burdened with enforced leisure it is unable to make constructive use of?

Neither massive chronic unemployment nor the twenty-hour week is to be expected in a fully collectivized economy making full use of automation. For new employment opportunities will be created both on higher technical levels and in mushrooming service enterprises. The number of the latter, skilled and unskilled, will be greatly increased. The growing complexity of the economy obviously will make stronger demands for highly trained and educated personnel, with consequent stimulating effects on the educational system. Far more teachers per capita will be required than at present, and teaching is one service enterprise that will be greatly expanded by the new developments. New services will be developed in great profusion, mostly under government direction.

The general effects of automation on the educational system, particularly the still embryonic branch of adult education, will be tremendously stimulating; but automation, in eliminating many purely routine tasks, will certainly serve to draw a line more pronounced than ever between the skilled and the unskilled, the educated and the uneducated. The line will become increasingly sharp between the more educable and the less educable.

The class lines in the future we are concerned with will be cultural rather than economic. For in the economic sphere the tendency will be increasingly toward equalization. The physically and mentally infirm and demoralized will be supported, work-free, at rather high minimal standards, although at lower real costs to society than at present.

There is, to be sure, much more to be said about the socioeconomic situation of the future but it must be left to later chapters.

The Political Structure

Technical changes induce economic changes. Economic changes bring political changes in their train. This is surely a general law of social development.

What we are witnessing today, even in the United States, is a recentralization of government power following upon the decentralizing movement that began in the eighteenth century. Decentralization took place in opposition to more or less arbitrary autocratic power, which with increasing economic development had become more and more burdensome and anachronistic. Society had become too complex to put up any longer with pleasure-oriented egocentric royal courts and a hereditary nobility.

Decentralization was most typically expressed in the gradual diffusion of political power throughout the populace by means of the popular franchise. Whereas those who wanted power and special favors under the autocratic regimes were obliged to flatter kings and their ministers, they were obliged, under the new so-called democratic dispensation, to flatter and woo the general public and its spokesmen. For those who would manipulate it in their own special interests must approach the general public in much the same way they approached the royal courts: by blandishments and flatteries. Hence the extravagances of election campaigns.

Recentralization, now proceeding at a rapid pace, is a cause of alarm to many, who profess to see in it a possible return to serfdom. While it is always no doubt possible that a system of state serfs may appear, as in Soviet Russia and China, strongly centralized government does not necessarily imply serfdom and does not seem likely to produce it in what are now the open societies.

Anti-centralists tacitly impute to government inherent and original sinfulness. With Thomas Paine they hold that the least government is the best government and that government at best is a necessary evil. Here they rub elbows with the anarchists. Such a theory was no doubt useful as propaganda while there was a struggle against entrenched autocracy. And the theory has been useful to socially anarchic business interests anxious to avoid profit-restricting regulation by freely elected, non-autocratic republican government. But intrinsically the theory is without merit. It is particularly without merit in a world crisscrossed with supercharged forces requiring regulation.

Decentralized government has been relatively weak government. Owing to its relatively isolated geographical position, the United States has not needed strong government to ward off external enemies. But rapidly increasing social complexity with accompanying disorganization as well as the external threat of totalitarianism is forcing into being strong centralized government in the United States.

The dispersed and relatively weak federal system of government, then, is historically temporary and not, as its admirers claim, representative of an immutable principle of the best in government. Localism and regionalism, while possible and even necessary in days of poor transportation and communication, are no longer functional. Under present conditions they serve only to retard development and to make administration woefully inefficient.

In its early days the United States was often spoken of as an experiment, which it was. And while many of the presuppositions on which it was founded have been verified by experience, a number have been found false. The supposed overriding value of decentralization has been one of these. At their strongest the forces of decentralization were defeated in the civil war of 1861–65. Since then the tide of centralization has been gradually rising, so much so that it is even seen in the encroachments of the individual states on county and municipal government powers.

Within less than 150 years, then, government in the United States will be completely centered in the national capital. Local affairs will be run from an American version of the English Home Office under something like a Secretary for Internal Affairs. City managers and state executives will probably be appointed or declared eligible from civil service lists by the national government, although there may still be vestigial elections of purely symbolic governors, mayors, and town councilmen. Forms of federalism may still be maintained in deference to established prejudices, just as the forms of monarchy are still maintained in England. This is not to say that local sentiments will be disregarded or, in every instance, overruled. They will, however, be subject to modification in the light of national policy and needs.

Each of the present American states, it seems evident, is destined to become pretty much of an administrative department of the central government, just as counties and cities will be subdepartments.

To some persons imbued with the conventional ideology of our times this prospect no doubt seems fantastical, even nightmarish. But the transition to it, already under way, will be very gradual, almost unnoticed by the general population. Can the strongly centralized government visualized here be averted? Not, surely, by any mere decision to avert it. If, however, there were a general decision to remove the conditions making for centralization, conditions such as mechanization and electrification, economic concentration and development, the decision would be effective. But who can believe there will be such a decision? People in general believe, it is true, that one can constantly introduce new productive and operational mechanisms without altering the functions of government. In this, of course, they are profoundly mistaken. Government, if it is to remain government, must adjust itself to new conditions brought about by new techniques.

What of Government in Europe?

As to Europe, this can be said: if it is to maintain its political independence, it must unite its separate parts under a single government. The most likely initial kind of government for a united Europe appears to be the federal type, which will best serve to produce some unity within diversity. Many giant steps toward the unification of Europe have already been taken: the European coal and iron community, Euratom, and the European Common Market, which is really a new unified government.

The possible failure of Europe to unite makes an alternate prediction necessary. A disunited Europe would unquestionably in time be nibbled up by Soviet Russia. In the end, then, Europe will be united. And the only question is whether it will be under independent European or under Soviet Communist auspices. Eastern Europe has already been seized by Soviet Russia. But in the event of some internal Soviet political convulsion it could well become part of a unified independent Europe.

What of England? Would it become part of a united Europe? For a brief time it appeared that England would resist incorporation in such a scheme, preferring to play its role within the Commonwealth of Nations. But England has now decided to join. She will no longer play her traditional balance-of-power role in Europe.

While the evidence is strong that federalism must in time be abandoned in the United States, and in Europe must either be transitionally adopted or dominance surrendered to Soviet Russia, the fortunes of groupings like the British Commonwealth of Nations appears to be extremely dubious. The Commonwealth is far more a historical accident than the logical outcome of economic or other necessity. And while modern means of transportation and communication make possible such a widely scattered entity, it has little economic rationale or coherence. It could not, furthermore, be successfully defended alone. However, it can continue with the support of a United Europe and a United States.

Soviet Russia appears, on the evidence, established to remain for 150 years or more. The question about Soviet Russia, however, is not whether it will survive but whether it will be liberalized. Liberalization, if it were to take place, would have to be the outcome of something very much like a palace revolution. For there is no reason to suppose that the thoroughly terrorized, misinformed, confused and illusion-ridden populace would ever be able to revolt effectively. Indeed, in view of the new weapons available to modern governments, violent revolution in a large modern state is no longer conceivable. Large-scale revolution has been made impossible by modern science.

Russia, particularly in the nineteenth century, experienced contact with liberal ideas. The Bolshevik revolution, indeed, would not have been achieved without much preliminary liberalization. Whether a liberalization like that under Czarism will ever take place within the Soviet government, leading to peaceful rapprochement with the liberal West, is entirely problematic. Most current evidence indicates Soviet Russia is irrevocably committed to the role of a modern Sparta. But the necessity for cultivating science and technology in a modern industrialized country makes it also necessary for the ruling group to allow some measure of free intelligence—that is, liberal intelligence—to develop. Whether enough will be developed to modify a political totalitarianism that sees its most dreaded enemy in its own people is something that clearly cannot be foreseen.

Red China also seems likely to survive, but that China will in fifty years be able to industrialize to the extent that Russia has in a similar period of time seems impossible.

It is not only that China is more backward in economic development and trained personnel than Russia was in 1917; it has other handicaps such as insufficient exploitable natural resources of the kind vital to industrialization, inadequate transportation facilities in a land of great distances, and a written language that makes the teaching of modern techniques very difficult. China, however, it is often said, has manpower; but as far as physical tasks are concerned this is the most inefficient and highest-cost power in the world. China's great population, instead of being a help, is actually a hindrance. In the virtual absence of mechanized farming it must put nearly all its effort into feeding itself.

This at least can be safely said: if China ever does succeed in industrializing herself to the level now attained by Russia, it will be surely in a much longer period of time. In Russia the Chinese have an extremely problematic reed to lean upon.

In India a vast, ignorant and superstitious peasant population poses an obstacle similar to the population of China. India similarly lacks many of the natural resources to sustain a full-fledged industrial economy. Relative advantages in the Indian position consist of her three-sided access to world sea lanes, useful even for internal coastwise operations, and her British-trained civil service and technicians. But even with the joint cooperative technical assistance of the West in a forceful effort to industrialize, it is difficult to see how India—even in a long period of time such as 150 years—will so much as approximate the present industrial development of the West.

The suggestion has been made that lack of natural resources impedes full industrial development in China and India. This is not to say that resources are entirely lacking in either country. But they are neither sufficiently diversified, accessible, nor sufficiently massive in quantity. Europe, it may be objected, similarly lacks basic resources. The point is hardly well taken, however, for Europe for several centuries has had available to it the sea-borne virgin natural resources of the known world. On the basis of domestic resources mainly in iron, coal, stone, wood, and clay, together with its own technical prowess, Europe in some 450 years laid the foundation for its present complex industrial economy. That economy now draws upon a large part of the outside world for the entire range of known materials. The United States, although possessing probably the richest resources in the world, is far from self-sufficient and also draws upon the entire world for materials. It was European industrial techniques used by a European population developing rich natural resources that produced the American economic system. (Without these no amount of capitalism and no entrepreneurial genius could have accomplished anything.)

Thus Europe and the United States, in order to develop themselves to their present level, have drawn heavily upon the world's raw-material resources, leaving less available for newcomers.

The prospect as of now, then, for a variety of reasons, is that neither China nor India will be fully industrialized even in 150 years, although India—if it remains part of the world economy, from which China, like Russia, has largely excluded itself—may be somewhat farther along. Internal upheavals in a country such as China are of course possible. In general, the prospects of China are at the moment quite obscure. India maintains relations with the whole world; China is chained for the most part to Soviet Russia, which would no doubt like to keep in power a regime subserviently oriented toward Moscow. But Russia is having difficulty doing this even with a regime she assisted into power in China with a view to excluding Western Europe and the United States.

At the moment this is written an ideological rift between Russia and China appears to be widening. China, in emulation of Stalin's policy vis-à-vis Hitler and the West, would apparently like to embroil Russia with the West, seeing each cut the other down in warfare. Hence the preaching of militant world revolution by China. Russia, aware of western strength and no doubt aware also of Chinese intentions, instead preaches co-existence between the Soviet and the non-Soviet blocs and draws back, as in the case of Cuba, when directly confronted by western power.

Four broad possibilities face China:

1. To isolate herself as an independent, nationalistic entity. This would be in harmony with traditional Chinese xenophobia and feelings of inherent superiority but would cut her off from technical aid and so retard development.

2. To accept Russian ideological leadership in return for some technical aid, which in any event the Russians will never provide in sufficient quantity to make China independent and hence a formidable nearby potential adversary.

3. To establish friendly relations with the West in part return for technical aid, which would require a complete abandonment of world revolutionary intentions.

4. To cooperate with Japan in the establishment of a Far Eastern common market, which would also require abandonment of world revolutionary ambitions.

The last is the most logical possible development but not necessarily the most likely. From their respective points of view, all the outside parties most concerned are justifiably suspicious of a huge nation like China when it is under totalitarian auspices. On any of these four courses aggressive Chinese nationalism is going to experience difficulties and delay.

What of Africa and South America?

Neither Africa nor South America shows any signs whatever of becoming an industrial rival of a United Europe, the United States, or of Soviet Russia. But both should remain important suppliers of raw materials to the world's economy. In Africa development promises to be spectacular, but under non-African auspices. Despite all agitation for native political independence, there is no likely near prospect for vast economic development under native auspices nor is there any apparent basis for independent political unification of the whole continent within 100 years. But urbanization, cultivation, and mechanization seem likely to continue apace, with consequent lifting of cultural and social standards—always, however, under direct or indirect non-African guidance.

Latin America will also continue to occupy a subsidiary position in the world economy unless she should be able first to achieve legitimate government and then to unite politically. Of such a union, though favored by a common language and culture, there is at present little sign. The future quite evidently belongs to big political entities like United Europe, the United States, and Soviet Russia. Sections of Africa once belonging to England, France, Spain, or Portugal might be attached, if only tenuously, to a United Europe.

The future of small countries, then, is dim. The smaller countries of Europe such as Sweden, Norway, Denmark, Finland, Holland, Austria, Portugal, Spain, Greece, Belgium, and Switzerland will all be more or less willing parts of a European union, exercising some local autonomy within a federal framework, or unwilling parts of an extended Soviet Union, having no local autonomy. For geographical reasons Finland will probably be absorbed by Russia, following the Baltic States, Poland, Czechoslovakia, East Germany, Hungary, Rumania, and Bulgaria. Yugoslavia will have to choose: Russia or Europe.

What of small new states such as Israel? Israel's future seems extremely problematical, particularly in the face of a rising Arab nationalism that seems likely to result eventually in some sort of Arab federation. Such a federation could hardly be independent in any real sense, being without sufficient resources to develop a strong industrial economy, and must rely either upon Europe, the United States, or upon Russia. The unduly harsh treatment meted out by Soviet Russia even to its own people, not excepting many of its leaders, should in the end serve to keep the Arab world as well as the rest of the African world from voluntarily falling under Soviet tutelage.

All of this no doubt seems very much like moving nations about as though they were inanimate chess pieces. But, as subsequent chapters will show, it is not without reason and not without high probability. A probability, it should be evident, represents a narrowing of mere possibility. Possibilities, of course, are multitudinous.

I do not mean to suggest that accidental or unforeseen events will not change the prospect sketched here. Personality clashes within governing circles, the rise of magnetic leaders and the like can change details, but they cannot change the general contour of necessary developments. For what the world is undergoing is a rather rapid process of sociocultural evolution unavoidable and necessary in the light of initial steps long ago taken.

First, no intervention by any man can alter the fact that small nations and split continents are destined to be distinctly subsidiary factors in future world affairs. No national leader in Europe, however compelling his intellect and personality, can widen Europe's choice of either becoming part of the U.S.S.R. or forming an independent union. But why should one not believe, as some misguided Europeans do, that there is some chance of the United States taking and organizing Europe? One reason that will not happen is that the United States, unlike Russia, has neither the political nor geographical orientation for such a task. Even if it had the desire it would not have the operational theory, the experience, nor the ready framework that Russia possesses. The Soviet process known externally as "infiltration" and "subversion," successfully practiced already in a number of countries, well expresses the Soviet drive to rule or ruin.

Would Russia, if she got control of Europe, operate it constructively—that is, with a view to maximizing Europe's welfare? This is entirely doubtful on the basis of past Soviet performances in countries she has taken over. Instead, Russia would dismantle and weaken Europe, transferring to her home territory as much of Europe's productive equipment and personnel as possible. Soviet Russia, one may be sure, would systematically "bleed" Europe if she ever got control of it, a prospect that no doubt spurs the Europeans most interested in achieving European unification.

Could China turn against Russia? Such a development is surely possible, but there is no present evidence to suggest that she will. China could, of course, change her main allegiance from Russia to Europe, Japan, or the United States, but this would not greatly alter China's world role. In the presence of the new weapons her excessive population as a serious war-making potential is nullified. She is neither a military nor an economic asset to either Europe or Russia. Japan and China, however, could be valuable to each other economically

—Japan because of her developed industry and China as a market for finished goods and a source of raw materials. A fusion of China with Japan, with Russia assisting in the fusion, is not inconceivable, although what would inspire Russia to build up such a formidable power on its eastern borders is not at present apparent. Instead, it seems to be in the narrower interests of Russia (and Europe and the United States as well) to keep Japan and China as separate as possible. But if Japan and China ever do unite, a consummation visualized by the Japanese war lords of World War II, there would be more chance of this Asiatic region's emulating Russia in industrial development than there is with the two separated.

And if Russia were to extend its rule over all of Europe, it seems likely that the United States would be solicited to fuse at least with the ethnically European parts of the Commonwealth of Nations— England, Canada, Australia and New Zealand to begin with. Such a contingency, however, seems remote, and what is most likely in the light of present evidence is the gradual union of Europe in a single federal system with the United States standing ready to give assistance against further Russian interference. Many Englishmen apparently do not relish the prospect of a united continent, which England has struggled for centuries to forestall, but England must concur in the achievement of European union in the face of the obvious Russian threat to take over the continent.

Another way of looking at future world development is to see it as becoming most advanced in areas most committed to realistic, scientific thinking and least advanced in those areas still in thrall to mythic and non-scientific thinking.

What has been roughly sketched in thus far is the organization of the nations vis-à-vis each other on the world stage in the next 150 years. To preserve its independence Europe must combine in at least a federal union or else be swallowed, piece by piece, by voracious Soviet Russia. It cannot long remain fractionalized unless Russia undergoes an internal upheaval, of which there is no present intimation. The dominant world powers, if Europe unites, will be the United States, United Europe, and Soviet Russia. China, India, Latin America, and the Arab Middle East will not have become industrial and cultural counterparts of these land masses. Even though they may greatly have improved their economic and cultural positions, they will be subsidiary to the main development unless Russia and the West knock each other out in nuclear warfare. The single, remotely probable chance of Asia's gaining world ascendency lies in the prospect that Russia and the West will destroy each other. South America will continue to play a distinctly subsidiary role as a raw materials producer until she matures politically and unites under a single flag. The fate of Africa is linked pretty closely to that of Europe.

In the light, then, of presently available evidence the United States, United Europe, and remnants of the Commonwealth of Nations should in 150 years in combination still be economically, culturally, and politically in the world lead. Soviet Russia may well have drawn abreast, but only if she has modified her political system so as to have permitted the emergence of considerable social and cultural freedom. For without such freedom there can be no genuine creativity, only imitativeness.

While there is much in the interrelationships of nations that holds potentialities for change either through cooperativeness, competition, or conflict—or a mixture of the three—the greatest potentialities are unquestionably to be found within the nations themselves. At least among the most advanced and creative nations, where there is cultural freedom, it is internally that factors of change are most operative; external factors making for change are secondary. With the obviously backward nations such as Russia it is the opposite; in their sudden convulsive attempts at development they are clearly reacting, but tardily, to the rise of the advanced nations to positions of unprecedented leadership.

Within all going societies at all times there exists a more or less stable equilibrium between threatened disorganization and efficient organization. A society is progressive in proportion as it achieves more efficient organization and reduces disorganization, efficiency being construed as effectiveness in meeting the individual needs and convenience of its members. A society is retrogressive as its organization becomes less efficient, failing to meet individual needs, and verges upon disorganization. Efficient organization is not synonymous with an imposed rigid pattern.

Nuclear Energy and Automation

Experimental flexibility must be constantly brought to bear with respect both to the accumulated factors making for change (which I shall discuss later) and to new factors entering the social scene. Two such new factors, potentially revolutionary in their combination, are the new nuclear-energy sources and automation or automatic factories, depending upon electronics. Here we may take passing note of a few of the many changes that will be wrought by the new energy sources and automation.

Man, as we know, has the ability to choose whether he wishes to embark on certain courses within a narrow range of selection. But once he has chosen, certain consequences are inexorable. A man may choose to step or not to step off a high building but, once having stepped, he has very little control over the consequences of his action. Russia in 1956 created a Ministry of Automation. And Great Britain, afraid of being crowded out of world markets by either Russia, the United States, West Germany, Japan, or all four, is strongly pushing automation. Its development is being methodically promoted in West Germany and in the United States.

Automation will produce many unsolicited results, some to be enumerated later, but one of its effects will be to require more highly trained technicians—engineers, scientists and industrial managers—even as it greatly diminishes the demand for the unskilled and semi-skilled factory-machine tender. In the long run—in one or two generations—it will tend to eliminate not only many factory workers (a recent study forecasts 200,000 a year for ten years) but also the traditional businessman or business entrepreneur. In place of these will appear highly trained economic administrators.

Although the insistent pressure of automation for more effective higher education will be spectacular enough, this is only part of the story. For automation, by increasing leisure time, confronts the public with the problem of how to employ leisure. Leisure can be used passively or actively, destructively or constructively, but hardly indifferently. The Western world confronts, in automation, a possible destiny similar to that which confronted the Roman Republic with the introduction of slavery. Following the acute analysis of Max Weber, we may note that slavery in ancient Rome displaced the free farmer and artisan, creating the unemployed, pleasure-loving urban citizenry that was from time to time appeased by conquest-financed bread and circuses. In the course of time this citizenry became thoroughly demoralized, public institutions consequently lost their vigor, graft and corruption became increasingly resorted to as ways of getting rich, and the stage was prepared for the final internal collapse. The devitalized citizens were unable in the end to resist the infiltrating barbarians from the north.

Automation obviously prepares the stage for similar events in a modern setting, and the outcome will obviously depend upon how leisure time is utilized. If it is utilized destructively, as in ancient Rome, internal collapse faces the errant society. If it is used merely passively, as already increased leisure time has been largely used in the modern world, it will place an even larger portion of the population than at present in hypnotic subservience to television, radio, films, sports events, circuses and hollow theatrical spectacles with inevitably stultifying effects.

But with the example of Rome before us—who said history teaches no lessons?—this result not only can, but surely will be avoided. It will be avoided because policy makers who otherwise might be willing to indulge the populace, cannot but be aware that malicious leaders of Soviet Russia and Red China would be first to profit by a demoralization of the Western population. Western policy makers, then, simply must turn the interests of a leisure-burdened populace to constructive ends—that is, to cultural ends.

One of these ends will certainly be educational. And it will largely be education for adults. These adults will already be thoroughly schooled or merely slightly schooled. Among those well schooled, some will be technically or purely vocationally educated.

Those originally not thoroughly schooled either in technical or humanistic studies will, as working adults, have the opportunity of resuming their studies. Whether college graduates or not, educated persons in the future cannot consider merely four years of conventional college education sufficient for the highly complex world in which they will be living. Actually a lifetime of supplementary formal education will be necessary.

The consequence of the continuous demand for adult higher education will be that the adult division of the universities and colleges will become the largest segment in the entire school system. It will be larger than the elementary division for the simple reason that there are far more adults between the ages of twenty-one and seventy than there are children between six and fourteen. Similarly there are more adults than children of secondary-school age or youths of college age. True, not all adults will spend part of their leisure time going to school, but enough will be making continuous use of school facilities to make this enrollment the largest.

The main social class distinction of the future, then, will be between those attending adult classes in higher education of all the standard varieties—that is, the educated—and those unable to assimilate further education.

But not only education as an intensive leisure-time pursuit will be given strong impetus by automation. World travel during vacations will be encouraged as a constructive leisure-time activity leading to feelings, directly acquired, of greater kinship with other peoples as well as knowledge of the world. Automation, in other words, will nurture a far more widely diffused liberal spirit than was nurtured either under agriculture or the manned factory system.

The emergence of a very large educated class with broad cultivated interests should stimulate more social activity for the sole pleasure in sociable interaction. The lost art of conversation may well be recaptured as people have the opportunity to learn some things worth talking about.

What can be predicted in detail, should one wish to be so explicit, about a single line of development such as automation may well be illustrated here. If automation is as widely adopted as it already shows many signs of being, then it is difficult to see how the following effects can be averted:

1. A great increase in fixed capital in the form of new machinery, requiring increased savings and investment by a broad section of the populace and some reduction in expenditures for consumer goods and services.

2. A tremendous increase in the production of uniform products and components.

3. The probable production of standard components of versatile use in the assembling of a great variety of different products.

4. A much larger volume of output under continuous operation of machines with consequent more rapid consumption of raw materials, further ransacking of the world for raw materials, and increasing usage of presently neglected materials.

5. A vast expansion of markets, including markets for consumer goods in underdeveloped regions as well as at home.

6. A much heavier demand for electricity, and concomitantly for fuels, with which to power automated factories.

7. Relative stabilization of the inflation-deflation, boom-depression cycle under a system of continuous production; for instead of savings

accruing from production slow-downs, costs will be increased as expensive equipment stands idle.

8. A marked reduction in the number of small businesses except in specialty, handcraft, and service lines. Handcrafts, which will exist in clothing, furniture, some textiles and decorative lines, will be in the luxury class.

9. A possible decline in the use of storage space for raw materials and component parts, owing to the rapidity of the production process.

10. A heavy all-around increase in the world freight load.

11. A relative decline in the price of finished products but a relative rise in the price of increasingly scarce raw materials.

12. Increased use of complex consumer products (television and radio sets, cameras, movie projectors, airplanes, etc.) and an increase in the variety of complex products (reading, dictating and translating machines, etc.). Instead of in theaters, movies will be shown in homes and before small groups on home projectors, with films rented from libraries.

13. Reduction in productive flexibility and much more central planning far ahead with respect to all economic dispositions.

14. A relatively great substitution of international or bloc planning for national planning, of national planning for individual corporate or organizational planning and, in general, group planning for individual planning.

15. As indicated earlier, a vast increase in the size of individual corporations and vastly more of the labor force concentrated in service (non-production) pursuits, from unskilled to highly skilled. There will be a reduction in the labor force engaged in manufacturing by half or more in a matter of three generations. Highly skilled services include engineering, industrial and social management, economic analysis and planning, scientific and medical research and application, teaching on all levels up to postgraduate and adult, physical and psychological correction, industrial designing, personal guidance and counseling with a view to maximizing individual satisfactions and reducing social friction, etc.

But with automation and other factors making for greater complexity there will be greater responsibility on the upper managerial and service levels, the personnel of which will be aided, however, by the vastly expanding line of automatic computational and cybernetics mechanisms.

No doubt hours of employment will be reduced from the present forty-plus, but whether they will sink below thirty hours a week for the average worker or will even go as low as thirty hours is doubtful. People operating automated equipment will not enjoy shorter hours, although these skeleton staffs (by comparison with the present heavily manned factory) may in some lines work in three shifts of eight hours each. People in service and skilled employments will have no grounds to ask for extremely short hours.

The idea of a work week of twenty hours and less, predicted by some, is based on the theory that present industrial jobs must be shared, with hours appropriately reduced as less input per worker is required to meet production norms. What is overlooked is that automation will create many new service jobs. Assuming that the entire manufacturing process is automated back to the acquisition of raw material from mine and field—and it is doubtful that all manufacture can be automated—one must now reckon with the vastly greater quantities of raw materials and finished goods to be transported. Although pipelines for petroleum and gas now represent automation in transportation, it is difficult to visualize an automated transportation system for dry bulk goods. Railroads, ships, and airplanes could in principle be operated by remote control, as subways well may be, but it will probably long remain cheaper to man them. A growth in manned transportation facilities can then be seen as absorbing many workers with the increase in production under automation. Transportation is, of course, a service industry. Other services and new specialties will absorb other workers. Repair and maintenance of a wide variety of consumer appliances as well as the new industrial mechanisms will absorb large numbers of trained workers. The automobile, the radio, and television brought in their train a huge army of specially trained repairmen.

With the unceasing demand for more highly trained and cultivated people attention will shift after not many decades from the school to the home.

In the future, and rather soon, government is going to be forced to bring scientific remedial attention to bear on families producing children with gross emotional disturbances and blockages, just as it already in advanced jurisdictions brings remedial attention to bear when the school discovers that children are undernourished, inadequately dressed, physically ill, or maltreated at home. The foot which government already has tentatively in the door of the home is going to be put farther forward. Families that refuse to cooperate are going to come under increasingly severe legal pressure.

One could cite hundreds of examples of this strong, already current, trend but the case of Newburgh, N.Y., versus the state and federal governments in 1961 is fully illustrative of what is happening. Newburgh is a small and old textile-manufacturing city some fifty miles north of New York City on the Hudson River. Early in 1961 the new city manager, acting for a majority of the city council, announced that the city was beginning a campaign against "chiselers, loafers and social parasites" who were on unemployment and sick relief and old-age care.

The campaign, which forced all the indigent on public relief to register at police stations as part of a policy of intimidation, met with national applause from self-styled conservatives. It was opposed by the State Board of Welfare, which won all subsequent decisions in the courts. The city of Newburgh, in other words, lost all along the line.

Public investigations disclosed that, contrary to the city's case, there was no fraud in relief payments and no outside migrants, as alleged, drawing relief at the expense of local taxpayers. In 1960, it was disclosed, only $205 had been spent on new arrivals out of a total relief budget of $1,000,000. Of this budget the locality contributed only $340,000, with state and federal governments contributing the lion's share. Furthermore, only 3 per cent of the local population was on relief and most of these were epileptic, blind, aged or physically disabled. Very few able to work were on relief.

The position of the dominant faction in the city was that all these cases should be cared for by churches, families, and private agencies despite the showing of experience that this meant little or no care. Government, beginning in the 1930s, had been forced into this area by human misery, which adversely affected public morale and jeopardized the desired international image of the United States as a humane nation.

An unexpected result of the Newburgh case was to bring about a re-examination by the federal government of its $4 billion national relief program and to find it inadequate. What was required, Washington concluded, was more and earlier expenditure in the prevention of relief cases. Another unexpected result was that outside intervention caused the local share of relief payments to rise $40,000 for 1962. In the end the city administration announced a plan of "psychological warfare" or intimidation against relief applicants and of "thought control" over new and untrained welfare workers brought in to pass on relief applications.

One dramatic fact finally stood out for all to see: in the face of unremitting propaganda against "Big Government" by unregulated special interests fearful of effective regulation it was clear that the central government, having many factors in mind, was more compassionate than was penny-pinching local government run by untutored, insensitive minds. It was, after all, the experience of generations of the indigent and incapacitated that had made "county poor farm" and "public poorhouse" dread bywords in the public mind. In this respect experience with flinty local government bore out the common experience of individuals among themselves, often testified to: when one is prosperous one has many friends, but when one is broke one has few or none. For now all the fair-weather friends fear they may be called upon for tangible personal sacrifices as a testimony to friendship.

Further Impressionistic Anticipations

We have, as I remarked earlier, been scanning impressionistically some vistas of future change as a preliminary to examining our terrain and its pros and cons more closely. As a finale to this chapter, then, I shall summarize changes almost certain to come that will be discussed in coming chapters along with the reasons for believing they will eventuate.

Some of these changes of the next 150 years will be as follows:

1. Western government as a whole will be converted into a gigantic social service institution relating to every department of modern life. This will be the much denounced Welfare State, which will contrast with the conceptions of the state as an impartial referee among contending individuals and social groups or the State as a special instrument of dominant social groups. The gradually emerging type of government will be manned within 150 years throughout its length and breadth by highly trained experts rather than by gifted amateurs, egocentric careerists or payrollers, as in the past. The politician of the future will be but the sum total of his expert advisers.

2. In the new state there will be a drastic reconstruction of the judicial system, particularly in the United States but also in Europe.

The present judicial system is but a latter-day improvisation upon an essentially medieval institution. There will also be radical changes made in the handling of persons convicted of law violation, with greater emphasis on rational treatment and effective rehabilitation than on ineffective punishment. As matters now stand, particularly in the United States, there is a steady yearly increase in the crime rate. Much of present-day crime, furthermore, is committed by repeaters, that is by persons whose original anti-social hostility has been intensified by caged confinement for periods of years. It makes little sense for society thus to provoke the commission of still more anti-social acts. Close confinement in the future will be reserved for the unrecoverable anti-social personality, who will be permanently confined whatever the kind of crime he has committed. Truly correctional institutions will be more on the order of sanitoria and schools. But owing to social and cultural changes toward greater efficiency, there should be a marked decline in criminality as such. The cost of coping with crime will be much lower than at present.

3. The armed forces of the great nations in the *very* near future will become relatively small in number, consisting of highly trained, well-paid career personnel, many of whom will be college-trained in the sciences. The rank and file of this army will be more highly trained than many general officers of the recent past! Mass conscription and the maintenance of mass reserves in the advanced nations will be abandoned. For in a modern war there would not be sufficient time to get a mass army deployed. Armored forces will be kept to a minimum as suitable only for brush-fire war against lightly armed mischief-makers or for internal police duty. The present pentomic division, employing long-range thermonuclear missiles, is a harbinger of the future military unit.

4. Social services under the supervision of government will be multiplied up and down the line. Embracing the mentally as well as physically retarded, a broader interpretation than ever before of the concept of dependency will emerge. The result will be greater governmental protection of dependent personalities from exploitation.

5. Owing to the present great emphasis on research, there can be foreseen further world progress in science, particularly in biology, medicine, and the behavioral sciences. The general stimulus to such research will be the emergence of massive problems attendant upon progressively increasing social complexity. Because of the heavy costs involved most research will be government-financed.

6. The economic system, multiplying in complexity, will be subject to increasing governmental regulation and control. Company directors, instead of being chosen exclusively by management and stockholder blocs as at present, will also be named on behalf of the public at large and by the government directly. On the boards of all the large corporations there will be directors representing (1) the national government, (2) the general public, (3) stockholders, and (4) management. And management will have to take into consideration in its planning far more factors and points of view than at present.

7. There will be a radical reconstruction of cities, already partly under way in the United States. As part of such reconstruction, there will be developed a public building program going far beyond anything thus far blueprinted by the most imaginative of today. Not only will it include apartment buildings, schools, clinics, hospitals and sanatoria for the ill and the aged, but it will also include neighborhood public indoor recreational facilities for teen-aged youth, public country summer camps for all children eight to sixteen, cultural centers, and government research centers.

8. Cities will expand until entire countrysides are more or less fully urbanized. Residential slums as well as unsightly factory districts will be entirely eliminated. While private passenger car operation will increase very much abroad, notably in Soviet Russia but also in Africa and Asia when more roads are opened, it will decline from the present high level in the United States. In the United States there will be greater dependence than at present on mass transportation facilities, particularly on high-speed buses; there will also be much renting of cars.

9. There will be increasing application of scientific method and findings to all institutions and areas of life. Racism, for example, will be virtually eliminated. Not only will it be well understood that there is no scientific basis for it but, more effectively, it will be politically inexpedient in a close-knit interdependent world. The pendulum in this quarter may well begin to swing in the opposite direction. Governments may positively encourage racially mixed marriages, for political as well as for biological reasons. Crossbreeding, as animal breeders know, produces stronger progeny. Any increase in genetically linked diseases among old stock could well induce policies in favor of crossbreeding. In any event, multiplied human contacts across extensive distances, made possible by rapid transportation, suggests

a great coming racial intermixture. In some 1000 to 1500 years of high world civilization, or thirty to forty-five generations, there might well be produced a single human race, with all ethnic lines blotted out.

As to this prediction, it may be noticed that all ethnic groups are more or less xenophobic, ethnocentric, self-segregated, and self-applauding. In a nation genetically heterogenous like the United States chauvinistic leaders of such groups, or at least of remnants of such groups, constantly warn against assimilation with contaminating "outsiders." Such assimilation nevertheless proceeds, particularly among the subvarieties of whites but also in lesser degree between whites and non-whites. Echoes of tribalism with overtones of shamanism will no doubt continue to be heard, but this can nevertheless confidently be said: the more interracial contact there is throughout the world, the more assimilation there will be.

10. Although often predicted by many seemingly interested parties, there will be no great religious revival in the world during the next 150 years unless, perhaps, there should be a particularly destructive war. In fact, what may be expected is a further steady and gradual decline in religious fervor and a dimming of the religious outlook in favor of the scientific and secularly philosophic. One might suppose the opposite, to consider the religious allusions of American politicians. But such, it is well understood, is merely vote-seeking.

Religion, as is well known, has thrived not on fear alone, but on fear of the unknown and feelings of helplessness. As knowledge has increased and man's control over his immediate environment has been made more secure, fear of the unknown has receded; the sense of helplessness has diminished. Increased opportunities in the modern world for distraction as well as creative self-realization have also dimmed the attractiveness of religion.

Technological changes, moreover, make religion less necessary to public policy and, in the view of such political leaders as the Russians, make it a positive hindrance. For, the feeling is, religious persons tend to rely less on their own efforts and more on mysterious supernatural forces. The leaders of Bolshevism no doubt had this aspect of self-reliance partly in mind when they launched their protracted crusade against religious belief.

11. Trade unions and service workers' associations of various kinds will no doubt continue in existence, but under far stricter governmental supervision than at present. The shift of workers out of manufacturing will cause the membership of many unions to decline, but

new unions will appear and some old ones will enjoy membership increases. Unions in transportation services will surely enjoy enlarged membership rolls. Among new workers' associations to arise will be those of scientists and upper-echelon technicians. If only to preserve relative economic positions, most members of the labor force will probably belong to some union or craft association. Not to belong, as in the case of teachers in the United States today, is to jeopardize one's economic and social position.

It is, then, along such lines as the foregoing that our predictions will take form. There remains now the important task of discussing how we arrive at our predictions. For unless the reader is convinced they follow pretty inevitably from evidence, they must seem like pure fantasy, to be summarily dismissed. But before we come to method we shall first, in the next chapter, briefly consider the importance of predicting in the history of mankind.

CHAPTER II

MAN, THE FUTURE AND PREDICTION

"All living things act to anticipate the future; this is what chiefly distinguishes them from lifeless things."

—JACOB BRONOWSKI

Life of all kinds is clearly anticipatory, differing in this respect only in range and extent. At its least obtrusive, anticipation is purely negative and defensive, shown as protective coloration, ability to flee, natural armoring as with shells or thick hides, unusually keen senses of sight and smell and the like. In all these instances the general anticipation is evidently of ever-threatening danger.

At the other extreme there is active anticipation as it shows itself in man, extending itself on to infinity.

Between these two extremes foresight and anticipation show themselves profusely in common animal behaviors: birds building nests, insects projecting antennae ahead of themselves, animals storing food against the coming of winter. Even though these actions may be involuntary, without formal forethought, they show life as anticipatory. And merely to anticipate is to engage in a general, if vague, sort of prediction. Anticipation at least implies the prediction that there will be a future, that there is continuity between the time that is now and a yet-to-be-experienced time that is not now.

For as far back as the record is visible, man has self-consciously sought both to predict and control the future—his own future—in his biological interests. The attempt at prediction and control has for most of known time been made through magic and religion. The task still remains to bring prediction in general fully under the jurisdiction of science. While the idea of controlling the future or any part of it may appear megalomaniacal, it is clear that prevision of the future in terms at least of probabilities may guide present actions and thereby influence cause-and-effect sequences extending into the future, thus influencing the future.

Man's predictions, history attests, are variously classifiable. Most of record are mythic-fantastic; they are fables invented to explain group destinies, foretell individual or group fortunes, or regulate individual conduct. Others are supposedly intuitional, as that evildoers at some future time will certainly be punished. Still others are based on common sense, what everybody agrees is clearly evident, as that the solar system will always continue, without wobbling, like an ever-running reliable clock. A much more advanced, semiscientific type is rationally systematic, elaborating deductions from a set of postulates; the results here are obviously limited by the appropriateness of the postulates as well as by the validity of the inferences. The most advanced type is conventionally scientific; here the premises from which deductions are drawn are inductively established rather than postulated—that is, they are empirical, factual, verifiable.

Man is so constituted biologically that he *must* predict. He has no choice at all in the matter. And to argue, as some persons do, that man cannot predict the future to any extent is to argue, contrary to fact, that man cannot exist. The farmer who plants a crop makes a prediction: that there will be a harvest and a market for it. If he could not make such a prediction he would have no reason to plant. The predictions men make may be wholly correct, wholly incorrect, or a varying mixture of both. Most ordinary human predictions are of the latter, mixed variety and the task is to devise a method of insuring far more correctness than incorrectness in predictions of human affairs, individual and collective.

Man exists wholly in the unstable present. The present, literally and exactly viewed, is an affair of the moment, quickly gone. It is constantly crumbling and disintegrating. But by means of recollection and anticipation man gives himself an illusion of living in more than a rapidly transitory present. He mentally expands the actual present into what philosophers have called a "specious present." Man, it is evident, must act in order to live, and few of man's actions can be consummated in the fleeting present. His acts, in other words, have continuity as conscious projects and are enmeshed in situations or complexes of various overlapping events. Man remembers earlier stages of his acts even as he is involved in present stages, and thus is made sensitively aware of temporal sequence and continuity. This experienced continuity he insensibly projects toward the anticipated completion of his act in consummation and satisfaction, hence arriving at the concept of the future. Men's acts are as bridges through time. Consciousness accompanies these acts.

The past, as man commonly views it, is something that very much resembles a recording, as if by camera and phonograph, in his memory. In a lifetime this memory fades, blurs and becomes indistinct, but it may be vividly preserved in writing or by frequent retelling aloud. The racial memory is also preserved, at first by hearsay through reports by one generation to the next and later in the course of evolution by writing. In relatively late cultural development a selective past is recorded, constructed and variously interpreted in the formal study we know as written history.

Man is interested in history not out of mere inquisitiveness, but actually because he feels uncertainty about the future. Before there was written history he depended on myths. By recalling and examining past events (and imagined events), some measure of future events, and possibly control over them, is thought to be obtained. Although the future contains novelty, much about the future turns out to resemble the past. Although some historians hold that history teaches no lessons, this is not completely true. Past experience, of the individual and of the race, does teach lessons that are sometimes applied, aptly or not, in the present and the future. The burning of one's hand in a fire is an individual historical experience. If there is any doubt left in the victim's mind that a similar juxtaposition of hand and fire will have similar consequences, a repetition of the experience will remove it. Experience—that is, historical events lived through—teaches that there is a stability and regularity about much phenomena. Remembered, such phenomena may be applied by the organism with satisfactory results in the future.

Most men probably make no attempt explicitly to predict even the immediate future. But in order to live, men must at least implicitly predict the future. This sort of implicit prediction, made every day by nearly everybody, shows itself most plainly in *policy*, individual or group. Implicit policy in the individual is expressed in *attitude*, and is often similarly expressed by groups. Attitudes are complexes of predictions, many of them unconscious, unconsciously constructed out of past experience.

Policies embodying predictions are revealed by many kinds of groups. They are evident in families wherein expenditures and savings, for example, are made on the basis of predictions of what will under varying conditions conduce to the welfare and the satisfaction of the family on the morrow, next year, and even some years into the future. Government, as the policy-making and policy-guiding center for a whole society, is the single institution that probably does most predicting, implicit and explicit, in all of human society. Most governmental prediction, furthermore, has thus far been extremely simple, not to say simple-minded, for it has held in general that the future will be very much like the past. This particular belief has probably done more than any other to undermine, overthrow, and destroy governments in this century. War and the effects of war, particularly in an age of rapidly advancing technology, turn out to be very different from war in the past. The results of World War I, for example, were very different from what was anticipated by any of the participating governments, winners and losers alike. World War II similarly held many surprises not only for its most aggressive promoter, Germany, but also for its next most active promoters: Russia, Italy, and Japan.

In domestic matters governments are on somewhat less perilous ground when they predict that the future will be pretty much like the past. Budgets, for example, represent predictions of what will be required in the way of expenditures for the coming year; many of these expenditures can be predicted exactly, while others are easily provided for by contingency allocations. Governmental capital budgets represent predictions extending far into the future.

While governments err in their predicting, as I have noted, they have in the past often been correct because the future has so strongly resembled the past. Their most grievous errors in this century stem from the fact that they have failed to take full account of drastically changed and highly relevant conditions that influence the future.

Most governmental predictions are made on a common-sense basis, and common sense has long been known to philosophers as likely to prove misleading. To common sense the earth seems flat, a straight stick projected into water at an angle seems bent, and many physical objects seem solid. Physics, on the other hand, testifies that there are no absolute solids, only energy complexes of different degrees of porosity. What appears to common sense as solid matter is known to physics to consist largely of empty space, of point events in space-time. If we are to achieve anything worth while in our predicting we must, without abandoning it entirely, go far beyond common sense, beyond what appears to be plainly evident to everybody. For what is plainly evident to everybody is often false.

Earlier, in distinguishing various kinds of human prediction, I gave the highest priority to the rationally systematic and the conventionally scientific methods. The difference between a rationally systematic and a scientific prediction lies, it would appear, in the validity of the premises. A fully scientific prediction is one with such high probability that it verges on certainty. But until methods yielding near certainty are devised, any methods that produce fairly strong probability will be welcome.

Divination, Prophecy, and Prediction

For the most part, man's attempts at long-range prediction in the past have not been fortunate, thus providing ample grounds for prevalent ingrown skepticism about his ability to predict. A few spectacularly successful predictions about historical developments of quite circumstantial detail, however, suggest that the method employed and the skill of the observer make a difference.

Divination, its methods now thoroughly discredited, has been found on all levels of culture from the most rudimentary to the very complex. The literature dealing with it is extensive, and is most notably represented by the four-volume *Histoire de la Divination dans l'Antiquité* by A. Bouché-Leclercq.* The sort of predicting practiced by augurs, necromancers, haruspices, and priests stands to scientific sociocultural predicting about as alchemy stands to chemistry. The Bible is, perhaps, the root cause for most skepticism about man's ability to predict the outcome of his own enterprises. For the Bible, both in the Old and New Testament, is replete with predictions proved false or in principle unverifiable.

With the rise of physical science, predictions of a mythical and fantastic order fell into increasing disrepute, at least among the informed. But the influence of physical science on belief about the efficacy of predicting was double-edged and contradictory. For it gave rise to exaggerated faith in the ability of science to make correct predictions about nature and, over the long range to the present, in-

---

* Short articles with extensive bibliographies may be found in the Encyclopaedia Britannica and other reference works under titles such as "Astrology," "Augurs," "Divination," "Oracle," "Prophet," and "Witchcraft."

directly reinforced skepticism about predicting in human affairs. The success of predicting in celestial mechanics was the impetus for both developments.

In mid-eighteenth-century France a royal physician, François Quesnay (1694–1774), applied the Cartesian model of a mechanical universe to the sphere of political economy to found the first rational system of economics under the name of "physiocracy." The name was coined from Greek roots meaning rule by or according to nature. The system strongly influenced later classical, Manchesterian, and Marxian economics, and its basic precepts live on in American Chamber of Commerce economics.

It was the aim of the physiocrats to base economics on supposedly correct cosmic principles or laws. And it was their general prediction that if that were done, prosperity and justice for all of society would be secured. Nature, the physiocrats assumed, was beneficent. *Ex natura jus.* Man, by frustrating nature, wrought harm—a strange conclusion in view of the obvious fact that man had survived by freely modifying nature in his own interests.

All wealth, the physiocrats held, was derived ultimately from the earth, the soil. Neither trade, banking, nor industry produced anything over and above what they were given to work with by the earth, a point they could make with seeming reasonableness as mechanized industry was not yet appreciably developed. Hence land was necessary to their system, naturally beneficent land. The possessor of land, the landowner, was also an obvious "natural" ingredient. Property was therefore part of the natural order and, derivatively, property in the products of land and ultimately in all movable goods. For cultivation, workers were obviously necessary and they, too, were part of the order of nature. And it was natural that some persons were stronger, some weaker; some owned property and some had only their labor to offer. This labor was the property of the landless and could be sold to landowners.

Any attempt by government to regulate or interfere with this system was, obviously, unscientific and unnatural. Whatever was unnatural was, as the Church had long taught, immoral and to be avoided. There was to be no regulation of this natural system, but everything was to be allowed to take its own God-inspired course in a freely competitive market. This doctrine became known as *laissez faire*, the greatest benefit to society purportedly accruing from allowing each individual in the process to maximize his own self-interest.

Perfect balance and justice would be obtained through natural free competition. Government would get its necessary revenues by taxing the surplus gain of the landowner, but would levy no taxes on trade or industry in order that their services to the land and its workers would be as cheap as possible. Neither tariffs on exports nor on imports were to be allowed, nor excise taxes nor road tolls. The free flow of capital to agriculture in order to enhance productivity should be encouraged in every possible way.

While the physiocrats, in concerning themselves with production first, hit upon the central problem of economics, it was soon noticed that as far as the system was practiced in eighteenth-century France, it did not diffuse well-being throughout the country. For the agricultural laborers, freely competing among themselves for jobs, did not fare well. They were, in fact, impoverished. The predicted general benefits did not show themselves.

In England, scene of the emerging Industrial Revolution, the economists, led by Adam Smith (1723–90), found the production problem centered on labor. It was labor, they held, that produced wealth. Capital itself was accumulated labor, which the capitalist, a onetime laborer, had saved by restricting his personal consumption. But most laborers were held in an iron vise. For if wages rose, they reproduced themselves at a higher rate, thus bringing into being more laborers who, by their excessive numbers, exerted a competitive downward influence on wage rates.

David Ricardo (1772–1823), a conservative London stockbroker who became perhaps the chief ornament of classical or capitalist industrial economics and was a prime influence through his writings on Karl Marx and socialist thought, ventured one of the most famous of erroneous early economic predictions in his *Principles of Political Economy and Taxation:* "In the natural advance of society, the wages of labour will have a tendency to fall, as far as they are regulated by supply and demand; for the supply of labourers will continue at the same rate, whilst the demand for them will increase at a slower rate." As everyone can see, this famous early nineteenth-century prediction, gratifying in the extreme to factory owners, has been wholly wrong.

Karl Marx (1818–83) incorporated this prediction into his thinking and, accepting the "laws" of classical economics as true, made many similar pessimistic predictions. In our own time orthodox Marxists believe that Marx forged in his historical dialectics an intellectual instrument of great social predictive power. For more than two decades after the Russian revolution the Kremlin, in the name of Marxism, freely published predictions of coming world events, mostly of a wishful nature. These were almost invariably wrong. Marxian Communism is a close parallel of Christianity in the nature of its general apocalyptic predictions, although it has shifted the main scene of action from heaven to earth. Thus Marxism holds that all industrialized non-Communist societies will someday very soon collapse during a downturn in the business cycle—an analogy to the Christian end of the world. In place of such societies there will quickly arise the secular New Jerusalem in the form of blissful Communist societies governed by the happy workers themselves. But in all history no such swift decline and rise of societies has ever been seen.

Apart from these general predictions, which have not yet been fulfilled nor even appear to be on the way to fulfillment, Marx made a number of other celebrated though unrealized predictions: that social and political revolution was imminent in most industrialized countries, that revolutions led by socialist parties would first take place in such countries, that the condition of the workers under capitalism would steadily grow worse (here echoing Ricardo), that most of the population would be proletarianized under capitalism, and so forth.

Such monumentally erroneous predictions by Marx have given a false sense of security to many who fail to see that Marx was nevertheless wholly correct in discerning that the post-Medieval, private business system, conjoined *a fortiori* with power-machine production, made for an extremely volatile and unstable social system peculiarly liable, unless carefully guided, to large-scale war, permanent inflation-deflation, economic crisis, and recurrent political upheaval. Marx, oddly enough, was kept by his Hobbesian theory of a tyrannical state from anticipating that legislative measures in parliamentary governments might forestall in detail many of his direst predictions. He somehow failed to notice that man, although held to some extent captive, self-hypnotized, in systems of thought and society, is nevertheless very much of an improvising creature of great ingenuity. Modern man, to escape the Marxian debacle, has merely altered the system bit by bit from crisis to crisis.

Another famous misprediction of the rationally systematic order is that of Thomas R. Malthus (1766–1834), English economist and professor. Malthus, in *An Essay on the Principle of Population*, stirred up controversy by coolly arguing against the probability of appreciable social progress on the ground that social miseries were constantly reinforced by the strong tendency of population to increase faster than the supply of food. Population, he held, always increases up to the limits of available means of subsistence. It does not go beyond these means, owing to natural checks in the way of war, famine, disease, vice, and general dejection of spirit spontaneously generated by the fact of overpopulation itself. There was not much prospect, he felt, of modifying this truly vicious cycle, even by adding the practice of sexual continence to the list of spontaneous checks. For very few persons, he predicted, would be sexually continent.

Malthus developed his famous thesis as the contradictory of a theme originally laid down by William Godwin in his *Enquiry Concerning Political Justice* (1793). On the point at issue Godwin was completely right and Malthus completely wrong. Yet, ironically, Malthus became the more famous and is still widely thought the more rational of the two. As to the possibility of an excessive population's impeding social improvement, Godwin said, "The obvious answer to this objection is, that to reason thus is to foresee difficulties at a great distance. Three-fourths of the habitable globe are now uncultivated. The parts already cultivated are capable of immeasurable improvement. Myriads of centuries of still increasing population may pass away, and the earth be still found sufficient for the subsistence of its inhabitants."

Godwin's views were similar to those of the Marquis de Condorcet, French theorist. Condorcet said, before Malthus, "Might there not then come a moment when these necessary laws begin to work in a contrary direction; when, the number of people in the world finally exceeding the means of subsistence, there will in consequence ensue a continual diminution of happiness and population, a true retrogression, or at best an oscillation between good and bad?" Condorcet admitted that as a matter of arithmetic a time of human overpopulation might sometime arrive, but he denied that the time was imminent and contended that the development of science would enable man to cope with such overpopulation when it became a fact.

Malthus, on the other hand, argued that the time of overpopulation was immediately present, and it is precisely this contention that that counts most heavily against him. Joining issue specifically with Condorcet, Malthus said, "M. de Condorcet thinks that it cannot possibly be applicable but at an era extremely distant . . . it will appear, on the contrary, that the period when the number of men surpasses their means of easy subsistence has long since arrived; and that this necessary oscillation, this constantly subsisting cause of periodical misery, has existed in most countries ever since we have had any histories of mankind, and continues to exist at the present moment." Malthus went on to take Condorcet to task for suggesting that mankind, in order to avert overpopulation, would resort to "promiscuous concubinage, which would prevent breeding, or to something else as unnatural." The "something else as unnatural" was an obvious reference to effective birth control. Malthus, in addition to taking inadequate stock of known world factors that might increase the supply of food, unscientifically denied the relevance of such possible forms of behavior as did not measure up to his moral standards. Malthus, then, was clearly wrong in his prediction.

Owing to the growing indubitable excess of population in the world, particularly in India, China, and Japan, many persons believe that Malthus was correct in his predictions. But the fact that population in these areas now outruns food supply is not attributable to any natural and general tendency to become excessive, as Malthus argued. The birth rate in those regions, in fact, has remained stable all along, near the biological maximum. The sharp rises in population have been produced not by an increase in the rate of reproduction, but by a reduction in death rates through the intervention of modern medicine and sanitary measures. There has been no corresponding increase in food supplies, owing to the maintenance of agriculture in an elementary state. Hence the reduction in caloric intake per capita.

Even though it alone would not elevate living standards to the levels in Europe and North America, better agriculture would greatly increase food supplies at least in India and China. And either the withdrawal of modern medicines or the wide practice of birth control, inconceivable to Malthus, would reduce total population.

A further count against Malthus is that the birth rate, along with the death rate, was in fact sharply reduced in industrialized Europe and the United States. The more recent increase in the American birth rate, however, is yet far from pressing against food supplies, which show a large yearly surplus.

In his extreme pessimism Malthus was like most of the classical economists. For it was their melancholy mission, no doubt in unconscious echo of views acquired in their Puritanic religious upbringing, to stress that as a matter of natural law man could introduce little improvement in an inherently imperfect and sinful world. Everything was necessarily, lawfully, as it had to be, and the rich would continue rich and the poor abjectly poor. In part because he believed these economists, Karl Marx was led later to call for the forcible overthrow of the existing economic system. For, as a believer in the possibility of improvement, Marx attributed mass impoverishment to the system. The economists, however, saw mass impoverishment as a natural necessity, bound to take place in any system.

To date most predicting in the social sciences has been done in economics and continues to be done in that field, with distinctly uneven results. Economic studies, however, are working their way out of earlier biases and becoming more reliable. They are used in much successful business forecasting. Although the early failures of prediction in economics reinforced skepticism about social predicting, the shift of prediction in human affairs from the earlier mythic and fantastic forms to the semiscientific marked the rise into view of social rationalism which has continued to show itself in the empirical development of the social sciences and in tentative steps toward basing public policy upon exact knowledge—that is, highly probable knowledge.

But, emboldened by Marx, Malthus, and the early economists, various writers about the social scene took to dramatic and often melodramatic predicting. H. G. Wells did much of this kind of social predicting, with uneven results, and achieved a considerable reputation as a seer. While some of his predictions were realized, e.g., the development of residential suburbs and the mechanization of the home, they were already discernible as definite trends when he made them. Wells, indeed, missed some stellar opportunities because of his excessive common-sense caution. Thus, in *Anticipations*, published in 1901 and giving predictions of things to happen before the year 2000, Wells wrote:

"I have said nothing in this chapter, devoted to locomotion, of the coming invention of flying. . . . I do not think it at all probable that aeronautics will ever come into play as a serious modification of transport and communication—the main question here under consideration." In this same book Wells also wrote:

"I must confess that my imagination . . . refuses to see any sort of submarine doing anything but suffocate its crew and founder at sea."

But Wells was almost certainly accurately anticipating our future, reaching over two devastating world wars, when he set down in the same book that "A people must develop and consolidate its educated efficient classes or be beaten in war. . . . The nation that produces . . . the largest proportional development of educated and intelligent engineers and agriculturists, of doctors, schoolmasters, professional soldiers, and intellectually active people of all sorts; the nation that most resolutely picks over, educates, sterilizes, exports, or poisons its people of the abyss; the nation that by wise interventions, death duties and the like, contrives to expropriate and extinguish incompetent rich families while leaving individual ambitions free; the nation, in a word, that turns the greatest proportion of its irresponsible adiposity into social muscle, will certainly be the nation that will be the most powerful in warfare as in peace, will certainly be the ascendant or dominant nation before the year 2,000."

Wells accurately foresaw "the power that will finally supersede democracy and monarchy altogether" as "the power of the scientifically educated, disciplined specialist" whose forte is "the power of sanity, the power of the thing that is provably right."

When they were not frankly fanciful, Wells's predictions were feeble and far short of the mark. At times he was dominated by palpable prejudices and the prey to wishful thinking, as indeed in his vision of an approaching world government. "We are only in the very beginning of a great Roman Catholic revival," he also wrote.

Except in the United States, Roman Catholicism has almost everywhere lost ground since Wells wrote this. Even in the United States it has shown no Wellsian efflorescence.

Wells also predicted, for obscure reasons, that the Russian and Spanish languages would decline in use. But again he saw the possibility that Russia would come to dominate China politically in a matter of decades. This issue is still in the balance.

Wells in his predicting—some of it surprisingly clairvoyant, much of it mistaken and even trivial—was always stimulating. But his predictions had no systematic rationale. They were the commonsense, intuitional visions of an intelligent man who was widely read in and stimulated by the literature of socialism.

Successful Sociocultural Predictions

What, then, of empirical or scientific predicting?

We have seen some examples of quasi-scientific, rationally systematic predicting by the early economists—examples, unfortunately, of rational, or at least rationalized, error. Has any significant correct predicting been done in the social sphere?

We may first go rather far back for a remarkable long-range prediction, ventured on the basis of knowledge and genuine insight, certainly an example of effective intuition in prediction. This stellar prediction was made by Roger Bacon (1214–94), English philosopher and scientist. "I will now enumerate the marvelous results of art and nature which will make all kinds of magic appear trivial and unworthy," Bacon wrote. "Instruments for navigation can be made which will do away with the necessity of rowers, so that great vessels, both in rivers and on the sea, shall be borne about with only a single man to guide them and with greater speed than if they were full of men. And carriages can be constructed to move without animals to draw them, and with incredible velocity. Machines for flying can be made in which a man sits and turns an ingenious device by which skillfully contrived wings are made to strike the air in the manner of a flying bird. Then arrangements can be devised, compact in themselves, for raising and lowering weights indefinitely great. . . . Bridges can be constructed ingeniously so as to span rivers without any supports."[1]

Such a series of specific predictions could be made only by someone who had a good preliminary grasp of technical principles. And when it comes to the prediction of mechanical inventions, the record of success in our own day is probably brightest and a standing rebuke to those who assert one cannot make correct predictions in human affairs. S. C. Gilfillan records that by 1936 George Sutherland, predicting many coming inventions in 1900, was 64 per cent accurate; T. Baron Russell, predicting in 1906, was 70 per cent accurate; Charles P. Steinmetz, predicting in 1915, was 76 per cent accurate; and A. C. Lescarboura, predicting in 1920, was 78 per cent accurate.

Technical inventions and at least some scientific discoveries can be anticipated with a high degree of accuracy by projecting trend lines, and "high degree of accuracy" here is taken to mean in the near vicinity of 75 per cent accuracy or better. One reason one cannot predict inventions and discoveries much nearer to 100 per cent in accuracy is that even though logic may point toward the possibility of some sort of oncoming invention, it cannot guarantee social acceptance and useful operation. An invention is not usually regarded as having been made until it is accepted as such. For example, on the basis of present knowledge there could probably be constructed a mechanism that would be a combined land transport, surface vessel, submarine, and aircraft. The fact that such a quadruple transport is not constructed is not that technical obstacles make it impossible, but that there is no known need or demand for it. It is not, then, an invention.

But far more precise long-range predicting has been seen in the field of social events when it is done by persons with extensive sociocultural knowledge, sensitive insight, and great reasoning powers.

For accuracy, specificity, and range of individual items probably the most spectacularly correct general long-range prediction on record is the one made by Marie Jean Antoine Nicholas de Caritat, Marquis de Condorcet, usually known simply as Condorcet (1743–94). One of the dazzling group of eighteenth-century French *philosophes*, savants and Encyclopedists, Condorcet in the final section of his *Sketch for a Historical Picture of the Progress of the Human Mind*, first published in 1795, predicted many salient facets of our own age, ranging ahead 100 to 150 years. Condorcet's predictions, rationally systematic, were based on his theory of history, which he divided into ten stages of which only the final one had not been realized to his day. Each stage had a causal relationship to the next. The ninth stage, in which he found himself, was in his view the inevitable cause of the tenth, which could be deduced. And this ninth stage was unique in that the fully developed human mind was finally freed from domination by myth, superstition, mysticism, and intellectual cowardice in general. With his mind freed, modern scientific man, as Condorcet saw the prospect, could only proceed in a more rational way than in the past and introduce those many innovations he predicted.

He saw the future condition of man working out under three general headings: (1) the abolition of inequality between nations, (2) the progress of equality within each nation, and (3) the full perfection of mankind. Since 1794 the most change has probably been seen in the second item. Efforts are now going forward with respect to the first item. But, alas, the most remains to be realized with respect to Condorcet's final item.

As to the coming rule of equality, Condorcet did not see it as canceling out natural differences among men. For he believed "the only kind of inequality to persist will be that which is in the interests of all and which favours the progress of civilization, of education, and of industry, without entailing either poverty, humiliation, or dependence." He then raised the question whether under such a circumstance men will "approach a condition in which everyone will have the knowledge necessary to conduct himself in the ordinary affairs of life, according to the light of his own reason, to preserve his mind free from prejudice, to understand his rights and to exercise them in accordance with his conscience and his creed; in which everyone will become able, through the development of his faculties, to find the means of providing for his needs; and in which at last misery and folly will be the exception, and no longer the habitual lot of a section of society."

This, at any rate, was the ideal he hoped would be attained.

Summarily listed in the order he gave them, here are Condorcet's remarkable series of predictions:

1. The principles of the French revolutionary constitution will spread and inspire the spirit of revolt in the downtrodden of many nations.

2. The colonies of the New World will be made politically independent of Europe.

3. The backward regions of Africa and Asia will be freed from European exploitation.

4. Instead of mercenary adventurers and superstition-mongering monks [missionaries], the advanced nations will send out to the backward peoples more cultivated types able to help propagate in remote regions liberty, knowledge, reason, and happiness.

5. "Meanwhile everything forecasts the imminent decadence of the great religions of the East. . . ."

6. The great differences among individuals in the past, despite formal assertions of legal and political equal rights, had three main causes that led to the destruction of the ancient republics: inequality in wealth, inequality of status as between the man of hereditary privilege and the man obliged to work for a living, and inequality in education. All these inequalities, Condorcet held, are traceable

to "artificial ways of perpetuating and uniting fortunes" by law, which ways, he predicted, will be radically altered.

7. As part of this process of financial leveling, Condorcet foresaw and predicted (or brought into being as a concept) what has since become known as Social Security, especially as it concerns the aged, widows, and orphans.

8. Universal formal education was predicted by Condorcet in these words: "by a suitable choice of syllabus and of methods of education, we can teach the citizen everything that he needs to know in order to be able to manage his household, administer his affairs and employ his labour and faculties in freedom; to know his rights and to be able to exercise them; to be acquainted with his duties and fulfil them satisfactorily; to judge his own and other men's actions according to his own lights and to be a stranger to none of the high and delicate feelings which honour human nature; not to be in a state of blind dependence upon those to whom he must entrust his affairs or the exercise of his rights; to be in a proper condition to choose and supervise them; to be no longer the dupe of those popular errors which torment man with superstitious fears and chimerical hopes; to defend himself against prejudice by the strength of his reason alone; and, finally, to escape the deceit of charlatans who would lay snares for his fortune, his health, his freedom of thought and his conscience under the pretext of granting him health, wealth and salvation."

9. Scientific discovery, involving knowledge of new facts about nature, the analysis of such facts and the relations between objects and all possible combinations of ideas, will continue indefinitely, said Condorcet, bringing more and more of nature within its scope, and more and more knowledge to mankind.

10. Equal opportunities for education will increase the number of scientists and, with them, the scope and number of the sciences.

11. The arts—by which Condorcet meant techniques in general—will flourish along with the sciences, limited only by the range of theory.

12. There will be a tremendous economic expansion, Condorcet predicted. "A very small amount of ground will be able to produce a great quantity of supplies of greater utility or higher quality; more goods will be obtained for a small outlay; the manufacture of articles will be achieved with less wastage in raw materials and will make better use of them.

"So not only will the same amount of ground support more people, but everyone will have less work to do, will produce more, and satisfy his wants more fully.

". . . each successive generation will have larger possessions, either as a result of this progress or through the preservation of the products of industry; and so, as a consequence of the physical constitution of the human race, the number of people will increase."

13. Inequalities of rights between the sexes will be abolished. Women will be educated as well as men.

14. War will come to be regarded "as the most dreadful of scourges, the most terrible of crimes. The first wars to disappear will be those into which usurpers have forced their subjects in defence of their pretended hereditary rights." (Here he foresaw the termination of wars involving dynastic claims.)

15. "Nations will learn that they cannot conquer other nations without losing their own liberty; that permanent confederations are their only means of preserving their independence; and that they should seek not power but security. Gradually mercantile prejudices will fade away: and a false sense of commercial interest will lose the fearful power it once had of drenching the earth in blood and of ruining nations under pretext of enriching them."

16. ". . . wars between countries will rank with assassinations as freakish atrocities, humiliating and vile in the eyes of nature and staining with indelible opprobrium the country or the age whose annals record them." (Here he anticipated a now widely popular view, incorporated in the United Nations Charter.)

17. "The progress of the sciences ensures the progress of the art of education which in turn advances that of the sciences. This reciprocal influence, whose activity is ceaselessly renewed, deserves to be seen as one of the most powerful and active causes working for the perfection of mankind."

18. "No one can doubt that, as preventive medicine improves and food and housing become healthier, as a way of life is established that develops our physical powers by exercise without ruining them by excess, as the two most virulent causes of deterioration, misery and excessive wealth, are eliminated, the average length of human life will be increased and a better health and a stronger physical constitution will be ensured."

19. "The improvement of medical practice, which will become more efficacious with the progress of reason and of the social order, will mean the end of infectious and hereditary diseases and illnesses

brought on by climate, food, or working conditions. It is reasonable to hope that all other diseases may likewise disappear as their distant causes are discovered."

All of this, it should be remembered, was predicted in 1794, when there was scarcely visible a single direct trend toward any of it. All of it was deduced from the progress made in the establishing of general principles by philosophical thought and abstract science.

Did Condorcet at any point overshoot his target, which was future actuality? It must be conceded that he did, although in only a few respects. He seemed to believe it possible for man in a relatively short time to make himself absolutely perfect in all respects, meaning by perfection the full development and realization in each individual of all constructive potentialities: physical, psychological, moral, and intellectual.

But, arguing against scoffers, he held—and correctly—that the average life span could be greatly extended. He went further and said that it could be extended *indefinitely*; he did not believe, however, that man could make himself immortal.

Although correctly foreseeing much change that could be interpreted as progress and much increase in human freedom in general, Condorcet did not foresee the rise of new anti-libertarian tyrannies in the form of Bonapartism, Communism, Fascism, Nazism, and Falangism. He did not see the rise on the heels of war of concentration camps, a peacetime version of war prison camps. Nor did he foresee wars of more terrible dimensions than ever seen before: the Napoleonic Wars that began soon after his death and continued for nearly twenty years and World Wars I and II. Condorcet, then, did not foresee every detail of the future, nor did he claim to. He did, however, quite precisely foresee the general world future for more than 150 years ahead.[2]

Another Frenchman, Alexis de Tocqueville, in his celebrated *Democracy in America*, in the 1840s predicted that Russia and the United States would eventually emerge as the dominant world powers, a skeptically received prediction now realized. In this century Bertrand Russell has made a large number of accurate and important long-range sociocultural predictions, as his biographer notes.[3]

Keynes, Hertz, and Others

We may now direct our attention to some additional successful predictions made in the far more empirical latter-day institutional economics.

John Maynard Keynes, for example, was an economist who showed by means of verified, systematically rational predictions the power of economics as a true science rather than as a quasi-science constructed in slavish imitation of physics. In 1919 Keynes published a book titled *The Economic Consequence of the Peace*. The entire composition was a general prediction: that Germany would be unable to make the reparations payments imposed on her by the victorious Allies and that the treaty would lead (1) to a world collapse of prices, (2) to the creation of a multiplicity of national trade barriers which would induce unemployment and despair all over, (3) to numerous corporate and national bankruptcies, (4) to the birth of violent new nationalisms, and (5) to ultimate political and economic chaos as well as (6) to new wars. His flat, unqualified predictions were publicly endorsed by a large number of prominent economists and political scientists. But they were not endorsed by the leading organs of opinion in the Allied countries, which backed the politicians. These latter, in turn, had the task of keeping their constituents in the dark. For the political constituencies of the Allied countries had been indoctrinated with the thoroughly false idea that Germany alone had caused the war. Now, the politicians argued, it was time for the culprit to pay for the damage it had caused. And this seemed like simple justice to the uninformed.

Keynes's prediction was, as everyone can now discern, completely vindicated by the world economic collapse of the 1930s and the rise to power of Hitler.

Why, we may ask at this point, was such a well-argued and expertly endorsed thesis so thoroughly ignored by responsible political leaders? They were aware of the Keynesian views from the beginning, for Keynes had been a technician with the British delegation to the peace conference, from which he resigned in protest. The answer is that down through history informed rationalism is almost invariably at loggerheads with the vested interests of the day.

What later became known as "Keynesian economics" is embodied in two thoroughly unorthodox books: A *Treatise on Money* (1930) and *The General Theory of Employment, Interest and Money* (1936). The immediate solvable problem underlying widespread unemployment, Keynes argued against many who held it to be underconsumption or overproduction, was actually underinvestment. For unemployment to be efficiently eliminated and minimized, Keynes said, investment in basic producing enterprises and in public works should be greatly increased. The complex economic process in modern society, Keynes held contrary to prevalent views, does not derive its chief impulse from demand of consumers for consumers' goods but from demand of investors for capital goods. Keynes also argued that credit should be made available to entrepreneurs at low interest rates, savings of the public should be reduced and consumption of consumers' goods encouraged. The national budget should be left at a deficit, more money being expended than was taken back in taxes. Building up the fundamental capital equipment of the country—that is, all equipment that produced material goods or services—would bring demand for a wide variety of products to bear against many diverse industries, Keynes pointed out, thus causing them to hire workers of all kinds. The employed workers, in turn, immediately begin spending their pay for all varieties of consumption goods and services, causing demand on the productive enterprises to be compounded.

While Keynes has not been formally vindicated as far as the chief organs of American public opinion are concerned, his policies have been adopted by the British Government, which elevated him to the peerage, and by American governments ever since Franklin D. Roosevelt. Keynes's doctrines were not fully implemented, to be sure, until vast capital sums began to be invested in the war industries and the huge wartime budget deficits were incurred, leading to inflation. Germany under Hitler had unconsciously practiced a part at least of Keynesian doctrine by making heavy capital investments in the munitions industries. Unemployment was eliminated in Germany before it was eliminated in Britain or the United States. To combat inflation Keynes suggested the reverse of his formula: forced savings with much buying deferred.

The shrill outcries of the chief representatives of the vested interests against Keynes in the United States were truly deafening, but by the 1950s many of these same representatives appeared to have quietly adopted Keynes's views without giving him due credit. One similarly encounters persons today who voice many of the original views of Marx and Freud although they formally denounce the two.

The Keynesian theory of employment can be incorporated in a thoroughly scientific, conditional, predictive statement as follows: if heavy investment is made in the productive industries and if a nation goes deeply into debt for the sake of such investment, then effects are produced throughout the economy that cause unemployment to be reduced in some rough proportion to the extent of investment and debt creation and cause prices to rise. The proposition, of course, is susceptible of much more precise extended formulation.

Keynes is not alone among latter-day social scientists in having made practical predictions fully borne out by events. As to the world situation after World War I, Dr. Friedrich Hertz, Austrian political economist, wrote in August, 1919:

"Certainly the subjugated nations will be quite ready to foster everything which may lead to the breaking of their chains. . . . Those states will be exposed to the most violent convulsions, to war, treason, revolution, and the breakdown of the social order. Indeed, there are in the peace terms the germs of new wars, which may involve the whole of Europe in terrible bloodshed again and end in chaos."

Writing in February 1919 in London, F. W. Pethwick Lawrence said:

"A still more serious problem to be faced by the Allies when they consider the imposition of a vast indemnity is the effect it would have on international relationships and the necessity for maintaining military, naval and aerial establishments after the war. . . . It might mean a permanent army of occupation of at least a million men, but even if this were avoided it would certainly imply a tension in Europe which would translate itself into big standing armies, great fleets and swarms of military aeroplanes."

Both these highly circumstantial predictions were fully borne out by events of the next two decades.

The factors that led to World War I itself were precisely warned against by experts. Thus J. A. Hobson, distinguished English economist, in *Imperialism* (1902) wrote:

"That this policy [of imperialism] marks a straight road to ruin there can be no doubt. But how to stop it? What principles of safety can we lay down? Only one—absolute repudiation of the right of British subjects to call upon their government to protect their person or property from injuries or dangers incurred in their private initiative.

. . . Analysis of imperialism with its natural supports, militarism, oligarchy, bureaucracy, [tariff] protection, concentration of capital, and violent trade fluctuations, has marked it out as the supreme danger of modern national states."

Writing in March, 1914, four months before Sarajevo, H. N. Brailsford, English writer, in *The War of Steel and Gold*, held that the coming war would be for exclusive market outlets and world monopoly control of basic natural resources. His analysis was confirmed in detail in the item-by-item provisions of the Treaty of Versailles. But the official propaganda on both sides falsely attributed the war to a struggle for the realization of high-minded ideals set in abstract philosophical frameworks.

One may go back farther than either Hobson or Brailsford for extremely accurate predictions about World War I and its effects. Thus Friedrich Engels, collaborator and associate of Karl Marx, in a letter dated February 23, 1888, to Marx's friend Wilhelm Liebknecht, wrote as follows:

"How things will turn out when it actually comes to war it is impossible to foresee. Attempts will no doubt be made to make it a sham war, but that will not be so easy. If things turn out as we would like it, and this is very probable, then it will be a war of positions with varied success on the French frontier, a war of attack leading to the capture of the Polish fortresses on the Russian frontier, and a revolution in Petersburg, which will at once make the gentlemen who are conducting the war see everything in an entirely different light. One thing is certain: there will be no more quick decisions and triumphal marches either to Berlin or Paris."

Here was a fairly circumstantial prediction of the Russian revolution twenty-nine years before the event!

In a separate prediction Engels forecast that the Germans would probably advance through Belgium by means of what later became known as the "Schlieffen swinging-door plan." This was actually the way the Germans advanced in 1914, although the plan was not developed by the German General Staff until 1905, long after Engels had foreseen it! Engels also predicted that Germany would treat the Belgian Neutrality Treaty as a mere "scrap of paper." It not only did this but used Engels's own words in officially characterizing the violated treaty! And when he made this prediction Engels also, in the early 1890s, predicted that the German advance would be halted at the Marne River, where in fact it was halted.

Writing about the looming World War I in 1891, Engels said:

"This war, where fifteen or twenty million armed men would slaughter one another and lay waste Europe as never before, must either bring about the immediate victory of Socialism, or so shatter the old order of things from top to bottom, and leave behind such a heap of ruins, that the old capitalist society will become more impossible than ever before, and the social revolution, though it might be set back for ten or fifteen years, would however, in this case also, have to conquer and in so much the more speedy and thorough fashion."

The outbreak of World War I found leading economists and historians accurately foretelling where it would lead.

Thus Irving Fisher, professor of political economy at Yale University, wrote in the New York *Times* for August 17, 1914, just two weeks after war broke out:

"The cost of the war is certain to be frightful, both in loss of wealth and loss of life. . . . The future historian will, I imagine, find it difficult to assign any considerable responsibility to anyone, even to those who play the central role in the war drama. . . . The present war will have been utterly in vain. The same causes will continue to produce the same effect. The nations will again vie with each other to have the biggest armies and navies. The people will again have to carry an increasing burden of military duty."

This was not only seeing beyond World War I but beyond World War II as well.

William Sloane, professor of history at Columbia University, in the New York *Times* of September 20, 1914, characterized the war "A disaster of unparalleled significance" and "a future menace to civilization." He warned the United States against becoming involved —one of the many expert warnings that were ignored by the vested financial interests that prevailed upon Woodrow Wilson to become pro-war—and disclosed the essential falsity of Sir Edward Grey's "White Paper." For more than ten years, incidentally, Edward Grey, in 1914 the British Foreign Secretary, had expounded to private upper-class groups his idea of the coming role of England in Continental politics. This role called for England's opposition to German aspirations. In these private talks Grey was repeatedly challenged by Bertrand Russell, then a little-known young logician but also a member of the upper class, his grandfather a former Foreign Secretary. Russell's view, vindicated by events, was that Grey's policy would be the ruin of Britain, but all it earned Russell was an undeserved reputation for being pro-German. This accusation seemed justified because Russell felt England should not oppose Germany in its designs on France. Russell was again monumentally correct when in 1920, after a trip to Bolshevik Russia, he informed world liberals that they had nothing to hope from Bolshevik Russia, which he accurately characterized even in those days as a centralized despotism devoted solely to its own aggrandizement. Many liberals rejected Russell's analysis, to their later chagrin and discomfiture.†

Again, after the war and in the years leading up to the world economic crisis of the 1930s, leading independent European and American economists repeatedly criticized the economic and financial policies of the governments, which they accurately predicted would lead to the difficulties of the 1930s. Such economists included Gustav Cassel, Sir George Paish, Hjalmar Schacht, Sir Arthur Salter, H. Parker Willis, Paul M. Warburg, Benjamin M. Anderson, and Max Winkler.[4]

As to various more specific and precisely formulated government measures, social scientists also have an impressive record in making predictions of what the effects would be. In 1930, for example, the Congress of the United States passed a measure called the Smoot-Hawley Tariff Act that provided for sharp increases in American tariffs, with the presumed intention of protecting American industry and employment from the competition of cheap foreign goods. Before the bill was passed it was publicly protested by several hundred economists who publicly circulated a round-robin statement predicting that the effects of the bill would be reduced world trade and sharply increased unemployment. As other countries passed similar measures in self-protection against the American colossus, this is precisely what happened. And suddenly swollen German unemployment, it is now well known, had much to do with assuring the elevation to power of Adolf Hitler in 1933.

The Roosevelt administration, in harmony with scientific recommendations in so many respects, scored perhaps its worst record in a quarter wherein it ignored expert and informed opinion. That quarter

---

† Bertrand Russell, one of the really acute minds of the twentieth century, long outlived his own brilliance. As an octogenarian his succession of contradictory pronouncements in the 1950s and early 1960s about Soviet Russia, nuclear policy, NATO, and disarmament served to bring into serious public question the intellectual stability of his final years.

had to do with Soviet Russia. Roosevelt's New Deal was not, as some partisans are quick to point out, pro-Soviet or pro-Communist. But Roosevelt, believing all other approaches barred, had determined on a policy of candid friendship, with the obvious intention of winning the Soviet to cooperation with the free world. He aimed, in brief, to seduce the Kremlin into the path of virtuous cooperation. The Kremlin by its many churlish responses and underhanded conduct showed that it understood precisely what he was up to.

Critical experts on Soviet affairs, however, warned Roosevelt publicly and privately that this approach could never succeed, would unduly expose the United States to harm, and advised instead a more cautious attitude toward the Kremlin. The extensive blood purges of the late 1930s in Russia, directed at a very large segment of Communist personnel, alone testified that the Kremlin could not play a cooperative role in the world.

The early predictions of these experts on Russian behavior have been repeatedly borne out in minute detail for more than twenty years.

What of the way Soviet Russia turned out under the leadership of Lenin and Stalin compared with the high hopes of socialists all over the world for the socialist revolution? Was the main Russian turn of events foreseen by anyone? It was indeed foreseen, long before the event, and by the founder of Lenin's Russian Social Democratic party itself, Georgi Plekhanov (1857–1918). Writing in 1884, Plekhanov predicted that the attempt to impose socialism on Russia by force, as was later done by the left-wing Bolsheviks in the Social Democratic Party under Lenin, would inevitably lead "to a political deformity after the image of the Chinese and Peruvian Empire, a renewed Czarist despotism with a Communist lining." And this is just what Soviet Russia is.

Leon Trotsky as early as 1905 predicted that Lenin's tactics would lead to a narrow party dictatorship contrary to Marxism. Trotsky later joined in establishing that very dictatorship.

Predictions about the future of Russia must wait until we come to consider, in later chapters, political and economic developments in the world.

Some Concluding Remarks

In conclusion, the social sciences are usually represented as of very low predictive power compared with the physical sciences. But the comparison is hardly valid for a number of reasons. First, since the rise of quantum physics, with its element of uncertainty in measurement, physical scientists no longer claim jurisdiction over exact prediction. In classical physics, which dealt in the larger phenomena such as celestial and terrestrial mechanics, the claim to make exact predictions was indeed made. Reality, in the classical conception, was like a gigantic clock, and if one knew the whereabouts of some of its parts one could tell the future whereabouts of other parts—an impressive feat to most beholders. Again, certain apparently invariable sequences of phenomena having been established, one could foretell the occurrence of these sequences if the relevant factors were present, thus giving us the conditional prediction.

But many such virtually invariable sequences were also present on the social scene. For example: If people Y wage war against people X, then people X will wage war against people Y. So the predictions of physics were not greatly different, although they were doubly impressive because they were made about impersonal, and mysterious, nature. It is only very recently that human nature has come to seem as baffling as non-human nature. Man for long has, perhaps through familiarity, felt that he knew himself sufficiently at least not to be impressed by predictive statements about people, especially if they were cynical statements.

There is, indeed, little difference between physical prediction and the sort of social prediction we are chiefly interested in. Both kinds of prediction hold only that if certain conditions are satisfied, then there will be a certain consequence.

This is just the sort of prediction, for a relatively short span of time to be sure, that I wish to make in the sociocultural sphere. We want to know certain things that will almost inevitably occur. We cannot, let me admit at once, pretend to have an inkling of everything that will occur, or exactly when it will occur, because we aren't aware of all the preconditions. But we want to know about certain important changes apart from more or less accidental events.

Physics has certain procedural rules or assumptions that are in fact predictions. One of these stipulates that nature is uniform and another that it is continuous. The prediction is that if one investigates, one will always discover at any future time that nature is uniform and that it is continuous. This procedural rule (disguised prediction) has always been verified in the sense that it has never—yet—been found to be false. But there is no theorem that will prove it.

Actually, if one confines one's attention to existing states of affairs, there is more power in the social sciences with which to make reliable probability predictions than in the physical sciences. The latter only rarely predict future states of affairs, but usually stipulate only the conditions that must hold if certain states of affairs are to be the case. Moreover, the consequences of stipulated antecedent conditions are rarely *exactly* as visualized.

As to social scientists, since 1936 they have predicted the outcome of American presidential elections within a maximum range of error of 6 per cent; in the election of 1960 they were within a margin of error of 1 per cent. Beyond the prediction of such events, social scientists are able to make innumerable valuable tendency predictions such as, "In a time of economic difficulty there is a strong tendency for an uncoerced electorate to vote against the party in power." Again, "In time of war there is a strong tendency for the suicide rate to fall."

Rather than deal with the power of the social sciences in detail, the reader may be referred to *Can Science Save Us?* by Professor George A. Lundberg of the University of Washington (Longmans, Green and Co., 1947) for a discussion of the predictive power of these sciences in coping with social problems.

As to science in general, conceptions of it are almost as varied as the great number of those who engage to interpret it to the public. What is science to one eminent interpreter, often a working scientist of great repute, turns out not to be science to another equally eminent interpreter. For this reason perhaps it might be helpful to let the reader know what, in general, is the view of science implicit in this book. It is put forward by that extremely sophisticated and subtle interpreter, Karl Popper, in *The Logic of Scientific Discovery*.

"Science is not a system of certain, or well-established, statements," Popper writes, "nor is it a system which steadily advances towards a state of finality. Our science is not knowledge (*epistēmē*): it can never claim to have attained truth, or even a substitute for it, such as probability.

"Yet science has more than mere biological survival value. It is not only a useful instrument. Although it can attain neither truth nor probability, the striving for knowledge and the search for truth are still the strongest motives of scientific discovery.

"*We do not know: we can only guess.* And our guesses are guided by the unscientific, the metaphysical (though biologically explicable) faith in laws, in regularities which we can uncover—discover. Like Bacon, we might describe our own contemporary science—'the method of reasoning which men now ordinarily apply to nature'—as consisting of 'anticipations, rash and premature' and as 'prejudices.' [The quotations by Popper are from Bacon's *Novum Organum*, I, 26.]

"But these marvellously imaginative and bold conjectures or 'anticipations' of ours are carefully and soberly controlled by systematic tests. Once put forward, none of our 'anticipations' are dogmatically upheld. Our method of research is not to defend them, in order to prove how right we are. On the contrary, we try to overthrow them. Using all the weapons of our logical, mathematical, and technical armoury we try to prove that our anticipations were false—in order to put forward, in their stead, new unjustified and unjustifiable anticipations, new 'rash and premature prejudices,' as Bacon derisively called them . . .

"The advance of science is not due to the fact that more and more perceptual experiences accumulate in the course of time. Nor is it due to the fact that we are making ever better use of our senses. Out of uninterpreted sense-experiences science cannot be distilled, no matter how industriously we gather and sort them. Bold ideas, unjustified anticipations, and speculative thought are our only means for interpreting nature: our only organon, our only instrument, for grasping her. And we must hazard them to win our prize. Those among us who are unwilling to expose their ideas to the hazard of refutation do not take part in the scientific game. . . .

"The old scientific ideal of *epistēmē*—of absolutely certain, demonstrable knowledge—has proved to be an idol. The demand for scientific objectivity makes it inevitable that every scientific statement must remain *tentative* forever. It may indeed be corroborated, but every corroboration is relative to other statements which, again, are tentative. Only in our subjective experiences of conviction, in our subjective faith, can we be 'absolutely certain.'

"With the idol of certainty (including that of degrees of imperfect certainty or probability) there falls one of the defences of obscurantism which bars the way of scientific advance, checking the boldness of our questions, and endangering the rigour and the integrity of our tests. The wrong view of science betrays itself in the craving to be right; for it is not his *possession* of knowledge, of irrefutable truth, that makes the man of science, but his persistent and recklessly critical *quest* for truth.

"Has our attitude, then, to be one of resignation? Have we to say that science can fulfill only its biological task; that it can, at best, merely prove its mettle in practical applications which may corroborate it? Are its intellectual problems insoluble? I do not think so. Science never pursues the illusory aim of making its answers final, or even probable. Its advance is, rather, towards the infinite yet attainable aim of ever discovering new, deeper, and more general problems, and of subjecting its ever tentative answers to ever renewed and ever more rigorous tests."[5]

It is far from my intention to suggest that the social sciences are as advanced as the physical sciences. But it can readily be shown that they are far more advanced than is commonly thought even by some rather careful students of science in general.[6] And by those thoroughly conversant with adequate methods, as I think I have established in this chapter, significant predictions of impressive power have often been made on a semiscientific basis. Indeed, as I hope to establish in this work, such significant predictions can be made quite systematically—that is, scientifically—which fact (if established) will do something to validate the scientific claims of the social sciences.

It will be the aim in the next chapter to isolate, one by one, the main factors that make for predictable sociocultural change in order to provide the groundwork for later additions by other workers in this same field. In the course of time, as fresh factors are uncovered, there will become available to mankind a new discipline that will allow better and more precise sociocultural forecasting, both general and particular. To this new and still-to-be-developed discipline I give the name of prognostics.

CHAPTER III

TOWARD A GENERAL THEORY
OF SOCIAL PREDICTION

When all is said and done there seems to be evidence that even the "laws of nature" are changing. Modern physics suggests the possibility that changes are taking place in the speed of light and the rates of chemical reactions. In other words, the universe is changing, and it becomes hazardous to attempt calculations concerning the very remote past and future. It appears that eternal natural stability is as improbable as its psychological corollary, eternal truth. This should worry no one except the seeker of eternal certainty. It may turn out that fundamental change and uncertainty are the nearest things we have to eternal principles.

—WILLIAM S. BECK

Can one make valid predictions in purely human—that is, sociocultural—affairs?

"There is a popular conception that prediction is impossible in human and social affairs," observes the sociologist William F. Ogburn; "at least, one often hears this opinion expressed, particularly among individuals who admire wisdom and conservatism and deplore recklessness. The person who essays to predict social events readily becomes the butt of criticism of wise elders.

"There are various sources of this popular belief. One lies in the fact that we all can see the unexpected happen. What seems certain does not occur. Forecasts go wrong. We gamble on the future and lose. . . . Another source is the popular belief in luck and chance. The movement of the stock market or the success of a theatrical production is believed to be due to chance or luck. Disasters come from the hands of Fate. In some religious groups, God's way is held unpredictable and His hand is often seen manifested in the affairs of men. This conception of luck or fate denies causation or inevitability, which is the basis of scientific prediction.

"Another source of disbelief in prediction of social affairs is the idea of freedom of the will. In some intellectual groups, it is admitted that prediction about the stars can be made because they are unaffected by human effort. But in society everything that is done is influenced by human will, and therefore is neither inevitable nor predictable.

"Finally, there is the cautious person, interested in his reputation for good judgment, who does not wish to undertake the hazard of forecasting the future; and, having a reputation to protect, he speaks impressively about the futility of trying to look into the future."[1]

Social scientists, made unduly sensitive by the miscarriages of predictions by some early precursors, seem chary of predicting. As Ogburn points out, "most social scientists prefer to be historians and are less willing to venture an estimate of the future than the businessman or the ordinary citizen. The ability to look ahead with some success is particularly important in a changing society. . . . What is needed is many social scientists working at the problem of forecasting the future as well as social scientists writing histories of past events. With many social scientists working on the future, we should gradually accumulate a set of useful procedures. . . . In the course of time, with others working on forecasting, a tradition of usages will be built up, and we shall know better how to do it."[2]

Thus far Ogburn's plea has borne little discernible fruit. Peter Drucker, a management economist, says flatly, "But no human being can possibly predict the future, let alone control it."[3] Professor Drucker makes this observation in a book titled *Landmarks of Tomorrow*. As he is the author of another book entitled *America's Next Twenty Years*, he is perhaps at least unconsciously a bit ambivalent on the subject.

Arnold Toynbee, the historian, places himself on record with the assertion that "I myself believe that prediction is not possible in the field of human affairs. I believe that the outcomes of human choices, purposes, and plans are unpredictable intrinsically, however fully we may be informed about the relevant past facts up to date. And I also believe that these intrinsically unpredictable plans, purposes, and choices play a large enough part in every human situation to invalidate predictions based on other elements in human affairs that might perhaps be predictable if ever they could be isolated."[4]

Toynbee's precept is contradicted by Toynbee's practice. For example, he has taken to issuing warnings of what dire consequences will probably ensue for mankind if certain "responses" are not made to certain "challenges" of the times. If certain actions X are not taken, he often predicts, then certain consequences Y may be expected to take place, even the downfall of Western civilization.

Thus Toynbee is reported in a *Reuter's* dispatch from Oxford as saying that "the human race is not likely to survive unless it succeeds in regulating the birth rate by means other than war, pestilence and famine."[5] In the same year, writing under the title of "The Pioneer Destiny of Judaism," he said, "As a historian, peering into the future in the light of the past, I spy the wave of the future in the Jewish Diaspora." He went on to argue that there is dawning a new age, which he calls "the Age of Diasporas." In this age, he predicts, the typical community will not be the present nation-state but a "world-encompassing" religious and "non-monopolistic association." The world will be united politically but will be religiously pluralistic.[6]

Again, Toynbee is on record as holding that American liberal democracy can become the "wave of the future" only if it recaptures the pioneer spirit.[7] And the fate of Athens and Rome awaits the United States if it practices national selfishness and overcentralization of power.[8]

All these statements, it is evident, are predictions, and Toynbee's historical writings are filled with predictions, direct and implicit. His formal denial of the possibility of predicting the future can therefore only be interpreted as meaning one cannot predict it correctly, in which case any prediction, including his own, is meaningless. History, too, becomes meaningless if any possibility of applying its lessons is denied. For such lessons must be applied, if at all, in a future.

If the widely prevalent view that one cannot predict the future is interpreted to mean that nobody can foretell everything about *all* of the future in minute detail, it is unquestionably correct but hardly more than a truism. If it is interpreted to mean that nobody can foretell everything about all of some *narrow segment* of the future such as the coming week, year, or decade it is equally correct and truistic. But if it is interpreted to mean that no reliable predictions whatever about the future can be made, no reliable forecasts about broad necessary developments as distinct from accidental details, then it is demonstrably and monumentally wrong. Business forecasters correctly predict business conditions for a year ahead and, in some spheres, for as far as ten years ahead. Governments, as already observed, must continually make predictions of long and short range, many of which turn out to be quite correct.

If the United States unilaterally dismantles its military establishment, as recommended by some, it will quickly fall under the absolute rule of Soviet Russia. This prediction is as certain as that the sun will first appear on the morrow over the eastern horizon. If the stipulated condition were met, the United States would very quickly attain the political status of Poland and Hungary, the main difference being that it would be a larger puppet.

Yet the denial of the possibility of making correct predictions has many followers, as Ogburn notes, and most social scientists would probably join in taking a more or less dubious view of predicting. But if one utilizes the same non-selective interpretation of the past, one could as reasonably say the historian cannot say anything valid about what is past.

It is otherwise with physical scientists, many of whom have been extremely active of late about making some extremely long-range social predictions. The mere fact that they are scientists concededly does not guarantee the accuracy of their predictions, but it is at least significant that they are not astrologers, theologians, fortunetellers, or rash speculators. Harrison Brown, geochemist with the California Institute of Technology, in 1954 published *The Challenge of Man's Future*, which makes reasoned empirical predictions about the future in the light of population pressure against natural resources. In collaboration with two colleagues he published in 1957 *The Next Hundred Years*, introducing technological and intellectual resources into the equations of the former book. Of the first book Albert Einstein said, "We may well be grateful to Harrison Brown for this book on the condition of mankind as it appears to an erudite, clear-sighted, critically appraising scientist. . . . The latest phase of technical-scientific progress, with its fantastic increase of population, has created a situation fraught with problems of hitherto unknown dimensions. . . . This objective book has high value."

Our Nuclear Future is the title of a book published in 1958 by Edward Teller and Albert L. Latter, both physicists, the former the "father" of the hydrogen bomb. Late in 1957 a seminar of physicists, chemists, and biologists met in New York City and made predictions on affairs extending up to the year 2057; some of their more imaginative flights were reported in the New York *Times Magazine* of December 8, 1957. Under the title of "The Next 10,000 Years" J. H. Rush, a physicist, contributed an article to *The Saturday Review* of January 25, 1958. "Planning for the Year 2,000" by J. Bronowski,

British physicist, appeared in *The Nation* of March 22, 1958. In "Science as Foresight" Bronowski contributes the final chapter to *What Is Science?* (1955), edited by James R. Newman. But Sir Charles Galton Darwin, grandson of the author of *The Origin of the Species* and himself a nuclear physicist, appears to be well ahead of everybody as far as time span of prediction is concerned with his *The Next Million Years*, a forecast published in 1953 of the long-term future of the human race. Many other such works could be cited.

What is decisive, however, on this question of whether or not one can make valid predictions in human affairs is that the logicians of science hold that one can. Professor Ernest Nagel of Columbia University, for instance, writes that "it is in fact sometimes possible to foresee, if only in a general way, what are the likely consequences for established social habits of the acquisition of new knowledge or new skills. For example, the manufacture of equipment required as a means of transportation and communication generally increases with the industrialization of a society. On the other hand, there is also evidence for the generalization that, when men discover the advantages of more rapid forms of transportation and communication, they tend to use these forms in preference to older but slower forms. In consequence, when knowledge of more rapid forms becomes widespread, the manufacture of equipment for the established forms will tend either to decrease altogether or to increase at a diminished rate, and at the same time the natural resources needed for that manufacture will either be exploited on a smaller scale or be assigned other uses. Even if the effects of the newly acquired knowledge upon patterns of social behavior may not be predictable in minute detail, at least a rough account can sometimes be supplied concerning the probable consequences of such innovations. In short, if the knowledge men possess of social processes is a variable that enters into the determination of social phenomena, there are no a priori grounds for maintaining that changes in that variable and the effects they may produce cannot be the subject of social laws."*

In another place Professor Nagel observes that "nothing comparable to quantum mechanics is available in the social sciences upon which to rest the assumption that human events are theoretically unpredictable. Nor does the actual evidence establish the claim that human actions are utterly unpredictable in fact. It would be ridiculous

* Ernest Nagel, *The Structure of Science* (New York: Harcourt, Brace & World, Inc., 1961), p. 471.

to maintain that every detail in man's future can be predicted, or even to pretend that every event in the human past can be inferred from the available data. On the other hand, it is no less ridiculous to hold that we are completely incompetent to predict anything about the human future with any assurance of being correct. It is almost truistic to note that our personal relations with other men, our political arrangements and social institutions, our transportation schedules and our administration of justice, could not be what they are unless fairly safe inferences were possible about the human past and future. To be sure, we cannot predict with any certainty who will be the next President of the United States. But if we take for granted current American attitudes toward domestic and foreign issues, and also take into account the present alignment of the world powers, we do have good grounds for confidence that there will be a presidential election during the next leap year, that neither major political party will nominate a Communist, and that the successful candidate will be neither a woman nor a Negro. These various predictions are indefinite in certain ways, for they do not foretell the future in a manner to exclude all but one conceivable alternative. Nevertheless, the predictions *do* exclude an enormous number of logical possibilities; and they do point up the fact that, though the human beings who will participate in the coming events may have considerable range of free choice in their actions, their actual choices and actions will fall within fairly definite limits. The obvious import of all this is that not everything which is logically possible is also historically possible during a given period and for a given society of men; and the equally obvious interpretation of this fact is that there are determining conditions for both what has happened and what will happen in human affairs."†

But a clear statement of the relevant theoretical laws or rules of procedure, as distinct from empirical or universal synthetic laws, will be required before we are ready to go ahead. Universal synthetic laws are apparently not widely applicable in the present condition of knowledge to sociocultural phenomena as such and may never be.

Before proceeding there is a further point to be made in reply to those who hold, inconsistently, that one cannot predict the future or any part of it. The very statement "One cannot predict the future or any part of it" contains a concealed prediction that the future will be found so unique that one cannot say anything accurate about it in advance. For saying "The future is unique" or "The future is novel

† *Ibid.*, pp. 598–99.

surprise" is the same as saying "The future will be found to be unique" or "The future will be found to be a novel surprise," predictions both. The only way to avoid making predictions about the future, right or wrong, is to deny the possibility of a future at all and thus go against common moment-to-moment experience. Merely saying there is coming such a state of affairs as a future is a prediction. Attaching predicates to this state of affairs is further prediction.

Change and the Universe

Paradoxically, the only invariably stable general feature about the world appears to be change. The universe, in the light of modern physics, is a wanton hyperbolic dance of ever-seething, perishable particles that mysteriously combine in certain definite proportions to produce the gross phenomena known as matter and form. As succinctly put by Heraclitus of Ephesus (536–470 B.C.) as cited by Plato, "All is flux." And human social and cultural affairs, no less than those of the environing impersonal universe studied in physics, chemistry, and biology, are also subject to constant alteration as history attests, to the perennial dismay of conservatives. For all that is conserved is change itself.

The larger physical and biological events are beyond the control of man, and at most can be somewhat anticipated, modified, and anthropocentrically utilized in certain respects. But on the social and cultural level man is the center, the agent as it were of environing nature.

The word "change," like many others in the natural languages, is imprecise. In physical science it refers, irreducibly, to the purely spatio-temporal motion and relationship of energy particles or collections of particles. Change is here understood as alteration in some overarching physical state, as when iron rusts, water changes to vapor, radiation occurs—that is, when some combination or separation of particles takes place. But social and cultural changes, with which we are primarily concerned, are quite different, more complex, and serve to mark off sharply the social and cultural sciences from the physical sciences.

Social change refers fundamentally to some alteration in the tangled maze of individual and group relationships among people and in the interconnections of such relationships.

The establishment, modification, or abolition of slavery, serfdom, free citizenship, hereditary titles, private property, laws of inheritance, marriage, constitutions, and civil liberties are examples that represent social change. Lest the impression be conveyed that social relations are also invariably relations in law, let it be noticed that the changes of people from hunters to grazing nomads, to agriculturalists, to artisans, to factory workers, to office workers, to professionals also represent changes in social relations.

Social relationships are so numerous and diverse that at first blush it seems almost impossible to encompass them all intellectually. Each person in society stands in thousands of specifiable relationships to hundreds of groups and millions of people all over the earth.

Because social change consists of changes in existing social relationships, it would be clarifying if one could succinctly indicate something precise about the nature and complexity of the relations in question. Fortunately the relations involved in discourse have been formally abstracted in the logic of relations. They are designated by degrees as dyadic, triadic, tetradic, and polyadic—that is to say, they involve two, three, four, or many terms or objects. Such degrees of relations, moreover, are subject to further abstract formal classification as (1) symmetric, asymmetric, and non-symmetric; (2) transitive, intransitive, and non-transitive; (3) reflexive, irreflexive, and non-reflexive; (4) connective and disconnective; (5) correlative, and on to still others.

Although social relations are reducible to abstract logical form, this does not mean that the same type of relation, logically speaking, has a uniform social or cultural status. The social meaning of any particular relationship is very different from its logical classification. There is again the cultural evaluation of the relation to be considered, although cultural evaluation does not always coincide with social utility. Culturally some relation may be rated high or low; socially it may be of opposite operational value.

But the possibility of abstractly rendering the structure of social relationships (which I will not attempt to do) indicates precisely what social change refers to. It is alterations in these relations. Each kind of logical relation is socially exemplified in many different ways and is reflected particularly in accurate statistics that show occupation, marital and parental status, education, level of income, religion, nativity, ethnic grouping, condition of health and the like. Such groups include subgroups as well as individual members.‡

‡ Some logical considerations relevant to this study are set forth in Appendix A.

The Nature of Social Change

Social change consists of alteration in numbers included or excluded in any of these socially expressed logical relationships and in creation of new relationships and abolition of old. But it is only when there are enough instances of alteration to be noticeable that social change is said to take place. One can, in other words, predict general social change by predicting detailed changes in social relationships. While in practice one can attempt to predict only a relatively few of these in which one is most interested, theoretically one could certainly predict what would happen to all within specified limits by isolating every single relationship and predicting what alteration it would undergo under pressure of known factors.

As to general social predictions, one must introduce various restrictions to guard against historically possible contingencies—that the society in question will be left to its own management, that it will not be conquered and subjected to a conqueror's will, that no presently unknown factors such as the appearance of a new kind of epidemic disease will be brought to bear, etc. What of sudden novel future arbitrary decisions by people in general to follow some uncharted course, such as a possible decision of the people of the United States to reunite with Britain under the British crown? Such arbitrary novel actions in history are few if not completely absent; for peoples and societies strongly tend to be guided in their collective actions by their *cultural style*, which amounts to a general broad programming for action. History is often the report of clashes of cultural styles.

While change in only one instance of any social relationship certainly represents some change, it is only when there are many changes adding up to a mass phenomenon that social change is acknowledged to take place. Here it is the same as with the gas laws of physics. The change in velocity or direction of one or a very few particles in a certain volume of gas is not considered to have altered the state of the gas; for the gas laws do not pretend to take account· of individual random particles, only of the average statistical action of particles. Social change is similarly detectable only in statistical aggregates. When the aggregate of blacksmiths or midwives increases or decreases by only a few there is no social change discerned. But when the occupation of blacksmith or midwife virtually disappears, the disappearance is seen to be an instance of and part of great social change. The subsequent appearance of automobile mechanics, aviation mechanics, and medical obstetricians reveals further evidence of social change.

But predictions of changes in social relationships can only validly take place on the basis of some evidence. A wild guess might by chance turn out to be correct, but this would hardly validate guessing as a reliable method of prediction. Evidence, however, never speaks for itself but must be interpreted. Care in interpretation should produce some convergence of predictions by various prognosticators to a certain range that is a great deal narrower than the entire range of ideal possibility. But sociocultural predictions cannot be absolutely certain. They must take place, as in the physical sciences, on the basis of relative probabilities, interpreting probability here as determined by the weight of evidence.

Culture and Society

Cultural change, although closely related to social change, is quite different. Culture, unlike society, is not so readily reducible to a complex of structurally connected logical relations. For culture, to cut through a mass of involved description, is most basically a tangled accumulation of group devices or inventions. It is the totality of what members of a group have acquired by learning and habitually express in acts, thoughts, techniques, tools, beliefs, hopes, statements and other symbolic representations. As E. B. Tylor put it in *Primitive Culture* (1871) it is "that complex whole which includes knowledge, belief, art, morals, law, custom and any other capabilities and habits acquired by man as a member of society." A society is itself a more or less confused cultural expression.

The term "culture" is used in this book as it is defined and discussed by the anthropologist A. L. Kroeber.[9]

As Ernst Cassirer noted, "All works of culture originate in an act of solidification and stabilization,"[10] which is what I refer to as an invention. Whatever is noticeable about a culture after the first invention, whatever it was, are the elements of relative permanence (retained old inventions) and change (new inventions). Nothing in human experience is absolutely permanent, and it is the mistake of the traditionalist to postulate permanence. The retained old inventions of a culture compose what is known as tradition, a habitual pattern, and conflict in a culture comes about through the appearance of new inventions that rival the traditional pattern, as modern science rose in rivalry against religion. Even what is believed to be most permanent, such as language or religion, is itself subject to slow change as many small new inventions are introduced into it. The English language of today, for example, is very different from the English of Chaucer's or of Shakespeare's day. Christian Catholicism today is very different from the Catholicism of A.D. 500, A.D. 1400, or even A.D. 1800.

Although cultures always change, their prescientific slow change gives some semblance of validity to the position of the traditionalist, who believes that certain things never change, among them human nature. But at times the introduction of certain new inventions accelerates the process of change and fundamentally challenges the traditional pattern both of culture and society. We live in a time of such accelerated change, owing to the introduction of powerful novelties such as science and machine technology. Through these everything that is old in Western culture—religion, social myth or ideology, and even language—is being fundamentally challenged. The introduction of machine technology into society, making obsolete almost all established tools and procedures, has had the effect of fundamentally altering the structure of society and its institutions and of forcing further alterations—the special object of our interest in this book.

While I do not wish to discuss the nature of culture at any length, leaving the interested reader to consult the authorities, the power of the culture over man is emphasized in a certain extreme view of it that the culture itself has autonomy, a life of its own, and directs man rather than being subject to man. This view is put forward by Leslie A. White.[11]

White supports his view by citing the long line of technical and scientific inventions that logically succeeded each other and the many inventions that were simultaneously produced by different men far removed from each other. The culture, as he sees it, simply made use of properly organized nervous systems to make new inventions as extensions of the old. In White's view, man is a puppet of his culture, responding to its prescriptions.

White's view, however, does not explain long periods of inventive sterility, as between the end of the Hellenic world and the Renaissance. Why, in other words, is man sometimes not visibly responsive to the promptings of the culture? Mass preoccupation with the problem of sheer survival could conceivably explain such culturally sterile periods. Again, White's view does not explain artistic creation which, unlike scientific creation, does not take place in a tight logical procession, each stage of which foretells the next. And in art, unlike science, two identical works from different minds, such as calculus or the Darwin-Wallace theory of evolution, are never seen. In music neither Bach, Beethoven, nor Wagner had successors who carried their styles to further heights. In painting neither Michelangelo nor El Greco had stylistic successors who followed as Newton followed Galileo, Kepler, Copernicus and Brahe, and Einstein followed Newton and others.

Some parts of culture, then, foreshadow coming inventions; but not all parts. Man, as Kroeber asserted, is the creator, not the culture, even though as a creator he interacts with his culture. In the matter of interaction with man the culture shows its power. What each culture knows as "human nature," for example, is largely a cultural perspective. And what some term such as "*basic* human nature"—that is, human nature stripped of all that is learned—means is no more than pristine animality.

It is not the culture, then, that invents, but man, although man works with materials given to him by the culture on the basis of motivations stimulated in him by his environment. Much of what man invents, moreover, is not seriously purposive but is invented in a spirit of play or diversion. It often takes men a long time to see any practical application for some inventions, as in the case of conic sections or the steam engine of Hero of Alexandria (third century A.D.).[12]

Whether an invention shall be applied, and how it shall be applied, remains for social determination. Expressing the dominant orientation of American society, the determination in the case of ingenious inventions like the radio and television was that they should be mainly used for the entertainment of the masses to bring them into range for persuasive advertising of items of consumption. In some possible other society they would have been used for the education of the masses and, indeed, steps were taken in this direction by the government-owned British Broadcasting Corporation in its "Third Programme." In Russia the radio is used for the persuasive advertising of political ideas.

Culture, in any event, is the repository of the objects, prescriptions, and conventions that help hold society together, although a peculiarity about culture is that, despite accepting new elements, it does not give up completely any element no matter how old or outmoded it may be. Society, to its discomfiture, often tries to apply disparate cultural elements, but in the long run society must accommodate itself to the most coercive of the cultural elements—that is, powerful technological inventions—or be abruptly reconstituted.

Improbable Factors of Change

Many possible developments of which no account is taken in our predictions could conceivably influence future events within our time limit, but such possible developments are not taken into account because there is no evidence they will be operative.

Unprecedentedly heavy showers of cosmic rays from outer space or unusual solar radiation might induce radical mutations in human germ cells, resulting in a radically new kind of person who proceeds to establish a new pattern of existence on earth. A new Ice Age might cover half the earth; the earth might tilt on its axis and thus alter climate, or climate might change for some other reason.

But for more than 10,000 years there has been no known change at all in basic human nature or in environing earthly nature. In the absence of positive evidence there seems no reason one should anticipate changes brought about either by changes in environing nature or in human nature. We may, then, take nature and human nature as broad constants for our purposes.

Man himself, cultural man, is the source to which we must look for the stimuli to change of the kind we can predict within broad limits. Since the last Ice Age man himself has produced the most spectacular alterations on earth in the form of cities and empires. Man himself is the great natural force with which we must reckon most carefully. He can now make nature's deserts bloom with life as well as he can destroy cities and consume forests. He can now literally remove mountains.

But are the changes wrought by man entirely random and casual? Are they spasmodic, the result of sudden novel decisions? Or can any order, pattern, or system be discerned in man-induced change?

The Cyclical Theory of Change

Since civilization first emerged, greatly impressing reflective men, many theories of social change have been put forward. Such theories have concerned change both in its larger outlines and in its microscopic, detailed, or bits-and-pieces aspects.

The oldest, most encompassing and perhaps best-known theory of social change, put forward by many persons with special variations and emphasis from Plato to Nietzsche, Pareto, Spengler, Toynbee, and Sorokin, is the cyclic theory, which holds that change takes place according to a recurrent discernible basic pattern or rhythm. Cycles that account for change are emotionally satisfying, perhaps because they are found in environing nature in the form of seasons, day and night, the rotation of the celestial system, the rise and fall of the tides, the life cycle, the lunar cycle and the like. It is simple and seemingly logical to say that all change is cyclical.

The cycle of social change as envisioned by its devotees may be circular, arguing that repetition is essentially the case over long periods of time. More favored currently is a cycle in ascending spiral form, allowing room for some novelty in the extension of the spiral —enlarging as it unwinds—but the argument remains that change takes place in a typical sequence of standard basic types of phenomena. A multicyclical theory is also a possibility, with different orders of change occurring at different periods.

There are also linear and multilinear theories of change, as in those that argue for progress, evolution, development from simplicity to complexity, and the emergence of basic novelty; and curvilinear and multicurvilinear theories. Changes within these larger patterns when they are cyclical may take place rhythmically or in pulsations, rhythm and pulsation being determined by inherent phenomenal limits.[13]

All orderly change, it is argued by the respective proponents, fits into one or another of these theories. The possibilities that remain are that social change is not patterned but is entirely random, irregular, and disorderly or that it is subdivisionally patterned but does not follow geometric designs.

At times, to be sure, social change is disorderly, as during the disintegration of a society. But in periods of increasing integration it appears to follow relatively orderly lines.

For our purposes it is not necessary to decide which of these theories relating to long-range sociocultural change is applicable. Far more evidence than has been adduced thus far is necessary before any of these abstract patterns can be established as controlling. The most serious objection to all these theories from a scientific point of view is that they are not at all informative about the future. They give no details. All the cyclical theories hold is that the distant future will, vaguely, be pretty much like the long-gone past. At most this yields a lulling emotional satisfaction. One feels one is being rocked in the cradle of a preordained destiny, that there is nothing really new, and that one will not miss anything novel.

The Harvard sociologist Sorokin has set up what is perhaps the most elaborately argued theory of long-term cyclical change, about which he writes at length in his *Social and Cultural Dynamics*. Sorokin calls the cycle a "super-rhythm" and holds that in Western culture it has cycled two and a half times in three distinct phases that he calls ideational, idealistic, and sensate. Not only are there enormous quantities of empirical data lacking with which to support the theory, but much of the argument rests upon the logical fallacies of equivocation and ambiguity with respect to the word "intuition."

In his final chapter Sorokin predicts the apocalyptic disintegration of sensate Western culture beginning within "a few decades" of his year of publication, which was 1941. With Spengler, in brief, Sorokin is a pessimist, forecasting a cultural debacle. Toynbee is by comparison only mildly pessimistic. Each of these three writers is essentially a mystic, Sorokin and Toynbee in empirical dress.

A disciple of Sorokin's, Amaury de Riencourt, has written *The Coming Caesars* (1957) as a forecast of what is going to happen to the United States and the world. The United States, in brief, is destined to play the role of ancient Rome in the spiraling historical cycle, Europe the role of Greece. The United States is to be ruled by men essentially like the Roman Caesars. And to know in general what is going to happen in the future we have only to read about the Greco-Roman past.

While this sort of prognosis may be satisfying to some readers it will not be the critical-minded, who fail to see signs of repetitive necessity in history. There are features about every age that resemble features of past ages: they all have people and the people have rulers. Analogies are not hard to find. What one is interested in, however, when it comes to predicting is relative novelty. And although the United States is going to have rulers, one thing that one can be certain of is that they will not remotely resemble the Roman Caesars except that they will be men. Because modern society is infinitely more complex than Roman society ever was, the rulers need far more loyal, willing, and highly trained collaborators than any Roman Caesar ever required. This requirement alone rules out anything culturally childish like Caesarism.

Other Theories of Change

Subordinate to such all-embracing abstract theories of sociocultural change as the cyclical, linear, and curvilinear are others relating more modestly to immediate factors of change.

Conflict, struggle, and competition are the chief ingredients in one major theory of change held to variously by Heraclitus, Hegel, Marx, Gumplowicz, Oppenheimer, and various others. Hegel (1770–1831) was the great systematizer of this view, creating from it a fascinating system of illogical logic which is the basis of the official Soviet way of thought today.

As anybody can see for himself by reading history, much readily discernible change comes as an aftermath to conflict, especially conflict in the form of war. The ecological struggle for existence in uncultured nature as defined by Malthus and Darwin is an example of the general struggle concept. Competition is involved, of course, in war and in ecological struggle for existence but it may also be stylized, as in a game, and take place under sociocultural rules. Economic competition, for example, is the official legal doctrine of the United States, at least ritualistically observed by many court decisions. Actually economic competition in the United States is highly qualified, much to the advantage of the people, its rigors softened until it is often much like a friendly tennis match.

But that most change has been wrought without conflict and that conflict is far from basic to sociocultural change is readily understood as soon as one considers all the change brought about through human cooperation, coordination, and friendly adaptation. Unquestionably cooperation has accounted for vastly more change than has conflict and competition—in some ratio such as 9,999 to 1. Science, for example, is almost wholly the product of voluntary cooperative effort; conflict has played no role whatsoever in the development of science as such although military conflict has concededly stimulated much scientific effort by inducing society to pay for it. Conflict did not contribute at all to the development of language, which arose out of the cooperative effort to communicate, or to the development of any of the fine arts. Certain social institutions may have arisen partly or wholly as reflexes to conflict, and the institution that seems most likely to have been a response to such stimulus is the state. But although carrying on much conflict, the chief task of the state historically has been to eliminate conflict over wider and wider areas. Culture as a whole, however, is obviously a product of cooperation almost entirely, and only in small part a reflex to conflict.

Even in conflict, it is noticeable, factions must cooperate within their own ranks in order to function successfully. Rome may have been developed in some degree by conflict but in order to carry on conflict, in order to destroy Carthage, Rome had first to establish itself as a highly cooperative body. The Roman military phalanx and legion were highly cooperative, efficient teams. Semicompetitive economic units in the form of corporations in the United States, too, are often marvels of internal cooperative effort. Were it not for this internal cooperativeness they would go out of business instead of becoming monopolies or semimonopolies.

Conflicts as such, like war or revolution, *never* produce constructive or creative change. At most they may break down man-made barriers to change. The changes instituted after a war or revolution, it is notable, themselves always stem from cooperation, voluntary or enforced. The post-conflict social elements gather together to repair and compensate for the damage inflicted by war and revolution.

Cooperation, then—particularly cultural cooperation—can easily be shown to account for far more change in human affairs than conflict, struggle, and competition, even though some change is traceable as an aftermath to conflict and even though much cooperation, if such it can be called, has been obtained under duress, coercively. Conflict, indeed, is a form of social disorganization and brings about constructive change only if it clears the way to a new peaceful synthesis. Perpetual conflict would destroy society and culture.

Cooperation and conflict, it must be conceded, are both rather imprecise terms although most readers no doubt are aware vaguely of what they indicate. But the terms themselves afford no clue to how they do produce change. Cooperation, indeed, and conflict too, could be resorted to in order to resist change, to attempt to keep affairs in a state of permanent equilibrium. One must look more deeply for what it is that produces the great, fairly slow but discernible changes in human affairs. But the general category to which one must look rather than to any other for guidance is that of cooperation. It has been a persistent and not unsuccessful sociocultural aim, shown in the very emergence of culture and society, to reduce the incidence and occasion of conflict in human affairs and to maximize cooperation.

Invention and Social Change

Change in human affairs, it may then be agreed, is produced for the most part cooperatively, but the special factor that produces change—that about which men cooperate—is invention. Here it should suffice to observe that the notion of invention's being at the basis of sociocultural change is very widely accepted by leading social scientists.

Invention refers to far more than the popular idea of a new patented gadget, although it includes that. Some writers distinguish between material and non-material invention. A material invention is anything from a stone hammer to a cyclotron. A non-material invention is a religion, a language, a philosophical system, a science like cybernetics, a new institution or the like. Others make the same distinction under the names of technological invention and cultural invention. Still others distinguish between means and ends in culture, with the material and the technological regarded as means and the non-material and non-technological as ends. Religion, in this view, is regarded as an end, although it is plain that historically and conceptually it is as much a means as an end in itself.

To make a long story short let it be noted that the entire fabric—the warp and woof—of culture, in every minute detail, is an invention. Culture is a collection, a stream, a repository, an inventory of inventions combined and recombined, combining and recombining. And it is new inventions of culture that alter social relations and thus induce social change, not vice versa. Fixed societies, as of bees and insects, remain fixed because they are instinctual expressions uninfluenced by a developing culture.

White, basing his ideas on observations extending back to the early nineteenth century, sees the cultural system as a series of three horizontal strata: the technological layer on the bottom, the sociological, including the economic, layer just above, and the philosophical or ideological on top. Energy flows into the system via the technology, beginning with the stone hammer, stone ax, spear, and fire and ending up in our day with the steam turbine, dynamo, and atomic furnace. The technological layer is basic and primary. The overlying social system is a function of the technological layer, not vice versa. The technological system, in other words, determines and operates the social system in the interests of the technological system. The philosophical system has the function of rationalizing the technological and social systems, professing to show that they function according to fixed eternal truths.

Man, however, utilizes his culture selectively. And, contrary to what White says, man can change his culture.

A good example of an aspect of culture that made puppets of some men for a long time is the way language bemused philosophers and others in the past, leading them to interpret reality according to the primitive rules of the spontaneous, long-evolving languages. Thus, because one could state an abstraction in the form of a noun, such as the Good, Beauty or Mind, philosophers thought the abstraction must have some kind of mysterious concrete and locatable existence. And many were the other ways in which language misled philosophers. But more recently, largely in this century, logical procedures have been developed that enable philosophers and whoever wish to follow them to escape the cultural dictation of languages. Although most of the populace, and its favorite tribunes, remains in thrall to the pitfalls in the common languages, the means are now at hand in modern logic and semantics for their liberation from subservience to a cultural phenomenon. The point is not that philosophers have changed language. The point is, rather, that they have destroyed its former power over the human mind by developing techniques of precise analysis. And this, I take it, amounts to changing an aspect of culture and of escaping from cultural puppethood.

But even if the culture implies only in science and technology the next steps to be taken, the step to be discerned by some special mind —as it can be conclusively shown by a mass of historical evidence that it does—then we are on the track of an important concrete influence to social change. For it is the sphere of physical, technological invention, as White holds, that generates the chief impetus to social change. *Hamlet, Faust,* and Beethoven's *Ninth Symphony* have not been without their influences. But who would contend that they have had anything like the social influence of Watt's steam engine, the electric motor and dynamo, the internal-combustion engine, or any single one other of a long line of technological productions? If only in that portion of culture labeled scientific and technological one can with any certainty make forecasts of at least some coming inventions, then one can forecast the probable effect of such inventions on already existent social relations. Unless the invention itself is forcibly repressed by society, the changes forced into being by it cannot be avoided. As to whether an invention is likely to be repressed, we must turn to the culture as a whole to determine whether the invention is in harmony or disharmony with the culture style as a whole.

Textile workers in England rioted and destroyed machine-powered weaving machines when they were first introduced. Here was a segment of society opposing a new invention, and had this segment been able to make its will prevail in England and elsewhere, the world would not have experienced the Industrial Revolution. But a dominant element of society, committed in the spirit of the culture to greater and more efficient production and to the amassing of wealth, had decided to accept the new machinery, and its will prevailed.

Today some leaders of organized labor feel that automation should be opposed or, if introduced, should be made to support without effort those unskilled job applicants who can no longer be given factory work. If their views should prevail, society will be little affected fundamentally by automation. But automation seems entirely in harmony with the worldly, physicalistic outlook of Occidental culture, so we can safely predict that efforts to halt it will come to naught and that society will be deeply affected by it.

The various Oriental and Middle Eastern cultures, strongly committed to the view that earthly life is of little importance in the light of an afterlife sure to come, were not impressed by the new technology and until very recently, except in Japan, would have nothing to do with it. Their social systems, in consequence, long remained relatively unchanged but are now being rapidly altered owing to strong exposure to the new technology, much of which was forced upon them by alien intruders.

And once the decision has been made to apply the new in technology, the social consequences of such application cannot be avoided. Such consequences thereupon become *necessary, unavoidable*, and it is with such consequences that we will be concerned in this book.

Particular historical events are contingent. That is, they could happen or not happen or could happen in some other way. But it is also historically evident that if certain initial steps are taken, inevitable developmental consequences immediately follow. There are consequences to be seen from technological innovations going back to the stone hammer. At first the consequences were few and far between and slow to show themselves. But with technological accumulation they became more evident and of greater dimensions. And eventually in the modern age the technological accumulation has become so great that it presses with ever-increasing insistence on the social fabric. It presses, in fact, with such insistence that the fabric must be altered in detail if it is to be preserved as a whole. About this last there is, humanly speaking, no choice. There is therefore a relative necessity about the social changes we are able to forecast. Although men may, exercising their power of choice, refuse to make them, the refusal will not be without a heavy price, and the price may well involve social dissolution. From the past behavior of men in the mass, however, we know they will not willingly choose destruction if there is an alternative. The alternative in our case is alteration in social relations. Society as constituted is not sacred.

Innovation and Invention

In the beginning, very probably, man did not realize that he was inventing any more than the average man today realizes that he is an inventor in that he cannot *exactly* repeat any action.

A distinction has been drawn between history and science to the effect that history is concerned with what is unique and science with what is similar. The world is dualistically divided, it would seem, between unique events and similar events. Earlier in this chapter the point was made that the only fixed feature about the world is the fact of invariable change. Change is the sole empirical absolute. Does this not contradict science, with its many regularities and laws?

Here it seems advisable to cite a contemporary interpreter of science, Richard von Mises of Harvard University, who wrote, "We may suppose that there is general agreement that the course of history as a whole is given as a *unique* phenomenon. The formation of the earth, and the evolution of the animal and plant species we also know only as an individual event that runs down in time and has not ended yet. . . . It is quite right to say that the natural sciences arrive at formulations of general laws only by dissecting the immediately given; that they arbitrarily simplify by neglecting the individual distinctions of the separate cases, thus doing an injustice to reality in this sense.

"In fact, there remains merely the truth that physical research tends to statements as general as possible, which comprise as many special cases as possible. But any special conclusion, for however few cases it may hold, even if it describes only a single case, is also a physical statement—even though the textbooks of physics usually are not filled with such propositions. Finally, there exist at any period new phenomena which are not yet subsumed in the theory and can be registered only individually."[14]

As I remarked a few paragraphs earlier, the average man does not realize that he is an inventor in that he cannot repeat any action and that, in fact, no action whatsoever can be repeated *exactly*. As far as exact repetition is concerned, no scientific experiment whatsoever can be repeated although it is true that, by ignoring differences, it can be *approximately* repeated.

"Every individual is basically innovative for two reasons. No two stimuli to which he reacts are ever identical. . . . When an individual steps across the traditionally accepted boundaries of sameness and treats two different things as the same, he is displaying originality. . . . The second reason for diversified reactions is that no one ever entirely or minutely duplicates his responses to what he regards as the same stimulus. Inevitably an organism is altered by its own responses; it is not the same after responding as it was before. This is so even when the reactions follow upon each other immediately. . . . Changes in his reactions are even more evident when the passage of a long interval of time brings about physiological, emotional, and intellectual transformations in an individual. And responding differently to the same stimulus is also counted as original when it overrides the cultural dictates which make prescribed allowances for it. This dynamic situation is pregnant with novelty; and it is continually bearing strange fruit, as anyone may observe by close attention to his own behavior and that of his associates."[15]

The answer, then, to the question of why man is an inventor is easily come by: man is an inventor because he cannot, try as he will, do anything twice in exactly the same way. What becomes generally regarded as a *significant* or culturally accepted invention represents an accumulation of innumerable deviations from some original act.

Culturally significant inventions, however, are those that are generally noticed and are put to use, such as tools, machines, institutions, philosophies, religions, and sciences.

Such highly developed, stylized inventions are accepted, made part of the culture. And after being accepted they tend to accumulate. Even the most rudimentary societies are found with a number of the more simple of such so-called "material" inventions, such artifacts as digging sticks, stone hammers, spears.

While a single invention produces change in human affairs by bringing about changed human behavior, many inventions bring about more change in the way of new inventions. In fact it has come to be regarded as pretty much of a cultural law that invention induces more invention, operating much like the exponential law in algebra or the rule of compound interest. We now have a growing capital stock of inventions, inducing an ever-increasing income of fresh inventions.

Inventions, humanly meaningful three-dimensional objects and organizational structures of symbolized functional meanings, make up culture; the three-dimensional items particularly are sometimes referred to as the cultural "base." They are, however, no more a base than are abstract ideas. The axioms of logic and geometry are certainly as much a part of our cultural "base" as any material object. Each little item in the cultural inventory is a cultural "trait."

Changes in neighboring cultures are often induced by diffusion, which has the same effect as original invention. Thus the wheel is thought to have had its origin about the year 2000 or 2500 B.C. in or near the Middle East, but its use spread rapidly.

But inventions that are accepted bring other changes, often tremendous, in their train. Our theoretical law therefore begins to take form as follows:

Social change is the effect, primarily, of more or less readily accepted inventions. For inventions, as has been noticed by many expert observers, set into motion an inventive chain reaction that is finally noticed by everybody as change in the social environment. It is then commonly said, "Times are changing."

A significant recent technological invention, for example, is television, which set in motion its own chain reaction. Once the idea of television had been actualized, the aim was to market it. Capital was provided, manufacturing establishments were set up to make receiving sets and transmitting equipment. Affected at once by this activity was the economic system, which now had incorporated into it a whole new industry with many ramifications. The effects of the new industry in terms of demand for goods and services were numerous and complex. New economic relationships were established.

There were also competitive effects on other industries—radio, motion pictures, and newspapers, all of which at an earlier stage had had similar competitive effects on other industries. The pattern of activity in the advertising industry was also affected.

The institution of government was affected, too, for new rules had to be devised to regulate the new industry, particularly with respect to what might be transmitted. Actually hundreds of minute changes were wrought at every level of government, so that one can say that the polity itself was very much, if only subtly, changed by the introduction of a single invention like television.

It is popularly supposed that the United States as a political entity has undergone no significant change since the Constitution first took effect but actually it is now, largely as the result of thousands of significant inventions incorporated in it, a very different political entity from what it was late in the eighteenth century. It bears only a superficial resemblance indeed to that political structure. In fact it is very different from what the United States, as a system of government, was in 1920—or even in 1940! The government of the United States, like other governments too, is constantly changing, incorporating in itself a constant stream of organizational and procedural inventions.

As Curtis Bok, late Associate Justice of the Supreme Court of Pennsylvania, pointedly remarked, "Every time a court case is decided the Constitution is amended just a little: the only difference between court decisions and constitutional amendments as such is the size of the question involved."[16]

Yet perhaps most Americans believe that, except for the formal amendments to it, the Constitution has not been changed since 1789.

Source of the Invention Theory of Change

Although it has been put forward by various persons since A. R. J. Turgot (1727–81) gave it prominent and perhaps initial expression, the idea of invention as the main stimulator of social change was no doubt most strongly suggested by the powerful effect of the invention of the modern steam engine. The consequences of that single invention are what is really described in all descriptions of the Industrial Revolution and its many aftereffects.

Institutional changes especially are induced by the introduction of inventions. Their effect is also to bring into being entirely new institutional forms, such as the League of Nations, the World Court and the United Nations, and new government departments. What I call the recreational institution is, at least in its extremely large dimensions, something new in society. Recreation itself, of course, is old in the history of civilization. And recreation as an institution was known to the Romans and even earlier. But in size, variety, and complexity the recreational institution of today is something entirely novel.

Such an institution, of such size and complexity, could develop only where large numbers of people had a considerable amount of economically supported leisure time at their disposal. The modern recreational institution, then, is largely a reflex to the introduction of labor-saving machinery, shortened hours of work, and higher rates of real income.

Changes as a result of technological inventions extend also into levels that are more commonly regarded as "cultural," levels such as language, art, science, and systems of thought. Such cultural changes are themselves inventions. Language has been very much affected by the new inventions and by their ramifying effects as well. For one thing, new words such as "television" and a host of others have been introduced. All the visual arts have been affected, too, and not only in the new objects given them to depict. Architecture has been vastly affected by modern machine technology. The skyscraper, for instance, could not have been produced without such technology. Nor would the economic conditions for the skyscraper, the concentration of many people in a small area, have been provided without the development of factories and offices using machine technology. Painting has been radically affected by the invention of photography, which largely did away with the demand for hand-wrought portraiture, landscapes, and the like.

The new inventions stimulate theoretical science by posing new problems for solution. As theoretical science is affected, philosophy and social theory are affected in countless ways. The successes of physical science, for example, suggested that a similar approach might produce a psychological, a social, and a cultural science—all of which we have with us today. To these have been added cybernetics and prognostics.

The effects of directly practical inventions, then, are more inventions on the purely theoretical cultural levels. Theoretical science possesses thousands of inventions of its own which the general public never sees and rarely hears about. Mathematics similarly, as new problems are put to it, burgeons with mathematical inventions which are both solutions to the new problems and the posing of fresh problems.

Our guiding maxim, then, amid all the complexity of the sociocultural sphere, is that invention plus the cooperative use of invention is the stimulus to further invention, particularly in social institutions and in the higher thought systems. This latter part of invention is recognized as social and cultural change. Ideas also change—among others, ideas of what is good and what is bad, desirable and undesirable, true and false, right and wrong. But it is mainly in the socially inventive reactions to complex inventions that significant social change takes place.

The Social Effects of Invention

Now, as Ogburn and others have shown, one can predict many of the sociocultural consequences of sharply defined accepted inventions like radio, television, and thermonuclear weapons. For one thing, as soon as practical models are produced—as of automation— one can discern at once that a new productive industry is about to be added to the economic system. This new industry, in turn, has foreseeable non-economic social effects of many kinds.

Prediction, then, may concern the spectrum of effects of one particular invention, of a small or large group of particular inventions, or of the totality of existing inventions. Furthermore, prediction may (as we have seen) require two steps: first, the forecasting of some as yet unachieved invention, and secondly, the social inventive effects of such an object. For example, such an invention might be a certain chemical preparation curing all kinds and varieties of cancer. There would be deductively foreseeable social effects of such an invention, such as the abrupt curtailment of research on cancer, the closing of cancer-treatment centers, the elimination of bequests for cancer research, the manufacture and sale of the new cure, a further reduction in the general death rate, a further increase in the older segment of the population, and a revision of the curriculum in medical schools.

Again, prediction may also concern the effects of a few particular coming inventions or the effects of all particular inventions within a certain span of time. Although, as we have seen, there has been some success in predicting something like 75 per cent of coming mechanical inventions within certain periods of time, nobody has as yet scored anything like 100 per cent in making such predictions. It is clear, then, that one cannot predict all coming inventions within a certain span of time and one cannot, therefore, predict the future effects of all inventions to come in a certain period of time.

Some inventions have more influence for change than others, and we may grant this even though any invention produces some change. But the question now arises: are we interested in all future changes or only in certain kinds of change? And the affirmative answer seems to apply more particularly to the second question even if, out of idle curiosity, we might say we were interested in all future changes.

We are as human beings no more interested in all aspects of the future than we are interested in all aspects of the present or the past. We are, with respect to past, present, and future, necessarily only selectively interested. And our selective interest is largely determined by the known problems and concerns of our times. So what I intend to do is to direct attention to those areas of life in which we are most interested and ascertain what invention—using the word in the broadest possible sense—will do to bring further invention to those areas of life and what those further life area inventions will be.

Automation, for example, is a recent invention applied to industrial production. As already noted, it seems very likely to be widely applied. And it is possible, so it is argued here, to predict systematically what many of its future effects will be as it is increasingly applied —that is, its effects on the various cultural sub-systems within which people live: the economic, the political, the educational, the recreational, the medical, the scientific, the familial, the military as well as on the cultural system as a whole.

As to automation, time will establish, it appears, that most of its effects and certainly most of its important effects can be readily anticipated by utilizing our methods. Certain of its effects, even important ones, may escape anticipation. But it seems that they must be few and, for the most part, obscure. And with respect to many of its effects we would hardly be interested.

Each prediction, at any rate, falls within a certain numerical range of effects, scaling down in degree of evaluation. What is most important, to be sure, is open to some dispute and depends upon what relevant norms are applied.

One may, it is true, selectively trace the future effects of a few so-called material inventions, as Ogburn did with radio and aviation. And while there is interest and the possibility of gain in knowledge in so doing, there is also the possibility, it would appear, of making more general predictions on a broader scale. Such predictions as the latter provide one in advance with at least the outlines of a working model or models of the future. Such hypothetical models may have many uses. They provide a tentative test of various current propositions in the social sciences. They also serve as means for criticism of the present by looking at it in the light of an anticipated future. Again, they may help policy makers mold their thoughts about the future. Not least, they may afford diversionary amusement, always a value to man.

Does this mean that some one person, such as myself, will be able to unlock the chief "secrets" of the future? Probably not. But if many persons start investigating and exploring the future by these methods, much of it will be unlocked in advance and the means may be forehandedly developed to cope with it. An entirely new and valuable discipline of sociocultural prognosis may thus be founded, a discipline that might well be named prognostics. In any event, it is under this handy rubric that this study is offered.

Cultural Inertia

Influences that resist, although they do not prevent, change have been collectively termed "cultural inertia." In general they include the human factor of fear of what is unknown and consequent hostility to the new, the prestige of religion-validated tradition, the force of habit asserting itself in mass social pressure for intellectual and behavioral conformity, the tendency of most people to look away from unpleasant problems that require solution, and ever-present mass apathy. More specifically, cultural inertia is reinforced by the constant hyperactive political and propaganda efforts of vested social interests which pervade and often dominate institutions such as those of government, religion, education, communications media, and even science. To these influences may be added the fact, as first pointed out by Freud, that everyone possesses a more or less "reactionary" personality shaped by influences surviving from an overvenerated dead past.

But the mere expectation of change, it has been noticed, is itself an aid to change, and Occidental culture exists in the expectation of change, of discovery, of invention. "Innovation flourishes in an atmosphere of anticipation of it."[17]

Social Movements and Change

Beyond well-patterned inventions expressed in some three-dimensional object or symbol system, there are also less well-defined inventions in the form of social movements, which arise from widespread dissatisfaction with conditions produced by some sort of antecedent inventive change. The social movement seeks some further change, which it specifies, and may be reactive, reformist, or revolutionary.

Social movements usually proceed on the basis of some document or documents, an invention in the philosophical-ideological layer of the culture as distinct from the technological layer, although the "document" may be no more than an impassioned political or religious exhortation.

The Bible, long withheld from the European populace by the Romanized Church, was eventually translated into the common languages and then distributed widely by means of the newly invented printing press. Many social movements, political as well as religious, had their origin in this single act of making the Bible generally available.

The famous French *Encyclopédie* was an invention, based like most inventions on an earlier invention: *Chambers' Cyclopaedia or an Universal Dictionary of Arts and Sciences*, first published in London in 1728. A condensed compilation of printed knowledge, the *Cyclopaedia* had been made necessary by the many publications since the invention of the printing press. The printing press and a great volume of already printed material, then, were inventions necessary to the *Encyclopédie*.

But none of these writings could have had the least influence had not what Kroeber terms the subsistence-economic-technological level been prepared to receive them.

Changes in laws by way of adjustment to new conditions also induce social change, and such changes—juridical inventions—are often a purely rational response to new conditions. What Marx termed capitalist society, for example, has immeasurably changed itself by means of reform legislation. Some of this legislation has been placed on the books in response to the demands of reformist social movements. Most has been made necessary by the social effects of machine technology.

The Influence of Social Problems, Scandals, and Social Crises

Despite changes we can see in the directly experienced past, there does not appear to be much change in the present on a day-to-day basis. Except perhaps in the middle of a revolution, the social scene appears to be as fixed as the earth, and this it is! But the earth, appearing to be fixed, is really in rapid motion, spiraling around the sun, moving with the solar system and changing within itself. Analogously, the social system is imperceptibly changing.

Tendencies resisting change, self-consciously led by the established interests who articulate these tendencies and celebrate them as part of a Higher Reality, succeed in keeping it to a minimum and therefore keep it from being apparent except over stretches of time. Formal social change perceptible to all takes place usually only in times of crisis, although each crisis situation itself expresses informal change that has already taken place. A crisis is itself a change.

Most unconscious, haphazard change of the kind introduced directly and immediately by technological inventions is not very thoroughgoing except in its disorganizing effects. It is the consciously controlled secondary changes induced by such inventions that are most spectacular and humanly most deeply significant. And such indirect or secondary changes in their fullest dimensions are seen usually as the formalized political aftermath of crises large and small. The crises in themselves represent problems in adjustment deferred but clamoring now, at the moment of crisis, for resolution. Such resolutions of crisis were seen in most of the measures of Franklin D. Roosevelt's "New Deal" in the United States.

Rational foresight rarely brings about change, although there are always persons, a small minority, urging certain rational changes before crisis supervenes. Such persons are almost invariably ignored by the apathetic majority and are usually stigmatized in various ways as nuisances in the continuous routine propaganda of the *status quo*. It appears to be the belief of the propagandists and their employers that if the spokesmen for formal changes can be discredited by ridicule or otherwise, then change itself can be avoided. But in this, history shows, they are woefully mistaken.

It takes problems to bring on crises, and problems—happily or not—abound in a complex volatile society such as that of the Occident. A crisis may concern only one specific problem or it may embrace at once a series of problems. In a time of general crisis many problems are faced. Failure to solve certain basic problems, and in particular certain combinations of problems, history attests, may cause the slow decay and dissolution of a society.

Precisely what, though, is a social crisis? A social crisis is some particular strain on social relations that induces sudden and unexpected physical pain or mental anguish in large numbers of people and the threat of pain, anguish, or great inconvenience and loss to other large numbers. History is replete with such crises, ranging from limited ones to revolutionary upheavals that profoundly altered the structure of societies as in the case of the French and Russian revolutions. An economic depression, for example, is a social crisis, its magnitude determined by its depth and extent.

In response to crises, societies either attempt to restore some fondly remembered pre-existent state of affairs (as in Spain since 1936), to adjust outmoded institutions to new conditions (as under Franklin D. Roosevelt in the United States), or to establish a new set of institutions (as in Russia after 1917). Changes may affect all institutions at once or only a single institution. Historically, attempts at restorations have invariably been short-lived, resulting in series of crises interspersed with realistic interim adjustments (as in France since 1815) or in eventual debacle (as in Germany under Hitler). Efforts to frustrate technologically stimulated change always fail. The most that can be done is to contain and control it. Only if the new techniques themselves are rejected can the old society be preserved, but then it loses competitive strength against societies that embrace the improved techniques.

In any case, people must be coerced through suffering or the immediate threat of suffering to acquiesce in conscious adjustment to unconscious, haphazard change precipitated by new inventions, mainly technical. Without suffering or the threat of it they almost always, as a group, resist formal change, governed as they are both by habit and established positions of relative advantage. Rational arguments favoring formal adjustments to change invariably fail to appeal to more than a very few. But the formal changes finally introduced under the influence of crisis (unless they aim at some blind restoration) usually reveal attempts on the part of frightened social managers to bring into play rational considerations.

When a crisis has moved beyond the point of rational management, when it evades all efforts at resolution or is handled irrationally, it leads to total disorganization and panic. A condition of anarchy or near anarchy then prevails (as in the Congo after 1960, Europe after the religious wars of the seventeenth century), with the outcome long in doubt.

The factor of rationality, it should be noticed, rarely plays any role in the process until the settlement of intensifying crisis faces society, and sometimes not even then. To believe that it does is to be misled by the philosophers' portrayal of man's nature as basically rational. Largely as a result of this portrayal it is everywhere assumed that man is a quick learner. And so he is, in comparison with the lower animals. But men as a whole are not quick learners in relation to problems that bring into play their emotional biases. And it is in this respect that men, for the sake of their own welfare, need to be extremely quick to learn amid conditions of increasing complexity like the present. In relation to their own best long-term interests men, on the whole, are rather obtuse—wishful, optimistic, almost blind, craving security in the sense of illusory certainty.

But, sooner or later, men in society must defer to rationality at least in facing up to the disorganizing effects of certain causes they have optimistically allowed to be put into play. Since the Industrial Revolution began they have had to cope with the socially disorganizing effects of machine production, and now they must begin coping with the disorganizing effects of automation, many formal adjustments to which will disturb existing social relationships.

If, for example, there is no effective restraint on procreation as death rates throughout the world are sharply reduced by medical technology, men must come to decisions on what to do with population that exceeds the means of maintenance and self-development. In the United States itself, it should be noted, the population has long exceeded the existing means to educate it properly for a technological age. The excess population may be destroyed, allowed to sicken and die, be maintained on a meager and minimal basis in a semiailing state (the policy of the United States at present), be adequately provided for, or allowed eventually to overwhelm and destroy the society as a whole.

But consequences there always are. And pain or the threat of it alone makes men face, more or less realistically, the consequences of earlier innovations.

Crisis-stimulating Problems

What are some of the problems to which we can look to precipitate crises that will produce remedial changes?

There is, first, the general problem of a highly volatile, mechanized economic system. This problem is too well known and too ramified to require detailed attention here. Suffice it to say here that the problem involves boom and depression, inflation and deflation, and the constant increase in capacity to produce without commensurate ability to distribute effectively. Whenever this complex and volatile economic system gets out of order, we find a social crisis impending and demanding urgent attention from many directions.

Next, and certainly closely interwoven with the economic problem, is the political problem of destructively competing large and small national sovereignties in a world made much too small by technology for such competition. Nationalism and nationalistic patriotism are all, in the light of the newest workings of the culture, anachronistic and suicidal cultural traits. Under present technological conditions the uncorking of the nationalist spirit is simply self-defeating and self-destructive.

Although in the advanced industrial states there is now considerable, though limited, awareness of the risks of nationalism under present conditions, this same intensified awareness is not evident in the non-industrialized countries, in Africa and Asia generally and in Latin America.

The more conventional and immediately familiar domestic social problems are present in the advanced countries, potential triggers for future crises. They are of the following order:

Conventional individual crime is on a rising world trend as social bonds are loosened or nullified by onrushing change. The problem here is how best to quell it at its sources.

The institution of the family is engulfed in increasing crisis, reflected in many individual behavior problems including criminality.

Religious and ethnic conflicts, basically traceable to ignorance, abound in nearly all quarters of the earth. Arbitrary social inequality as distinct from inevitable or inherent inequality, despite all the protests there have been against it, is still with us on every hand. Both of these facts generate problems.

Unprecedentedly sharp increases in population pose a general explosive problem and many derivative problems with many ramifications in many parts of the world.

Mental and emotional illnesses of problematic proportions appear to be increasing rapidly in industrial countries with large-scale accompaniments such as alcoholism, indulgence by vast populations in demoralizing gambling, widespread delinquency, drug addiction, and general popular apathy. Apathy evidences itself most perceptibly by popular immersion in what has come to be known as "mass culture."[18]

Propaganda in and of itself constitutes an acute modern social problem, lighting the fuse for many future angry explosions because so much of it instills monumental public delusions. The common undesirable feature about all propaganda is that it relies on uncritical emotional reaction to approved or disapproved symbols rather than on rational argument about facts; in so doing it manipulates and victimizes rather than leads, instructs, and enlightens. While many lines of propaganda are in their ends fairly harmless, apart from their manipulation of emotion, the most frequently encountered lines of propaganda instill in millions conclusions on important topics that are either demonstrably false or misleading. The manipulation of the victims has as its end making them think or act in ways desired by the self-appointed propagandist, who fills the role of a social puppet-master. Propaganda fosters social myths.

As this is not the place for an extended treatment of the propaganda question, the most that can be done is to refer the reader to useful sources of information.[19] But it should be observed that although propaganda may be as old as civilization, it emerges as a modern problem mainly because the technology of communication has been developed and makes it broadly effective.

The vested interests in militant form as "pressure groups" also constitute a social problem and are treated as such by sociologists. By reason of their self-aggrandizing activities they gradually build up opposition to themselves, leading to clamors for changes.[20] Over the long run the specific vested interests never win. But in the long run, as John Maynard Keynes noted, we are all dead.

Inadequate or pseudo education, the kind probably most persons obtain under the canopy of universal education, where it exists (making them ready targets for propagandists and ready victims of mass culture), constitutes a basic problem in complex modern society. For the fact is that multitudes, although formally processed through schools, are far from educated or even partially educated. What is called universal education is still largely a façade, kept from development into a sound institution by many factors that require later examination.

Increasing urbanization poses a problem with many facets, chief of which are slums, inadequate public services, run-down and overcrowded neighborhoods, and socially unbalanced communities in city and suburb alike. To this problem of urbanization is linked a worldwide housing shortage and sharp growth in population.

Which of these foregoing problems is most basic, and which most explosive, is a question. The general economic problem appears to require the most adroit handling and seems to be the one which, mishandled, can be most incendiary, most like a fuse apt to lead to explosive social change. Next is the political problem, overlying the economic. Most basic rather than most explosive or incendiary appears to be the problem of inadequate education, which has left us in a highly complex society with a mass of the unduly ignorant, maladroit, and half educated. Failures of education are not traceable alone or directly to an inadequate school system, but also to difficulties in the family system that trace down to other social maladjustments. The general failure in education is, as a matter of fact, a failure in the whole process of *enculturation*, about which more will be said in a subsequent chapter on education.[21]

To the very general failure in the process of enculturation are traceable many social conflicts abetted by cultural tensions. This latter phenomenon is most often shown to view in Western society in tension between mythic elements in the culture on the one hand and the newer empirical, rational elements on the other. Most prominently this tension has shown itself in the conflict between institutionalized religion and rising science, a conflict which, far from being ended or resolved, continues as a general protracted and damped-down skirmish.

There is, it may be conceded, no lack of explosive material with which to trigger crises. And not yet even mentioned is the gnawing problem of extreme poverty and malnutrition that besets the backward, raw-material-producing countries. One cannot determine just when a crisis will befall and what its nature will be. All one can be sure of is that potential frequent crisis is built in, as it were, in the modern sociocultural structure. Avoidance of crises by specific solutions of the crisis-generating social problems in question would itself represent social change, so whether the problems are solved through rational foresight before they become explosive or are allowed to explode and so induce social change, they will in either case be instruments of social change.

Other efficient levers of sudden change, as history tells us, are public scandals of various kinds. We cannot predict their incidence but, knowing the behavior of persons in power in the past, we can say for the future that such persons will again commit acts that provoke extreme public reaction. The masses, bemused and delusion-ridden as a consequence of saturation in steady propaganda and the narcotic products of mass culture, are suddenly stung out of their torpor by crisis or scandal. Some figure or figures about whom they had one set of expectations turn out to have betrayed those expectations. The masses then suddenly line up with the spokesmen for change, sometimes with the spokesmen for the most extreme change possible.

It will be seen that our theory of change does not visualize change deriving from willing decisions or from the foresighted exercise of rational free will. If changes were based on such decisions, many that are almost surely coming should have been made long ago. Social adjustments take place owing to eventual necessity, and the necessity is always and invariably one forced by existing or impending crisis. Reasonableness plays no initiating role whatever in the process. For the elements and factors opposing change are always irrationally obdurate. Those responsible for the formalities of the changes, those in charge as it were of protocol, are finally forced against their will to act in certain ways. They behave as though they were acting on the basis of a decision, but the decision is always one of choice between order and chaos and seldom any more.

Dean Acheson, former Secretary of State, in testifying before a Congressional Committee about whether the United States should enter into reciprocal economic agreements with the European Common Market countries said, "We have no choice." What he meant was that the United States had no choice if it wished for maximum beneficial results for itself. The United States, clearly, could choose not to make such agreements. But, whatever its choice, there would be foreseeable consequences, better in one case than in the other.

The range of choice in the resolution of nearly every social crisis, as in most human affairs, is similarly narrow although man, imbedded in a deterministic natural and social scheme, has the illusion of having before him a wide range of choice. If in his choice, however, he steps outside of an extremely narrow range, he is threatened by disastrous consequences.

It is the anticipated consequences that bring actual choices, particularly in social management, down to an extremely narrow range. The absence of full rationality in making choices does indeed often have an influence on the choice made. In Spain, for example, the elements of superior force in the culture, combining with circumstances of the times, determined that the irrational choice was made. The consequences of continuing in power a dominant social class that had failed to modernize the country in competition with neighboring countries were inescapably those of condemning the Spanish people to fall farther behind the procession of modern, scientific-minded and technic-minded nations.

American society, in order to eliminate the threat of atomic warfare, could choose to bow to Russian power. That it will never do so is determined by the culture, which dictates struggle and resistance on the basis of faith in self-reliance and superior ingenuity. In the effort to overthrow the United States, Russia is more likely, should it persist, to overthrow itself.

The Theory of Historicism

There is a theory, known as historicism, that holds future history can be prophesied on the basis of past history. Karl Popper, agreeing with us that piecemeal social developments can be predicted by appropriate methods, not only denies the claims of the historicists but subjects them to devastating logical analysis.[22] He contrasts the mystic *prophesying* of the historicists with the rational *predicting* of social scientists.

An important issue underlying this seemingly trivial dispute about the words "prophesy" and "predict" is that the historicists believe no action can be taken in the present to alter the future, that the future has already been completely and entirely determined by the past; whereas empirical-minded social scientists believe that the impending future can be altered and shaped by appropriate actions in the present, by—to use the word of our time most unpleasantly provocative to vested interests—planning. Historicists believe planning is futile; the die of the future has long since been completely cast. Various vested interests fear the word "planning" because they suspect, not without some justification, that if rationality prevails they will be planned out of existence.

Apart from the already examined fundamental type of social change resulting from cultural alterations—inventions—introduced on the "subsistence-economic-technological level," we are left with initiating ideational changes coming from exercise of the play impulse and slow growth changes. Such play impulses have shown themselves in the construction of various utopias. Such activities and slow growth, resulting in new religions, new idea systems, social reconstructions, and basically altered culture patterns, are of a long-term nature and difficult if not impossible to predict, and perhaps all that one could do would be to prophesy them. I shall not, however, attempt such prophecy.

These are, however, referring now to White's three-strata pattern, essentially (1) philosophical and ideological changes, which arise to justify and elucidate earlier (2) technological and (3) sociological changes. The minute steady technological changes born of the culture are primary and at once directly affect the social level, producing changes in social relationships. In the course of time a slow growth, which amounts to an accumulation of changes, produces the basic alteration in cultural patterns as shown in systems of ideas intended to be justifying and elucidating.

Games Theory and the Future

A question to be faced for those aware of the newest theoretical developments is whether mathematicized games theory can be applied to our problem of predicting. If games theory undergoes very considerable further mathematical development it should indeed apply, giving effect to various factors we have encountered. Games theory, we may remind ourselves, deals with the choices and decisions people may or should make on the basis of available relevant information in conflict situations involving two or more persons (players) and some element of uncertainty. The object of the "game" is to maximize advantages and minimize disadvantages. The theory, mathematicized, is applied literally to games, such as parlor games, as well as to economic and military situations, career prospects, serious or playful encounters with aspects of nature, statistical computations, financial problems, two-person encounters as in "the battle of the sexes" and, indeed, in all manner of situations involving conflict of interest and choices of strategies and decisions.

But games theory in its present state of development as a mathematical tool is notoriously weakest in *n*-person games where *n* gets to be a very large number. It is just this sort of *n*-person theory that is of greatest interest in social science.

Occidental culture, moreover, is changing slowly but very significantly as its "game" is played—that is, the rules are subtly changing. What the modified rules are is sometimes not very clear for a long time to anybody in the game. And, to begin with, the rules all along were not wholly consistent; these rules, in the form of the culture, contained several overlapping and even contrary and contradictory sets of rules which the objects or counters of the game—individual people and groups—may apply as they are disposed to in the light of surrounding conditions.

But we know, in the perspective of Occidental culture and what it is likely to become, that certain scores, positive and negative, can be rapidly read off as the game begins, as far as Europe and America at least are concerned. Under other cultures other results might be obtained. Thus one can say, for example, with almost absolute certainty that in the next 150 years no legally established legislature in Europe or America will legalize cannibalism, human or animal sacrifice, parent-child or brother-sister incest, multiple marriage, the blood feud, infanticide, suttee or purdah, the revival of chattel slavery or serfdom, dueling, replacement of the national language, public performance of the primal sexual act, teaching astrology in the schools, general confiscation of private property, and obliging scientific laboratories to begin the day with a session of prayer.

One can, as is readily to be seen, and contrary to the sage remarks of many skeptics, make a long string of virtually certain predictions about the future. But one cannot, as suggested by fairly recent world events, with the same degree of certainty say these legislatures will not legalize physical torture or cruel and inhuman punishment like burning or burial alive or that nations will eschew genocide or the bombing of cities. While the odds, I think, are in the main against such developments and repetitions, they are not prohibitive odds as in the case of the first set cited.

As for positive as opposed to negative predictions, the chances seem good for the legalization of euthanasia under public safeguards, the sterilization of persons almost certain to make grossly unfit parents or to have grossly unfit progeny, mandatory birth control and the issuance of special permits for couples to have more than one or two children, gratis public application of psychological therapy at least as widely as physical therapy is now applied, the absolute prohibition of formal social discrimination on any arbitrarily chosen ground whatever, extremely easy divorce by mutual consent in the absence of dependent children, small armed forces, and liberalized and broadened social security allowances of all sorts.

CHAPTER IV

THE POPULATION PROBLEM

Coming events and developments will inevitably be shaped and modified by the sudden influx of additional people in various world regions. At the outset, therefore, I shall consider some of the influences of world populations on future events.

By their mere presence, it is evident, an excessive number of people retards industrial development by consuming, like swarms of invading locusts, the substance needed to form creative capital. And by their participation in a long chain of social processes, surplus people become causative factors in producing disruptive events, which themselves operate to delay development.

Whether or not a population is excessive or surplus depends upon a variety of factors. The first of these is the per capita availability of fresh water and food, arable land, and forests and minerals. Next there is the factor of favorable climate and terrain, geographical configuration of mountains, plains, waterways, harbors, and deserts and positional relationship to other large populations. Third, and in modern times as important as any of these, there is the factor of popular diffusion of knowledge and grasp of sophisticated techniques. And a final factor in determining whether or not a population is surplus is the ready availability of cultural instruments for training, such as schools, libraries, laboratories, clinics, and systems of adequate communication such as widely shared, readily used languages.

Regions are commonly classified as developed and underdeveloped, with Europe and North America the prime models of development. But all that are underdeveloped, it should be noticed, are also culturally backward by European standards and grossly overpopulated in relation to all the factors enumerated above. Practically all of Asia (notably China and India), Africa, and Central and South America rate as underdeveloped.

A prediction that may be ventured at once, simply with the factor of excess population in mind, is that none of these underdeveloped regions in the next 150 years is at all likely to achieve a status or standard of consumption remotely comparable to Europe, North America, or even contemporary Russia, whether or not Russia and the West destroy each other.

Even if such regions improved their present state of development by ten or twenty times, which is in itself impossible owing to the pressure of excess population, they would not even come close to Soviet Russia and the West. This is not to deny that the condition of the underdeveloped regions can be vastly improved with the tutelage and help of the advanced nations. Achievable improvement, however, in view of concrete difficulties must fall far short of the fantasies of those who see these regions as "catching up" with the West. Even Soviet Russia, for all she has undeniably achieved in industrialization, is still far from catching up.

Nor will these regions as a whole for a long time to come achieve much in the way of a voluntary reduction in birth rates, owing to the weight of ancient cultural biases.

The sudden inflation of world population, unlike that in the United States since World War II, has not been induced by any significant increase in birth rates or the operation of anything like a Malthusian law. It has come about entirely owing to science-derived improvements in public health measures and in the distribution of medical assistance, the latter made possible by governments and private agencies of the developed areas.

Throughout the world, excepting Europe and North America, the birth rate has long stood near the biological maximum and population excess has been avoided through the impersonal operation of disease, famine, and warfare. As better health measures have reduced the incidence of disease, so somewhat better crop cultivation and food storage have functioned to reduce but not eliminate famine.

But the cycle of spontaneous population control constantly struggles to reassert itself. As less food is regularly available per person owing to the survival of more persons, lower per-person caloric intake and lack of variety in diet paves the way for diet-deficiency diseases and a lowering of physical vigor in entire populations such as competent observers find today in China, India, and Egypt. The very lack of physical vigor in the population acts as a drag on any great burst of national activity.[1]

Although the governments of India and Japan promote birth control and the government of China attempted to popularize it in the face of public indifference, the movement makes little headway where it is most needed, owing to ignorance-rooted apathy and inertia and traditional cultural patterns that have long outlived their usefulness. Every birth was once socially necessary, and as a consequence was celebrated, in the face of a high and early death rate. Without many births societies would not have survived. Now the converse is true but the local cultural patterns survive, imbedded and sanctified in ancient religions. The medical and sanitary measures that have reduced death rates are intrusions from an alien, more powerful, and very often disliked culture, the European.

In the West the birth-control movement is most strongly opposed by the Catholic Church and by non-Catholic fundamentalists. Both dogmatically continue to recommend what was once socially useful and has of late become socially disruptive. Their remedy for an excessive number of children is sexual continence, which in practice is often a euphemism for auto-erotic practices.

Beyond true continence, unquestionably accomplished through effective sublimation of nervous energy in a few cases or leading to neurotic behavior or symptoms in most of its rarely dedicated practitioners, there is no effective middle ground short of birth control by chemical or mechanical means. Sexual moderation is no solution, for a single exposure a year can cause a woman to conceive up to her biological maximum. But effective birth control requires some initiative. To offset the lack of such initiative scientists have developed a contraceptive pill which, taken daily, insures female sterility. As yet the pill is too costly for mass public distribution. And there is no guarantee that all or even most of its recipients would use it faithfully.

The broad reason for this is that most of the people of the backward regions are fatalistic. Accustomed to a long-established, monotonous life rhythm, they believe that what has always been must always be. Religious tenets here enter to reinforce deeply inculcated attitudes.

Many investigators report, furthermore, that probably in most people of the backward regions there is little particular desire for birth control. Contrary to Western supposition, children among culturally backward people are not usually the accidental, unsought by-products of the sexual act. They are wanted, for a variety of reasons. Often they are mere status symbols, proving adulthood and virility in their parents; childless women are widely looked down upon, their husbands commiserated or twitted. They are, too, often regarded as valuable additions to the local work force and as continuers of a long and revered family line extending back to some great hero or god. They are also welcomed as recruits for one of the sides in local feuds, and for the brute reinforcement of religious sects, castes and tribes that, it is feared, would die out without replenishment. In most societies, advanced and retarded, they are probably valued more as means than as ends.

The Chinese peasantry, for example, has long felt the need of many children to insure future attention to the graves of parents and to participate in ancestor worship, without which the souls of the dead are thought to expire.

Multitudes of surviving children are not recognized by the populace (whatever leaders and intellectuals may think) as connected with environmental difficulties. As they have always been more or less beset by uncontrolled calamities—flood, drought, insect invasions, disease, famine, and war—the populations do not seriously visualize the possibility of any other condition. Illiterate and (contrary to the assertions of political leaders) unaware of world conditions, they interpret reality in terms of myth, as indeed do orthodox religionists in the West. To combat basic illiteracy tens of thousands of schools are needed, and books, libraries, paper, pencils, and other equipment. Even if, overnight, all the necessary physical equipment were made available to educate only children, there would be needed millions of trained teachers. These can be trained, in an illiterate population, only very slowly, over at least a period of several generations. There is, however, no one to train the necessary teachers. A relative handful are being trained abroad.

Even the United States, under the pressure of population increase since 1945, feels itself undersupplied with one and a half million classroom teachers, nearly all college graduates. If the United States is undersupplied with this many, China and India, which have few teachers, would be undersupplied with three times as many.

Without a sufficiency of teachers to instill basic skills with numbers and letters, there is little chance that backward populations will be able to acquire mastery of the higher techniques in any great hurry. Improvement must therefore necessarily be slow where it takes place, spreading out in very slowly widening circles. Only the exceptionally apt can be singled out for thorough education.

Nor is there any sign, apart from the assurance of Westernized intellectuals, that the broad populations desire basic changes and are willing to change themselves in harmony with them. It is true that they would everywhere like to be more comfortable, free of hunger and disease. But they are unaware that in order to achieve this minimum of comfort they must radically alter their traditional ways of thinking and acting. This they show themselves, thus far, unwilling to do.

In every region marked for development one finds Western-educated intellectuals in political charge. The idea that the countries should Westernize stems entirely from them, not from the people or their religious leaders. In order to obtain the cooperation of the peasantry in China, as earlier in Russia, such intellectuals have had to resort to extremes of coercion and every trick known to propaganda. In India and elsewhere cooperation is being sought through persuasion, with final results in the balance. Coercion in China has already produced a condition bordering upon chaos.

Even with help from the West, now available to a total of four billion dollars annually and destined soon to attain eight billion dollars annually, progress must necessarily be slow, owing to hampering local conditions. But the worst of these local conditions is overpopulation. Because of the continued rise in populations what is often called developmental aid would be more aptly called emergency aid designed merely to keep the *status quo* in balance. For against the background of industrialism the overpopulated, underdeveloped regions rate, sociologically, as little more than huge disorganized disaster areas. Such a description applies with particular force to China but also to India, Egypt, and large sections of Brazil as well as a variety of smaller places. Central Africa has not yet felt the extremes of population pressure, but in view of the falling death rate and a stable birth rate it may soon do so.

A Few Figures to the Point

A look at a few broad figures at this point will be helpful in understanding what the situation is. According to the United Nations *Statistical Yearbook*, world population crossed three billion in 1961 and is now increasing by fifty-four million or nearly 2 per cent each year. At this rate world population must double every thirty-five years.

Some 2000 years ago there were only 250 million persons on earth, a total it took some fifty to one hundred thousand years to achieve. But by 1620, when the Pilgrims came to America, world population had doubled. By 1860 it had doubled again, now crossing a billion for the first time. Tripled over this figure now, the rate of increase is rapidly accelerating.

At present rates world population in A.D. 2000 would be six billion and in 150 years fifty billion. But, because there are not in sight the resources, physical or cultural, to support such a population, it may be predicted at once that this figure will not be even nearly approached. It even seems very, very doubtful that six billion will be attained by A.D. 2000.

As lower fertility rates will very probably not be reached either through rational birth control or sexual abstinence, owing to cultural resistance, it is clear that population will be held down only by high mortality rates. Such will be achieved by famine, diet-deficiency diseases and localized warfare.

For the next fifty and more years, then, the world may expect as regular items of news either the spectacle of apathetic half-starved backward populations exhorted and prodded by their government propaganda to greater efforts at raising themselves by the bootstraps or reports of riots, rebellions, insurrections, demonstrations, and assassinations in the underdeveloped areas. Most of the deaths, however, will be from diet-deficiency diseases or outright starvation.

It is far from generally realized—a point made by Harrison Brown —that the population volcano now erupting in the underdeveloped areas could not manifest itself without technical aid, medical and agricultural, from the industrialized world. This world has an economic interest in obtaining raw materials from the underdeveloped countries. But it is highly doubtful that it will continue giving aid when its scale exceeds the value of the raw materials obtained or in prospect or the strategic political advantages to be gained. It is at this point that the situation may be expected to express itself in the form of spectacular news events.

And it is situations such as these that Russia deviously exploits in her own interests, with communism blamed as the initiating factor. This it is not, for if conditions were favorable nobody would listen to the bizarre communist analysis. As it is, people want to blame someone or something for their misery and communism has tailor-made scapegoats to offer: capitalism, imperialism, colonialism, and the

United States. Were it not for these, the communists argue, peoples would be living in lands flowing with milk and honey. Yet prior to the rise of capitalism they weren't better off.

Of world population increase in the 1950s, which saw India adding the stupendous total of 100 million people, six out of ten were born in Asia, two out of ten in Latin America and Africa. At present rates, demographers point out, the population of Asia from 1950 to A.D. 2000 will expand by a total equal to the entire world population of 1958. By A.D. 2000, if present trends hold, the population of Latin America will have quadrupled over 1950.

As to troubles stemming from overpopulation, my prediction thus far has been vague as to place. Such troubles will, indeed, sweep the overpopulated portions of the world but will be especially severe in China, India, Indonesia, Egypt, and Brazil for some time to come. Desperate barter dealings with the Soviet of overpopulated regions such as Ceylon and Cuba, while economically and politically beneficial to Russia, can only have the effect of lowering native standards of living and intensifying misery in the underdeveloped areas. This is inescapable because products bartered for low-priced Russian oil and timber instead of sold in exchange for a variety of needed world goods are thrown on the world market at depressed prices by the Russians in their ceaseless quest for foreign exchange with which to purchase machinery and scientific equipment. On world markets such "dumped" commodities break down the prices of what underdeveloped regions have remaining for sale. And once foreign installations, seized on Russian advice, are worn out, the Russians will be unable to replace them and foreign investors will be understandably disinterested. Stripped, the underdeveloped areas that have relied on self-serving Soviet formulas will be deeper than ever in severe crisis. Except where their governments hold power by naked force they must all, eventually, turn back to the West for reasonable solutions.

What China shows is that communism is not the solution to the problem. And India and Egypt clearly show that nationalism and political independence are not in and of themselves solutions.

The rational solution, as I have indicated, would be birth control. But the theory I outlined excludes rationality from consideration in solving problems of adjustment to change until the crisis has become so deep that it leaves few if any feasible alternates open to choice. Ultimately, it is true, all peoples must come over to the practice of birth control.

But although individual experts can say this, as they do, the heads of Western governments cannot. They are inhibited by the political vengefulness of religious anti-birth-control elements at home and by the need to avoid the appearance of interfering in the internal affairs of other sovereign states. Nor can native political leaders, even when they recommend birth control, make their counsels prevail. Both the Chinese and Indians have thus far resisted the recommendations of their leaders.

Whether a particular region is overpopulated cannot be determined by comparing absolute numbers. The Netherlands, with 869 persons per square mile, has the densest national population in the world; Belgium has 758 persons. Underlying and supporting these populations is the most advanced intensive agriculture in the world and the highest concentration of industrial and scientific techniques. These in turn rest upon some of the most advanced technical and scientific schools. The populations per square mile of the United Kingdom, Western Germany and Japan all exceed 500 persons, compared with fifty-six for the United States and twenty-three for the U.S.S.R. (U. S. Statistical Abstract, 1958).

But Indonesia with 146, China with 165, and India with 305 per square mile are relatively overcrowded owing to lack of resources, natural and cultural. Giving the population per square mile for these countries and comparing the totals with densely populated advanced countries is highly misleading in consideration of the inhabitability of huge tracts. In China, for example, most of the population, due to mountainous terrain and deserts, is crowded into a very small part of the country. Much of China, in fact is like the "Badlands" of Montana. Prior to the Japanese invasion of the 1930s most Chinese were crowded in at 1000 to the square mile. In the rice-growing regions of Kiangsu and Chekiang they were nearly 7000 to the square mile. Such crowding, a frequent occurrence in the Orient, make the population densities of Western Europe look like underpopulation. Most of the areas of these countries, as of Brazil and Egypt, that one sees on the maps are largely uninhabited and inhospitable to man.

Nor is it always the lack of food that enhances the miseries of these swollen populations. Religious taboos keep starving orthodox Hindus from eating beef and allow tens of thousands of cows, considered sacred, to roam the countryside, eating fodder and reducing the fertility of the land. Any government that herded in these cattle for slaughter would face insurrection. The Chinese have an aversion to milk and milk products; they therefore use cattle only as draft animals and for meat. But meat, compared with cereals, is the highest-cost source of proteins in the world.

A Scientific Analysis

Just how large world population might become if famine and disease failed to intervene, as it is absolutely sure to do, we learn from the California Institute of Technology geochemist Harrison Brown in *The Challenge of Man's Future*, 1954. If one could obtain from the 36 billion acres on earth the same crop yields now seen in Western Europe, "The earth could support 35 billion persons living at American levels of food consumption or 90 billion persons living at the nutritional levels which now exist in Eastern Asia."[2] But such a world yield is impossible owing to soil deficiencies and unfavorable climates.

After considering known resources, natural and technological, and known potentials, Brown concludes:

"If we were willing to be crowded together closely enough, to eat foods which would bear little resemblance to foods we eat today, and to be deprived of simple but satisfying luxuries such as fireplaces, gardens, and lawns, a world population of 50 billion persons would not be out of the question. And if we really put our minds to the problems we could construct floating islands where people might live and where algae farms could function, and perhaps 100 billion persons could be provided for. If we set strict limits to physical activities so that caloric requirements could be kept at very low levels, perhaps we could provide for 200 billion persons.

"At this point the reader is probably saying to himself that he would have little desire to live in such a world, and he can rest assured that the author is thinking exactly the same thing. But a substantial fraction of humanity today is behaving as if it would like to create such a world. It is behaving as if it were engaged in a contest to test nature's willingness to support humanity and, if it had its way, it would not rest content until the earth is covered completely and to a considerable depth with a writhing mass of human beings, much as a dead cow is covered with a pulsating mass of maggots."[3]

As Brown points out, for some two to three thousand years before 1850 the population of India was stabilized somewhere between 50 and 100 million people. The country was comparatively prosperous, with the death rate balancing a birth rate that was then, as now, close to the biological maximum. But improved public health measures introduced by the British after 1850 and the cessation of almost permanent civil war under British rule have so operated to increase population that the country is now impoverished, an ironical example of an instance wherein progress produced large-scale misery. As Brown further points out, more than 90 per cent of the total man-hours worked in India are devoted to the production, handling, and transportation of food. A similar state of affairs prevails in China and other overpopulated regions.

At this point we may note that the population difficulties of the world are attributable to what sociologists call "cultural lag," one part of the culture failing to keep up with another. The world situation is that the Industrial Revolution has burst far beyond its original confines in Europe and America. The new techniques were first introduced into distant lands by colonialists and imperialists. Westernized intellectuals and politicians now want more. Much of the population, while glad to accept the new techniques and even to acquiesce in changes in the institutional layers of the culture, hold tenaciously to the older religious, ideological, and philosophical layers. They cannot bring themselves to realize that their codes of personal conduct and inner dispositions must undergo changes in harmony with the new techniques and altered political institutions. Painful demonstration rather than argument alone will alter conduct, and the process is a slow one.

But before any of the staggering trend-indicated totals of population were produced by a continuation of present rates of increase, one may be certain that the already developed regions would curtail the means to maintain the increase. When, as, and if internal difficulties interrupted the outward flow of raw materials, there would be an attendant interruption of the inward flow of machinery, drugs, chemicals, and technical assistance. And if Russia and the West knocked each other out in atomic warfare the repercussions in famine and pestilence in China, India, and elsewhere would be enormous and long continued. Whatever remnants of humanity survived, perhaps in patches of the southern hemisphere, would swiftly find themselves living on levels prevalent five and ten thousand years ago. Practically the entire development known as civilization would be wiped out, with the possibility of recovery, if any, requiring thousands of years.

Retardation in Development

A certain effect of the population boom in the underdeveloped regions, already indicated, is that it will greatly retard industrialization and general internal development. Extravagant prospects of early significant improvement held forth by native political leaders will be greatly reduced in the realization, for a long time to come. The most that can be hoped for is a slowly spreading circle of improvement from the top down, very gradually enveloping successive layers of the population. Technicians, scientists, teachers, and administrators must be provided for before the masses are reached. From these masses, from time to time, only the most promising elements will be selected for higher training.

All present evidence, therefore, strongly implies that neither China nor India, about whom the most extravagant fantasies of sudden development have been spun, will be industrialized to nearly the same extent as the United States, Western Europe, and even Soviet Russia are industrialized.

And while production may increase in the less developed areas, despite the sodden weight of bloated populations, it is increasing at a much faster rate in developed countries. A study under the Rockefeller Brothers Fund, for example, indicates that in 1956 per capita gross national product in the industrial open societies was ten times that of the less industrialized open societies; and it was predicted that by 1976 it seemed likely to be fifteen times as great. Both the open and closed or "communist" industrial societies showed an annual growth in production of 4.5 per cent. If this rate continued to hold all around, the "communist" nations would never catch up, owing to the tremendous head start of the open societies, which have been historically favored.

The Shadow of Automation

Whether they are closed or open, the societies with populations that press against minimal resources are storing up much competitive trouble for themselves vis-à-vis the already industrialized world in connection with emerging automation. It is going to be a problem even for the United States, Europe, the Soviet Union, and Japan to give their populations constructive employment as the full advent of automation displaces factory workers. This problem will in the West be solved in ways we shall consider later. But the solutions possible in Japan, the United States, the U.S.S.R. and Europe will be far more difficult—or impossible—to apply in countries like India and China.

Just what this difficulty is may be brought out as follows: Increase in agricultural productivity, which is sought, drives people out of agriculture. In India as well as China and other undeveloped countries agriculture has been carried on by primitive means on tiny plots. As more efficient methods are introduced, plots are made larger and hand labor is displaced. The displaced labor drifts to the cities where, if industrialization is taking place, it finds employment in factories and offices. This has been the slow pattern of development in Europe and the United States, and promises to be the pattern in China and other industrializing regions.

But just as China is beginning to fill factories, mines, roads, and collective farms with abundant hand labor, the West, and even Soviet Russia, is turning to automation, which displaces unskilled and semi-skilled factory workers. Many persons displaced must in time, as it shall be argued later, be given higher skills for employment in highly complex societies.

Automation greatly increases productivity, putting it far beyond the productivity of the manned factory even if the pay of factory workers is kept low, as it undoubtedly will be under dictatorial totalitarian regimes. Should the presently undeveloped societies themselves turn to automation, seeking a short cut in the process of industrialization, they will be left with huge absolutely unemployable populations, which cannot soon be lifted from the level of ignorant peasants and workers to that of skilled technicians and creators. Even if the schools were available, such a sudden transformation would be culturally impossible. And if they do not automate they will be unable to compete in world markets with goods produced by automated processes.

It is for this as well as other reasons that it can be said with virtual certainty that it will be a very long time, more than 150 years, if ever, before the present undeveloped societies catch up with the developed societies technically, economically, and culturally.

But even without automation China seems very likely to have a permanent surplus population. Some of this surplus will no doubt be devoted to the manning of a large standing army and police force for use in keeping a restive, overworked population in subjection to the ruling totalitarian party. But such forces are a drain on productivity, not an addition to it.

Russia and China both no doubt believe their military establishments may pay rich dividends by capturing the industrial societies of Western Germany and Japan. They may also be used to capture the oil-rich Middle East. Only one power thus far bars the way of these vaulting ambitions, and that is the United States. Western Europe alone could not frustrate them. Hence the extreme animosity of Soviet Russian and Chinese politicians toward the United States.

Since Stalin's death there have been signs of relaxation in Russia and some indications of a better life for the people. But the level of subsistence had for decades been so low that almost any change would be an improvement. After various vacillations it seems that the Communist Party is going to be very slow about terminating the Stalinist austerity policy. Russia remains a closely guarded military fortress and there is no present evidence of early significant liberalization.

The Outlook for Liberal Government

The pressure of overpopulation against resources in the backward countries makes it certain that the prospects for the spread of liberal government in the world are extremely dark. Stronger and stronger governmental measures will be required as population keeps increasing. The large numbers of young people, preserved from epidemics and the like, will be an impatient lot as the promised better life does not appreciably materialize.

Except where dictatorships have been established there will from time to time be open unrest. The dictatorships that emerge will not necessarily be communist or even friendly to Soviet Russia and China. Many dictatorships of the present time are anti-communist, as in Spain, Portugal, the Dominican Republic, and the Union of South Africa. There are, too, so-called socialist police states, as in Yugoslavia and Egypt.

For the excess of population in relation to resources, as I have noted, makes liberal government impossible. An oversized population, if it is to be organized, must be controlled by stringent measures. These stringent measures will be increasingly manifest. For most of the world, then, the future belongs to dictatorship for all the time that is readily foreseeable. This, in fact, is the great age of dictatorships, not of republics. Perhaps a cause for regret, it is nevertheless a fact that needs to be recognized.

Non-relevance of the Russian Model

Many of the undeveloped regions are said to be interested in the Russian way of doing things because of Russian success in becoming the second-greatest power in the world. But even though, concededly, Russia has achieved much in building up its heavy industry, it isn't this achievement alone that gave it its present high position. Rather did Europe in two wars of unusual ferocity whittle down her relative strength, allowing Russia to pull ahead of such one-time political giants as Germany, France, and Great Britain.

Again, the communists exaggerate for self-serving purposes the backwardness of Russia in 1917, at the time of the Bolshevik seizure of power. In the nineteenth century several Russians emerged as first-rank scientists, more indeed than have appeared since 1917. Russian literature and music also attained world rank under the Czars. Furthermore, an extensive railroad system had been built before 1917, linking Leningrad and Vladivostok. Precommunist Russia, too, contained quite a few factories, made its own locomotives and other heavy goods. And, not least, Russia contained a number of first-class universities and technical schools. Much of scientific work carried on since 1917 has represented but the continuation of what had earlier been established as a tradition. The names of Czarist scientists like Mendeleev, Lobachevski, Pavlov, Metchnikov, and Kropotkin come readily to mind.

The undeveloped countries that look to the Russian development for their cues have nothing resembling this historical background and therefore, even at best, cannot be expected to make so much progress as Russia has made since 1917 or to attain to such a relatively high world position. But isn't China, with Russian aid, technical assistance, and tutelage and her own pertinacity, apt to emulate Soviet Russia and become a great politico-economic power? If China were a closely controlled Russian colony, one might regard this outcome as having some probability despite unpromising Chinese conditions. But if China is politically independent, as she appears to be, it is hard to see power monopolists like the Russian Communists collaborating in such a development. In fifty years, then, Red China even with vacillating Russian assistance will not have achieved what Russia has achieved from 1917 to the present.

The Actual Line of Development

Instead of educating the masses, for which both schools and teachers are lacking, the initial effort in underdeveloped lands will be to single out the most readily educable, the most intelligent, with a view to producing scientists, technicians, engineers, and the like. Some of the newly educated will go into teaching, but there will not be enough of these to increase the flow of the educated by very much. In the meantime some of those being educated are attending schools abroad. Many Chinese are being educated in Russia. Indians and others are attending schools in Europe and the United States. Although the number of those educated will in every case increase as the effort is made, the gain will not be sufficient to meet the need for rapid development.

It has taken more than 1000 years for Europe to develop its educational system. Even if this system is taken as a blueprint in its present state of development, it is not easily imitated. The center of any university or school system is the library, which requires usually a separate building and tens of thousands of basic volumes. Each of the backward countries needs scores if not hundreds of libraries, and in many cases the basic books are not even available in the native languages. In addition, universities and secondary schools (if they are to amount to anything) require laboratories, much of the equipment of which is expensive. With sufficient capital the physical plant for the needed schools and universities could no doubt be created, but the capital is precisely what is lacking. And even if the plant and equipment were supplied, the trained faculties would be lacking.

It is therefore going to be a difficult, virtually impossible job to raise appreciably the cultural level of populations in undeveloped lands, even with the aid of newspapers, films, radio, and television. These adjuncts will no doubt be pressed into service, and may help up to a certain point. But more will be needed in order to turn out scientists and engineers.

Summary of the Prospects

In summary, then:

1. World population will by A.D. 2100 fall far short of the theoretically possible totals indicated in present trends, owing to the lack of developed facilities and resources to care for such a population. But wherever population increase becomes critically excessive it can, as Japan has shown, be reduced rather rapidly by ruthless government action in initiating abortion, sterilization, and enforced contraception. Only if government is supplanted by anarchy in certain regions would it be impossible to institute such measures, and then the conditions of anarchy themselves would serve to reduce population and population increase in internecine warfare and famine.

2. Industrialization in all undeveloped countries will be greatly retarded by the population boom. It will not draw even nearly abreast of industrialization in Western Europe or the United States within 150 years.

3. The rate of industrial growth in the more developed societies is going to increase slowly and steadily over the rate of industrial growth in the undeveloped societies. Automation will enable the developed societies to draw far ahead of those dependent upon unskilled and semiskilled manpower.

4. The outlook for liberal government in the world, often called "democratic" government, is extremely dark. Even its beginnings in some of the undeveloped countries will be nullified and supplanted by dictatorial trends. There are many reasons why this should be so, but the population explosion itself practically guarantees it. Strong measures will be needed to apportion scarce resources and privileges among a surplus population. India is an extremely likely candidate for dictatorship. Dictatorships, however, will not necessarily be either Moscow-oriented or independent communist. We already see a communist dictatorship in Yugoslavia that is not under the thumb of Moscow. And most governments in the world today, by far, are of dictatorial though non-communist inclination.

5. With or without dictatorships civil disturbances can be looked for from time to time in the countries with surplus populations although they will no doubt be fewer under dictatorships. But when civil disturbances do take place there will be an interruption in the

flow of raw materials from the undeveloped countries to the fully industrialized countries.

6. Lacking natural resources, few of the undeveloped countries will ever be fully industrialized, at least not under their present separate and independent existence. A possible candidate for full industrialization is China but, it is our prediction, even in 150 years she will not even nearly have drawn abreast of the United States or Western Europe or other possible political entities. In that time, barring disasters in the rest of the world for which there is no unequivocal premonitory evidence at present, she will not even have drawn abreast of Russia. For this laggardness there are reasons other than excess population, although excess population is itself a significant drag.

7. In the meantime population will have continued to increase moderately in the developed parts of the world, but at a rate that makes possible the integration of a large percentage of the people in a higher culture. As these developed portions of the world are preponderantly populated today by whites, it can be said that after 150 years, even though non-white portions of the world may be somewhat better off materially, they will still lag far behind the white world.

However, before the lapse of 150 years they should have brought their crude birth rates down significantly, giving rise to a rate of population increase more or less parallel to present European rates. For a high standard of consumption will never be compatible with an extraordinarily large birth rate.

At the present time the proportion of Europeans and European-descended people in the world is declining. In 1950 Europeans and European-extracted came to about 30 per cent of world population. At the present rates of population increase, which will very probably not hold, the European proportion of world population would be no more than 20 per cent. Numbers, however, by no means tell the whole story here as the cultural quality of the European population vastly surpasses that of non-European world population. This cultural superiority will continue to prevail and, there is evidence to suggest, may even be enhanced.[4]

The Effect of Population Rise in the United States

In conclusion, a few remarks on the effect of population growth in the United States seem pertinent. Like the European, the American birth rate is far more flexible than that of the underdeveloped nations and can be expected to contract more or less spontaneously in response to evolving conditions rather than to continue blindly in disregard of environing circumstances. Nevertheless, the increases since 1940 will have strong effects the rest of this century, mainly adverse to traditional social outlooks. This is more than a little ironic as traditionalism has always valued fertility and family formation in the interests of social stability and continuity.

But under complex modern conditions numerous offspring are a factor making for social instability, as the economic system cannot absorb all youth into the work force either early or at a sufficiently rapid rate to keep unemployment within manageable limits. A numerous young population makes for change first in that it requires a greatly expanded school system as the price of maintaining social standards at established levels. Again, with the increasing introduction of automation into office and factory, the entry of larger and larger numbers into the work force must be deferred in order that they may obtain additional expensive education fitting them for useful employments other than in factories and business offices.

The crisis in this quarter is going to come in the United States, and soon, when factories and offices severely reduce their rates of hiring low-skilled young workers. Those who are congenitally unable to prepare for higher employments, at least half or more of the population, will contribute greatly to the number of outright social changes. For their presence will reinforce, among other things, demands for measures of personal assistance—such as unemployment insurance—associated with the concept of the Welfare State. All such measures will require for their implementation more taxes.

It is thus evident that as far as traditionalism and political conservatism are concerned, the recent upward surge of family formation will be a boomerang. Only policies identified with modern liberalism will be applicable to the situation if harsh extremist measures of either Right or Left are to be avoided; in the underdeveloped nations, as I have noted, population pressure on resources is a stimulus to the emergence of dictatorship. In the developed nations political conservatism, preaching adherence to old procedures, has no solutions whatever to offer young people out of work and unable to find employment. Even if the birth rate should begin to decline, there will be many such young people for several decades.

CHAPTER V

THE WORLD ECONOMIC KALEIDOSCOPE

Economic systems underlie government, as technology and culture in general underlie economic systems. Although they can each be separately distinguished, all are inextricably interwoven in patterns of relationships that sustain and enfold peoples as individuals, groups, and populations. Because economic systems logically, historically, and functionally precede, support, and stimulate government, I here consider them first. Government—more touched with drama than economics no doubt because it is the great instrument of eventual decision in human affairs—will next be surveyed in relation to probable changes to come.

Any economic system, as part of a social system, is a complex of more or less tangled interrelationships which, in principle at least, can be delineated abstractly in minute detail as indicated in Chapter III. The gross or over-all changes that from time to time stand out most conspicuously involve myriad changes in many of these details which, although of interest in the construction of economic and social models, are not within the range of our present interest. These economic relations in turn are subject to such human valuations as efficiency, imbalance, obsolescence, appropriateness, cost, and productivity.

But before general economic change can be considered, one ought first, before attempting any exercise in prognostics, to obtain some impression of what it is that is to undergo specific changes. I shall therefore sketch in a preliminary way the general world economic position.

The Lopsided World Economy

Both for geographical, climatic, cultural, and historical reasons, as is readily shown, the world is extremely lopsided economically, a statement given detailed justification in statistics cited in Appendix B. Actually virtually everything denoted by such words as modern, industrial, developed, and scientific is concentrated in Western Europe and America north of the Rio Grande River. Prominent exceptions to this generalization exist only in Russia, Japan, and fringe areas such as the Union of South Africa.

With only 25 per cent of the world's population and 19 per cent of its land area, Western Europe and Anglo-America (Canada and the United States) significantly produce and consume 90 per cent of the world's coal and operate nearly all its sea traffic. In portions varying from 60 to 90 per cent they own and operate most of its railroads and telephones and produce most of its aluminum, electric energy, cement, steel, and coke. They also possess nearly all of its leading universities, technical schools, and laboratories.

No other land mass or combination of multiple land masses is remotely close to them either in development or potential, a statement that does not imply any invulnerability to disaster. The very wealth of the North Atlantic Community harbors its greatest danger because it is a constant temptation to demagogic adventurers. For hundreds of years most of the troubles of this Community have come, it is noteworthy, from inside itself. At the center of these troubles have been extremist messiahs and their gullible followers who have challenged established but enfeebled myths with the even more incredible myths of pan-Slavism and pan-Germanism, Bonapartism, proletarian rule, Aryan mastery, and neo-Romanism. If the Community is destroyed it is far more likely that destruction will come about in a suicidal contest of internal myths and saviors rather than by the invasion of alien conquerors. For no combination of external forces has even the potential strength to overcome it.

If one includes Japanese and Russian production with the European and Anglo-American, nearly all of the world economy beyond the elementary agricultural stage is accounted for. Except for scattered mining operations and occasional plantation agriculture closely related to the North Atlantic economy, most of the world's economic effort outside the indicated areas is concentrated in low-yield subsistence hand agriculture and subsistence grazing. About 75 per cent of the world's peoples are hand cultivators of the soil. Most of them are peasants—illiterate, uninformed, credulous, and superstition-soaked.

The most poorly endowed continents from the point of view of generally helpful climate, fertile soil, abundant minerals, navigable rivers, and manageable terrain are, in order from least endowed upward, Australia, Africa, Latin America, and Asia (allocating Siberia to the Soviet Union). Yet Asia, economically still largely in the stage of subsistence agriculture, contains more than 50 per cent of the world's population. With a much poorer natural endowment Australia manages to produce a high standard of living for a proportionately much smaller population.

It is the mixed natural endowment, vitiated soils and the inadequacy of native cultures in relation to modern standards rather than the convenient scapegoats of colonialism or imperialism that are responsible for most world poverty. This is so even if it may be conceded that neither colonialism nor imperialism did much in most places to elevate local standards.

But though agriculture is almost the sole economic activity of most of the world, even in this department Anglo-America and non-Russian Europe lead by extremely wide margins. Europe, buttressed by a chemical industry that traces back to the European invention of the science of chemistry, has the most intensively and skillfully cultivated land in the world. In proportions of from 50 to 90 per cent non-Russian Europe and North America above the Rio Grande produce most of the world's wheat, citrus fruit, lumber, sugar, oats, and olive oil. They produce nearly 50 per cent of the fish, even though the seas touch nearly every land, and a third of its cotton.

Although the world has been impressed by the relatively swift industrial and technical ascent of Russia since about 1930, Russia is as yet not even close to the achievements of Western Europe and North America. About one third as large and four fifths as populous as the Soviet Union, the United States alone outproduces it by fantastically large margins largely accounted for by intensive mechanization.

In percentages of Russian production, current United States production stands as follows:

PRODUCT	PER CENT
Corn	2,300
Motor Vehicles	2,000
Copper and cotton	800
Aluminum and petroleum	500
Electricity and tobacco	400

PRODUCT	PER CENT
Synthetic rubber	300
Aluminum ore, pig iron, steel, cement, fertilizer, and zinc	200
Lead	166
Coal and cotton yardage	150
Iron ore	133

In agriculture average yields per acre in the United States, which could easily practice more intensive cultivation, are one and a half times those in the Soviet and in some categories two times. The United States has twice the cattle and one fifth more swine per thousand persons. Furthermore the United States has six times the total road mileage of the Soviet Union and twelve and a half times the surfaced roads. It operates more than twenty times the number of trucks, buses, and passenger cars. Despite its smaller land area, the United States has three times the railroad trackage and operates twice as many freight cars that carry three times more tonnage.

What makes Russia a leading political power, a modern Sparta, is its military establishment and a sufficiently large basic industrial development to support it. Outside the military sphere Russian deficiencies are tremendous. The United States has four times the housing per person and is constructing new housing four and a half times faster. It also has 25 per cent more primary and secondary schools per capita and twice the colleges and universities. Americans enrolled at the university level exceed Russians by three and a half to one although, significantly, more Russians than Americans take degrees in solid technical and scientific fields related to military applications. In the opinion of many leading American educators a large portion of the American system of higher education is woefully inadequate, a contention that receives some external evidential support in the more or less institutionalized low level of debate and editorial comment on public policies.

In the Soviet Union the common people are very much worse off than the common people of Western Europe and North America. For the means to buy a loaf of bread the average Soviet worker must work three times as long as an American. He must work six times as long for a pound of beef or quart of milk, twelve times as long for a suit of clothes or pound of butter, twenty-five times as long for a pound of tea and thirty times as long for a pound of sugar.[1]

First in the total of cultivated land in the world with about a third of all acreage, Asia has little to export beyond what is produced in industrialized Japan. The second in size of the world's land masses with about a fifth of all land, it is almost literally weighed down by its excessive population. It eats meagerly mainly in order to reproduce itself on a sharply rising scale.

Latin America, embracing the entire land mass and islands south of the Rio Grande River, is the next most significant world economic region. Fourth in land area, fifth in area of cultivated land, and sixth in total world population, it is as yet industrially almost negligible. It ranks even below Asia in output of cement. Like Asia it is enormously handicapped by difficulties of terrain and climate, soil deficiencies, cultural backwardness, shortages of well-placed mineral fuels and possesses population composed mainly of Indians and Negroes with intermixtures of these and Europeans. Relatively few are of pure Spanish or Portuguese descent.

Africa, first in land area in the world if Siberia is taken as non-Asian, ranks third with 13 per cent of world population. Most of its people are still culturally in the Stone Age and most of them resemble the North American Indians at the first arrival of Europeans. It is negligible in all categories of industrial output or has none at all. It has only 5 per cent of the world's railway mileage and 6 per cent of international trade. Terrain and climate are difficult and soils are widely eroded and leached.

The vast qualitative differences between the industrialized parts of the world, nearly all concentrated west of the Ural Mountains in Europe and in northeastern North America, and the difficult environmental conditions for significant development in Asia, Africa, and Latin America are little appreciated and are seldom taken account of in glib references to great impending development. The great difference in development as well as in potential (for development proceeds on the basis of earlier development) is shown in the tables of Appendix B.

With the facts as indicated in these tables we are now in a position to consider some predictions about the world economic future, about which there is much ill-informed expectation.

Aspects of the Economic Future

As far as significant balanced and integrated development and expansion are concerned, the world economic future belongs almost entirely to Europe, Anglo-America, and Soviet Russia. An integrated or even very extensive one-sided development will probably not take place within 150 years or even longer in Africa or Asia. The economic future for these areas is heavily clouded not only by the environmental and cultural conditions just cited, but because of the serious problem of overpopulation. Development stands a somewhat better chance in Latin America owing to its partial Europeanization; but even there not much can be expected for a long time to come.

The Future of Africa

As to Africa, careful economic geographers write:

"So much has been written in recent years about the remarkable economic developments now going on in certain parts of Africa that the impression has been created that a radical transformation is taking place throughout the continent. The actual situation, however, is considerably less spectacular. . . . Evidences of advancement are confined to relatively limited sections of Africa; the greater proportion of the continent has yet to experience an economic awakening."[2]

Apart from foreign-financed mining and primitive indigenous subsistence agriculture, almost all modern African economic activity is confined to the Europeanized Mediterranean coast and the temperate southern tip. About half the continent consists of arid desert, most of which serves as an effective barrier between the Mediterranean and the rest of the continent. Africa has few navigable streams and although it has a huge water-power potential the water-power sites are for the most part not located near any settlements or workable natural resources. Oil has been discovered in the torrid Sahara Desert and, if the reserves are large, will provide the foundation of an extractive export industry. But Africa has a poor soil endowment. "For with a few notable exceptions, such as deltas, flood plains, marsh lands, and areas of volcanic rocks, most of the richer soils are limited to regions of light or deficient precipitation."[3]

Even though various parts of Africa may attain nominal political independence, as has recently been the fact, the continent is going to remain for long economically and technically dependent upon Europe, Anglo-America and/or Soviet Russia. Africa may be a bone of contention among these, as she already appears to be; but she will never in the foreseeable future be economically independent by present European standards.

In order to achieve an integrated independent industrial economy, Africa would need the twin supports of rich coal and iron deposits. Iron is lacking, although there are secondary rich coal deposits in the southern, Europeanized segment. This same southern region is also known to be rich in copper, cobalt, gold, silver, tin, lead, radium, uranium, vanadium, asbestos, platinum, chromium, zinc, diamonds, manganese, and corundum—all of which practically guarantees that it will remain a mineral source in European hands, Russian or non-Russian.

Africa has only five cities of more than 500,000 population—Cairo, Alexandria, and Algiers on the north coast and Capetown and Johannesburg at the southern tip. Except for Cairo all are non-indigenous. Its geography is hostile to the growth of large cities on the long east and west coasts because the shorelines are smooth, devoid of natural harbors; river mouths are shallow and silt-clogged, and the shorelines are deeply lined with mangrove forests where they are not overshadowed by high cliffs. Again, most of the continent is hot and extremely dry or hot and excessively humid. There are few highlands; most of the continent consists of flat lands, either lowlands or plateaus.

Africa, in fact, next to Australia is the most poorly endowed of all the world's large land masses. It is clearly destined to remain an economic colony of Europe, mainly supplying raw materials. As it gains in stature as a producer of raw materials it will no doubt undergo concomitant social and cultural development, but not enough to place it within hailing distance of present-day Europe or North America. On the basis of all concrete present evidence Africa will never scale the economic, political, and cultural heights and it is very doubtful that its indigenes will for a very long time be Europeanized. It may be objected that many Africans brought to North and South America have been fully acculturated; but a difference is that these were subjected to total and exclusive influence of the alien, higher culture.

What of parts of Africa, such as the Arab north combined with southwestern Arabic Asia? The same holds true for this oil-rich, overpopulated region because of the lack of varied basic mineral resources. Contrary to the apparent dream of Arab politicians, there will never be a rebirth of the unquestionably great Arabian civilization because there are not the basic material resources regionally available to sustain such a civilization under modern conditions. The Arab world, however constituted politically, will remain within the foreseeable future an economic colony of Europe or Russia.

This is not to say that there cannot be much improvement in the present African position, in whole or in part. Almost any change on that continent represents improvement. But Africa does not have the geographic, climatic, positional, cultural, or natural resource base to be anything except an economic colony. For Africans to think otherwise is to be misled by wishfulness in disregard of obvious facts.

The Asian Awakening

Asia is the next large land mass in which the people are, as the saying goes, "awakening." Many enthusiastic observers predict a bright cultural and economic future for it, and particularly for India and China.

Here, and for reasons very similar to those applicable to Africa, there will be found a wide gap between expectancy and possible realization.

China, rich in coal, is deficient in iron ore and the nonferrous minerals. No matter how advanced the methods that are applied, without minerals, and particularly without iron ore, Chinese industrial development cannot emulate Europe's, America's, or the Soviet's. "China's total known high-grade iron ore reserves would meet the requirements of the steel industry of the United States for less than a decade; its known petroleum supply would be exhausted in a few days if used at the current American rate. Copper, lead, zinc, and sulphur —all essential pillars of industry—are exceedingly limited in quantity."[4]

But more recent reports have greatly increased the estimate of Chinese iron ore reserves. Dr. Edward C. T. Chao of the United States Geological Survey, according to the New York Times of December 27, 1960, reported to the annual meeting of the American Association for the Advancement of Science that in the preceding ten years two hitherto unknown deposits aggregating ten billion tons had been found, about ten times the ore removed from the Mesabi Range in the United States from 1892 to 1950. Reserves of molybdenum had also been found, the largest in the world, and important deposits of ilmenite. Reports of discoveries of large nickel deposits were, however, questioned as doubtful. The location of the Chinese coal deposits, it was pointed out by other Chinese experts from the government, posed difficult transportation problems.

If these latest reports of extensive iron ore deposits prove to be correct, important modifications will have to be made in predictions about the Chinese industrial future, at least as far as the very long range is concerned.

China is additionally handicapped by being burdened with extensive highly mountainous, hilly, and desert-dry terrain, while its more fertile parts are subject to heavy rains and periodic devastating floods. Although the country is impressively large in gross territory, one is progressively less and less favorably impressed as one studies topographical and climatic maps. Sinkiang, western and eastern Tibet, Inner Mongolia, and much of Manchuria can be written off totally as very dry, inclement, sandy or rocky regions hard to get to and good for little except extremely light grazing and scrappy agriculture. Only the eastern half of eastern China or China proper is territory of rich agriculture and even there much of the land has been ruined by peasant ineptitude and heavy rains or is extremely hilly. The western part of China proper is a region of rugged terrain, poor for agriculture and, as far as is known, sparsely provided with minerals.

In combination with these two factors—lack of adequate minerals and difficult terrain—there is the third factor of gross overpopulation, which in relation to the meager resources makes absolutely impossible, unless population totals are greatly reduced, any achievement of vast industrialization.

The Chinese railroad network is chiefly located on the eastern plains. Even if it were extended into the deep interior, a gigantic task, there are no known resources there to be brought out. Nor will the deep interior sustain the population hordes of the agriculturally rich coastal regions.

As there cannot, owing to lack of minerals, be full-fledged integrated industrialization to absorb excess population forced off the land by improved methods of cultivation, the Chinese must find some other solution to their most gnawing problem. Manchuria and parts of western China may absorb a few migrants but not enough. Immigration is barred by law in most countries that might find room for some of the excess Chinese. As the Chinese living standard is right now hovering just above the starvation level, it cannot be further reduced. Unless the Chinese are to invade en masse the climatically inhospitable Russian-held north or the already overcrowded southeast of Asia, they must reduce their net birth rate very sharply, either by contraception, abortion, the incidence of famine and disease, or a combination of all these.

It is therefore my prediction that the Chinese population, instead of increasing much further or even stabilizing, will begin to be reduced in this century. The present government has blown both hot and cold about contraception and abortion, with its latest attitude apparently pro-fertility after a giant public campaign on behalf of contraception proved unpopular. But like the Soviet Russian Government under Stalin, the Chinese Government can make famine an instrument of national policy and it may be confidently predicted that it will do so once it fully understands that its present vast population as well as its birth rate is a political as well as economic handicap rather than an asset. So a combination of famine, abortion, and officially stimulated contraception may be expected to bring the swollen Chinese population down.

Invasion of southern territories by the numerically superior Chinese is clearly barred by superior weapons in the hands of the Western powers, which stand ready to defend Japan, Burma, Indochina, Malaya, and India against onslaught. The possession of a few demonstration atom bombs would give China little additional power without the vast and expensive systems to deliver them.

It would be a resource-rich India that would be the most likely object of a Chinese invasion. For the acquisition of any other territory would provide insufficient outlet for its masses of people, even though the advanced industry of Japan would be a valuable acquisition. Although a Russian-style pogrom against neighboring large populations would not violate the scruples of the Chinese Communist Party, the effort would hardly pay sufficiently unless it took place in resource-rich India.*

The Russian-style pogrom as a political method has become rather widespread in the modern world. Adopted by the Bolsheviks for use against dissidents, particularly property-minded peasants, it was emu-

---

* This paragraph was written in 1960 and was in the hands of the publishers in June 1962, four months before the invasion of northern India by Communist China that astonished Prime Minister Nehru, Defense Minister V. K. Krishna Menon and others, who thought it unlikely ever to take place. But the only unpredictable feature of the Chinese invasion was the particular moment it would take place, just as the only unpredictable aspect of the Soviet-Nazi pact (and Hitler's subsequent violation of it) was in the particular time selected for the denouement. An eventual hostile confrontation between expansionist China and expansionist Soviet Russia can similarly be predicted, whatever their ideological similarity.

lated by Hitler for use against the Jews, Poles, and Balkan peoples. The Russian Communists have also employed it against Poles and Hungarians. In the twenty-year struggle of the Chinese Communists with the armies of the Kuomintang both sides staged many large-scale massacres of unarmed civilians, so it may be concluded that the mercy they failed to show their own countrymen would hardly be shown to foreigners in possession of valuable resources.

China's abundant supply of coal, second only to that of the United States, foreshadows not only abundant electric power for the country but also an extensive chemical industry. But as China industrializes one-sidedly without the presence of great or handy metallic mineral resources, it follows that she must soon look abroad for pig-iron and other processed ores. This means she must participate in world trade. As the ocean route is cheap and the long rail haul from Russia and western Siberia costly, unless unexpected workable iron and other mineral deposits are found either in China or eastern Siberia, it is inevitable that China must eventually again look to the outside world for trade—to Japan, India, the United States, and even Europe. In time the arguments of terrain, land distance, and economics must work against the strange political marriage of culturally and ethnically disparate China and Russia. Again, the Russians are as alien to Asia as the English, French, or Americans, and xenophobic China cannot forever ignore the fact that Siberia, a huge Asiatic tract, is held by an essentially European power.

As China necessarily turns to the outside world for needed industrial materials, not immediately but certainly within 150 years and very probably within fifty years her government must moderate its present truculence. The time may well come when she will be anxious to enlist the cooperation of the Western world.

But in any event China will never, short of mutual destruction by Russia and the West, become one of the leading world powers—unless she secures Siberia, Japan, and India. It is highly doubtful that Russia and the West, whatever the signs, will oblige by destroying each other; and it is equally doubtful that China will get Siberia, Japan, and India. Too much force stands in her way. To speak of China at the present, therefore, as the world's fifth great power, entitled by might to sit at the same table with the United States, Russia, Great Britain, and France, is to take great liberties with meanings. China may indeed have close to 25 per cent of the world's population, but most of this population is a national liability.

World Mineral Reserves

The world distribution of reserves rather than production of the basic minerals, coal and iron, is a present factor that will have much influence on the future course of developments. Appendix C shows that the present industrialized nations are, with few exceptions, very preponderantly favored by the placing of the reserves of these two fundamental ingredients. Indeed it might well be argued that much of existing industrial development depends simply upon the distribution of coal and iron.

It is a combination of these two, and not one without the other, that provides the firm basis for pre-eminent industrial power and supporting military power in the modern world. No amount of human ingenuity has so far been able to make up for the lack of either one. The United States leads in the possession of both coal and iron reserves. In concert with Canada its lead is awesome. Taking the United States, Canada, non-Soviet Europe, Australia, the Union of South Africa, and Brazil together, all part of the dollar-sterling economy, it is clear that they impressively dominate the world in coal and iron reserves.

Iron is the most widely and abundantly distributed in the earth's crust of the industrially needful minerals. There is known to be much more iron present than is considered usable, and usability depends upon advances in techniques of recovery. What is not now considered usable may as the result of new techniques become usable, so that one cannot say further usable deposits of ore will not be found in China. But as of right now China has little more iron ore readily available than is sufficient to give her some initial momentum toward full industrialization.

Whether China makes this turn depends, of course, on the will of its dictators. For although economics influences political actions, it by no means fully determines them. A man may choose to starve rather than capitulate politically, as has been shown by many hunger strikers. The situational basis unquestionably exists, however, for Chinese cooperation with the Western world and the economic and geographic facts strongly argue that the Chinese-Russian partnership is an artificial product of unrealistic Leninist doctrine. It is in fact, like the entire economic and political development in both countries, completely un-Marxist, heedless of economic facts.

In any event, Red China is not going to be able to emulate Soviet Russia in its industrialization, for it simply lacks the resources.

The Future Prospects of India

India, like China, also possesses disadvantages. A similar disadvantage is serious overpopulation. Basically the Indian subcontinent is naturally wealthy, far wealthier than China. But this natural wealth does not prevent her myriad people from being poverty-stricken any more than the Nile Valley, one of the richest spots on earth, keeps the people of overpopulated Egypt from being among the poorest in the world.

India, unlike China, is replete with mineral deposits of almost all kinds, well located with respect to each other and with respect to easy access to industrial cities and seaports. India of the two is lower in coal reserves, of which China has the second largest in the world. But India is well endowed with huge, readily workable iron-ore deposits, ranking next to Canada in this mineral. She is also well supplied with well-placed deposits of the nonferrous metals.

She has navigable streams, manageable terrain and, fringing her extensive coast lines, extremely fertile soils. Unlike China she possesses a dense railway network, a heritage of long British rule. Her long coast line, with several large harbors, is excellent for domestic transport as well as commerce with foreign lands via the Indian Ocean.

But, after excessive population, climate is India's big handicap. Mild in the winter except for torrential rains in the north, most of India is torrid in the summer. The heat is enervating, sapping human ambition and energy.

India, like China, also possesses a multiplicity of languages and dialects, a handicap that can and no doubt will be overcome, but only in the course of a considerable passage of time. In the meantime the language disparity will be a drag on cultural and technical development.

India, unlike China, possesses a superb British-trained civil service and, through the knowledge of the English language in the small educated class, has readier access to the technical learning of Europe.

The Chinese, in thus far choosing Russian for ideological reasons as the predominant foreign language of their educated class, have a second language that gives access to less of accumulated Western learning. China has proportionately fewer people than India educated in the Western manner, and fewer good schools.

As in China, there is room for much improvement in India, in agriculture and notably in industry. Most Indian agriculture is still of the primitive subsistence type. India no doubt will improve, but very slowly.

Whereas in China the prohibitive-coercive type of government has been installed by the Communists, in India an experiment is taking place with the English permissive-persuasive type of government commonly styled "democratic." India, however, if it is to accelerate its industrial progress, will find that it must be less permissive and persuasive and more coercive. For the Indian masses will take a long time to emerge voluntarily from the cocoon of their myth-ridden culture. If they are to develop rapidly, coercive methods similar to those used by the Russian Communists against superstition-steeped peasants will have to be employed.

Such methods are deplored among civilized peoples but it is overlooked that Europe voluntarily left the myth-ridden maze of stuporous inertia only by a series of unrelated, haphazard steps that took hundreds of years. There was, first, the Italian Renaissance or revival of learning that struck at the medieval Christian Church as the guarantor and defender of inherited myth. Next came the rise of Protestantism, which split and dispersed the once formidable power of the Church, making its retrogressive rulings increasingly ineffective. Then came the emergence of modern science, modern technology, and popular learning, producing the extremely mixed cultural situation now prevailing in the North Atlantic Community. For developmental events to proceed at a similar leisurely pace in India and China is to guarantee very little modernization for a long time to come.

But even if the issue is forced in India as it is now in China, development will be exceedingly slow because of the lack of capital. As we have noted, India, like China, eats up the surplus produce of its land every day. Both countries are poor in capital because of their excessive population. The term "excessive" here relates to capital requirements for development.

India's hot summer climate need not, fortunately, be a permanent handicap. For she may in time install central air-cooling systems in buildings much as central heating systems are now installed in Europe and Anglo-America. For such air-cooling systems India needs more electric power as well as expensive equipment, and India, like China, has many undeveloped hydroelectric power sites. Unlike China, India will no doubt need to conserve her coal for converting her iron ore into steel. But atomic energy in the course of time may aid her in this respect. Were India to acquire generally cooled structures in its cities, the temperamental effectiveness of the people in relation to the environment would no doubt be greatly enhanced.

But, as in the case of China, no spectacular sudden economic, social, and cultural efflorescence can be expected in India. Neither China nor India will develop with anything like the rapidity of Russia, for reasons we shall now examine.

The Rise of Soviet Russia

The Soviet Union has of course made giant strides in industrialization and in raising the cultural level of a nearly 100 per cent peasant population in the less than fifty years since the revolution that overthrew the Czarist regime. But it could not have made such strides by effort alone. There had to be, and were, basic favorable circumstances.

Russia, in the first place, was already well on the road to development before the revolution. European technicians had been imported. Factory production had been begun. The country was making its own locomotives and much other heavy machinery. Foreign companies like the International Harvester Company and the Singer Sewing Machine Company were manufacturing in Russia. Again, the Czarist regime had provided the main regions of the country with railroads, one line of which, the trans-Siberian, was the longest in the world.

The Czarist regime had been able to mobilize millions of soldiers and had held out against greatly superior German forces in World War I for three years, until its military collapse for sheer lack of equipment. The Russian military record in World War I, as a matter of fact, was far more impressive than in World War II under the Communists, as is shown by the deep penetration and near triumph in the field of the German armies in the second war. Although prostrate as a result of the war, in 1917 Russia was not backward in the same sense that Asian and African nations today are backward. She was backward only by the most advanced European standards. The Russia of 1914 had since the eighteenth century been rated one of the leading world powers, and with good reason. India, China, and the other contemporary nations of Asia and Africa have never been so rated.

Once they had extirpated political dissidence and were able to turn to economics, the Bolsheviks took up where Czarism had left off, resuming the building of factories and bridges, the digging of canals, the laying of railroad trackage, and the erection of hydroelectric dams, schools, factories, hospitals, and laboratories.

But the Bolsheviks had natural factors in their favor that the underdeveloped nations of today do not possess. The agricultural and industrial heartland of the country, in the first place, was relatively compact, occupying an area at the eastern end of the fertile north European plain about 1000 miles wide by 1500 miles deep. In this area is now located most of Russia's population, most of its agriculture, most of its useful navigable streams, its moderate rainfall and temperate climate, nearly all of its rich and contiguous coal and iron-ore deposits and virtually all its manufacturing. It is its possession of coal and iron, as well as secondary minerals, that makes Russia a power to be reckoned with in the world today and not its adherence to a certain politico-economic ideology. The same holds true of the United States and of Western Europe. If depth and intensity of democracy were the determining factor, Sweden and Switzerland would be the leading world powers.

This Russian heartland is about half the size of the United States, an area very much smaller than the one sixth of the earth's surface usually attributed to the Soviet Union. Actually, as far as wholly desirable or manageable land area is concerned, Russia has far less than the United States. To the south, and east of the Caspian Sea, Russia has another region of about the same size but dry and sandy, sparsely populated, and fit mainly for subsistence pasturage and farming under great difficulties. As far as is known, it holds no petroleum reserves. The northeast of European Russia consists of dark coniferous forests that extend eastward beyond the Ural Mountains and cover all of Siberia except for harsh tundra along the Arctic coast and patches of grassland on the southern fringe. The soils of Siberia are acid and leached, poor for agriculture; moreover, the growing season is too short, as the region is very cool. Very little of this huge coniferous zone, therefore, is cultivable. Again, Siberia beyond the southern fringe cannot, as in the almost identical case of Canada, be inhabited except under extreme difficulties. It is as a potentially mineral-rich area that Siberia holds its chief significance, standing to Russia in this respect as Canada stands to the Western world.

Most of the cities and heavily settled rural areas of Russia are in what has been designated the heartland. But only about 33 per cent of the Soviet population is urban, with 67 per cent rural. The percentages are approximately reversed for the United States.

So-called Great Russians compose only half of a population that now well exceeds 200,000,000. Ukrainians account for 20 per cent and White Russians for about 5 per cent. These three groups constitute the dominant Slavic element. The remaining 25 per cent is composed of scores of other ethnic groups, most of them primitive hunters or grazers—Uzbeks, Turkmen, Tadzhiks, Kirgiz, Kazakhs, Azerbaijanians, Georgians, Tuvinians, Tatars, Mongols, Lapps, Komi, Khanty, Nentsy, Nga Nasany, Evenki, Eveny, Chukchis, Koryaks, Ud, Yukats and others. All these are mostly found in the more sparsely inhabited, less desirable living spaces, either the hot dry southeast or the cold north.

But all in all, the various necessary ingredients are present in the Soviet Union for reaching industrial and cultural levels that will at least equal those of Western Europe and could, with historical luck, surpass them. Most of the difficulties within Russia are conquerable. And when, as, and if they are conquered it will be despite the Communist Party and not because of it, although Communist politicians will no doubt claim the credit for all successes. But the Russian Communists did not endow European Russia with its good black earth, its rainfall and climate, its rivers, its deposits of coal, iron, and other minerals; nor did they develop science and modern technology or invent power-driven machinery. In this sense they are precisely like the entrepreneurs of European and American capitalism.

It is the challenging upthrust of Russia on the basis of its natural endowment that is partly responsible for the desire of other peoples to develop economically also. This desire is stimulated by oratorical native politicians obviously seeking positions for themselves and their followers. And it is given additional stimulation by the commercial daily newspaper press of the world that long ago found a useful simple circulation formula in stressing conflict and contests of all kinds. This press outdoes the Soviet press in depicting the forward march of

Russia to "overtake and surpass" the West, meaning Western Europe and Anglo-America. And this same press pounces upon China, India, and Africa and presents them as additional contestants in the exciting sweepstakes of progress.

But aside from Russia, a world power since the eighteenth century, all the evidence indicates that the others in the so-called race will fall far short of reaching the heights attained by Russia either in the same period of time or in a much longer period. The chief alteration in the world economy since the Russian revolution is that industrialized Europe has been extended eastward.

As a consequence of the reckless propaganda by politicians and newspapers, however, there is going to be a gradual disillusionment among many peoples of the world as results fall far short of expectations. At the moment it is hard to see what there may be to compensate them for their coming bitter disappointment. And out of this disappointment will no doubt come repercussions in the form of a politics of despair.

CHAPTER VI

WORLD ECONOMICS IN THE NEXT 150 YEARS

Now that we have a general impression of what the present world economic position is, we may turn to the future. How is the world economic system most likely to change?

As I have already mentioned, not nearly so much can be expected of coming developments in Africa and Asia as prognostications of recent enthusiasts may have led one to believe. Latin America, partly because it is not handicapped by the population excess of Asia, partly because it is in the trade orbit of Europe and Anglo-America, and partly because it is to some extent well-endowed with resources, could do much better if it had a leadership committed to modern development and if it initiated fundamental political changes. But special internal difficulties confront Latin America.

The chief areas of advanced industrial and cultural activity, as we have already indicated, will continue for 150 years or more to be Anglo-America, Europe, and European Russia, whatever the political auspices of these or other areas. Neither China nor India is going to pull abreast of them or even come close to emulating them, though both China and India will, no doubt, see some progress, particularly if they reduce population. The means are present for much improvement, provided both countries get sound management, which is itself questionable. Perhaps the greatest underlying obstacle facing any national management is the particular culture complex it must deal with.

Government and Non-government Ownership

One question before the world concerns the method of ownership and control of the economic establishment. In Russia title to all productive property is vested in the national state, which acts in theory as the trustee for the people. The self-appointed administrator of this trusteeship is the Communist Party, which in itself is held in supposed trusteeship for the members by a small number of self-appointed and co-opted leaders. The citizen cannot dispose of his ownership, cannot sell it, give it away, or otherwise alter the way the title is held. Even if it is still maintained that the citizens do exercise ownership, it must be conceded that it is ownership in some sense other than the direct ownership of personal property. There is an inescapable inertia about the supposed general ownership that keeps title vested perpetually in the state and qualifies personal benefits.

Looking at the question of ownership in this way we find that in Western Europe and Anglo-America there is some governmental ownership of productive property, there is considerable private ownership by individuals and small numbers of individuals banded together either in closely held corporations or partnerships, and there is public ownership in the sense that large sections of the public, like stockholders, bondholders, bank depositors, certificate holders and policyholders, are fractional titleholders of enterprises. The United States and Western Europe, then, do not have private-ownership systems, as is often erroneously stated, but a mixed governmental, private and public ownership system. For when large numbers of people participate in direct ownership it begins to amount at least to semipublic ownership. Full public ownership would involve a participation in ownership by everybody, and an equitable full public ownership would involve exactly equal participation in ownership by everybody, a condition not even remotely approached in Soviet Russia.

In addition to ownership there is the question of control. Owners, as is well understood, do not always control what they own. In Russia the government both owns and controls all productive property. The managers, in the persons of the few leaders of the Communist Party, hold no titles to productive property; but as they exercise control and as no rivals for control are tolerated, they are in effect the same as owners for life. For, concretely, they *are* the state; they *are* its will and wishes. If it is argued that a broad section of the citizenry concurs with their will and wishes and therefore is identical with them in intent, one must observe in the history of the Soviet Union that sudden reversals take place in the will and wishes of the leadership which the supporting citizenry, taken unaware, must be convinced by propaganda campaigns to accept. The citizens, it often turns out, do not know what their political will is until informed by the party leadership!

In Western Europe and Anglo-America individuals sometimes control their property directly, as landlords their houses or lands, partners and stockholder-directors in closely held corporations their businesses, and entrepreneurs their own, usually small, enterprises. But most property, governmental and non-governmental, is controlled by non-owning managements or by owners of a relatively large minority stake in an enterprise having many lesser owners. Most owners—of stocks, bonds, bank accounts, certificates of trust and insurance policies—have no direct voice in the management of their property and very little indirect voice unless they are able and willing to act in concert.

As to direct control, most citizens in Western Europe and Anglo-America have no more decisive economic voice than Soviet citizens. Indirectly, however, the citizens of Western Europe and Anglo-America possess lawful, although slow and cumbersome, ways of dislodging from authority both political and economic managers who do not attain prescribed ends, a fact which makes European and American political and economic managers somewhat more responsive to the popular will than is the case in the Soviet Union. As mere numbers do not guarantee the presence of wisdom, this ultimate popular veto power does not, true enough, always produce the best possible results. Of course a dialogue sometimes takes place between populace and managers in which issues are clarified and the populace is induced by the force of argument to see things as the managers see them, or vice versa.

A radical difference between economic management in the Soviet Union and management in Western Europe and America is that in the Soviet there is ultimately a single monolithic management, whereas in the non-totalitarian societies there are thousands of managements, operating under a generally loose governmental policy.

Whether government is to exercise more or less ownership in the next 150 years appears to some observers as a major issue. But it is not really open to a free decision. Just what ownership role government is going to play in various parts of the world will be determined by social circumstances. And the way circumstances now appear to be shaping is that in the Soviet Union, of all places, there is going to be some diminution of government ownership or at least of managerial centralization. In the first place, government ownership could not be increased there as it now stands at 100 per cent. Change there will be, however, and the only change possible is in the direction of less government ownership and managerial centralization. Just what the form of the coming Soviet non-governmental ownership will be one cannot, of course, say with any certainty, but it might take the form of collective ownership by members of producers' collectives. Such revived non-governmental ownership might well begin on the farms, where production has been consistently unsatisfactory.

The Soviet Union, contrary to its original intention, in time resorted to differential incentive wages, and it is not too much to expect that if it believes production will thereby be increased it will resort to differential incentive ownership. And there is no doubt that, within limits, differential returns in the way of wages and ownership participation stimulate effort in the simpler elements of mankind. If shares were allotted to workers in all Soviet enterprises, with the rate of return on the shares depending on the success of the individual enterprise in production, it might be argued that there had been a departure from the basic Soviet principle. But there would be no more departure than in the installation of differential wage rates. And the Soviets have never held principle above expediency.

Whereas differential wage rates no doubt stimulate individual effort, differential ownership would stimulate collective effort, which is the sort the Soviets appear to be seeking. The final word of government in all decisions would not be infringed by such an arrangement, although immediate decisions would be made by the management of each enterprise, in harmony with the national plan. If it is argued that this sort of change would be a step back to capitalism and away from communism, it should be noticed that what the Soviet Union now has is not communism in the sense of joint and equal participation, opportunity, and ownership. What Soviet Russia now has is monopolistic state capitalism. Unequally rewarded workers and consumers have little opportunity to protest and must be constantly rallied to the support of the system by means of managerial propaganda and bonuses.

Increasing State Ownership

Whereas less state ownership and centralized control can be visualized on the basis of insistent circumstance for the Soviet Union, far more state ownership and centralized control of elements of the economic system is due in Western Europe and Anglo-America. State ownership and control is much more prevalent in all parts of Western Europe than in Anglo-America and will probably be extended in Europe even as Anglo-America catches up to the present European position. There is no circumstantial reason, of course, for the degree of various kinds of ownership ever to be precisely the same in Soviet Russia, Western Europe and Anglo-America.

But already government ownership of economically productive enterprises is far more prevalent in both Europe and the United States than is generally recognized in the public prints. In most of Europe and in many parts of the United States municipal railroads and bus lines are government-owned. There are frequent demands in the United States for the government to take over the ownership and operation of the railroads, which were built, not by free enterprise alone (as often claimed) but partly by means of heavy government subsidies. Also, as concerns the argument that free enterprise is the most efficient in operation, the important case of the American railroads constitutes an adverse instance. For from their very beginning the American railroads have been consistently mismanaged by private operators both in their finances and in their functioning. Investors, patrons, and workers have been repeatedly let down.

So-called public roads, highways and streets are not generally recognized as what they are in fact: government-owned, -operated, and -maintained economic enterprises worth billions of dollars. Owing to the difficulty of financing them and paying for the cost through the levying of a commercial toll, private entrepreneurs did not even attempt to build and operate them. If it had been left to private enterprise, there would be very few roads and highways. As it was, the proliferation of roads and highways amounted to an indirect governmental subsidy of the privately owned and privately operated automobile-manufacturing and freight-trucking industries.

In Western Europe nearly all railroads, municipal transport systems, electric power and light and gas utilities, telephones, telegraphs, and a variety of other enterprises are owned and run by government. In France the national government is a shareholding partner in many so-called private industrial corporations. Banking and insurance enterprises are government-owned in many European countries, as they are in some states of the United States, such as Wisconsin and North Dakota.

In the United States as well as Europe a large and increasing amount of civilian housing is government-built, government-owned, and government-operated. For private housing, like railroading and road building, is one of the major economic spheres in which private enterprise has made a signally poor record for itself, providing inadequate and insufficient facilities at costs too high in relation to other costs.

Various factors draw government into different economic fields. Inability of private operators to make a profit with enterprises necessary to the public welfare, as in the case of municipal transit systems, find them usually eager to sell out to government. Reluctance of private capital to support some needed enterprise, such as housing and education, finds government forced to step into the breech. What has kept private operators out of most economic areas left to government is probably the inability to devise some way of charging for the service. How, for example, is a charge to be levied on users for lighthouse service? And if sewers were privately owned, would service be cut off if monthly fees were not paid?

Business Activities of the United States Government

What the board of governors of the Federal Reserve System describes as straight business-type activities of the federal government, leaving aside any such activities by state and local government, have already reached impressive proportions little realized by the public. In 1958, for example, total assets in federal business activities amounted to $106.96 billion compared with $36.15 billion in 1953, an increase of almost 200 per cent during a Republican administration! Of this huge sum $20.9 billion was alloted to so-called public-enterprise funds: $5.17 billion to the Commodity Credit Corporation for farm subsidies; $3.13 billion to the Export-Import Bank; $2.07 billion to the Tennessee Valley Authority; $2.4 billion to the Federal National Mortgage Association for home-owners' mortgages, and $1.37 billion for the General Service Administration. The Department of Defense accounted for $12.5 billion of the assets. Other activities swallowed $65.2 billion: $2.9 billion to the Rural Electric Administration; $9.45 billion to the Atomic Energy Commission (atomic energy is being made available to the world primarily by government, not private, enterprise); $8.7 billion to the engineering corps of the Defense Department; $5.07 billion to the Department of Commerce for maritime activities, and $4.1 billion to the International Cooperation Administration. There was $4.9 billion of deposit funds covering bank and other insurance and $3.06 billion of revolving trust funds for the Federal National Mortgage Association, the Federal Intermediate Credit Banks, and other purely banking activities of the federal government. In practically none of these affairs has it been a case of the federal government's thrusting aside private enterprise. Rather has it invariably been a case of the federal government's stepping in to make up for the absence, deficiency, or incapacity of private enterprise.[1]

Government in the United States, furthermore, right now accounts for more than 10 per cent of the national income, which is what is left from gross national product after deductions for depreciation charges, accidental damage to fixed capital, and capital outlays charged to current expense. In 1957 the contribution by all divisions of government to national income was $42.6 billion.[2]

We see, then, that there is a great deal more economic activity carried on by government in a so-called free-enterprise economy like that of the United States than is acknowledged by the ideologically one-sided daily newspapers.[3] In Russia the official ideology holds that only governmental ownership and operation of economic enterprise, dubbed socialism, is of maximum effectiveness; whereas in the United States the dominant ideology is that private enterprise is of maximum effectiveness and government enterprise is invariably wasteful, inefficient, unprogressive, and uniquely corrupt.

It is the general social function of newspapers, whatever their political orientation, to be the more or less openly avowed purveyors of an ideology. The fundamental difference between ideology and philosophy, it may be remarked, is that ideology erroneously purports to have found the truth, whereas philosophy, like science, professes only to be seeking the truth with ever-sharpening critical instruments. Many supposed philosophies, however, are in reality ideologies.

Key Concept: Collectivism

The key concept in the future economics of industrial society, Russian and non-Russian, is collectivism, with government in the non-

Russian sectors destined to play an increasingly forceful although far from exclusive role. While there may be little relish for this prediction in the world of open societies and there may even be futile protest against it, a strongly established trend toward collectivism is already unmistakable. There is no evidence that the trend will be reversed or will even level out; there is much evidence, on the contrary, that it will continue to gain momentum. Government is going to play an increasing economic role in the industrial societies of the next 150 and more years.

The full extent of governmental intervention in the economy in terms of general statistics is shown in Appendix D. And having thus made clear that contemporary government is a momentous economic factor in the United States as well as Western Europe and tends to enlarge in time of internal and external emergency, we may proceed to other aspects of the economy. It should be noticed, however, that many technical observers feel that governmental expenditures in the United States are being kept disadvantageously low in relation to internal needs. For the sake merely of keeping taxes down, it is alleged, the United States is neglecting many areas, such as education, that will ultimately cost it much more to remedy.

Whether there is peace or war, an avalanche of governmental economic activity hangs over the future and it is not difficult to see governmental economic activity's accounting *directly* for much more than 20 per cent of gross national product. It will probably not, in Western Europe and Anglo-America, account within 150 years for as much as 50 per cent of gross national product unless there should be unforeseen and, on the evidence, unlikely political overturns of the Leninist type. But government economic activities accounting for at least 35 per cent of gross national product *directly* is not unlikely. This estimate, if anything, may be too low. For a greatly expanded role for government is impending, especially in the United States, but also in already government-oriented Europe.

Collectivism in the United States

Collectivism, in the form of operation through large collectivities, is going to be the spreading economic style during the next 150 years. Just what is meant by this use of the term, which is usually associated in the minds of sketchily informed newspaper readers with economic organization in the Soviet Union?

The United States, it may surprise some persons to learn, is already a highly collectivized country. All our large corporations, such as American Telephone and Telegraph, United States Steel, and General Motors, are examples of collectivized enterprises. They warrant designation as collectivized simply because they have each collected so many functions, employees, stockholders, and customers within a single monolithic organization. There are no other reasons for employing the term in any context.

Most economic activity in the United States now, governmental and non-governmental, takes place under large-scale collectivized (although far from totalitarian) auspices, as a survey of the facts quickly shows.

Big Economic Units

A salient fact the general public is unaware of, although it is bluntly reported by the government statistical service, is that the 500 largest industrial corporations of the United States, employing no fewer than 9,079,000 persons—close to 15 per cent of the labor force—and having about 15 per cent of all corporate assets, registered aggregate sales of $188.3 billion in 1957. In the same year gross national product was $440.3 billion.[4]

Gross national product is an economic concept that relates to the total of goods and services, including governmental, delivered to ultimate buyers. Sales of industrial corporations are not all made to ultimate buyers but enter in part into interbusiness transactions of finished and semifinished goods that at a later stage become part of gross national product. If we allow an average markup of only 20 per cent to yield a total final price to the ultimate consumer for the sales of the 500 industrial corporations, we obtain a figure of $225.0 billion or slightly more than half of gross national product for the year.[5]

The way in which a variety of criteria sustain the contention that the United States is becoming a country of large economic units under concentrated ownership and operation is shown in Appendix E, to which skeptics who still think in terms of small and dispersed business enterprise should turn.

All facts, indeed, point to the conclusion that a few enterprises, managed and owned by relatively few people, account for very large and ever-enlarging portions of the gross economic activity of the nation.

What, if anything, does the general public possess? Seventy per cent of the population was covered by life insurance in 1955, but with an average coverage of only $6,900[6] and an average insurance premium per family of less than $200 per year. Of owner-occupied dwelling units in 1950, which numbered 19,901,646, 44 per cent were mortgaged.[7] No less than 45 per cent of occupied dwelling units housed non-owners—that is to say, tenants.[8] A portion of the general public has savings accounts, but little more in each individual case than enough to provide for personal emergencies. Government and corporate bonds are similarly held by the general public on the same comparatively meager basis.

The point is that there is not a particularly large propertied constituency in the United States, supposedly the center of non-governmental property sentiment in the world. As far as the general public is concerned, it is a matter of titular indifference whether or not government extends its economic activity. To the common man the monolithic corporations seem just as remote and abstract as the government—in fact seem themselves like the government and as far as the ordering of people's lives is concerned they are indeed part of the government, the Establishment.

Continued Corporate Mergers

All evidence points to the fact that corporation mergers will continue and that fewer and fewer enlarging enterprises in all fields of economic activity will dominate the economic situation. It will in time be a case of a few large non-governmental corporations, over which the government will have increased regulatory control, the government itself dominating if not owning the economic system. Individual or small enterprise will have only an interstitial and marginal role. There will be small enterprises, but only in areas not sufficiently lucrative or important enough to attract large capital or the government. Shoeshine stands, specialty shops, crossroads stores, repair shops, filling stations in lightly traveled areas, and retail stores in sparsely settled regions will be left to small operators. But virtually everything else will be in the hands of a few large enterprises or the government. The day of the so-called "little man" in business is over. True, new enterprises may arise from small beginnings on the basis of some invention or discovery; but such will in most cases quickly be absorbed by the larger agglomerations or will themselves grow large.

Only in the United States, of all countries in the world, does such a prospect seem alarming to numbers of people. In Europe, for example, there is no strong sentiment against bigness, as is shown by the long-established monopolistic cartels flourishing there. Illustrating the trend toward bigness in the world, even in the so-called free world, we find that in ultrademocratic Australia the Broken Hill Proprietary Company, the largest industrial enterprise in the country, controls about a third of the metals industries, while the second largest enterprise, the Colonial Sugar Refining Company, controls all sugar refining in Australia and New Zealand.

The extreme opposite of many enterprises in an industry is a single enterprise in each industry, with one management in charge. While this appears to be what the world is heading toward in each country —rather, on each continent—history invariably leaves behind it many raveled edges so that one is not justified in positively predicting such a neat outcome as a single enterprise for each industry. But the trend is clearly toward such an outcome, perhaps asymptotically. The future, in any event, belongs to collectivistic monopoly in the economic sphere. Already a condition close to such monopoly exists in many basic United States industries, and an extremely prevalent condition in basic industries is what economists term oligopoly, wherein two or three big companies account for some 90 per cent or more of all business in an industry and many tiny ones divide an extremely small percentage of the remaining business among them.

It is the work of a brief moment to merge the few remaining giants in any particular industry, replacing informal monopoly by formal monopoly. For the idea of oligopoly itself seems questionable when, as is often the demonstrated case, the industry giants tacitly agree among themselves on prices, models, quality and the like.

Future Producing Trusts

The foreseeable economic future, then, belongs to one or two industrial giants in each industry, perhaps even to interindustry giants like a Metallurgical Trust embracing ferrous and non-ferrous metals, a Fuel Trust embracing coal, petroleum, and natural gas, possibly a Power and Fuel Trust including such a product as electricity, a Food Trust that processes and retails all food and perhaps makes itself responsible for the primary process of raising the food, a National Housing Authority, and a single branch-banking system.

Embryonically the idea of such a development is present in the very names of many extremely large American companies: General Foods Corporation, American Metals Corporation, General Electric Company, International Business Machines Corporation, General American Transportation Company, United States Steel Corporation, National Biscuit Company and the like. The men who titled these and other companies at least unconsciously had in mind extremely wide domains.

But the prospect is more than embryonic, we see, when we turn to look at American Telephone and Telegraph, United States Steel Corporation, Great Atlantic and Pacific Tea Company, a few score other giant corporations, and a literal handful of the biggest banks and insurance companies.

Even as this is being written it is being publicly proposed by large private promoters to take the 139 remaining separate railroads in the United States and merge them into six regional systems. Such a merger would obviously prepare the way for the day when they would all be put into the same system—perhaps even a single system including railroads, bus lines, trucks, and air lines.

What would be the impetus toward the outcome of a single enterprise in each industry? The same, clearly, that has produced the present prevalence of bigness—lower costs, greater efficiency, wider availability, larger volume of business, readier access to capital, more efficient organization all around.

Is there any reason to believe that the economic situation will stabilize itself on its present level? There is no evidence at all that tendencies toward greater efficiency and centralization will be arrested. Basically the thrust for greater efficiency comes from the machine itself, which underlies the entire process of modern economic development. It is the machine that is dictating greater efficiency to the world, greater efficiency not only in the economic sphere but in all spheres of life. In this sense at least, the machine has come to dominate man.

The Decline of the Factory Worker

As enterprises are merged into larger and larger entities and as they install more and more labor-saving machinery, particularly of the automatic variety, they will no longer draw workers into factories and offices in large numbers. Such workers now fill large categories of the labor force; industrial society, until the present, has flaunted the distinctive feature of the factory worker. But the factory worker is now destined, and in the short run, to lose prominence much as the agricultural worker has already done. Both the factory worker and the office worker are on the way out as dominant categories of the labor force; both will remain, but in greatly diminished numbers.

It is with the prospect in view of displacement of factory workers that some labor-union officers are now calling for shorter hours of work at unreduced weekly wages, ostensibly in order to share prospective scarce employment. Some have predicted a work week as short as twenty hours. However, this is hardly likely. It is not probable that organized factory workers would be allowed by the rest of society to put in such short hours while others worked much longer. Nor is it likely that everybody else would be reduced as a matter of equity to such short hours, resulting in general part-time *functional unemployment* and attendant demoralization. But vacation periods will lengthen, to perhaps a month per year.

What will happen is not difficult to anticipate. As fewer and fewer are employed by automated offices and factories, more and more persons will be forced to offer special skills in the labor market in order to get jobs. In the past people in organized society have obtained employment on the basis of relatively little skill and in easy ways—as agricultural laborers, factory workers, office workers, and sales personnel. Most such have been unskilled in any real sense and it has been purely courtesy to refer to most of them as semiskilled.

Some persons, under the new dispensation, will be unable to develop skills, and these will merely sink into the more or less dependent mass of the unskilled. But others, capable of acquiring special skills, will acquire them. There will be many more persons engaged in highly skilled occupations requiring elaborate education. The number of factory workers in the United States today is about 12,000,000. This number, let us say, will be reduced to the vicinity of 3,000,000. That leaves 9,000,000, plus increments from population growth, to place in other employments. The country now has somewhat more than 1,500,000 teachers and this total can easily be more than doubled, considering not only population growth but the necessity for bringing teaching up to standard in all communities.

To a large extent the educational system is still a façade. It must be brought up to standard, and once the present standard has been achieved, education must be expanded and improved *in depth.*

Education the Key

It is only education that serves to differentiate man systematically from the lower animals. The more it is realized that true and full education enhances the worth of the individual and also serves society, the more rapidly will the educational system be expanded and deepened. By deepening I mean supplementing class work with individual work as in tutoring, psychological assistance, special coaching, and dealing with exceptional types of individuals. A great many more skilled workers can be readily absorbed in education, where they will be of much greater usefulness than if they worked in factories or offices.

The educational enterprise cannot, however, absorb all who would otherwise have found employment in office, factory, or store. But the professions, new and old, can absorb many.

With mechanical appliances proliferating both for production and direct use, the repair and servicing of such appliances will absorb many workers. The appearance of machinery—engines, automobiles, airplanes, radios, television, and mechanical household appliances— has brought into being many service and repair people. As more appliances make their appearance, both in number and variety, there will be more demand for servicing and repairs.

Factories, offices, and stores in the past have drawn people out of domestic employment, but one will now see a reversal of this trend as factories, offices, and stores reduce employment. Domestic help, now relatively scarce, will once again become plentiful. Persons of higher and rarer skills will once again be ministered to domestically by persons of lower and more common skills. Domestic employment may be counted upon to absorb a large slice of those refused employment by offices and factories.

What we shall see, then, is a much finer division of labor than at present and increasing professionalization. There will be more *types* of employment, particularly more specialized types. It seems that this development will represent improvement, although there will always be the danger in a mechanized society of surplus population— that is, population in excess of available employment opportunities.

Both the United States and Europe, however, will export much highly skilled surplus personnel to the rest of the world—Asia, Africa and Latin America—where it is needed in almost all categories. Such personnel will include teachers, librarians, physicians, surgeons, engineers, agronomists, and veterinarians.

The Coming Decline of Labor Unions

Labor unions, historically now at maximum power, are destined by accelerating, uncounterbalanced trends for a significant reduction in size and influence. While a few here and there may increase in size, they will not increase in power.

Automation, autocomputation, and telemation are all bound to reduce memberships as they eliminate jobs. Even installation workers in many lines will be less in demand as prefabricated parts are increasingly produced by automated machinery.

Unionism is fully effective from a union point of view only where there are concentrations of workers and heavy investments of capital, the managers of which can be coerced by strikes that halt extensive operations. Strikes cause lower returns on capital and often also strike against public convenience and necessity. Where workers are scattered, as among farm laborers at present and as will be the case more and more with the full onset of automation, wide-ranging strikes cannot be made effective. Where workers are few, except in technically sheltered crafts, they can be easily replaced; where places of work are isolated, mass support from sister unions is hard to mobilize. Strikes of many individual service workers and of consumer-appliance repairmen, for example, cannot even now be made very effective as they cannot bring pressure to bear against a single vulnerable point. Their concentrated impact is slight.

The constant demand of organized labor, constituting about 25 per cent of the labor force, for more pay and shorter hours is in fact a prime stimulus toward the installation of automated equipment in search of competitive economy related not only to the domestic but to the world market. The worker, whether he knows it or not, is increasingly a part of the world market, competing more and more with workers of other countries as the latter industrialize. The higher costs are in any given national industrial economy, the more difficult it is for that economy to earn foreign money with which to pay for needed raw materials. If foreign money is bought with domestic money, then foreign purchasing power in the domestic economy is enhanced, driving domestic prices higher and domestic living standards lower.

A few particular unions, sometimes locals confined to one area, whose workers' pay now exceeds that of most university professors and other highly educated professionals, may be able to retain relative positions; but the high pay in such special fields stimulates the search for economies lower down at the expense of less strategically placed unionized workers, whose very jobs may be permanently forfeit.

An illustration of what is meant may be helpful here. Since World War II, building-trades workers in New York City have consistently improved their wages, hours, and working conditions at the expense of real estate investors, tenants, and builders. In part compensation for higher costs of building, the entrepreneurs have successfully sought for lower operating costs in order, necessarily, to provide for proper return of capital. One area of economy was found in the installation of automatic or pushbutton elevators, long banks of which in many buildings once required two or three dozen operators. As new office buildings, apartment houses, and hotels installed automatic elevators, many older buildings, in order to achieve competitive economies, replaced their man-operated elevators with the automatics. The consequence was that thousands of elevator operators, engaged in what was known as vertical transportation, lost jobs they had held for twenty and thirty years and in which they thought they had life tenure. Prior to World War II the union of vertical transportation workers had been able to dictate wages, hours, and working conditions by calling strikes that forced tenants, employees, and customers to walk up thirty to sixty or more flights of stairs. Undefeated in the competitive bargaining arena, they were eventually bypassed by technological development spurred by their demands.

In other contexts similar consequences are possible, the workers of higher skills generating pressures by their demands that cause workers of lower skills to be displaced by automatic apparatus.

People in general, skilled and unskilled, will be far better off in every way when, as, and if full automation is attained. Better instrumentalities enable men more successfully to attain their goals, and what the goals are determines ultimate value. Labor leaders and unionists who look with hostility on automation and wish to impede it are in the same position as the machine-wreckers in the early days of the English Industrial Revolution.

But ultimately unskilled, low-skilled and so-called semiskilled work will command relatively lower wages than at present, although in an economy of true abundance, should disarmament ever make it possible, they may well draw wages higher than at present. Skilled and highly skilled effort will draw premium pay, which will be less the result of union organization than of personal value input made possible with better tools. High productivity, either of volume or quality, will be better rewarded than ever.

What all this foreshadows is the gradual slow decline of the labor-union boss. Much of this decline will be seen over the relatively near term, in the next twenty-five years. While the present generation of labor leaders may be little affected, the successor generation will be fully aware of the currents.

There will no doubt continue to be associations of workers. But, gradually replacing the unions we are familiar with, they will encompass workers of higher skill and will be more like the American Medical Association, which is actually run by a succession of elected officers who are skilled practitioners themselves—a different state of affairs from that in which organizational manipulators manage to get for themselves life tenure as bureaucratic heads of large bodies of mostly untutored followers. For all of union talk about democracy, most unions are not democratic; their procedures are rigged to perpetuate officers in their positions until death.

Public sympathy, once extended to organized labor engaged in severe contests with employers, is now swinging the other way as it becomes plain that organized labor is seeking differential advantages at the expense of other members of the labor force and does not hesitate to inconvenience the public by strikes. As the number of trained technical workers increase, enlarging the upper white-collar labor force, there will be further loss of sympathy. With more and more high technology in use, "blue-collar" workers will be increasingly displaced by "white-collar" workers.

As in the case of labor leaders, the managerial class also seems likely to experience some dilution of power, although less so than in labor. Aside from free lances in the performing arts, whose professional lives are generally short, business-industrial managers at present enjoy high status and maximum pay, even when their duties are routine and relatively non-competitive. The President of the United States is paid $100,000 yearly before taxes, the Vice-president $35,000. Most heads of Stock Exchange corporations exceed the latter figure, and very many far exceed the presidential figure with salaries ranging up to $250,000 and more annually plus pro rata pension and expense-account benefits. Corporate heads usually also have longer tenure, although not usually life tenure like labor leaders.

What will in time serve to reduce relative pay as well as powers of corporation managers will be alterations in the way they are selected and a reduction in the number of enterprises through mergers. There will be relatively fewer managers and more competitors for their posts. Already, through mergers, many corporation officials are thrown out of jobs in their forties and fifties and find it difficult to obtain comparable employment; this trend will increase. As to manner of selecting such managers: at present they are selected and retained by self-perpetuating boards of private directors, most of them officials of other companies. Interlocking directors in corporations sustain each other in their positions. The interlock is usually not direct but is of a serial nature, extending through chains of companies.

The pay of corporation officers is often said to be based on competitive factors—the need to attract the men best able to maximize returns for their companies. Yet the data shows little variation in the pay of officers of companies doing well and companies doing poorly. Leading railroad presidents, whether their companies run at a consistent deficit or show good profits, nearly all seem to be paid a minimal $100,000 annually. Except where bonuses are involved, the pay of company officers is only occasionally related to the showings the companies make. Ordinarily it takes a difficult-to-obtain concentration of stockholders to dislodge entrenched corporate managements.

But this situation may be expected to alter when large enterprises come to include government directors and public directors, who will not belong to the inner clique of company managers and directors. The more the public interest is seen to be affected by the very large companies, the nearer will be the day when such directors appear.

As officers and directors now only rarely own a considerable share in any company, they are at most trustees for other interests—stockholders, bondholders, employees, and public. They do not hold titles to their posts.

But the managers of the future will have far more theoretical education than do most managers at present. The day is not far distant when the familiar style of self-made, intuitive business executive will be a rarity, replaced by a highly educated, broadly reflective type. As matters stand now, only about 10 per cent of the labor force, including professionals as well as some industrial executives, is thoroughly educated. The necessities of the society and economic system shaping up for the future will require that nearly 25 per cent have comparable education—a task for the educational system (of which more later).

Corporate Operations

Will the big economic organizations—corporations and trusts—be operated as at present, even if somewhat more closely regulated by the government? Operation, it seems, will be different in the sense of being more responsible to general needs for goods and services rather than to particularistic needs for profits. To insure a different emphasis it seems likely that all large economic enterprise will, as indicated, have a wider representation of directors, some representing the point of view of government, some perhaps of labor, and some the general public. Such a development is what is minimally possible if non-governmental ownership is to be preserved. The alternative to such an arrangement could hardly be anything less than full socialism. For the public market, contrary to what some businessmen seem to believe, is not a private preserve. There is always the historical chance that governmental ownership will in the end prevail, thus pushing aside all mere modifications of present arrangements.

Will there be more or less personal freedom under such dispensation? The prevalent view no doubt would be that there would be less freedom. And it is true that there would be less freedom of choice about what might be done by economic entrepreneurs in the market. Market freedom, we may agree, will be considerably circumscribed by increasing government controls and regulations. But it does not necessarily follow that personal freedom will be reduced. Personal freedom, in fact, may be enhanced. For with fewer persons employed in the offices and factories of large enterprises there will be fewer dependent on the vagaries of the merchandise market, there will be more reliance on personal capabilities. Even if this formulation doesn't hold, there is no reason to believe that general civil freedom and intellectual freedom are necessarily bound to the market for goods. As matters stand now, many persons, perhaps a majority, have their actual freedom of action and expression severely circumscribed merely by being members or employees of an organization. In a world of fewer organization people there might well be more actual freedom.

Non-Leninist government, in any event, is going to play a much larger regulatory role in relation to all the big economic enterprises, although not necessarily an unduly limiting role with respect to personal freedom. There is going to be a much greater variety of jobs and skills in the developed societies, and more complex skills. The economic system as a whole, as office and factory forces are reduced generation by generation, is going to produce more value in the way of humanly needful services even as it produces as much or more than ever in the way of physical goods.

The big organizing factor of the future, through which the needs of society as shown in each period of crisis are expressed, will be government. And to the future development of government we now turn.

CHAPTER VII

POLIS, OR THE FUTURE OF GOVERNMENT

Since 1800 the central institutional role as far as experiencing change and forcing change in other social institutions is concerned has been played by the world economic system in its process of assimilating and applying advancing technology. And much of the economic system, particularly in primarily agricultural countries, remains to be brought up to the level of operation of the advanced industrial countries.

But in the next century and a half the most prominent—and turbulent—institutional role will, without any question, be played by government, the state. The political institution will itself experience notable changes and will guide and induce social, cultural, and economic changes of a far-reaching nature. In the more backward economies government is already playing this role with the assistance of governments of the advanced economies, or is about to; but in the advanced economies it will necessarily also assume an enlarged and clearly dominating role.

The political revolutions of the eighteenth and early nineteenth centuries destroyed the old-style dynastic autocracies. They were replaced by relatively weak, commercial-minded polities. Since then government has had to adjust itself more or less unconsciously, by fits and starts, willy-nilly and in bits and pieces, to mostly unguided economic developments, which became explosively expansive under the influence of population growth and applied power technology. In the next 150 years economic and other institutions will be very strongly affected and remolded by the self-conscious intervention of government. Such intervention will not take place, over the long run, because government or any individual in government necessarily desires to intervene—in government as elsewhere people find it easier not to bestir themselves—but it will be the whiplash of immediate necessity that brings government increasingly to the fore.

As in the past, there will of course continue to take place reciprocal stimuli to adjustment, growth, and change among the various social institutions.

Government in the form of the state is the great regulating institution of society, receiving and interpreting stimuli from every quarter and reacting. It has been important ever since the onset of civilization, but owing to the fundamental character and multiplicity of urgent problems in the contemporary world it is clearly faced with enlarging positive responsibilities. When it fails to measure up to these responsibilities, for any reason, unfortunate complications result.

Political management, not economics, will occupy the center of the stage in the impending era, even though economic affairs will continue to be a dominant interest of citizens and government. Political leaders, rather than industrial, commercial, and financial leaders, will be outstanding. After them will rank the technological, scientific, and philosophic leaders—the latter in the form of educators, management consultants, social critics, etc.

Government faces the same general problem it has faced down through history, now multiplied and intensified many times in urgency. The problem is analyzable into the two traditional parts of external and internal affairs, expressed in foreign policy and domestic policy, although the parts are not basically separable. No government can be externally strong and internally weak and decentralized. Most governments have always had some sort of foreign problem. But all governments today have an acute foreign problem in a world wherein extremely rapid transportation, communication, and the new weapons have transformed each society into a problematic, often volatile, next-door neighbor. At the same time a large part of each national economic system is enmeshed in a world economic system the course of which profoundly affects the inner stability of every society.

Each government, each society, is today closer together by far in travel time and in important reciprocal economic and cultural effects than were the ancient city-states of the tiny Greek peninsula. Russia and the United States, for example, can reciprocally place troops on each other's territories and deal each other military blows much more rapidly and effectively than could nearby Athens and Sparta. And each can affect the other economically, culturally, and politically in all available territories, which are now world-wide, much more significantly than could Athens and Sparta in the ancient eastern Mediterranean world. Russia, the United States, and others can do all this today, in fact, much more effectively than could the nations of 1900 or even of 1940.

The external problem for all nations, then, is extremely urgent and complex in every way—political, military, economic, and cultural. Enhanced vigilance, care, and effort is obviously required of government. Failure of any government to meet the challenge of this general situation produces disaster—and thus far in this century weak, business-dominated government has largely failed. In varying measure most societies, particularly those of Europe and Asia, have already in this century experienced disaster. The issue is now one of simple survival.

Government, as always, faces the internal or domestic problem. But the domestic problem, once relatively simple, is of enormous complexity and menace in our time under the impact of an avalanche of developments in science, technology, and industry, all of which are impersonally increasing the requirement for intensified rationality and scientific method in formulating public policy. The problem remains of assimilating and regulating these new cultural forces in order to assure stability, tranquillity, and orderly development on the domestic scene. The internal race is one between organization and disorganization, with disorganization ever threatening to gain the upper hand as traditional ideologies doggedly assert their claims to represent the wisdom of the ages. Flexibility is needed; rigidity is a hindrance.

Disorganization is seen on every hand in societies—such as our own—still organized mainly along untenable, traditional lines in the age of power technology—in labor-management conflict and in what appears to be an insoluble recurrent unemployment problem; in extremist political movements and propaganda; in apparently rising rates of already excessive crime at both the bottom and the top of the social pyramid; in grave overpopulation; in frequent group clashes on the basis of class, religious and ethnic classification (race); in the widespread infringement of civil rights by local groups; in deteriorated interpersonal relations in many families, to name only a few. Some problems are classified by sociologists as social pathologies and some as traceable to value conflicts; but those that do not stem from social disorganization induced by dislocations brought into being directly or indirectly by modern technology at least contribute to disorganization. So all may be viewed as stemming from or leading to disorganization.

The general domestic problem, then, of all modern governments is one of coping with increasingly insistent internal disorganization in many sectors. The strategy of the traditionalists is to temporize, hoping the problem will solve itself. On the side of the entrenched traditionalist is the whole force of social inertia and popular apathy, so it might seem that the traditionalist is bound to win out. But in addition, as we have noted, pressure is great and intensifying from outside society, from the foreign quarter. Under the impact of successive painful crises enveloping larger and larger sections of the population, the traditional point of view, we may confidently assert, is going to be pushed farther and farther into the background. Change, in any event, will be the result, either the change of disaster under extremism of Right or Left or the change of rational, planned adjustment under moderate legal methods.

Can the old institutions carry on in the traditional ways? Not successfully. The attempt to carry on blindly in traditional ways, which may be made here and there as it has been more or less up to recently in countries like Spain, Portugal, Poland, Hungary, Rumania, Italy, Ireland, and to a lesser extent elsewhere in Europe and in the United States, will lead only to disaster or decay for the societies concerned. They will be stricken from without or from within, or from both quarters simultaneously. All, in order to survive, must sooner or later candidly face the challenges of the day. And as these challenges are faced and, let us suppose, successfully overcome, the result will be sweeping change of the kind I am about to predict. Even if the challenges are not overcome there will be change—for the worse. Societies are either going to reorganize themselves and keep in step with developments or they are going to fall behind and into political extremism, Left or Right. Then there can only be government by decree.

While there is plenty of room for choice in the situation, there is absolutely none between great change on the one hand and no change or little change on the other. The choice is really only between guided change that has a relatively favorable outcome and unguided change that has a relatively unfavorable or disastrous outcome. The traditionalists will not only be defeated either way, they will be overwhelmed. And even though, under guidance, traditional values gained at great cost may be preserved (and one may individually hope they will be), the traditional arrangements for securing them will be swept away precisely because they no longer preserve and conserve those values.

The institution that must meet the general challenge directly and consciously is the institution of government. The problem is quite beyond private solution. Governments must not only be the midwives for extensive social change but they must themselves, in the process, undergo great change.

Government in the United States

Let us examine, first, the outline of changes as they affect the government of the United States. Contrary to the popular view, government in the United States has undergone vast changes, some far from gradual, since the Constitution of 1789. It is, in fact, like most other governments, undergoing piecemeal change from year to year in both its functions and agencies. The United States Government today is responsible for many functions and now possesses many agencies completely foreign to it as recently as 1940 or 1950. It will take on more functions, produce more agencies, increase in efficiency, and undergo many, many internal adjustments.

The general change in this system is going to be one from federalism to a unitary government, with power that is now local, regional, and particular concentrated increasingly and, finally, definitively in the central government. In view of the American bias against big and concentrated government such a prediction may seem farfetched. But it will be under the repeated pressure of crises of various kinds, arising from social, economic, and foreign-policy problems, that the mood may confidently be expected to change. Such crises will relate to unemployment, one-sided educational opportunities, family disintegration, overpopulation, minority persecutions, medical care, housing, uncontrolled crime, and other problems.

Does this mean that a rewriting of the Constitution is to be expected? Not necessarily, and very probably not, such is ideological inertia. Under its own rules it is extremely difficult to alter the formal provisions of the Constitution. But the Constitution, as we know, is subject to interpretation and reinterpretation by the courts. What is held constitutional in one period is often held unconstitutional at a later period, as witness rulings on racial segregation.

Steadily Increasing Central Power

One way in which the federal power over the states has increased in the past three decades is by means of money grants for specific purposes that the states, under the burden of their many urgent problems, are unable to finance. The federal government has made huge outright grants and grants that require a dollar-for-dollar matching by the states, some of which have not accepted these conditional gifts. In cases of acceptance the federal government has drawn the rules governing the expenditures, so that federal power is exercised through the granting of funds, matched and unmatched, in connection with specific projects. As these projects include the building of schools, paying of teachers' salaries at least in part, the building and maintenance of highways, housing projects for low-income recipients, installation of sewage plants, the erection of hospitals, and maintenance of special health services, it is evident that federal economic power is increasing in many areas not directly related to interstate transactions. Federal moneys are also payable to persons out of work, the aged, many young dependents, persons eligible for Social Security, federal pensioners such as superannuated civil servants, injured war veterans and the like. Localism and regionalism is everywhere losing power.

The already enlarged federal role is reflected in the federal budgets, which have increased by astronomical proportions since 1914. The budgets divide into military and non-military items, with the former preponderating but both large. Each division of the budget makes the federal government an extremely potent influence in the economic system, so potent indeed that without the federal presence the economy would simply collapse. To speak of the economy, then, as non-governmental and private is already anachronistic.

Furthermore, if federal subsidies were withdrawn from various parts of the economy—from agriculture, defense industries, steamship and air lines, railroads and the like—there would be serious trouble not only in the directly subsidized areas but in many dependent areas. World disarmament to any appreciable extent would introduce a momentary crisis to this economy, which could be solved eventually by finding other outlets for production, such as perhaps development of backward economies and extensive public works programs. But while it lasted, the crisis would be serious.

Already, despite rhetorical objections, whenever a private enterprise finds itself engulfed in difficulties, government is called upon by the entrepreneurs to make loans or to take over the entire enterprise—as in the case of municipal bus and rapid-transit lines and railroads. Unable to meet the housing needs of people, private enterprise stands by, helpless before the magnitude of the problem, and allows the government to do the necessary building or to subsidize private builders. Railroads, despite subsidies, are in financial straits.

Government funds, either for capital improvements or immediate service expenditures, are raised immediately or ultimately from taxes. Government borrowing must be paid for ultimately out of taxes unless the government is to default on its obligations, always a possibility but not a likelihood in a viable economy. As increasing amounts are drawn from citizens for taxes, the amount of money remaining for both private investment and private consumer expenditure will be reduced. The size of the so-called private market will be reduced relative to the so-called public sector of the economy. It is here that the shoe begins to pinch the private entrepreneurs, whether government-subsidized or not. And it is with this rising prospect in mind that it is evident fundamental alterations are in prospect for the economy.

Newspapers and Their Ideological Role

Newspapers, privately subsidized via advertising, are the principal media for tirelessly inveighing against the evils of government and of politicians. They have convinced many people that government is inherently and unavoidably wasteful, mischievous, and dishonest. The evidence presented in support of the thesis is, however, obviously prejudiced.

Although newspapers can be counted upon to continue their monotonous campaign, the position of newspapers themselves is being undermined by technological advance (radio and TV) and one can see very clearly that their influence is going to diminish. But first, before considering this aspect, let us ask what is the general nature and role of newspapers the world over?

The general commodity offered by every newspaper—left, right,

center, and all gradations in between—is ideology. And ideology is
a non-empirical theory, often misnamed a philosophy, that is developed on an a priori basis to defend some special interest. The two
dominant politico-economic ideologies of the world are those of private economic enterprise and government economic enterprise. The
partisans of each hold that the key to salvation lies in their particular
outlook and that the contrary system holds forth the promise of nothing but grief and destruction. Obviously, however, there is something
to be said for each form of enterprise. Neither could exist without the
other. The Soviet ideologists ignore the fact that were it not for many
private free contributions to technology and administration Russia
would still be in the oxcart stage. The American ideologists ignore the
fact that without massive government aid—beginning more than 100
years ago—to agriculture, to railroads, to waterways, to schools, to a
multiplicity of other enterprises, so-called free enterprise could never
have developed the present American economy.

The newspapers, in making out their continuing case against government, whose effective intrusion the supporters of the newspapers
fear, have consistently failed to keep as vigilant a critical eye on the
private entrepreneurs. Had they done so they might be entitled to be
hailed as devoted partisans of the truth. This brings us to another
step in our predictions. Unless disaster is to be the outcome, the
police power of government is in the future going to be brought to
bear with increasing force against the private market. Not only is that
market going to be greatly shrunken in relation to the government
role in the economic institution, owing to increased siphoning off of
taxes, but it is going to be much more thoroughly regulated by government than in the past.

The Market Place as a Focal Point for Crime

The reason for this coming intensified regulation is that the
fulsomely extolled private market, in the United States as elsewhere
in the world, is the medium for so very much chicanery, deceit, and
fraud as to foster impaired public morale and spreading cynicism,
with threatening reverberations throughout society. In their selective
presentation of statements the newspapers have largely concealed this
fact, and have even succeeded in ignoring, concealing, or glossing over
scientific analyses relating to the situation. One such analysis, already

a sociological classic the findings of which are by now reproduced in most general treatises on criminology, is *White Collar Crime*, written by the then dean of American criminologists, Professor Edwin H. Sutherland.[1]

Sutherland shows, on the basis of official convictions, that in terms of money losses by far most crime is committed by the upper socio-economic "white-collar class"—businessmen and employees, professionals and labor leaders (most findings with respect to which have been made of record since Sutherland published). While crimes of violence and most small crimes against property, mostly committed by the lower classes, are met with heavy penalties, the upper socioeconomic crimes (with the exception of embezzlement and a few others) draw light penalties, often only fines. For that is the way the laws are written by upper-class-oriented legislators, their campaign funds largely subscribed for by upper-class elements.

A white-collar crime is defined by Sutherland as "a crime committed by a person of respectability and high social status in the course of his occupation." (It does not include such things as murder or other traditional crimes.) They are crimes peculiar to a business and pecuniary system. The culprits are not only individuals; corporations stand high in the roster of convicts. Furthermore, as in the lower classes, many of the culprits are repeaters, committing the same crimes over and over again for decades and, upon conviction in cases involving millions and hundreds of millions of dollars, drawing only light fines. Such culprits, as Sutherland points out, correspond to the criminologists' concept of the ideal delinquent: the professional thief, aristocrat of the underworld.

What are these crimes? They consist of fraud in general and, more specifically, of embezzlement; restraint of trade; misrepresentation in advertising; mislabeling; infringement of patents, trade-marks, and copyrights; unfair labor practices and misuse of labor-union funds; secret rebates; violation of trust; misappropriation of funds; conspiracy to defraud; income-tax falsification; bribery; adulteration of foods and drugs; price gouging; commercial and industrial espionage; false weighing, measuring, and grading; price rigging and discrimination; dilution of equities; secret payments to obtain unwarranted business; wash sales; stock jobbing.

Over a forty-year period, Sutherland found, seventy of the largest United States corporations had *average* convictions of thirteen, with ranges up to 222 adverse decisions for some. He cites the Comptroller of the Currency as reporting that in one quarter 75 per cent of the national banks violated the national banking laws. Dishonesty was found in more than 50 per cent of bank failures from the Civil War to 1919.

With crimes like these the test, says Sutherland, people of the business world are probably more criminalistic than are people of the slums. In cities and states they are the elements largely responsible for bribing officials—in the purchase of supplies, making of contracts, enforcement of regulations, and enactment of legislation.[2]

At times one single case makes the front pages of newspapers, as when in 1961 virtually the entire electrical-equipment manufacturing industry was convicted in federal court for an elaborate conspiracy extending over more than twenty years to rig the market by prearranged price bids. The illegal gain was judicially estimated to run into hundreds of millions of dollars. Moderate fines and thirty-day jail sentences were imposed on a few lower-echelon company executives by a vocally indignant judge. Newspapers, in reporting the event, treated the case as exceptional whereas it was, in fact, typical of many others.

Following this decision the United States Department of Justice in an unusual action went to court to ask that the General Electric Company be enjoined against future similar law-breaking. The Justice Department informed the court that since 1910 this very large company had undergone twenty-nine convictions! The effect of an injunction would be that its violation could draw fines running into millions of dollars.

In the meantime business publications like *Fortune* magazine and *The Wall Street Journal* have published long analyses showing that the same sort of conduct is now being seen in thousands of business employees who, in one way and another, are stealing money and merchandise from their employers to the tune of up to $3 billion annually.

Standard business practices in violation of poorly enforced and loosely drawn laws remind many observers of old-style unscrupulous adventurer-traders who, while neglecting no opportunity to cheat among themselves, proffered cheap whisky, beads, ribbons, wet gunpowder, and obsolete guns to Stone Age aborigines in return for valuable ivory, furs, jewels, and gold.

The point of these remarks is that there is inevitably going to be stricter policing of the market place by government, if only to prevent collapse of public morale.

But if the public is indifferent and the market place is difficult to police, how can one look forward to any change? First, public indifference stems from lack of information owing to failure of newspapers to report the facts in all their massiveness. Before the government can proceed on the basis of public support, this ideological barrier must be broken. Second, the market place is so large and so complex as to baffle regulation by any ordinary means. How then may one expect any change?

Changes in both features will be wrought by means of technological innovations, which will be irresistible. To show the nature of such innovations, and consequent changes, it will be necessary to discuss first the prospects of the newspapers and then the means for policing the market effectively.

Journalistic Method

What is culturally and socially significant about the entire panorama here sketched is how the facts have been successfully kept from the general public. Books such as Sutherland's are published, reviewed, and incorporated in other professional evaluations. They are known to students. But they are reviewed by newspapers in such an inconspicuous way as not to attract the notice of others than specialists—an example of "soft censorship" that is evident with respect to many other authoritative socially critical treatises as well. What such novel theses obviously require is careful and prolonged discussion, pro and con, in the daily press. Their unwelcome nature is made crystally apparent in that the scholarly interpretations of the phenomena in full perspective are not allowed to replace in the daily reports the threadbare clichés and stereotypes that perpetuate in the public mind an outmoded and essentially false picture or a pure myth about the nature of wrongdoing.

As to newspaper technique, which is neither scientific, scholarly, nor philosophic, how does it accomplish its ends? That technique has been studied by logicians who find in use, rather than the method of solid logic, the methods of rhetoric and eristic, the arts of invalid persuasion. The technical name for the method is "slanting," which employs one-sided selection of facts and achieves distortion through the use of suggestion and hyperbole. Slanted and suggestive discourse, as distinguished from direct discourse, usually contains some minor element of truth but its chief effect is to be misleading. Unwarranted connotations, either honorific or depreciatory, are attached to the terms employed, such as in "politician," and no responsibility is assumed for the hidden indirect argument. A man in public life cannot deny that he is a politician. Although he may be every bit as much of a politician in the depreciatory connotation of the term, the man in business is referred to as "a business leader" or "captain of industry," conveying honorific connotations. True statements are made, such as one that President Kennedy has given various members of his family government jobs, thus implying nepotism. Omitted is the fact that the appointees are independently wealthy, have left or refused lucrative private jobs and, in some cases, serve without salary. True on a very low level of meaning, slanted statements are not true, as they should be in order to be logically sound, on all the levels. Nor are they true in major effect.[3]

Although slanting is common to all newspapers without exception it is less used, and perhaps only unconsciously, in the more reputable ones. Such, however, are few in number; the intellectually disreputable practitioners predominate in number and circulation. But the more closely issues tend to involve a newspaper's basic ideology, the more likely are news reports to be slanted. Soviet newspapers, as everyone knows and can see, are grossly slanted, and in general the less tutored one's audience is, the more effective the method is. What Americans and Europeans usually fail to recognize is that their own publications employ the same technique, but more deftly, on questions foreign and domestic. This is not to suggest that Soviet journalism is the same or as good as American and European journalism, for some non-Soviet publications, even though they can be shown to be slanted in particulars from time to time, come much nearer to the norms of truth as established by logicians and epistemologists. It would be difficult, however, to find more than a dozen of the larger newspapers in the United States and a similar number in Europe that are even relatively free of slanting.

The Coming Decline of Newspapers

But if newspapers systematically conceal the facts and if the public is apathetic and inert, as many studies show it to be, how is change possible? And if there is change will it be for better or worse?

Technology here, as elsewhere, is the potent ingredient in the forces that bring about change.

Newspapers, up to the present, have been the leading factor in shaping the modern public mood, a fact well recognized by the Communists in their home campaign for low-level literacy. But newspapers now are under pressure from new techniques, mainly those of radio and television, but also from enlarging and deepening higher education. Newspapers no longer have a constitutionally protected monopoly on daily free (and often irresponsible) utterance, and in the past forty years, since radio appeared, a large number of newspapers, some of them long established, has gradually gone out of existence. This fact has alarmed some observers, who see many cities left with only one news medium and, necessarily, a one-sided editorial point of view.

Such alarm would probably be justified if there were no other media for purveying and interpreting news, but other media, and more powerful ones, are at hand in radio, television, and video tape for television projection. People now, in many instances, are no longer dependent upon third-person reports of something happening; they can see it happening, they can see and hear the person being interviewed. Not only is the experience more vivid but the viewer is nearer actuality, often without the necessity for interpretation. The universities perform a delayed corrective role. And books, such as Sutherland's, finally disclose the true situation where it has been distorted.

As radio and television, like newspapers, are patronized by advertisers, it might appear that they are subject to the same economic influences. But radio and television necessarily operate on channels apportioned and supervised by government, to which they must necessarily be at least as respectful as to corporate advertisers. Newspapers, under the blanket license given by free-press laws, have been under no similar compulsion. Again, although newspapers have aroused the justified wrath of elected officials on many occasions, they are mainly local enterprises, and for officials to move against newspapers has been much like attacking a hydra-headed national monster. This monster, however, is now being sapped at its source by having to share its advertising revenue with radio and television, which in turn are neither local nor hydra-headed but operate in vast centrally directed national networks. For loading the rhetorical dice against government officials on public questions, furthermore, they are under the double threat of being investigated and penalized for misuse of a public franchise to the operating channel and of having the government itself establish competing networks, which may well be done in any case.

In response to much criticism of the low caliber of pioneer radio and television programing considerable improvement has been achieved, at least in the New York City area. Television in New York is now beginning to explore the world, including the social world, and is bringing much in the way of immediate event vividly to public attention that most people would not take the trouble to read about in newspapers. Since 1959 important documentary reports have been televised on political, economic, and social problems as well as distant regions. Good discussions are growing in number. Sunday programs in New York approach the ideal and probably represent the best television in the world.

With public attention fixed on these media, and with the pressure of media managers to find ever new material, public attention is increasingly relaxed with respect to the newspapers, which more and more seem to be reporting twice-told tales that have already had vivid exposure on radio and television. Free of exclusive one-sided newspaper indoctrination, the public attitude with respect to government is bound to become more favorable, more balanced.

Few radio and television stations now editorialize. In their necessity to avoid taking sides they must, as the newspapers never did, give equal attention to many points of view. They cannot, as did the newspapers, blandly and repeatedly commit the logical fallacy of neglected aspect, so that the public obtains a broader acquaintance with the facts and issues and comes by its broadened insight in an easier and more entertaining way.

The new techniques of radio and television have, perhaps most dramatically, placed new power in the hands of high elected officials. In the past, under the plea of necessarily abridging their statements, newspapers could play fast and loose with slanting and suggestion either for or against them, depending upon the requirements of the newspapers' ideology. Now public officials can simply bypass the newspapers and their rhetorical tricks.

The first American President to do this was Franklin Delano Roosevelt, who won four elections against the opposition of more than 90 per cent of the nation's newspapers. With television now available to him the American President has more power in reaching and influencing the public mood than any President before him in history. The business interests behind the newspapers, as Roosevelt showed, can be thoroughly frustrated if the President so wills, an example of the way in which government, through advancing technology, is eclipsing the anti-governmental business influence over the public mind.

In 1900, or even in 1920, a Pericles could not have reached the public, unedited, in so vast a domain as the United States. Now he can at any instant stand right before every citizen in the intimacy of his own home. No nimble-witted editors can intervene.

The newspaper pattern, as a whole and in detail, is going to change very much in the future under the further impact of radio and television. As the purveying of spot news and the on-the-spot showing of sports events is taken over more and more by the newer media, newspapers in general, fewer in number, are going to be driven more and more toward background reporting and reporting in detail and in depth. The more reputable newspapers are going to do this better in the future in response to the enlargement under educational influence of a sophisticated audience that craves facts and their judicious interpretation. The less reputable newspapers, for which there will always be an audience among the emotionally immature, will be similarly driven to background material but will probably specialize, as they do now, in the exploitation of individual psychopathology and aberrancy ruled off radio and TV.

Newspapers falling in between the reputable and disreputable will tend to go out of business entirely. The better newspapers, furthermore, may well come to publish national editions, distributed either by airplane or simultaneously printed by photoelectronic processes in distant plants. The New York *Times* has established a West Coast edition and *The Wall Street Journal* a national newspaper. The *Christian Science Monitor* is already national. Such national editions could well be supplemented with editions bearing purely local news. But the local news region is enlarging with advancing urbanization. Many villages and even small towns are now without newspapers, and thus dependent on nearby city papers that publish news of local subdivisions. It will be the trend of the future for all villages, small towns, and even for small cities to be dependent for local news, apart from local radio stations, on newspapers printed in large urban centers or on local weeklies.

A few high-quality national newspapers, however, could easily meet the market, which is not likely to be extremely large, for reliably presented and interpreted news relating to politics, economics, finance, science, and public policy. These will reach about 25 per cent of the public, the educated.

Radio and television, both powerful influences for shaping the public mind, cannot forever remain principally at the service of private advertisers. In Europe, government radio and television is a reality and it is not very much to expect that someday government in the United States will also establish its own domestic broadcasting stations. There are already local municipal and federal foreign-broadcast radio stations. Even if government does not go into television, the private holders of public broadcasting franchises must give government and government personnel so much respectfully neutral and even sympathetic attention that in effect they become semigovernmental agencies, media for the full expression of governmental and general public views as contrasted with private ideological views.[4]

Government and Market Crime

Faith in government being somewhat restored as the populace is no longer monotonously indoctrinated with an exclusively anti-governmental point of view, government is going to be in a more advantageous psychological position to deal with the vast amount of crime now concentrated in the market place. But, although in a position to do so, will it do so? It is almost certain that it will do so, that it will make penalties for illegal economic behavior much harsher and that it will have the will and the means to enforce its laws.

In the first place, technological developments make possible a more effective policing of the market place than in the past. Secondly, government is the institution that must deal with the many influences toward disorganization operative within contemporary society. Thirdly, the presence of an enlarging educated class, basing its views on scientific social analyses rather than on the utterances of slanted newspapers or narrow-minded political figures, makes it imperative as a matter of morale that government act to enforce intellectually respectable criteria for the protection of society and its members. To fail to do so is to allow everything to go by default to the forces of disintegration and demoralization.

In a country as large and complex as the United States effective policing of the market place is notoriously difficult. But with larger and larger economic units involved, policing is somewhat simplified. The greatest aid to government in the policing of a complex market place, however, is now ready at hand in the technological innovation of high-speed electronic and photographic data-processing machines. Government is now on the threshold of installing such apparatus in quantity for the gathering, compilation, and processing of records of all sorts. Business firms, too, increasingly use these machines for their own records of transactions.

Private chicaneries of all sorts, difficult to detect in the past, will be more readily detectable in the very near future. Bookkeeping evasions are going to be more difficult to contrive. Discrepancies are going to be uncovered quickly under the electronic process. Financial fraud, internal peculation, income-tax falsification, suspicious pricing practices, balance-sheet juggling, concealment of assets are all going to be operations more difficult to carry out undetected. This is not to say that all market-place crime is going to be eliminated. But more criminals are going to be caught, and as more are caught more are going to be deterred. And as more are deterred the relative improper emoluments, direct and indirect, from business enterprise are going to be reduced, often, however, to the benefit of stockholders and customers who in the absence of adequate regulation have often, as the record shows, been shortchanged by corporate managers.

Strict government regulation of the market, or even absolute government control of it, would not eliminate all market crime. This is concretely evident on the basis of Soviet experience. In Russia almost all of the market is governmental. Yet Soviet newspapers from time to time report instances, some of them involving highly placed personalities, wherein criminal statutes governing market practices have been violated wholesale. Stiff prison sentences have been meted out to those found guilty. In view of the censorship imposed on the Soviet press, which is itself a governmental enterprise, there is little reason to suppose that all cases are reported. So serious and widespread is the situation that the death penalty was invoked early in 1961 for embezzlement and similar offenses. Very probably only those cases lending themselves to some special desire of the government ever see the light of day. Despite the strong influence of government in Russia, the many Russian convictions for crimes in general, some of them involving the very highest governmental personalities in alleged conspiracies against the stability of the government itself, show that strong sanctions alone do not completely eliminate crime; although it is the Soviet ideological contention, contrary to the Soviet record itself, that crime, and particularly market crime, is a peculiarly capitalistic phenomenon. Such a contention flies in the face of all history as well as of all contemporary non-capitalistic experience.

But widely prevalent crime, nevertheless, can be reduced, and must be reduced where its prevalence, as in the United States and perhaps also in Russia, seriously compromises the social system at its foundations.

For many decades increasing regulation of the market place by government under the spur of threatened disorganization and demoralization has been a noticeable trend. Such tightening regulation, concededly uneven in benefits, is seen in the establishment of the Interstate Commerce Commission, the Federal Trade Commission, the United States Tariff Commission, the Federal Reserve System, the Small Business Administration, the National Labor Relations Board, the Civil Aeronautics Board, the Farm Credit Administration, the Federal Aviation Agency, the Federal Communications Commission, the Railroad Retirement Board, the Federal Deposit Insurance Corporation, the Federal Power Commission, the Federal Home Loan Bank Board, the Federal Mediation and Reconciliation Service, the Housing and Home Finance Agency, the National Mediation Board, the Securities and Exchange Commission, and in the Sherman and Clayton anti-trust acts, the Food and Drug Act, the Banking Act of 1935, the Investment Trust Act of 1940 and a host of other similar laws and measures. There are, in addition, the Departments of Agriculture, Commerce and Labor, regulating and aiding their constituent spheres.

Businessmen in government have heretofore been common, both in elected and appointed posts. Government civil servants in business enterprise, representing government policy, are going to be even more common unless, which seems unlikely on cultural and historical grounds, the governmental intrusion into the economic institution should take the Leninist form of being exclusively governmental. A decreasingly self-oriented free hand, at any rate, is almost a certainty both for business and for labor organizations. On the face of it, this appears like an invasion of a "private" domain, and will be vigorously resisted as such. How private, however, are these enterprises, embracing millions of stockholders and employees and affecting all of society? Such is ideological lag amid social change that the phrase "private enterprise," when it is employed, is usually applied to what in actuality is public enterprise.

Already in Europe government has a direct stockholding interest in many large corporations, as in England, France, Germany, Sweden and elsewhere. The acquisition of an ownership stake in corporations by government in the United States is not beyond the realm of possibility. Short of such a step, however, corporations are certainly going to be made more and more amenable to government policies, probably via directorships of the kind already indicated, and are going to lose much of their present irresponsible autonomy. Government does not need to be a titular owner in order to exercise internal influence.

Preference for Government Service

Another sign of the dominant upthrust of government as an institution is that the ablest men, when they are in a position to make a choice, already prefer to make a career in government rather than in economic management. It is often said in the newspapers that government, because of its relatively low pay, is unable to attract able men. Yet Roosevelt, Eisenhower, and Kennedy had little difficulty, when they wanted a man, inducing him to leave a lucrative private job for government service. The newspapers made much of the financial sacrifice involved, which is not really so great in view of the fact that very high salaries must pay up to 50 per cent and more in taxes (another evidence of government intrusion into the "private" economic domain).

Wealthy men in American government are no novelty. In the nineteenth century they were found in cabinet posts and, notably, in the United States Senate, "The Rich Man's Club," under the constitutional rule then in force that senators were to be named by state legislatures. Since 1913, however, senators have been popularly elected. A point about wealthy men then in government is that they were uniformly pro-business and anti-labor and anti-agriculture and worked directly in the service of their private interests. Now they are either somewhat anti-business, as were Roosevelt and Wallace, or neutral with respect to business and markedly friendly toward labor and agriculture, and concerned about the general welfare. President Kennedy appears to be a neutralist with respect to business although a short-term prediction that may be ventured is that he cannot be a neutralist with respect to irresponsible business if his administration is to be a complete success. Irresponsible business and labor practices surely are in for a very rough time over the very near term, and this has been shown by President Kennedy's attitude toward both corporations and unions. For, as we have seen, a large section of the populace is now taking its cue from the illegitimate entrepreneurs, down to workmen who fail to perform their tasks properly. Unless public morale is to erode still further at a time of rising pressure from abroad and disorganization internally, there must be a cracking of the political whip over the irresponsible operators. Common business practices are surely going to be circumscribed.

Regulation of Legal Market Activities

But the hand of government is going to be felt increasingly over the next 150 years with respect to purely legal economic activities as well as the many illegal activities. Business enterprises, losing full autonomy, are not going to be allowed to do various things that they can now legally do in enticing a heedless public to buy.

For one thing, there is going to be allocation on the basis of social need of increasingly scarce raw materials, such as iron, copper, and perhaps even petroleum. Whether such allocations will be a hindrance or a help to business enterprise remains to be seen. It could be the latter if advanced technology comes to the aid of business enterprise by developing substitute materials that conserve scarce resources.

Many products now made for the open market are regarded by many experts, in the light of basic future necessities, as either superfluous or wasteful. It is the view of such experts that the United States is grossly oversupplied, for one thing, with its seventy million automobiles, in the making of which vast quantities of steel are used that might better be used elsewhere—for example, in the needed extensive rebuilding of cities, the construction of schools and hospitals, the replacement of bridges and tunnels, and the erection of many new plants and structures. Even the proliferation of office buildings and hotels is regarded by some observers as a misapplication of manpower and materials in view of the acute need for schools, supportive institutions, and residential housing.

But even though steel may come into short supply because of necessary demands, substitute materials may well come to the fore. In the case of automobiles, already making increasing use of aluminum made from plentiful bauxite and electric power, one may see bodies made of aluminum and even of plastics. In the upshot only the frames may be made of steel. Already many products formerly made with wood and steel, such as radio and television sets, are now made largely of plastics and aluminum and are being made on more compact scales.

Plastics, now utilizing coal, petroleum, and a variety of other materials, in the course of time will unquestionably make more use of abundant supplies of coal. Other sources of materials for making plastics may well be discovered. Wool and cotton can already be completely discarded in favor of more effective synthetic fibers for clothing, rugs, draperies and the like. With the almost certain prospect of such further developments one can well see that the chemical industry is going to grow by leaps and bounds beyond its present already swollen proportions. We are already heavily dependent upon the chemical industry for medicines, fertilizers, plastics, paints, textiles, rubber and the like, and plastic furniture is already present and seems likely in the course of time to replace wooden furniture.

Cement appears to be in adequate prospective supply for whatever replacement and expansion is to take place. Steel, however, has largely supplanted stone and wood for structural reinforcement, but not necessarily forever. Short of a bridge type of skyscraper construction, stone may well come back into favor as a construction material. If it does it is in abundant supply, with efficient means for obtaining it. Our mountain ranges guarantee us ample stone for all building purposes, and the new explosives guarantee that we can easily break up the mountains to obtain the stone. If we wished to employ them, we have the technical means for razing entire mountain ranges, after which it is merely a mechanical problem of transportation to move the stone into place.

The chief and most valuable use for steel in the future to which we have reference will be for the building of productive machinery. Its overuse now for articles of individual consumption like pleasure automobiles may well make for difficult problems in the future, for it is by means of productive machinery of all sorts that modern society will be able to survive. Modern society itself is to a considerable extent a machine; social relations, in fact, are now often mechanized relations.

Meeting acute social needs, in short, will be the requirement of the future on the economic system, not producing goods that by means of persuasive and extremely illogical advertising can be sold to the unthinking at a profit. No doubt many such goods will continue to be sold, but not until after government, representing an informed social consensus, has given its approval. Many types of business are going to have trouble obtaining the sort of raw materials they would prefer.

Allocations at present are being made, but by means of the price system. The highest bidder gets the materials he wants. Materials are sold with only the immediate profit of the project in mind. Philanthropic aims are not seriously regarded in the decision to sell. A skating rink will be able to purchase materials more readily than a hospital.

It is the argument of economic individualists that if individuals, relying on their own choice, fail to make adequate provision for the future, then the well-merited blame and pain is on the sinful individual. Many individuals in need, however, have acquired dependents. And other individuals, as in the case of school children, are already dependents without ever having had a chance to make sinful market choices. Again, individuals who have chosen wrongly in the market place are a burden not only to themselves but a burden and a positive danger, in many cases, to society. Persons unable to pay for needed medical and hospital care, having been systematically enticed into spending their money on frivolous choices, hold jobs wherein their illnesses—such as alcoholism—may be a threat to the safety and welfare of strangers. To deny them necessary medical care simply on the ground that they are unable at a certain time to pay market prices for high-priced services is to jeopardize all of society, including the economically sensible who have made prudent expenditures and investments all along.

It is the role of *persuasive* advertising, using all the intellectually disreputable tricks in violation of logic, to induce people to purchase basically unnecessary or even personally harmful merchandise (such as excessive quantities of liquor, candy, and tobacco). Purely descriptive advertising, catering to inherent needs, is in another category entirely. Many of the claims of persuasive advertising take the form of pseudo statements in that they can neither be affirmed nor denied. Others are so vague as to be meaningless or hopelessly ambiguous.

False claims in advertising can be proceeded against under laws against fraud, but pseudo claims are more difficult to proceed against under the rule of press freedom. But making merchandise advertised in this way less available through direct governmental allocations would undercut the entire process.

The Influence of Foreign Instability

Unstable conditions in a changing world are also having the effect of enlarging the operations and authority of the national government, presaging a superstate. World War II left the United States in a position of unsought leadership and responsibility for which it was ill-prepared. In time it will come to share this leadership with another rapidly emerging superstate, United Europe.

Foreign economic, military, technical, and general cultural aid given to the world since World War II at a cost of hundreds of billions have greatly enlarged the scope of the United States Government abroad. Even if an absence of domestic problems made it possible to restrict the expansion of the national government at home, the pull of the foreign situation would make it impossible. The United States Government can hardly be the giant abroad all agree it must be and the midget at home that anachronistic ideologists believe it ought to be. While playing an historically unique material and theoretical role abroad it can hardly remain small, timorous, restricted, and functionally divided at home. If it can be frustrated at home by the governments of Mississippi and other culturally retarded states, and by the electoral manipulations of ubiquitous rustic Machiavellis, how can it ever expect to hold its own against an entity like Soviet Russia? If the entrenched rustics prove too strong for it how can it prevail against the Khrushchevs, Gromykos, Mao Tse-tungs *et al.?*

Local autonomists are doomed by the interlocking pincers of unguided domestic change and foreign change. Guidance can be exercised only by a strong central government. Soviet Russia is merely one additional, though important, unruly factor in an unstable, shifting world disequilibrium. Even if Soviet Russia didn't exist, even if it were cooperative, there would remain many difficulties—enough to give any State Department insomnia.

Localists appear unaware that the United States is dependent on the outside world for many scarce resources, is close to exhaustion of many others. Countries such as China, India, and Russia have yet scarcely touched theirs. In order to obtain needed imports and market outlets for agricultural products and finished goods, the United States requires some stability in the world. To obtain this it must put forth effort, thereby building up government.

Whether or not Soviet Russia will continue to disrupt stability wherever it can, one cannot foretell. In its own interests—for it now has much to lose—it may come around to cooperating in the establishment of stability.

Future American Presidents

It may be further predicted that American Presidents are going to be of the active rather than the passive type, the new style having been brought into being by Roosevelt, Truman, and Kennedy. Most American Presidents, per contra, have been passivists, allowing the political and social system to follow pretty much its own lead. Crises and times of crisis bring to the fore more determined, decisive types, which will be indispensable in the next 150 years. Types represented by Eisenhower, Hoover, Coolidge, and Harding, beloved of traditionalists and standpatters, while they may manage to be elected from time to time in the confusions of politics, will become increasingly untypical. Accidents, it must be noted, also play a role in bringing certain men to the fore, and accidents cannot be predicted. Passivists in office, however, are going to make a very poor showing.

The center of government, furthermore, is going to be the executive branch rather than Congress or the Supreme Court. For the times will increasingly call for strong executive action.

All this, it is clear, amounts to statism and the Welfare State, terms used by traditionalists in accusing tones. The accusation happens to be true, but no amount of objection can avoid the general outcome that has been sketched. Epithets and oratory won't halt the trend. Crises, many of which are already upon us, will only hasten it. If some way could be found to avoid the external clashes and the internal crises, the traditionalists might hope to save some of their threatened procedures.

As we look about the world we see a variety of models of political systems. The totalitarian models in which government is the sole entrepreneur, such as we see in Russia and China, do not harmonize with the American cultural outlook and may be ruled out as eventualities except under extreme stress.

If all works out relatively well, and there is naturally no guarantee that it will, there will be a near approach in the United States and Western Europe to the politico-economic system now partially presented to view in Sweden. That system was established pretty much as a matter of forethought because Sweden was free of many problems besetting other nations. She had the advantage, in industrializing rather late, of seeing what mistakes others had made. Through her location to one side and her foreign policy she was able to avoid involvement in wasteful wars for more than 150 years. She was, in effect, freer to be rational.

The inexorable emergence of the Welfare State under the pressure of multitudes of problems, internal and external, all of them created by the emergence of advanced technology, will have many effects other than those mentioned. These effects will be surveyed in later chapters, institution by institution.

It remains for us now to turn to government on a global scale.

CHAPTER VIII

GOVERNMENT THROUGHOUT THE WORLD

As the influence of advanced machine technology and overpopulation grows, the most successful government over the next 150 years will be continent-wide in scope. In this respect Europe will, if it evolves in its own cultural terms, emulate the United States, Soviet Russia, Communist China and India. Europe cannot remain fragmented, as it has since the medieval period, and still survive as an independent entity.

Toward European Unification

Already Europe has taken the decisive step toward a federal type of unification in the Treaty of Rome, signed March 25, 1957. As commonly reported, this treaty did no more than create the European Economic Community or Common Market, an extension of the European Coal and Steel Community of 1951. But what has been widely overlooked is that the Treaty of Rome is really a constitution for a United Europe, opening with words reminiscent of the preamble to the United States Constitution: "to establish the foundations of an ever closer union among the European peoples."

Like the American Constitution, the Treaty of Rome establishes divisions of government—a Council of Ministers, a Commission, an Assembly, and a Court of Justice to interpret the document and adjudicate disputes.

The Council of Ministers, with wide powers, consists at present of representatives of the participating states, with four votes each for France, Germany, and Italy, two each for Belgium and the Netherlands, and one for Luxembourg. Greece, an associate member, has lesser powers. Council decisions are not subject to ratification by national cabinets or parliaments and in some cases may be made by majority vote, in others unanimously.

Located in Brussels, the Commission, the executive branch, applies the rules and policies handed down by the Council. Only two of its nine members may be from the same state. They are removable only by two-thirds vote of the Assembly, to which they are answerable.

The Assembly consists of thirty-six members each from France, Germany, and Italy, fourteen each from Belgium and the Netherlands, and six from Luxembourg. In the beginning these members are drawn from the national parliaments, but in time may be directly elected by party preference. In relation to it the Council may in time be purely advisory.

The Court of Justice consists of seven judges, and may rule against a member state, the Commission, the Council, or any natural or legal person. Provided with its own budget, the Community organization draws revenue from the member states on a percentage basis. It also has a social fund, an investment bank, an overseas development fund for associated territories, as in Africa, and jurisdiction over atomic power.

The organization now sends diplomatic representatives to more than twenty countries, including the United States.

The Constitution of the United States was similarly written, in Baltimore, by what was ostensibly a commercial convention of sovereign states. The far-reaching nature of the decisions taken was understood by few persons at the time or by many even seventy-five years later. Even today some persons fail to understand them fully.

The European Economic Community established a uniform tariff against certain goods from outside and is successively reducing tariffs between its members, providing an end to all inter-member tariffs by 1970. Reciprocally it also reduces tariffs against other countries, including the United States. Its aim goes far beyond this, however, being nothing less than uniformity of economic policy throughout the Community in order to facilitate free competition and trade. In its first stage, for example, it provides for equal remuneration for equal work to men and women workers. Uniform standards are applied throughout with respect to capital, labor, monopolies, and state purchases.

England, the leader in establishing the rival European Free Trade Association with Sweden, Norway, Denmark, Portugal, Austria, and Switzerland as members, has since decided to join. Polls early showed popular opinion in England was 70 per cent in favor of joining and leading government officials and members of parliament long favored joining. The European countries in the Free Trade Association will all eventually follow England's lead.

So Western Europe, if it survives as an independent entity, will certainly be unified—economically, politically, and to a considerable extent culturally. And if it is not self-unified, by whatever means, it will in time become a unified extension of Soviet Russia. It will not, in any case, survive in its traditional fragmented condition. Such fragmentation, and an accompanying partial cultural fragmentation (as expressed in the development of different languages from similar bases), took place in a time of slow transportation and poor communication. As a set of distinct nations, Europe today is an anachronism in a technic-minded world that requires centralized government supervising large territories.

The Fate of Eastern Europe

What of Eastern Europe? Its prospective fate is similar. Eastern Europe will either be integrated into a unified Western Europe or into Soviet Russia. The latter eventuality appears at the present time to be the more likely, although the cultural inclination is all toward the West. When, as, and if the Eastern European states are absorbed by Russia (like Latvia, Estonia, Lithuania, Turkistan, Georgia, Kazakhstan, and various other Soviet territories), they will unquestionably be brought in as Soviet Republics. For Russia, with its regional administrative departments formally designated as "republics," already possesses the framework for such absorption, which would take place whenever Russia considers it timely. In the course of time the rise of new generations in Eastern Europe without traditional loyalties will make such absorption less difficult than at present, a fact that Russian long-range political planners no doubt keep in mind.

But if some historical crisis should develop, such as a bid by China for world communist leadership or an internal struggle over leadership that frustrates Russia in this evident plan, then Poland, East Germany, Hungary, Czechoslovakia, Rumania, and Bulgaria must either be incorporated into Western Europe, with which it is traditionally bound, or slump into anarchic stagnation. Yugoslavia must also join with Western Europe or come under Russian rule and eventual absorption.

What of the possibility of a Russian rapprochement with Western Europe, leading to cooperative endeavors in a peaceful world? Such a rapprochement, while not impossible, is virtually ruled out by Leninist ideology. So deeply committed is Russia to this ideology that she would be without orientation if she deviated from it very much although the Russians are apt at reinterpretations. It enables her political leaders, for one thing, to explain at home all Soviet shortcomings —and they are many—as caused by a hostile outside world operating on "capitalist" lines. All evil, according to this ideology, stems from private ownership of property, an absurd contention. Against this ideological commitment there is no substantial evidence to support the probabilty of a Russian-European rapprochement.

These remarks appear to foretell some sort of absolutely symmetrical outcome, one way or the other, such as the unification of all Europe. But it is undeniable that unforeseen historic events, such as the rise of strong personalities, may produce temporary deviations from the line of prediction. Although a distinct trend may be foreseen as inevitable, this does not imply that every element must be included in the trend. With the rise of machine industrialization in England it could readily be foretold that industrialization would spread to the European continent and even beyond, being taken up successively by all countries that wished to emulate English power and standards of consumption. But there was no reason to suppose that every European country, including those without coal and iron, would industrialize. Nor was there any reason to suppose that there might be holdouts such as Spain and Portugal, which under the rule of landholders and the Church clung desperately to traditional ways and were consequently left far behind the mainstream of development and rendered culturally sterile.

The unification of Europe, then, may be looked upon as inevitable, with the possibility that some small areas will successfully remain aloof. All that is in question is whether the unification will be under Russian or autonomous auspices.

Creative Europe

The more advanced sections of Europe, such as Scandinavia, England, Germany, France, Switzerland, Austria, Belgium, and Holland, are already in many ways more advanced than the United States, institutionally and technically—as in social services and, on the Continent, more modern production plants. Competitive pressures alone will force the United States to emulate Europe despite domestic ideological opposition. Because of the immediate experience of destructive, tradition-shattering wars Europe has been forced to be more pragmatic, less ideological, than the United States, with the result that its social services and social planning are more developed than in the United States. Neutralist Sweden in particular is the European showcase in these respects.

In saying that the United States will someday approximate Sweden in its social services and social welfare schemes it is not being suggested that the people of the United States, seeing a good thing, will set out to copy it. Such rational procedures are rarely seen in nations. What is being said is that the pressures leading to internal disorganization—intensifying labor-management disputes, structural unemployment, family dissolution, increase of the aged, juvenile delinquency, an increase in ever-continuing economic crimes, lack of adequate housing for an expanding population, surplus rural populations, shortages of schools, teachers, playgrounds, and supportive institutions in general—will force remedial actions in the United States similar to those that have taken place or are imminent in Europe. It will be the coercion of crises rather than the foresighted application of reason that will bring positive governmental action in the United States more and more to the fore, in contravention of the still-dominant American ideology that equates government action in the social sphere with tyranny.

Contrary to cherished American belief, Europe has long been ahead of it in many respects. For example, Europe had the dial system of telephone and the cradle hand telephone for decades while the American system still required an operator and the old-style two-piece upright telephone. More dramatically, Europe added jet propulsion to the American airplane and converted the original American rocket from a toy to a formidable missile. Such European improvements and use of advanced models while the United States is clinging to technically obsolete equipment could be cited in thousands and even tens of thousands of instances. By present advanced European standards, for example, most American industrial plants are conceded by American experts to be obsolete.

The United States, in fact, has borrowed from Europe (with certain special details altered) the ideas for its entire cultural, social, political, and economic systems and, from time to time, it has obtained from Europe most of its people.

Europe, in fact, is the most creative continent in human history. It has been infinitely more creative in the span of 2500 years than all other continents and peoples combined throughout all of the one to ten million possible years of human history. The whole world, it may well be said, is no more than the halting pupil of Europe.

While the United States on the basis of European theory has contributed certain practical innovations, such as the telephone, the telegraph, the reaping machine, the electric light, the phonograph, and mass-production methods, in the all-important theoretical underpinnings of modern culture the United States has just begun to make contributions. Atomic theory, relativity theory, the germ theory of disease, genetics, psychoanalysis, evolution, democracy, republicanism, post-biblical ideas of law and the like are all European. Only in cybernetics and electronics has the United States been markedly original.

The United States as Europe's Pupil

It is long since the United States could be regarded as a mere apprentice to Europe. But at best the United States can be reasonably rated yet as no more than a worthy and somewhat awkward pupil, possibly the worthiest in a world where only Russia thus far has shown a similar insatiable desire to engage in wholesale cultural borrowing. On the basis of an incredibly naturally rich continent, which Europe does not possess, and a favorable climate, the United States has so far been successful at every step with Europeanization.

American pride, much of it unjustified, was dealt a severe blow in recent years by Soviet Russia when the first space satellites, manned and unmanned, were launched. The Russian achievements shook American opinion in two respects: (1) that Russia was hopelessly laggard, and (2) that the United States was by inherent merit pre-eminent. But if Russian contributions antedating the Soviet are considered, then it is extremely doubtful that the United States can point to world scientists of its own development transcending in importance leading pre-Soviet Russians.

It is often said that the Soviet-dominated Russian people are the prisoners of their own propaganda, but the same can be said of the Americans, who suffer from a severe case of insufficiently justified cultural chauvinism, fostered mainly by newspapers and provincial politicians.

What has kept Europe from realizing fully on its unique creativeness has been the prolonged internecine European political struggle since the dissolution of the Roman Empire. But this struggle, which nearly brought Europe to final ruin in World War II, has done much, by now, to destroy the inertia of traditional local nationalisms. Now Europe is once again freely extemporizing and inventing, trying to solve profound problems. To argue that the United States, as successive crises grip it in whole or in part, will ignore solutions found elsewhere is merely to contend that the United States will prefer outmoded ideology, such as that of eighteenth-century Europe, to survival. The prediction here is that the United States, plentifully supplied with intellectual acumen, will elect to survive as it increasingly feels the pinch of crisis. At first, though, the rhetoricians of stale ideology will have it all their own way; but as they are discredited by concrete situations they will, one by one, drop out of sight, remembered like Warren G. Harding and Calvin Coolidge only as exemplars of folly.

Economic Differences

One respect in which the European economic system differs from that of the United States is that much of European industry, a fact soft-pedaled in the private-enterprise American press, is nationalized —in telephones, telegraphs, electric power and gas, railroads, municipal transportation, steamship and air lines, and even in some important manufacturing and resource extraction. For most of Europe, whether nominally socialist or not, most of these services are government-owned and government-operated. Some manufacturing and extraction industries have the government present as a large stockholder.

Other large sections of enterprise are government-subsidized, in which respect the United States has in many directions already followed suit—in steamship and air lines, defense industries, periodical and package postal rates, agriculture, and residential housing.

But the fact that public utilities are largely government-owned in Europe is no reason that they will be in the United States. Nevertheless the United States Government from time to time is forced to enter into the development of hydroelectric power, especially in underpopulated and underdeveloped areas when private companies feel such an undertaking would long be unprofitable. The impressive highway network in the United States is entirely governmental. In these respects the United States is following the European pattern.

In addition to nationalization, part ownership and subsidy by government, in Europe one finds more stringent regulation of economic enterprises and more planning by economic enterprises in concert with government. In Europe, in fact, government is felt to be helpful to enterprise. In the United States, despite the dependence on government of many business interests in quest of tariffs, contracts, loans, tax concessions, subsidies, and accelerated amortization of capital investments, government is publicly held to be basically inimical to enterprise. For in the United States government supervision and intervention is believed to lead to "control" and control is considered harmful, in theory, because it is supposed to lead to deterioration of individual character, loss of creativeness, and absolute tyranny. In actuality government regulation and control is fought off as much as possible because there is so very much managerial impropriety and, in fact, as we have seen, criminal wrongdoing. Government regulation, leading to "control" and planning, means that standards would be more rigidly imposed, reducing kickbacks, payola, bribery, extortionate bonuses, inflated expense accounts, excessive managerial salaries and the like. What newspapers refer to as "crooked politicians"—seen mainly in local government—are people corrupted by business interests and business ideology. But on higher governmental levels, where there is more critical scrutiny, politicians are necessarily more honest than secretive business interests.

The United States, it cannot reasonably be denied, when faced with disorganization within and pressure from without as brought to bear by Russia, China, and their satellites, must raise its standards. And the only effective instrumentality for enforcing higher standards, in a situation wherein various vested interests fight to preserve socially destructive privileges, is the central government. It follows that government is going to be just as prominent and forceful in internal affairs in the United States as in Europe, even though it may not exert itself in precisely the same way in the same aspects of social life. But just as Europe has had much to learn from the American experience, as in mass-production techniques, the United States has much still to learn from Europe. The borrowings of each will continue to be reciprocal. And they will stimulate each other competitively.

The Future of Liberty

According to American business ideology, the presence of government foreshadows the loss of liberty; but this contention is not true unless liberty is equated with economic brigandage.

While liberty, as history shows, can undoubtedly be destroyed by government, it is nevertheless a fact that wherever liberty exists or has existed it has been produced and guaranteed by government. What determines the outcome is the kind of government one has. Liberty is never absolute, for absolute liberty leads at once to anarchy. When there is no restraint upon anyone, all are in ever-present danger. Liberty, then, is necessarily relative, and consists of an intricate structure of governmentally guaranteed restraints and permissions. There is restraint first upon individuals and upon government, forbidding certain actions by people and by the government. The people are made free *from* encroachments by others and by the government. On the other hand, the structure of liberty produces freedom for individuals *to* engage in certain specific activities, which are protected.

Historically, the freedom to engage in specified activities has been identified by Mortimer Adler and associates in an exhaustive analytic study[1] as (a) the natural freedom of self-determination, (b) the acquired freedom of self-perfection, of which a number of forms of collective freedom are theoretical variants, and (c) the circumstantial freedom of self-realization, of which doctrines of political liberty are variants. Natural freedom must be limited by government lest one person's self-determination cancel another's.

When the main emphasis in obtaining liberty is placed on diminishing the powers of government, particularly in the supervision of economic affairs, then the liberties of the many in the private sphere can readily be encroached upon by the liberties left to a few aggressive, sometimes psychopathic, private operators. This is what has happened historically in the United States and what is at issue in Chamber of Commerce arguments against "government interference" as the spokesmen for the many invoke governmental aid against a few.

The Chamber of Commerce libertarians, who dominate newspaper space, are the spokesmen for natural freedom of self-determination, in which the organized and established readily triumph over unorganized newcomers. The self-determination they are mainly interested in is chiefly economic, as they are open partisans of the highly questionable doctrine of ethical materialism, that all well-being flows from the maximum realization of individual pecuniary self-interest. Where stress upon freedom has general human creativeness in view, chiefly by intellectuals who are freely stigmatized by newspapers as crackpots, eggheads, and impractical visionaries, it is circumstantial and acquired freedom that is most valued.

For the United States, it may confidently be predicted, the conception of freedom as natural and providing extremely wide scope for self-determination, especially for private economic self-determination, is due in the next 150 years for increasing stringent limitation.

But the conceptions of freedom as circumstantial, enabling self-realization, and of acquired, visualizing self-perfection, will be increasingly in the ascendency. Thus the conceptions of freedom that foster creativity, spoken for by a vast preponderance of philosophers down through history, as Adler shows, will come more and more to the fore. Liberty, contrary to Chamber of Commerce orators, will not be lost but will, in fact, be strengthened for the many. Nor is this to say that natural self-determination will be entirely ruled out. But its operative overemphasis in American history to date will certainly be reduced very much.

The Economic Future of Europe

Europe, with the establishment of a huge tariff-free internal market, will be in a state of long-term economic boom rivaling that seen in the United States since its Civil War. But as Europe does not possess the raw material resources found in Anglo-America, her economic boom must necessarily involve other regions that are able to exchange raw materials for capital and finished goods. These regions are relatively near at hand, by modern standards, in Africa and South America.

There will be, as there already is, American participation in the European Common Market. For many American companies, in order to avail themselves of its advantages, have already established branches in Europe, just as many European companies have been long established in the United States. While Europe was fragmented and crisscrossed with tariff walls it was not attractive to many American companies. And Congress has already given the President power to make reciprocal tariff reductions.

The general task of the revived and unified European economy, in addition to taking care of home needs, will be the economic development of Africa and Latin America to whatever extent possible in the face of certain possibly inescapable isolated gains by Soviet Russia in the same areas. Aiding Europe in this task will be Anglo-America.

The future of Europe and the United States is clearly enmeshed with the establishment of a North and South Atlantic political and economic community, the colossal counterpart in the modern world of the Mediterranean community in the ancient world. Barring anything like a new global war, the preponderance of evidence strongly suggests that this community will emerge in stronger and stronger outline in the next 150 years, eventually perhaps as a formalized Atlantic Union. With it will come unprecedented economic prosperity, cultural advance, and social well-being for all its sectors—Europe, North America, South America and Africa—going far beyond anything promised by communism.

The Future of Latin America

When it comes to Latin America, it is evident we deal with an area without the well-established trends of either disorganization or organization to be discerned in Europe and Anglo-America. Prediction is consequently more hazardous, and must be ventured by considering equally likely alternative probabilities. And although there are unifying threads throughout Latin America, there is also much variety—geographic, climatic, economic, ethnic, and social—among its nineteen independent nations and three European dependencies.

Three broad possibilities present themselves for Latin America.

First, it could remain approximately and uneasily the same, a source of agricultural and mineral raw materials for Europe and North America and a modest outlet for finished consumer goods. But even if we did not have the example of Soviet Cuba before us this possibility is hardly probable; for by many indications Latin America, under the impact of technology in the outside world, is in a ferment, has indeed been in a slow ferment since the Mexican revolution of 1910.

Second, each country or a cluster of countries could follow the example of Cuba, wherein a group of political-minded intellectuals, basing itself ultimately on the lowest and most readily malleable stratum of the population, seizes power and establishes a Soviet-style dictatorship for the collective rigid organization of the country. As dictatorship, basing itself on small circles of landowners, has been until recently the dominant political style in Latin America, it should be evident, even without the example of Cuba, that it is far from foreign to Latin American experience. While a Soviet-style dictatorship can take advantage only of situations wherein a large section of the population is desperate, perhaps mainly from self-frustration as in pre-Castro Cuba, and finds itself amid widespread poverty, it is far from true that it brings the impoverished into a desirable life. The experience of the Russian and Chinese masses, still obviously poor, terrorized, and from time to time near the starvation level, testifies to that. For the Soviet-style dictatorship must devote so much of the produce of new technology to maintaining itself in power—to supporting an extensive internal police, a huge bureaucracy, an elaborate censorship and propaganda apparatus to hide its defeats, and a well-paid and well-equipped army—that not much beyond subsistence remains for the former peasants, now tied to state farms and factories rather than privately owned estates. The Leninist solution, then, is a dead end as far as social creativity is concerned, leading to industrial serfdom—although Latin America, if neglected by Europe and Anglo-America, could succumb to it, particularly as frustrated youth asserts itself as in Cuba.

The *third* possibility is that Latin America, either in whole or in part, will receive cooperation from Europe and Anglo-America in effecting non-dictatorial reorganization in order to adjust to new conditions such as sudden population growth under the application of modern medicines. Such orderly solutions, however, require the collaboration of Latin American authorities, some of which are hostile to change in the belief that by grimly holding on they may be able to perpetuate conditions to their own narrow local advantage. Since World War II the United States has found that economic aid in some countries has been frittered away by entrenched traditionalist elements instead of being used to elevate the standard of living of the masses. Europe and Anglo-America, once they have determined to move, require cooperative local authorities, which in the nature of the case must be flexible-minded.

It is assumed here—and it is a very large assumption—that Europe and Anglo-America will for the most part prevail in Latin America. The main trend of organization must be either to the Soviet-style or the liberal-style development, with the landowning, Church-supported traditionalists losing out in either case. At times the new development will be gradual, at times spasmodic. There is too small a lower middle class for an extreme Rightist solution to be imposed.

Latin America, despite the general label given it, is far from integrated. It is true that it is influenced by European tradition but it is also true that this is the least creative, the most backward strand— the Spanish-Portuguese. Latin America is dominated also by two European languages, Spanish and Portuguese, each with the most meager artistic and theoretical literature of all European languages in extensive use. A less ambiguous advantage is that Latin America already contains many of the ingredients of an advanced civilization in its chief cities—Buenos Aires, Rio de Janeiro, São Paulo, Caracas, Lima, Valparaíso, Montevideo and Mexico City—although its universities and technical schools are comparatively provincial, like those of Spain. Their approach to subject-matter is not typically that of free critical inquiry, as in the best of the European and American universities.

Positive handicaps to the modernization of Latin America beyond the coastal areas are unfavorable terrain and climate, which is why most development of the continent to date has been coastal. Again, beyond the coasts the culture itself is not unambiguously European. For the basic ethnic stock is Indian, with a mixture of European and African. Although the religion is almost uniformly Catholic, it is not Catholic in either the European or American sense, but Catholic with often considerable accretions from the local Indian religions.

The population of close to 150 million in all Latin America, now multiplying rapidly, is by no means distributed evenly in its ethnic composition. Most of the people are of mixed Indian and European ancestry (*mestizos*) and of mixed Indian and African ancestry (*zambos*). There are also mixtures of Europeans and Africans and of *mestizos* and *zambos*. Both in terms of recent mixtures and of different genetic strains living close together, Latin America is the world's outstanding multiracial continent.

Argentina, with a population of about eighteen million, possesses no Negroes to speak of and only about 2 per cent of its people contain traces of Indian genes. But the basic Spanish stock has been reinforced by heavy immigration of Italians and of some Germans, who also cluster in the more temperate parts of Brazil and Chile. Uruguay, population three million, is similarly composed. Brazil, on the other hand, in a population of some fifty-three million contains about five million Negroes and various mixtures, making it the most multiracial of the Latin American countries; less than half its people are white. The remaining countries are mainly non-white, with many mixed strains. Not more than 3.5 per cent of twenty-five million Mexicans are wholly European; the country is for the remainder mostly *mestizo*, with Indian strains predominating.

The populations of Latin America are concentrated for the most part in a few countries and in a few areas, mainly urban. Most of the region is, by North American and European standards, empty and difficult to live in. Nearly half the population of South America itself is contained in Brazil. For this reason and owing also to its territorial size, latent resources, and relatively advanced industry, Brazil must play a key role in the modernization of Latin America. Argentina, smaller, less tropical, also holds a key position.

Most of the populations are peasant or unskilled workers, largely illiterate, although in a few of the smaller countries, such as Uruguay, the educational level is comparatively high.

Formally there is no racial discrimination in Latin America such as one sees in the Union of South Africa or the North American South; but there is indirect discrimination, showing itself most obviously on the economic level, as a consequence of cultural attainment and cultural transmission within the educated classes. The lowest elements from an economic and political point of view, in most of the multi-racial countries, are the Indians and next above them the Negroes. Then in ascending strata are found the *zambos*, mulattoes and quadroons, the *mestizos* and finally, at the top, Europeans, with the Spanish and Portuguese predominating. Many of the Europeans have been schooled in Europe and the United States, have connections abroad and possess what in the United States is called "knowhow." They are too, predominantly, the property owners.

Indians and Negroes are largely passive politically. Changes of regime, although supposed to be by means of elections, have usually been achieved by means of *coups d'état* in which the military forces, like the Roman Praetorian Guard, invariably play a crucial role. The ruling elements have, for the most part, been illiberal. Mexico was the first and, thus far, the only country to have contrived an independent distributive revolution, with many favorable internal results.

If Latin America is to modernize it must first, taking into consideration that there is little tillable soil, make better living arrangements for a preponderantly peasant population. Such will be made under Centrist or Leftist auspices, with the Left solution, expropriative, leaving the peasants employed on state farms *à la Russe*, rather than on the present Rightist estates. Latin America must also expand its own machine manufacture of clothing, furniture, and many household appliances, building up a larger class of factory, office, and professional workers beyond present levels. In the absence of local heavy industry, machinery would need to be imported. A tremendous potential market exists in Latin America for European and North American dynamos, motors, machine tools, food, textile and shoe machinery, oil refineries, road-building equipment and the like. All such development requires large infusions of capital from outside, which in the existing state of affairs can come only from governments or be guaranteed by governments.

Although far below its potential, Latin America is not on nearly so low an economic level on the whole as Asia or Africa. Among the continents it stands third in its partial development, after Anglo-America and Europe. Yet, owing to difficulties of terrain, its economy is extremely lopsided, compartmentalized, unintegrated. Its basic resources are widely separated—iron-ore reserves in Venezuela and Cuba, low-grade coal reserves, iron ore, and bauxite in Brazil, copper and iron ore in Chile and Peru, petroleum in Venezuela and Mexico, bauxite and manganese in Cuba. To join these reserves with railroad and pipeline systems is, on grounds of cost, almost impossible because of intervening high mountains, dense tropical forests, and wide rivers. Some resources are almost inaccessible, and subject to extremely difficult conditions of recovery. High-grade coal reserves are lacking. Sea and air lines are the best means of communicating among all the parts.

In exchange for external goods, such as machinery and consumers' goods, most of the countries export one or two major products for the world market—copper from Chile and Peru; iron ore and petroleum from Venezuela; tin from Bolivia; silver, gold and petroleum from Mexico; sugar from Cuba; coffee from Brazil; meat and preserved foods from Argentina; vanadium, petroleum, lead, zinc, and tungsten from Peru. The internal economy of each country is, then, mercurially affected by variations in world-market prices, collapsing and bringing with it political unrest each time the world price falls. Until 1913 Brazil produced most of the world's rubber, but was hard hit in this product when Malaya became a big producer; now synthetic rubber production has brought difficulties to Malaya as well as Brazil. Chile was a big producer of natural nitrates until World War I, when German chemists found a way of making synthetic nitrates for the production of agricultural fertilizers. Bolivian tin production now appears to be in dark prospect as cans begin to be manufactured of aluminum. It is readily seen that advancing technology often brings boons to Latin America and then suddenly removes them. The region is peculiarly vulnerable to the effects of technological changes.

Government necessarily plays a large role in the economics of the region, often being the owner, senior partner, or close regulator of the leading industries, many of which were started by foreign investors since bought out, squeezed out by taxation, or deprived of their holdings by force. In general the public utilities, including railroads, are government-owned, and Argentina is notably well supplied with railroads, with more mileage per person than the United States. In most of Latin America the railroads are bridges to seaports; they are not transcontinental. In the most advanced countries, such as Argentina, Brazil, Chile, Uruguay, Venezuela, and Mexico, manufacture for domestic needs is quite diversified, although lack of sufficient contiguous coal and iron-ore deposits precludes heavy manufacturing, as of locomotives, machinery, automobiles, and ships.

To further the generalized well-being of its people and lift the cultural level, making the continent fully creative, political solutions are inescapable. And unless Latin America is to remain slavishly dependent on the outside world for whatever well-being it has, the form this political solution must take is eventual unification along the line pursued in Europe. Like the United States, Latin America borrows ideas from Europe, albeit much more slowly. It borrowed the idea of political independence and then the idea of separate republics. The separatist idea was carried to extremes owing to the influence of geography, which operated to keep regions apart.

But while Latin American unification must aim at general goals similar to those of European unification, it will not be carried out for identical reasons. In economics, for example, tariff walls between manufacturing countries are not a problem, as in Europe. The problem is basically one of obtaining capital for development and then of mutual and reciprocal stabilization of price fluctuations for exports. The latter could, it seems, be achieved by means of a joint insurance scheme into which each country pays a certain agreed percentage of profits on exports, the payments building up a fund under the disposal of a superstate such as that set up for Europe by the Treaty of Rome. When difficult times were encountered by one commodity, the resources of the central fund could be drawn upon to cushion the impact on a member country. At the same time uniform tariffs on imported manufactured goods could be drawn so as to favor goods manufactured by member countries. Again, such uniform tariffs would place the region as a whole in a better bargaining position vis-à-vis Europe and Anglo-America, which in exchange for tariff concessions might be induced to make price concessions on raw materials exported by Latin America. As in Europe, the superstate would pool military resources and set up a regional central bank and related institutions. Local affairs would be left to each country, but international and interregional affairs would be under the superstate.

Under the collective guarantee of a superstate, loans would be easier to negotiate for the development of the whole area. As basic capital investments were made, there would be a radiating effect on the economy of the entire region.

Although Brazil already makes about half its own steel, the outlook for heavy metallurgical industry for the region as a whole is not extremely promising. Coal is not readily available for west coast and Venezuelan iron ore. Bauxite deposits and abundant hydroelectric power in Brazil provide the basis for a regional aluminum industry. The outlook for coal chemicals and petrochemicals where coal and petroleum exist is promising, provided plant capital becomes available.

Large-scale regional development under the auspices of a European-like superstate would provide the means for establishing a better educational system and reducing the high rate of illiteracy and technical backwardness in the region. Widespread cultural backwardness is a barrier it will take several generations to eliminate. Eventually, in 100 years or so, the upper branches of the educational system would be in a position to make creative world contributions of the kind made by European and North American universities.

Brazil and Argentina would necessarily be the key factors in starting such a superstate, with advanced Uruguay perhaps participating from the beginning. Steps taken under the Treaty of Rome, it should be remembered, began with agreements among merely Belgium, the Netherlands, and Luxembourg (Benelux). As to the traditional rivalry between Argentina and Brazil, it was never so severe as that between France and Germany. It should be bridgeable, although what is lacking thus far is the persuasive urgency of extreme crisis and looming disaster that brought France and Germany together. Although it has problems, Argentina, mainly a food producer, does not have such severe ones as Brazil. Advantages to both from such a superstate could, however, be clearly demonstrated.

Venezuela, Colombia, and Peru, all of which adjoin Brazil but are not in overland connection due to intervening mountains and jungle, would be next for logical inclusion. Ecuador, Bolivia, and Paraguay, each of relatively minor importance, could come into the plan, perhaps as associates, whenever they chose. Administratively, the north and west coasts are more closely connected to each other by ocean and the Panama Canal than to the east coast. Mexico, the central American republics, and the Caribbean states would find many advantages in joining the scheme.

Although the details may be different, something along the line of what is here sketched will be seen, the beginnings within less than twenty-five years, *if* the region is to avoid profound recurrent civil disturbances and possibly Communist penetration. As matters stand, vis-à-vis world commerce and world culture all regimes in Latin America are necessarily agents of some one or more of the outside Great Powers. Communist critics hold that the regimes are agents of North American or European imperialism. But Communist regimes are no less agents of Russian imperialism, as in Castro's Cuba. If Russia gets into difficulties or decides to withdraw its support, Castro's puppet regime will fall like the proverbial house of cards.

But although no nation or regime is completely independent, as the need of Europe and the United States for alliances shows, Latin America could make itself more nearly independent by its own political effort. There is a limit, too, on the aid that can be provided by Europe and the United States, both of which must allocate a large part of their resources for defense against the Russian war machine. According to Soviet propaganda, the United States is the initiator of world superarmaments; but the most superficial reading of American history will convince anyone that the United States, prior to the advent of Russian military expansion, always maintained a small standing army, never had peacetime conscription, and was invariably materially unprepared for every war it ever entered. Russian armaments thus serve a dual purpose, deflecting capital from world development and, in the process, keeping large regions so poverty-stricken as to be vulnerable to Communist penetration. It is Russia that has thus far been adamant against any effective plan of scaling down armaments. But as the strain of heavy armaments retards its development far more than it does that of the more advanced West, Russia may not always block a reduction of armaments.

The prediction for Latin America, then, is that it will forge ahead to prosperity and copartnership with Europe and Anglo-America under an effective superstate, or will, in its various parts, remain economically and politically dependent on outside countries—North American, West European, or Russian, with the Chinese possibly taking a hand. The most probable outcome is that it will, following the lead of Europe, gradually form a superstate and become an advanced member of the Atlantic Community.

In the meantime partially industrialized Brazil appears to be the country in which the most can be achieved by material aid from abroad. Internal political disputes appear to pose the greatest difficulties. Improvement of conditions in Brazil, making it more nearly self-sufficient, would have radiating effects throughout the region, although if Latin American organization is to become fully effective, the region must follow the way blazed by Europe in the Treaty of Rome.

The Prospects for Africa

Africa, far behind Latin America in development, has only recently achieved precarious political independence in its various parts. But if it is to modernize, Africa must rely on European and North American economic and cultural tutelage for a very long time to come, for

150 years or more. In the meantime chaotic internal conditions could cause it again to lose independence.

Even more so than Latin America, Africa is culturally, climatically, geographically, and economically disparate. Not integrated in any respect, ultimately it too, in an age when effective government is continental in scope, must unify. But although beginnings toward such unification may well take place in the span of 150 years, it is by no means on the immediate agenda. Aid for development must come from abroad, and such aid is clearly limited at present by the Russian-initiated armaments race. In the meantime Russia endeavors, and will continue to endeavor, to establish political footholds, as it appears to have done in certain places.

As long as it maintains its present racist ideology, the Union of South Africa has little role to play in the development of interior Africa, most of whose people are non-white. Going it alone for as long as it can, the best the Union can do is to be a producer of gold, diamonds, uranium, coal, steel, and other raw materials for itself and the outside world.

The most Europeanized parts of Africa are the Arab Mohammedan north, along the Mediterranean Sea, effectively separated from the main body of the continent by the Sahara Desert, and the extreme south. The destiny of indigenous Africa is evidently something separate. The key country of this region, apparently destined to play a political role similar to that of Brazil in evolving Latin America, is the former British colony of Nigeria, which has the largest population of all the African nations, around thirty million.

What is shaping up in this region, although it will no doubt be long in coming, is a Central African Federation, semicontinental in scope and organized along the line of the European Union and the incipient Latin American Union. The now independent states of Guinea and Republic of Congo, and the former Belgian Congo, will very probably eventually join such a union. Other nearby regions such as Ghana, and adjacent areas should also logically belong although there well may be, in the upshot, anomalous holdouts.

Available known resources strongly suggest that such a union will for long be, at best, a trading nation doing some light manufacturing at home and maintaining close economic political and cultural relations with the European Union. Thanks to simple propinquity and the prevalence among the educated of the French and English languages, ties are already close, the leaders in most of the regions having been educated in France, England, or in local French or English schools. The pattern of education in the local schools through the university level is European.

Most of the people in this region, however, are still tribal-minded and still have far to go under intellectual leaders that are themselves far in advance of the populace. But economic development alone is a potent uprooter of tribal life. Urbanization and individualization must be the outcome of any modern economic upsurge.

In time the Union of South Africa will inevitably establish close economic relations with the nearby Central African Federation. And, as the latter grows in influence with the outside world owing to its increasing economic weight, it may be able to bring effective political pressure on the Union to modify its racist policies. These latter, however, are almost sure, before such a hypothetical time, to bring their own liquidation. For the Union needs to bring in native Africans from the north as workers in mines, fields, and factories. In a population of about thirteen million, only some two and a half million are of European descent. In view of the presence of such a large proportion of non-whites and the growth of independent political power in non-white Africa to the north it is evident that the racist policies cannot endure. South Africa is a place in the world surely marked for violent internal explosions. Had the Europeans of the region been consistent in their racist policy, which excludes non-Europeans even from an education, they would on principle have brought in European immigrants. But these they would have had to pay much higher wages. The dominant Boers wished, impossibly, to have it both ways: the cheapest possible labor and permanent white dominance.

For a time Southern and Northern Rhodesia may join, under white rule, with the Union to maintain a precarious white dominance in the region. But in the long run, owing to the relative scarcity of whites and the high cost of bringing in more, this policy must fail. The eastern half of Africa extending north to the Gulf of Aden will also be dominantly non-European and in the course of time must, if it is to be truly independent in a world wherein government is increasingly continental in scope, either join with the central African union that has Nigeria as its nucleus or form an East African Federation. In the meantime there will no doubt be much political maneuvering and intriguing, with the Great Powers from time to time intervening directly.

When, as, and if southern Africa is joined politically to the central part, the continent will be in a much better position industrially. In the meantime new resources may be discovered in various parts and developing technology will convert into resources many substances not now valued as resources. Remaining European colonies, such as the Portuguese, are sure to go the way of the British, French, Italian, and Belgian to independence.

The Mediterranean North

The northern portion of Africa, Arab and Mohammedan, falls into a separate category. Already largely independent it, too, must fuse in union unless its parts are to be the political and economic cat's paws of continent-sized powers. Already the first steps toward such a fusion have been taken in the short-lived United Arab Republic, which in time may be part of a grouping that includes Libya, Tunisia, Syria, Algeria, Morocco, Jordan and Iraq.

Whether united or not, there are not the resources in this region to support heavy industry, so the economic prospect is for another trading region with some light manufacturing. With the nearby industrial nations in a position to supply fine instruments and heavy machinery, there is room for much social and cultural development in the region, parts of which are richly endowed with petroleum. This last fact makes it of special interest to the Great Powers.

What of Israel, neither Arab nor Mohammedan, in this situation? Israel, like small countries everywhere, must function in a large coalition, and the only coalition available to her is the one that is adjacent. Israel and the Arab states clearly must make up, and such a reconciliation has been already suggested by Ben-Gurion, Israeli Prime Minister. If it is argued that bad feeling will prevent such a reconciliation, one needs only point to the now close relations between long-embattled France and Germany.

Israel has been dependent for much of her support upon aid from the United States, official and private. But she cannot forever depend upon such aid, even from private Jews. Two or three generations from now most of the descendants of present-day Zionist Jews will unquestionably have lost touch with Israel, despite efforts to prevent it, just as European-descended Americans of the second and third generation have lost touch with the countries of their ancestors' origin.

Israel, technic-minded and with European scientific theory at her finger tips, would be, as she has already been, a stimulating factor in an African Mediterranean Union. At its maximum this Union might extend from the Atlantic to the Red Sea and include the Middle East.

It may be argued that the Great Powers will intervene to prevent such unions as sketched for Latin America, Central Africa, and the Mediterranean. But as it is clearly to the advantage at least of the West European and Anglo-American powers for such unions to take place for the sake of the political stability and economic opportunities they provide and resistance to Communist maneuverings, it is almost certain that instead of being resisted they will be welcomed. In addition to political stability world economic development would be facilitated by these unions, which would be dependent upon Europe and North America for advanced theory, higher personnel, techniques, and complicated mechanisms. Only the Soviet bloc, if it continues its dog-in-the-manger policies, could conceivably be opposed.

It would take hundreds of pages to assess fully all the evidence for and against the probability of such unions, patterned after the Treaty of Rome, but as I assay the evidence the probabilities seem weighted by more than 75 per cent in favor of the outcome sketched, always provided the world is not subjected to the holocaust of another general war. Localized wars there may well be, but the existence of the new weapons confronts governments resorting to them with the high probability of mutual destruction, in which case the pattern of the human future is anybody's guess. China and India, by reason of their masses, alone seem to have what would be necessary to wield some feeble influence in such a ruined world.

The Far East

The outlook in the Far East is far less clear than in any region we have confronted. For it largely depends, in the present highly fluid state of affairs, on the resoluteness and aptness of European and United States policy, which in the past have been contradictory, weak, and largely ineffective.

At this writing overpopulated India alone appears to be modernizing at a notable rate, with aid from the outside world. And if the relatively open society has any future in the region, that future lies with India in its strong cultural ties with Europe. In her present course of political and economic development India, like the visualized Latin American, Central African, and Mediterranean unions, seems likely to maintain close relations with the European Union and Anglo-America.

As for Burma, Thailand, Laos, South Vietnam, Malaya, Indonesia, South Korea, the Philippines, and Japan, their future is clearly at issue and depends not only on the strength but on the skill and subtlety with which they are supported by Europe and the United States. Both Japan and the Philippines have made great strides toward economic and social betterment since World War II, but improperly or insufficiently aided, they cannot forever hold out against the counterpull of Communist China.

It is in the Far East, filled with resentful, apathetic, superstitious, and long-abused populations for which European ideological slogans have no meaning, that the Soviet bloc is most likely to make gains, as it already has in China, North Korea, Afghanistan, North Vietnam, and Laos. But in reaching out for more territories it is not the local territories primarily that are desired, for these for the most part are difficult and unrewarding. The long-range target of Communist maneuvering in the Far East is obviously Japan. Possessed with Japan's advanced industries, Communism in this region would have a more favorable future. The effect of taking over nearby countries is to shut off trade for Japan, which like all industrial countries needs raw materials, special products, and markets.

The fall of Southeast Asia to the Chinese and their puppets would signalize extreme danger for Japan and perhaps also India.

While politically, socially, and culturally distasteful to modern Japan, China is nevertheless a strong economic attraction. Economically the two regions need each other; the main question is, of course, which is to dominate. Western policy has been opposed to either Japanese or Chinese dominance over the region, although the West would now, no doubt, like to see a non-bellicose Japan reinstalled in Korea, Manchuria, and Formosa.

While a union of the Far East excluding China and supported by Europe and the United States is not an impossibility, it would be achieved only with great difficulty and cost. Communist gains in the region, however, are not necessarily permanent. If India, against the difficulties of illiteracy and overpopulation, succeeds in developing herself by means of permissive-persuasive rather than repressive-prohibitive government, it will have a tremendous effect on the region, serving to recover for its autonomous life sections that may in the meantime have gone Communist. The strong probability, however, is that India must resort to dictatorship if she is to overcome a backward culture.

Lacking Japan, Southeast Asia can be only a drain on the limited resources of the Chinese. Russia is almost as far removed from this situation as the United States. For a long time to come the most the Chinese could do in the region would be to grind down the population as it does its own. What the Communists and the western societies alike have to offer the peoples of the world is always evident in how they treat their own. People do not strive to immigrate into Russia or China, but they do seek to establish themselves in Western Europe, the United States, Canada, Africa, and parts of Latin America.

If Chinese Communist domination is avoided, a Far Eastern political union that had India and Japan as anchor points would be a distinct possibility if not a lively probability. Burma, Indonesia, Malaya, Thailand, Iran, Pakistan, South Vietnam, and the Philippines could well be parts of such a union and, less possibly, Australia, New Zealand and, perhaps, parts of East Africa. But the way is not yet clear to such a development and much reorganization and building must take place, particularly in India.

The Communist Bloc

Owing to the lack of precise uncensored information about many aspects of Russian and Chinese affairs, the Western world oscillates between underestimating and exaggerating Communist growth and unity. As Russia demonstrates, there has been Soviet growth since 1917, mainly in the establishment of heavy industry and heavy armaments but also in the creation and development of schools, scientific institutes, and administrative services. But growth and successes are almost all along the line subject to severe qualifications.

Communist political gains everywhere except in Cuba have taken place after the disruption of wars and by means of military action, as in Eastern Europe, Tibet, North Korea and North Vietnam. In no part of the world, not even in Russia of 1917, has the Communist Party led an uprising of politically conscious factory workers to victory in accordance with the Marxist formula. Except in Czechoslovakia, even Communist military success has taken place in undeveloped or only slightly developed peasant countries, including Russia, where the general cultural level was always extremely low. Communism is historically no more than a receiver in bankruptcy. Southeast Asia today, it is true, meets these conditions. And all over, even in Russia, extreme repressive and minutely tutelary measures are required to keep vast populations in subjugation. Russia does not even dare to allow its people to listen to foreign radio broadcasts, which it jams, travel freely about the country, or visit abroad except as members of official, conducted delegations.

Communist organization is overorganization and is necessary because people, once having discovered what the actual situation is, will not voluntarily support it. The regimes of Western Europe, even if sometimes for mistaken reasons, are voluntarily supported by the broad masses of people. Serious dissidents, actual and potential, are very few. Restrictive measures, except in a few minor and anomalous countries such as Spain, Turkey, Iran, the Union of South Africa, Paraguay, and the Dominican Republic, are consequently much lighter. Extremist regimes, Left or Right, by their very nature require harsh repressive measures.

Censorship serves to hide many serious defects within the Communist countries, although from time to time severe crises such as famine, internal political violence, housing shortages, lack of consumers' goods, juvenile delinquency, large-scale economic crime and the like bring conditions partially into view. Russia itself is a major exhibit in rebuttal to the Communist thesis that all social difficulties are traceable to the private ownership of property.

Most Communist gains, including the original upthrust in Russia, have been produced not by Communist adroitness or cunning, as is often suggested, but by the inappropriateness of the opposing traditionalist point of view. Czarist inflexibility and obtuseness had more to do with the Communist triumph in Russia than Leninist theory, which was devised merely to take advantage of what it combatted. Communist inroads in Eastern Europe stemmed from a war engendered by traditional obtuseness in trying, by treaty provisions and tariffs, to keep Germany in a condition of permanent ailing convalescence after World War I. The chaotic consequences of Allied policy in the Versailles peace treaty were clearly foretold by John Maynard

Keynes, the English economist, in his brilliant *The Economic Consequences of the Peace*, published in 1919, as I noted earlier.

Soviet Russia and the West, when Germany had somewhat recovered, each strove to deflect a desperate berserk Germany against the other. The maneuvers backfired against both. Only a cooperative Germany fully integrated into Europe, as we see now with Western Germany and as Keynes foresaw, could be part of a peaceable community.

Russia in the outcome of the war of maddened Hitlerite Germany against the world had the opportunity of taking over Eastern Europe. With her own power alone Russia could not have done it and she could not do it today if Eastern Europe were part of the European Union. The Communist Party in every country has been an abysmal failure except where Russian arms have come in to enthrone it.

The same is true in the Orient. Had not Japan first ravaged China and had not the United States after the war pursued a weak, ineffective, and misinformed policy with respect to China, that land would not today be under Communist rule, even though China was weak after a prolonged revolution that began in 1912 and possessed a government very deficient by Western standards. Here Russian arms, again, served to help the Communist Party of China.

But China, regarded by some as a counterpart of Russia in the Far East and destined to undergo a similar development, is far from being another Russia. China, in fact, could well be the means to Soviet Russia's undoing, in the one possibility by emerging as a nearby rival, with eyes turned to Siberian resources and living space, and in the other possibility by absorbing technical aid and machine resources needed for the further upbuilding of Russia.

We have already scrutinized the inventory of China's known resources and the difficulty of its internal terrain as well as its vast surplus of population. The latter, far from being an advantage in development, is a grievous handicap, requiring for its mere sustenance what might otherwise go into capital development.

In forty years China cannot even nearly emulate Soviet Russia in its development. In the first place, it does not have the means at its disposal that Soviet Russia received from Czarist Russia. Again, Russia had surplus space in relation to population, with room for an expanding population, which China does not have. Again, Russia had rich, readily available resources while China does not.

As this is written, talk is rife to the effect that China in a very few years will join the world "nuclear club" by exploding an atomic bomb, in which case there will no doubt be renewed fears of a formidable China. But even if China shows the technical capability of producing an atomic bomb it won't be much more than a prestige symbol. In order to be a military power along the lines of the United States, Russia, and the European Union she must be able to produce such bombs in large quantities as well as possess the means of delivering them over great distances. If China ever does attain first-class military status it will be as awkward for Russia as for anyone else. China, on the whole, will for long be little more militarily than a paper dragon.

Expected wars, when they materialize, do not follow anticipated lines. Italy was supposed to join with Germany and Austria-Hungary in World War I but instead threw in with the Allies. The pattern taken by World War II was an unpleasant surprise to each of the major participants, including the victors. Nobody gained anything decisive in that war except the Chinese Communists, who were minor figures in it. Russia's so-called gains in Eastern Europe are highly ambiguous.

China as a factor in the Far East for long cannot be much more than a Russian tool and may not even be that. And Russian influence in the world is not more than that of a great military power. Its vaunted ideology does not do more for it than organize, here and there in troubled areas, a small nucleus of fanatics, useful in mobilizing opinion against weak and friendless governments. It will not be by means of Communist doctrines, which have failed in the past, that Russia will make territorial gains. They can come only from military power.

If the Far East succumbs to communism it will be by military rather than non-military political means. And the military means cannot succeed if they are countered with equal military means plus rational development of poverty-stricken areas. It is the false promise of quick development that brings the Communists whatever support they have.

The outlook for the Far East is nevertheless clouded because, on the record of the past, one does not know how much reliance to place on the resolution or adroitness of the West, the disinterested populations of which are always more concerned about enjoying near pleasures rather than facing up to clearly looming dangers. But adroit and realistic policies could do much to insure the orderly development of the parts of the Far East outside the Communist orbit. Russia, in the meantime, maintains its strong military posture at the expense of the basic needs of its people. It cannot forever continue to do so, nor is it any more able than was Germany to conquer the world by military power. In order to conquer, it must subjugate all of Europe and Anglo-America, which could count on most of Latin America, Africa, and India for economic defensive aid—a clearly impossible task and one that would ruin Russia itself. Russia, however, will no doubt continue to maneuver for advantage wherever it can, but even such maneuverings, as they stimulate efforts at reorganization in the West, will only be self-defeating.

As it cannot supply its expanding population by successful conquest, Russia must in time necessarily do so by internal creativity, in which direction she has almost limitless opportunities. Among other things, Russia must liberalize its policies vis-à-vis its own population, and since the death of Stalin has already taken steps along the road to liberalization. It must, for one thing, produce much more consumer goods unless the Communist Party is to suffer loss of what it may have of internal prestige. It must, increasingly, deliver for its own people.

Although education in Russia is one-sidedly technical, the country is not today, as in 1917, made up principally of gullible peasants. A large technically educated class has been created, and one that has access at least to the literature of the outside world. While ability to think rationally in one discipline does not, as many studies show, guarantee ability to think rationally with respect to all subject matters, it is nevertheless no doubt true that, pro rata, there are more disciplined and capable thinkers in Russia today than at any time before. This class, and many of those with which it works, is not going to be forever easy victims of ideological myths. In what they know is a short life at best they are going to demand, increasingly, more of the amenities of living—a basic problem for latter-day Bolshevism.

One reason one can realistically foresee increasing liberalization in Russia is that the pendulum of possibility does not have far to swing to the extreme of illiberality. Under Stalin, the teacher of Hitler in this respect, the absolute of repression had been reached, and upon Stalin's death there was only one course short of social suicide that change could take: up. While under Khrushchev there has been some relaxation of repression, with concentration camps nearly emptied, there is much room for further relaxation, not only with respect to civil liberties but also in consumer economics. One cannot keep people working forever for wages without giving them something tangible to buy.

Where Russia will continue to make gains at the expense of the rest of the world will be, as in the past, mainly through weaknesses, faults, and miscalculations by the West. Russia would not be likely to take on the entire outside world in a war unless—a very unlikely event—she came up with a monopoly of some new irresistible weapon, and her mere presence usefully serves to cement the rest of the world together. The nations outside are not likely to bicker and quarrel very seriously in the presence of Russia. So that, while aiming to be divisive, Russia is having the effect of gradually unifying the rest of the world against her and of isolating herself, a dangerous thing for any nation to do.

Nevertheless as a purely military power, liberalized or not, Russia remains to be reckoned with. On the score of communism it is worth noting that although at various times and places she attracts members to her captive parties, she does not hold them. The Communist parties of the world have had a multiplicity of membership turnovers, with the vast majority eventually leaving in disillusionment with each twist of Soviet foreign policy. The Communist parties have been the greatest school of anti-Soviet politics in the world, have done more than anything else to trample down the once widely attractive idea of socialism. The most dedicated anti-Communists are former Communists.

Scattered gains for communism are, nevertheless, more than probable in some of the world's various highly disorganized spots such as Iran, Laos, Cuba and wherever comparable conditions exist. But any profound intrusion into Latin America is practically ruled out by the near presence of the United States, which blocked a Communist take-over in distant South Korea. Without military and other support Southeast Asia could succumb. If the Communists took Iran they would acquire at once a large quantity of the world's oil reserves as well as a vantage point from which to threaten both India and Saudi Arabia, also rich in oil. As events in the former Belgian Congo showed, the Communists are also busy in Africa, but thus far only with meager results.

Not much that is worth while to them is available without great difficulties and risks. And local violence and intrigue can always be countered in kind.

The Commonwealth of Nations

There isn't much to be said of the Commonwealth of Nations, formerly the British Commonwealth and the British Empire. It is now an informal consultative body and may continue to be of importance in exchanging views among its various members. But its constituents in Africa and Asia are all destined to belong to independent regional unions, whatever relations they maintain with England and among themselves. There remains for consideration, then, only Canada, Australia, and New Zealand. The last two clearly belong in a Southeast Asia and East Africa union and may in time join although, owing to geographic separation and sharp cultural differences, they could well be anomalous holdouts in the looming organization of the world in continental collectivities.

Canada, however, is in a different position. Geographically, culturally, economically, politically, and diplomatically she is entwined with the United States. Sentimentally she is entwined with England and the former British Empire.

In the course of time, perhaps a long period such as 100 years, Canada will unquestionably unite with the United States, of her own volition and for her own advantage. Such an assertion may well set the teeth of contemporary Canadians on edge, but the reasons for it are not far to seek.

With the British Empire and Commonwealth gone, there is no large framework into which Canada can fit other than that offered by the United States. Already Canada has many close interrelationships with the United States in every field. Far more citizens of Canada come to the United States to live and work than vice versa. Many policies of the United States, however, irritate Canada, and meetings must be held from time to time on the highest official levels to modify them.

As matters stand, Canada has no voice in shaping the policies of the United States. But if she were part of it, on a basis of parity, she would have a strong voice in the national councils of a world power, a stronger voice indeed than she ever had in the British Empire or Commonwealth.

On a basis of parity the ten Canadian provinces would be admitted as states, for which role they nearly all qualify already by United

States standards. Such admission would at once give Canada twenty votes, or one sixth, in the powerful United States Senate. In the House of Representatives, elected on the basis of population in congressional districts, the voice of this region would be smaller but of strategic parliamentary importance nevertheless. With representation in the Congress would go much patronage in federal government jobs.

Local administration in the new Canadian states would be left entirely in Canadian hands, as at present, but Canadians might aspire to the presidency of the United States and would, from time to time, be elected to that office in line with normal probabilities. It would, for electoral reasons, from time to time be of advantage to the political parties to have a Canadian run for Vice-President.

In general, opportunities on a continental scope would be opened to every Canadian citizen.

No doubt there are many thorny questions that would require attention in effecting such a union, resembling in spirit that between Scotland and England. But such questions could be taken up by a special long-term commission. For those who may be skeptical of this probability, giving it a low rating, there is again the case of France and Germany joining political forces under the Treaty of Rome. If France and Germany and the European powers can unite under external pressures, then it is clear that other unions of the kind sketched in this chapter are far from out of the question.

While many arguments pro and con could be mobilized on the subject of a union of Canada and the United States, ultimate union will not come about or be prevented on the basis of such arguments, so it would be quite futile to give them. The union will come about, like the European Union and others predicted, under the simple pressure of necessity in a world wherein large collectivities have a distinct advantage over regions divided into a multiplicity of separate states.

But why, if unions are foreseen, should one not anticipate the union of Russia and China into an irresistible superunion? The unions discussed, it will be noticed, are all regional and for the most part of culturally and economically like-minded societies. The main bodies of Russia and China are located in widely separate regions and there is little cultural similarity between the two and no ethnic affinity. What there is of a bond between the two is wholly ideological, not going very deep in either society. The incorporation of Eastern Europe into Russia, however, while offering nationalistic and cultural difficulties, is on the other hand a distinct eventual possibility.

The Prospects of World Federation

What, first, of the prospects of Communist conquest and unification of the world in a single system? Communism by direct power cannot overthrow Western Europe and North America, as any survey of the relative possession of resources, people, and techniques will clearly show. To put the entire world under its control the Communists would require exclusive possession of some effective super-weapon, of which there is yet no sign. And Communism cannot indirectly conquer—as by conversion, subversion, infiltration, and conspiracy—unless the non-Communist world obliges by continuing to make the egregious mistakes of the past, such as bickering, quarreling, and overreaching.

Could not, however, important areas be honestly converted to communism, seeing in it a humanly better system? Too much water has passed over the dam for this to happen; communism has shown its limitations, intellectual shallowness, and absolute amoralism too clearly to view. Once they understand the issues, people prefer the ambiguous morality-amorality of the West as offering more hope.

Instead of world rule by the Comintern, what is a much more likely prospect is eventual rule of most of the world by a federation of the continental regional superstates outlined—United Europe, the United States (eventually including Canada), United Latin America, United Central Africa, United North Africa, and a United Far East. It is understood, I hope, that the actual names of these coming entities are not being given nor their precise composition, owing to lack of any evidence whatever for such assertions. Nor is it being asserted that all will emerge at once, full-blown. Rather is the development to be seen as a gradual snowballing process, with the chief incentive the already existent large entities of United Europe, the United States, Soviet Russia, and Red China.

Owing to long-established European influences in all the regions and the desire of indigenous intellectuals to emulate the European development, the outcome must inevitably follow along the general lines sketched. As to a federation of the interregional superstates, the world has already groped its way toward such organization in the League of Nations and the United Nations. A factor that has hampered both, however, has been the multiplicity of voices in such large collections of sovereign nation-states. Purely local questions have constantly intruded into the foreground of discussion and consideration, questions better left within each region. The task of the representatives of the regional superstates in a federation will be confined to the adjudication of interregional problems, with intraregional questions left to the regional organizations.

It is not necessary to expect that the entire world will be included in such a federation. For there may well be anomalous holdouts, as indicated before, that find it to their seeming advantage to remain aloof much as Switzerland has remained aloof from European blocs. Nor will the world necessarily see a single such federation. Already the Communists, in the Comintern, have such an organization and the strong tendency of the non-Communist world to form one, seen in NATO and SEATO, shows the drift of affairs. If the stresses between Moscow and Peking intensify, there may be two Communist blocs.

The United Nations will very probably not survive, at least in its present form. For it has been converted into too much of a cockpit of struggle by the Communists. In time it must give way to a more effective cooperative organization. While it is possible that communism in a modified form might eventually join in such a federation, at the present time it is hardly probable. At present the world is tending to form into two federations, with the Communists in a minority federation as far as resources, skills, and numbers are concerned. They are also left with the most difficult environmental problems—overpopulation, difficult geography and climate, backward cultures, and so forth.

The Theoretical Understructure of Prediction

The political unifications predicted as generally probable in varying, not precisely determined, degrees may seem to be out of harmony with the theory of social change laid down in Chapter III in that they depend upon conscious decisions. And decisions, as is well understood, may take different directions. Social change, as we see it, is not in the main a collective conscious process. We say therefore that these unifications must take place only *if* patently undesirable consequences are to be avoided, and that people, if they are able, will seek to avoid such consequences.

Our theory is applicable in terms of the flux of organization and disorganization. Cultural innovations—which creative man is constantly producing and in the modern world, through the instrumentality of science and technology, is producing in greater profusion than in all previous history—insensibly induce dislocations in seemingly solidly established societies, which increasingly are unable to attain their basic ends in the old ways.

To cope with the myriad problems that followed upon the introduction of machine technology, for example, there ensued a long train of *ad hoc* piecemeal legislation, all designed to cope with disorganization, to produce new organization suitable to machine production. The inventors of the machine did not foresee the havoc they would produce. Decision entered the situation only when the havoc became discernible. The decision could theoretically have gone against doing anything about conditions, but this would have been implicitly a choice in favor of disintegration, the choice the traditionalists and the apathetic invariably stand for implicitly. But directly confronted with the issue, man the organizer will, whenever he is able, favor revised organization instead of disintegration. Only when the issues are not clearly understood will societies grimly hold onto traditional ways and, unaware of what is happening, slowly disintegrate or stagnate. But in the light of widely dispersed knowledge the issues are fairly clear and well understood, by the Communists among others, as demanding another type of social and political organization. Where the Communists are mistaken is in believing that only the simplistic Leninist concept of proper organization is possible. Its concept of organization throws out much that is useful and hard-won along with what is outmoded.

But the Communists are correct in discerning that the institution of government must play the initiating and leading role in reorganizing the world. In all of what has been said in this and the preceding chapter it is evident that it is government that must take the lead, mobilizing what there is of private enterprise in its support. The task is beyond the capacity, vision, or taste of private enterprise. Can anyone seriously believe that the combined organizational resources of the United States Chamber of Commerce and National Association of Manufacturers, joined with their counterparts in other countries, could do what is necessary? And, if they could, is there any evidence of a desire on their part to do it?

A relatively pat outcome may appear to have been forecast. But while such regional unions and federations must be the inevitable outcome, in terms of our prediction, if operative organization is to prevail in the world, they will, in the light of what history shows us, not be achieved without difficulties. There will no doubt be opposition and obstacles encountered from place to place, chiefly of an internal nature as various vested interests and traditionalists are disturbed by necessary decisions. Civil commotions and even civil wars may well take place and, indeed, Latin America, Africa, and Southeast Asia are now experiencing both in varying degrees from time to time and from place to place. Setbacks, however, will tend to be temporary, with the general current in the direction forecast.

The emerging governmental constellations will not necessarily be what is considered democratic in Europe and the United States. Democracy is itself an ideology. But all government, it may be stated as an unrestricted general proposition or law, is by its very nature oligarchic, an affair of the relatively few. No extensive society was ever ruled by one man, so the idea of monarchy as a possibility must be discarded. Again, no extensive society was ever ruled by the many.

Rule is invariably *of* the many but *by* the few and, in its maximum benefits, *for* far fewer than the many—a realistic modification of Lincoln's sweeping formulation in the Gettysburg Address. But although necessarily and invariably oligarchical, the oligarchies differ in composition and technique, depending upon underlying conditions. They may be narrow or broad in point of view and base, producing results in accordance with techniques ranging from coercive-prohibitive to permissive-persuasive. The more mature, stable, and environmentally favored an oligarchy is the more permissive and persuasive it is apt to be. Harsh conditions produce harsh governments.

Latin America appears to have the best chance of evolving, in union, toward permissive-persuasive rule. Africa and much of the Far East appear, on the basis of local conditions and problems, to be limited for a good while to come to stricter rule, although the time may well come—in several hundred years—when all people are subjected to mild rule. But general tightening of governmental restrictions in the United States under the pressure of many converging problems is a distinct prospect. Loosely held reins of government will be more and more a thing of the past for a good while to come in the United States, until the world is more organized in large cooperative regional political systems and various serious internal American problems are solved.

Under loose government in the United States, for example, a small number of whites are allowed in the South to tyrannize in major and petty ways over Negroes, consisting in a state like Mississippi of about half the population. Such action will be terminated soon, but there are hundreds of problems in the United States, some of them already mentioned, requiring similar more stringent governmental intervention.

The salient requirement of the next 150 years, and one that will in the main be satisfied, is more and better government.

CHAPTER IX

SHACKLED GIANT: THE STATE OF EDUCATION

Government and the economic system, as we have just seen, are social institutions in the process of undergoing thoroughgoing change and facing further great change, but in education we confront an institution clearly destined for even deeper, wider, and more minute change. For education is faced with complex pressures of political and social dislocations unprecedented in world history.

Here we may conveniently recall our general theory: in its initial stages social change is unconscious and unwitting, and takes place willy-nilly, unnoticed. The change is produced by the sporadic or concentrated introduction of cultural novelties, initially believed to have only limited effects or no effects at all. In modern times most of the influential cultural novelties are scientific and technical. As it is seen that they more or less gradually disorganize established social patterns, sometimes even coming to induce chaotic anarchy, conscious intervention takes place, inducing institutional change. If intervention involves rejection of the cultural novelty, as sometimes happens, the given society differentiates itself for better or worse from others that accept it. Conscious rejection of cultural innovation in the form of science and machine technology was for long the social strategy of Spain and Portugal, with direct consequences that mark them off negatively from the rest of western Europe.

Ill-informed social managers in a complex, mechanized world inevitably find themselves presiding over repeated, deep, unresolved crises, stagnation, decay, or collapse. And ill-informed social management has been a conspicuous feature of the modern world, shown to view by the imperial bureaucracy and its successors in China; the military usurpers in latter-day Japan; the sultans in Turkey; czars, nobility, and commissars in Russia; nobility, military, and Fascists in Italy; the Hohenzollerns, military, and National Socialists in Germany; the Church, military, landowners, and Falangists in Spain;

landowners and military in much of Latin America; Hapsburgs in Austria-Hungary and, as coming events will almost certainly show, the Boers in South Africa.

But it is plainly evident that comparatively informed social management, even in the presence of dangerous currents, can produce relatively favorable results, as in Sweden, Mexico, Finland, Norway, Uruguay, Iceland, Denmark, and Switzerland—all small, homogeneous, and readily manageable. Despite mistakes and vicissitudes, informed management has produced what are on the whole relatively favorable results in postwar England, Austria, Holland, Belgium, and West Germany. France has been confused and self-contradictory.

Social management in the United States has been far from wholly remiss but whenever it fails, owing to insufficient insight at the level of decision, it produces long chains of troubles. A few managerial errors of American judgment in this century have, for example, been: (1) unnecessarily going far afield to intervene in World War I, prolonging that conflict to an embittering conclusion; (2) refusing to join the League of Nations, policies of which could have been influenced for the better; (3) repeatedly raising tariffs between the two world wars and thereby greatly contributing to world economic disorganization and the rise of Hitler; (4) persistently blundering with respect to Soviet Russia; (5) misjudging the aspirations of submerged peoples for liberation from internal and external exploitation, poverty, disease, ignorance, and misery, giving Russia many political opportunities; (6) endlessly fumbling at home about exacerbated labor-management relations, civil rights, urban blight, inflation-deflation, crime control, education and a host of other serious problems.

All public policies, whether effective or destructive, are invariably the creations of men schooled in certain ways. It follows that some of the responsibility for success or failure must be borne by the national educational system. The Battle of Waterloo may not have been won on the playing fields of Eton but it is certain that the British Empire was unwittingly dismantled in the pre-1914 classrooms of Oxford and Cambridge, whence the British Foreign Office drew most of its personnel. In defense of these old universities, however, it ought to be added that some of their brightest lights, notably Bertrand Russell and John Maynard Keynes, were in articulately detailed opposition to the Foreign Office, the first before the war and the second afterward. Had their views prevailed, Russell's prior to 1910, Keynes's in 1919, the British Empire would now be far less shrunken, a desirable state of affairs from a traditionalist point of view.

While social policy may not measure up to the best insights of the best minds, it can rarely transcend it. The schools, with which the best minds have usually had at least developmental connection, may not be the first or even the second lines of defense of a society; but the experience of the modern world shows that they have the makings of the *main* line. Government or the economic system under modern conditions can hardly be stronger than the schools.

Europe the Leader

The pre-eminent educational region of the modern world with respect to quality is Europe roughly north of latitude 43 degrees north and west of longitude 18 degrees east. If it is asked how Europe nevertheless could have floundered on into her contemporary difficulties the answer is simple: her best minds were ignored from time to time, particularly on political questions. This could easily be shown going back some 300 years, although it would require a fairly long digression.

Popular education was first established with state support throughout Germany, Holland, and Scandinavia under the influence of the Protestant Reformation, long before the United States was founded. In 1696 Protestant Scotland decreed the establishment of public schools in every parish. Denmark in 1814 established free compulsory secular elementary education and, later in the century, established vocational public high schools. The United States was a distinct latecomer to this procession. The first compulsory-attendance law in the United States was seen in Massachusetts as recently as 1852.

But in no other large country, pro rata, are so many students now carried to the college level (twenty times more than in England or France and twenty-five times more than in Germany) although the general qualitative performance, upon analysis by increasingly sharp critics within education itself, turns out to be less than impressive. In Europe it is determined by examination of students between the ages of eleven and fourteen, who shall be prepared for college and who shall enter terminal vocational training. In the United States such a determination is never formally made.

Mass Education

"About 45 million children, youths and adults are enrolled in the schools, colleges and universities, and some 1,667,000 teachers and administrators teach and manage the educational system and institutions" in the United States.[1] In 1955–56 there were 24,290,000 enrolled in elementary public schools and 3,886,000 in private schools, with about 90 per cent of the latter in Catholic schools. In 28,000 high schools in the same year there were 6,873,000 students compared with 823,000 in mainly Catholic private secondary schools. As of October 1957, there were 8,270,000 adults in some form of class attendance, not including 942,000 part-time college students. The American system has approximately 53,000 basic administrative units, with the public system of the first two levels directed by locally elected, unpaid, highly tax-conscious school boards, mostly non-educators. There is no outside regulation of private schools and colleges and there is no central regulation of public schools. Standards, in consequence, are extremely uneven, preponderantly inclined toward the low side.

In 1959–60, according to the United States Office of Education, there were 2,011 institutions of higher learning: 585 two-year junior colleges, approaching the final levels of the *Oberschule, Gymnasium,* and *lycée* in Germany and France, 718 four-year colleges conferring the bachelor's or first professional degree, 462 institutions conferring higher degrees, including the doctorate in philosophy or science, and 41 irregularly classified institutions. Impressive numerically, only 1,058 of this total were accredited by any of six regional and various professional accrediting associations. Only a small minority have exacting entrance examinations.

There are 141 institutions recognized as universities by the United States Office of Education although 250 enterprises, some obscure affairs with faculties of as few as eight members, claim the designation. The American Association of Universities includes only thirty-nine, which in their intensive survey are called by the sociologists Caplow and McGee "the major league."[2]

Coexisting with the 141 officially classified as universities are 789 colleges and non-university special professional schools, mainly of law and medicine. Among universities and colleges are about 100 segregated Negro institutions, nearly all in the South, ironic symbols of liberalism and the humanities.

By type of control, according to the Office of Education, there are the following:

Federal:
    12, including the military academies and special schools.
State:
    375, including 50 universities and state-wide university-college systems, some 162 teachers' training colleges (formerly called normal schools) and the rest junior colleges. Mostly second- and third-class in quality.
Local, City or County:
    311, mostly junior colleges (195) but including a few self-styled universities and four-year colleges. Mostly third- and fourth-class.
Private, Nonsectarian:
    520, including the oldest and most highly rated universities and colleges. Mostly second- and third-class.
Church-related:
    494 Protestant, 294 Catholic. Mostly third- and fourth-class. Of these 193 are outright theological seminaries.
Jewish:
    5, including three rabbinical schools.

Unlike the European, American college education is usually vocational. European education beyond secondary school is technical-professional or theoretical, the latter the intellectual apex. In the United States theoretical studies are most emphasized in the old private institutions, with a small minority of state universities ever so slowly drawing abreast; general or academic studies are emphasized in private colleges, vocational generally in public institutions. Most so-called professional training in the United States is recognized by insiders as strictly vocational, mechanistic.

Of the church-related schools about 200 are called "Bible colleges" and prepare for missionary as well as pastoral work. Located for the most part in rural regions of the South and West, few conform to modern educational prescriptions. Church-related schools in general emphasize mythic as opposed to evidential thinking; they are committed to the proposition that knowledge may be self-evident, broadly intuitive, and non-objective, but are unable under challenge to point to intellectual procedures for verifying such alleged knowledge.

Illusory Ratings

But, as educational analysts well know, the fact that an institution rates generally high constitutes no uniform guarantee. The best have weak departments. And the best have a monopoly neither on the best teachers nor the best researchers because, as is pointed out by Jacques Barzun, dean at Columbia University, "the chief criteria used in making appointments are prestige and compatibility, but that prestige, which rests on scholarly achievement and not on teaching ability, is judged by a survey of opinion rather than a survey of published work: the printed material gathered or submitted for judgment is looked at but not read."[3]

What is most emphasized in American higher education is revealed by the areas of concentration of degree recipients. Most undergraduate diplomas in 1958, for example, were given in education to prospective elementary school teachers. The next largest group took degrees in business and commerce—that is, accounting, office procedures, and business field techniques such as advertising, salesmanship, merchandising, etc. The third largest group took degrees in social sciences—history, government, economics, and sociology; much of this group unquestionably planned to enter high school teaching, miscellaneous journalism, and civil service. The fourth group took degrees in engineering, about 33 per cent of the number Russia is now graduating annually.

By European standards many American studies are not of university standard: business and commerce, management, journalism, agriculture, home economics, library science, forestry, and trade and industrial training. Leading American graduate schools in the arts and sciences will not accept most of the undergraduate credits in such studies as preparation for graduate work in more complex fields, pointedly showing the present ambiguous status of the bachelor's degree. It is not a certification of general intellectual ability.

Studies and National Power

Except for engineering few of these studies relate to competitive national power in an acutely rivalrous and dangerous world. Many can hardly be called intellectual. In an age when science is considered crucial to national power and well-being only 14,352 graduates specialized in the physical sciences, with 3,182 in physics; 14,408 in the biological sciences; 6,930 in psychology; 6,924 in mathematics, and 2,981 in philosophy. Only 8,942 took non-medical doctorates and of these only 4,133 were concentrated in sciences, physical or social.[4]

"But the vast majority of the Americans are *not* university students in the European sense of the term—that is, students preparing for a profession. Actually, the percentage of young men who are preparing to be doctors, lawyers, engineers, scientists, scholars, and teachers of academic subjects is about the same in this country as in Europe—a surprisingly small percentage, by the way—something like 6 per cent of an age group."[5]

As to accreditation, it is worth noting, approximately half the institutions of higher learning lack it. And accreditation in itself is almost uniformly recognized by educators as no guarantee of academic excellence. As one educational specialist puts it, "accreditation appears to be mainly a finding that an institution is not conspicuously defective in physical and staff resources. That is obviously not enough; there are far too many accredited institutions lacking other essential elements; or, if that pessimistic view is disputed, it is at least obvious that institutions which are miles apart in quality receive the same simple approval in terms of certification to the public."[6]

The High School

James B. Conant, as a consequence of his highly selective study of the American high school, found that the preponderating small ones, with graduating classes of fewer than 100, were entirely inadequate and that there was room for improvement in the larger vocational, academic, and comprehensive or multicurricular schools. Finding no problem in the basic pattern of these, he nevertheless found what is usually true also in the first two years of college— much overload on teachers. He found as a prevalent state of affairs, duplicated on the college level it may be said in passing, teachers of English composition with as many as 180 pupils. Conant found insufficient attention to social studies in some schools, insufficient ability grouping and so on.

The situation in both public and private secondary schools is much the same as that among the colleges and universities—a pyramidal structure of four qualitative layers with the lower layers accounting for most of the pyramid.

Out of 21,000 public high schools Conant and his staff surveyed only 103, plus four urban school systems. Out of twenty-two comprehensive high schools he found eight that in his judgment fulfilled the three main objectives of such a school: adequate instruction in English and social studies, adequate non-academic elective programs, and special arrangements for the academically talented. But foreign-language study he found unsatisfactory even in the eight top schools.

The two basic reasons for popular support of education in the United States, where it is supported, is that it will (1) supposedly make chances of pecuniary success in life better for the individual and that it (2) enhances social status, puts a status-hungry middle class on a level equal to that of the educated former landed gentry of England. But the high school, in its quantitative emergence during the twentieth century, had another utility, which Robert M. Hutchins calls "custodial care." The proliferation of machinery in agriculture and industry had the effect of making "structurally unemployed" youngsters of fourteen to eighteen who had once been able to find jobs or apprenticeships. What to do with a rising tide of unplaced adolescents became a problem, and high schools provided a convenient dumping ground, at once practical and seemingly idealistic. Poorly motivated by their culturally meager home backgrounds and in overcrowded, routinized classes, most merely marked dull time until graduation.

Reflecting the gross overloading of teachers there was seen, in college as well as high school, the advent of the mechanical examination, in which the student merely checks off the right answers among a selection offered. Not only are such examinations easily graded, they can even be zipped through computing machines. All they test is the student's range of information, not his general ability to perform in the abstract symbol systems. One consequence of this system is many Ph.D.s who cannot write plain grammatical prose in their native tongue.

Deceptive Features in Mass Education

One deceptive feature about mass education in the United States is the numerous enrollment, suggesting large numbers intent upon acquiring skills of some sort, manual or intellectual. Size of total enrollment, however, does not reflect the number who drop out of high school as well as college long before they complete prescribed courses. In recent years the graduating class of high schools has been only around 20 per cent of total enrollment and of colleges only around 10 per cent. Enrollments are heaviest in the first two years.

As to retention in school, in the period 1949-57 only 58 per cent remained to graduate from high school in 1956.[7] This compares with the period 1937-45 when only 39 per cent remained to graduate. In the 1949-57 group 30 per cent entered the first year of college compared with only 12 per cent for the earlier group.

Like the size of enrollment, the fact of graduation is not unambiguously meaningful. And the ambiguity extends even to graduate degrees. Leaving to one side the stature of the degree-granting institution, no educator contends that non-medical doctorates are of equal weight as between the sciences, physical and social, and the humanities on the one hand and agriculture, business and commerce, education, forestry, home economics, library science, religion and the like on the other hand. The only degree granted in the United States unequivocal in its designation of skills and significant of uniform high minimum competence in the holder is the M.D.

In itself, again, the Ph.D., even in the sciences and humanities and issued by a leading school, is far from precise in what it indicates either about ability to teach, to investigate, or to integrate existing knowledge. This is shown by the relevance and quality of dissertations, all of which are open to public inspection. Dissertations, furthermore, even if good, are no certain portent of future scholarly productivity. Many holders of Ph.D.s are at their pinnacles in their dissertations and are never heard of again in the extension of certifiable knowledge. Robert M. Hutchins notes that 75 per cent never again publish anything. Still others, under the pretense of conducting research, engage in what is no more than academic boondoggling, collecting scattered data on tenuously obscure themes. The light they shed, if any, is of low candle power.

The only way of determining the true weight of a Ph.D. holder is by his lifetime productivity. The winning of a Nobel prize is one of a variety of possible certifications of such productivity. Some merited certifications never come in the lifetime of the scholar, a fact that provides a partial screen for the non-performers and boondogglers. If this seems like an overcritical view it should be noticed that the Ph.D. academically has a meaning similar to that of the M.D. The holder of the latter is certified as able to dispel disease, in however small measure; the holder of the former is certified as able to dispel ignorance, extend the corpus of knowledge and wisdom. Among the many strange American awards of the Ph.D., Hutchins found one Far West institution had conferred it in automobile driver training.

Impediments to the Educational Process

The failure of more enrollees to complete the undergraduate college program has many causes known to educators—lack of funds, inability or unwillingness to meet academic requirements, poor prior preparation, desire to enter the labor force and earn money, etc. But one cause of many dropouts, especially among potentially capable students, is simple boredom with confused academic programs and abstract presentations, the relevance to reality of which the institution has failed to show. While the student may be deficient in many and perhaps most instances, the institution is deficient in others, in large part because it is operating under a variety of paralyzing inhibitions. Even a first-class contemporary American university is much like a Gulliver held to earth by myriads of tiny threads tied by Lilliputians. These inhibitions are imposed from the outside by powerful anti-intellectual social elements and tend to make many colleges and universities dull, routine, bureaucratic, in whole or in spots—staffed by people evaluated from the beginning as not likely seriously to challenge dominant cultural values, people who are considered "safe."

This fact is well recognized by authorities on the sociology of the educational institution. Wrote Charles Horton Cooley, a founder of American sociology: "It is strange that we have so few men of genius on our faculties; we are always trying to get them. Of course, they must have undergone the regular academic training (say ten years in graduate study and subordinate positions) and be gentlemanly, dependable, pleasant to live with, and not apt to make trouble by urging eccentric ideas."[8]

But eccentricity has invariably and necessarily been the mark of new knowledge, from Socrates through Galileo and Newton down to Einstein, Freud, Fleming, and Keynes. If an idea is not eccentric, even grotesquely eccentric, it is certain that it is not new and probably not fruitful. What idea could be more eccentric than the notion that molds and fungi have in them powers to cure some of the most deadly diseases? Had anyone speculatively ventured such a notion as recently as 1935 he'd have been derided, as indeed Freud, Darwin, Pasteur, and Keynes were derided for their extremely eccentric ideas. Scoffing, ridicule, anger, and violent persecution have almost invariably been the portion of the person working on the frontiers of knowledge; deference has usually been willingly accorded only to the scholar playing with thoroughly embalmed ideas and truisms. In this respect the present is little different from the past.

"Institutions and genius," said Cooley as quoted by Caplow and McGee, "are in the nature of things antithetical, and if a man of genius is found living contentedly in a university, it is peculiarly creditable to both. As a rule professors, like successful lawyers or doctors, are just hard-working men of some talent." Again, "It is true in university life as elsewhere that early success, as distinguished from eventual fame, usually implies an opportunism scarcely compatible with genius."

Not only is the *average* academician, as careful studies show, justifiably timorous about expressing his views in public; he is just as inhibited in his teaching, which on the college level at least in most cases boils down to the use, well or ill, of the lecture method. The inhibition that most besets the teacher, and which in time deadens many perceptive minds that have entered teaching, relates to his range of vital allusions and obiter dicta. As everyone knows who has taught, in teaching either by lecturing or demonstration it is almost mandatory that one proceed from the familiar, which may be questionable, to the unfamiliar. Otherwise the non-specialist listener is left, if not completely in the dark, at least in a fog. Without some background at least of what the misconceptions involved may be, much reading is just over any reader's head. Listeners, like readers, bring no more than their own preconceptions with them.

How does the teacher avoid difficult or controversial problems? He has a simple way: in most jurisdictions he treats the subject superficially and in the abstract, as though it had no relation to extant states of affairs in the world. It is true that allusion may be made to actual contemporary situations, but only if they are relatively free of controversy or if he follows an approved ideological line. But it is the controversial questions that are, from the average student's point of view, the interesting ones. They are also often the most significant ones. It was in his gadfly role that Socrates was most effective. Teachers who are gadflies are not wanted in most schools. A Socrates or anyone modeled after him would not be welcome in most American colleges.

The Educational Process

The educational process, often discussed as if simple, is known to be extremely complex. A multiplicity of neurological and psychological events occur within a person who is being authentically educated. The education itself is a general response to many stimuli, not all of which by any means come within the formal educational framework. Antecedent environmental stimuli from within the home and community also operate in provoking and inhibiting responses. Genetic neurological endowment, emotional conditioning, and extracurricular cultural influences impede or aid.

What is aimed at in education? As is well known, education is variously interpreted. Much of what is commonly taken to be education, however, amounts to little more than training in some established routine, an apprenticeship served in school rather than, as formerly, in a shop. Included is the absorption of assorted facts. And while trained technicians are indispensable for complex modern society, it is highly questionable whether, merely as technicians, they are truly educated. For they are little more than were the journeymen mechanics of earlier societies, a designation that some educators even apply to many routinely competent physicians, teachers, surgeons, and lawyers.

What educators have in mind when they mean serious completed education is, generally, the trained ability to investigate and reason analytically and creatively against a background of reliable information or evidence in both general and special fields. What passes for education in some schools and school systems is what educators term indoctrination or the habituation of the mind to move—sometimes in disregard or in the absence of evidence—in predetermined grooves. Forthright devotees of this method, which some secularists also practice, are the Catholic and many other religious sects. Soviet Russia is also an adherent of the method, although the Soviet approach is fundamentally split, for it must seek to encourage critical thinking in the area of the physical sciences. Its social science, however, and even much of its biology and psychology rest on Marxist-Leninist dogma and abound in strained interpretations.

In practice Russian scientists must ignore this dogma, which at least formally also frames the Russian physical sciences, because the process of change in nature—nuclear fission and fusion, for example, and photosynthesis—simply does not take place "dialectically" as prescribed by Marx, Engels, and Lenin. Nor does social change take place "dialectically." While the Russian dogmatic bias does not prevent scientists from emulating and accepting what is done abroad, it does limit new discoveries. Soviet Russia will never be a creative fountainhead so long as it retains its dogmatic commitments. Marx, far from having said the last word, represents only a transitional stage in the evolution of social science.

As to what it takes to induce a student to develop trained ability to investigate and reason analytically and creatively, not much is certainly known. It is evident that the student must be motivated, must develop an aggressive desire to study. Some seem endowed with such an attitude, others appear to have been conditioned by accidental features of their upbringing. But often a single experience, such as encountering a stimulating teacher or reading a certain book, or living through a set of disturbing experiences, such as participation in a desperate war or social or personal calamity, will open a person previously impervious to the formal educational process. As a result of such an experience or prior conditioning the student becomes an autodidact, a self-educator. For it has been well said that nobody is truly educated who is not self-educated, either in school or out. Neither schools nor educators can educate anybody who is not aggressively reaching out for education. All they can do is supply the framework, the guidelines and often ineffective stimuli.

By his own testimony John Dewey, regarded by some as America's major philosopher and educational theorist, was not awakened by the educational or environmental stimuli of the nineteenth century and remained unawakened until, reaching outside the curriculum in his fourth year at the University of Vermont, he read Thomas Henry Huxley. Thereafter he became his own educator while working for advanced degrees and beyond. Dewey's experience, variants of which are reported by others, justifies educators in the belief that some intellectual awakenings come late, some even after formal studies have been left behind. Many American college graduates, as educators well know, are never awakened and instead of being fully educated are mere Babbitt-like diploma holders, addicted to class-reunion jollifications, who clamor for winning football teams and protest against professors who make public utterances in violation of what John Kenneth Galbraith terms "conventional wisdom."

The educational process aims at inculcating the ability to make better personal choices and decisions in a free society where poor choices and decisions are being tirelessly argued for by advertisers, public relations counselors, compulsive traditionalists and the like. But, far beyond this, it is basically intended to develop facility in (1) theory formation expressed in the number- and letter-symbol systems and (2) the application of such theory to the management of materials and/or people, including oneself. As such management, commonly known as practice, may be socially or individually beneficial, neutral, or harmful, it is subject to evaluation by the educated—that is, to value-theory analysis—in order to determine whether the application is humanly good or bad, right or wrong, efficient or inefficient, progressive or retrogressive, etc., and whether it ought or ought not to take place. Usually this is the professional task of the philosopher, although in a free society anyone may play the role and make judgments in terms of nothing more than immediate personal convenience. Such egocentric judgments, it is interesting to observe, need to be attired in theoretical dress in order to command attention. Pseudo philosophy or ideology consequently abounds.

Theory is often popularly decried by the so-called hardheaded practical man although it is difficult to find any normal person who does not live within a framework of at least tacitly assumed theories. The only point is: are the theories correct, economically accounting for the underlying facts? Mere pursuit of individual unrelated facts is a waste, without any guiding theory, whether done in the field or via books. A sound theory not only explains millions of apparently unrelated facts but at a single sweep points the way to uncovering millions of relevant facts previously unsuspected.

Stimuli to Self-scrutiny

Although professional educators have long been aware of weaknesses in American education, several events in the past two decades have served to cast doubt on its general effectiveness.

1. The demonstrated success of nuclear physicists with the first

atomic bombs pointed up the fact to the sophisticated that success was attributable mainly to theory developed by Europeans. German successes with jet-propulsion rockets and other devices reinforced this general conclusion. Dr. Robert H. Goddard, American pioneer in rocketry, had been—typically—ignored in his own country.

2. The rapid Russian applications in nuclear physics and rocketry, shown by a country regarded as technically backward, provided more instruction along the same lines. But doubts about American educational supremacy could well have been expressed much earlier—when nuclear, genetic, psychoanalytic, evolutionary, neomathematical, logistic, and Keynesian economic theory were first made known to the world.

3. Another development that called much of American education into question, this one internal, was the heavy postwar college attendance under the Servicemen's Readjustment Act of 1944 (GI Bill). Many veterans, some by their own testimony not very promising in high school, consistently scored so high in intramural examinations as to cast reflection on the curricular standards of the colleges. What educators call "spoon feeding" had long been a feature of American college education, with the intention of most students before World War II being not to exert themselves or excel in studies. In the eastern "Ivy League" schools the ideal grade aimed at was what students called a "gentleman's C." Only students looked at by the majority as personally peculiar, referred to disparagingly as "grinds" and "grade hunters," took an interest in studies and achieved high academic standings.

What probably was the strongest educational spur in the military experience was the marked distinction in the armed forces between officers and men. Brought up in a supposedly egalitarian society wherein outward distinctions except those of money are blurred almost beyond recognition, men in the armed forces were suddenly disagreeably confronted with the fact of marked functional distinctions among personnel that were graded and expressed by insignia, pay, privileges, immunities, and deference accorded by rank. And the direct distinguishing feature between the "dogfaces" of the ranks and the officers was that the latter were products either of the military academies or the colleges. Not only did the United States Government in a time of peril recognize this distinction, it reinforced it at every opportunity. The officers were an obviously privileged class. And it was to wipe out the objective basis of this distinction that many soldiers, previously undistinguished as students but now alert to realities, set enviable academic records after the war.

Society as a whole is arranged in a hierarchy much like the army, only with many functional distinctions blurred. But society is similarly functionally constituted of officers and lower ranks. As in the army, so in peacetime society some find themselves classified as officers who really belong in the lower ranks; and some in the lower ranks could, with training, be good officers.

4. The postwar population boom, by straining school facilities to overflowing, in itself provoked a critical look at the system in view of demands for costly expansion.

5. The unification of Europe, now under way, by its economic pressure requiring an augmentation of American economic and supporting technical activity, also puts pressure on the American educational system to produce more upper-level personnel. For example, the electronics and chemical industries, as well as others, under pressure from more effective European competition require more persons with high-level skills to meet world competition. The United States can no longer proceed complacently behind protective tariffs, as in the past, unless it wishes to be edged out of world markets, with disastrous effects on its balance-of-payments position. Adequately mobilized trained intelligence is needed for new world conditions shaping up, and only an adequate school system can supply such intelligence.

Educational Lopsidedness

That American education is extremely lopsided in availability as well as quality is evident at once if we consider the outlay by states per pupil for primary and secondary schools, ranging from $426 in 1956 for New York down to $158 for backward Mississippi.[9] Northeastern private-school tuition at the same time was around $1,000 or more per year, primary and secondary.

The median for all states was $294, and well below that line were all the culturally retarded southern states, including oil-rich Texas and Oklahoma, and Maine, Vermont, New Hampshire, Idaho, and a scattering of others. In the upper twenty-five were such relatively poor states as Rhode Island and Wyoming. Although poverty, comparative in some of these instances, is often pleaded as the reason for the low quality of education, there is no American state unable to afford education as good as that offered in Iceland, Denmark, Finland, or Norway, where the levels are relatively high.

College and university standards, public and private, are to some extent revealed by scales of faculty salaries, all extremely low by prevailing American income standards. Many students immediately upon graduation enjoy higher rates of pay in industry than the faculty average in most colleges.

Although most of the lower-grade universities and colleges keep their pay schedules conspiratorially secret, the American Association of University Professors for several years has collected as many as are available, some 20 per cent. Many institutions have an average pay scale below that for factory workers, which as of June 1961, was at an annual rate of $4,908. In only eighty-five institutions, according to the A.A.U.P., are the average salaries as of 1961 at $8,500 per annum or above, with Harvard University paying $12,000 and higher and Massachusetts Institute of Technology $11,500 to $11,999. Although most institutions decline to report, the lowest admitted average salary for a full professor in 1960–61 was $5,200 and the lowest admitted average for all ranks combined was $4,631. Teachers' colleges and church-related schools were especially low in their rates of compensation. Public universities and liberal-arts colleges paid less than their private counterparts. In some an extraordinarily heavy class load and hourly schedule accompanies low pay.[10]

The pay of scientists, too, runs at similar low levels, according to the National Science Foundation, rarely rising above the $6,000–$15,000 range.[11]

"There are dozens of liberal arts colleges which pay average salaries as low as $3,000 per year and minimum salaries much lower still," writes Paul Woodring, educational consultant to the Fund for the Advancement of Education of the Ford Foundation. He characterizes such payment as "starvation wages."[12]

Actual average pay for teaching ranges even far below gross figures in a goodly number of institutions through the device of having graduate students teach freshmen and sophomores, even in such crucial subjects as mathematics and logic. While such experience may be valuable for graduate students, it is oftentimes of questionable value to the undergraduates. And even the A.A.U.P. figures relate only to full-time faculty. If part-time faculty is added—some of it, such as outside doctors in the medical schools, serving for no pay at all—one finds that the average compensation for teaching in the universities and colleges sinks abysmally low.

There is a cultural bias, inherited from the eighteenth century, that books and teaching ought to be inexpensively available to all, especially to the poor. Through books and teaching, it was felt, the general cultural level would be lifted. This bias, perhaps laudable in itself, survives as an anomaly, a cultural lag, in the "affluent society" when there are no longer any institutionalized poor. And those who are poor by circumstance—through personal deficiency or illness, residence in blighted economic areas or the possession of more children than they can support—are seldom interested either in reading or education. But teachers are expected to subsidize in part this anomalous bias. At one time many teachers, regarding their work as uplifting humanity, were idealistically willing to sacrifice themselves. But now, as they see many of their former students proceeding to enrich themselves in a money-oriented world, they are increasingly soured and turn to other pursuits. But ingenious college-faculty members are far from absolutely limited by low pay. A number derive supplementary income from writing profitable textbooks, lecturing to lay audiences for fees, editing and reading for commercial publishers, functioning as industry consultants (especially lucrative for professors in technological departments and schools) and advisers to governmental bodies, inventing mechanical and electronic devices that in some cases have earned millions, compiling myriads of anthologies, writing novels and plays, engaging in private tutoring, entertaining on television, conducting independent research for private agencies and the like. Time and energy so spent, it goes without saying, is obviously subtracted from necessary preparation for teaching or academic research. In known instances full professors engage in humbler income-supplementing occupations, such as part-time selling, summer-camp counseling, housebuilding, dog breeding and the like. Some few are shrewd investors, even extensive stock market operators.

As the elite of the teaching profession, college and university faculties are paid more in general than elementary- or secondary-school teachers (except for a few of the latter with long tenure in advanced jurisdictions, mainly a few residential suburbs near large northern cities—New York, Cleveland, Los Angeles, Chicago—and eastern private schools). Public grade-school teachers in a few advanced jurisdictions are paid up to $10,000, a sum by no means very high when one considers the crucial role a teacher may play in orienting many children toward future educational achievement. Salaries of administrators in the school and college system, the intermediaries between teachers and the public, run somewhat higher than those of teachers.

Another broad approach that suggests much about the kind of instruction available in an institution is the student-faculty ratio. At Harvard it is less than 3 to 1, at California Institute of Technology 3 to 1, and at Massachusetts Institute of Technology 5 to 1. The farther it is below 10 to 1, everything else being equal, the more favorable a general sign it is. Yet a ratio of 20 to 1 is not unusual as one descends the academic pyramid. In some very large municipal institutions, particularly junior colleges, there is a ratio of 30 to 1. Combined with teaching schedules that often go well beyond the maximum prescribed of twelve per week, some as high as 18 hours, there is an insupportable load on teachers. As the load cannot be carried, it is the students who are defrauded, receiving only the vaguest of vague outlines of an education. All a teacher can do under such circumstances is to go through the motions of teaching. With the best will in the world he cannot be effective.

When veterans flooded the schools after World War II one of the major universities had classes of 800 in introductory economics, presented in a huge gymnasium equipped with loudspeakers. Another major university had *graduate* "seminars" of 100 in philosophy! Since the postwar influx of students abated, conditions are not this abnormal but many schools have obviously overpopulated classes, to the detriment of educational quality.

In many overcrowded high schools the best the teacher can do is to maintain some semblance of order in the classes.

Academic Freedom

It is well recognized in educational theory that unless the teacher is free to adopt methods and procedures he is not going to have much success in developing people able to investigate and reason independently. The term academic freedom is almost as complex as that of freedom itself, being very little restricted by the adjective, and about the term in its broadly accepted usages there is much illusion even among academicians themselves. The term as it is used does not provide, as it obviously should, that students should be free from indoctrination, against which the immature are helpless and as a result of which very many are severely crippled intellectually for life. Public policy not only permits various kinds of indoctrination in the schools, public and private, but positively endorses it.

Students aside, academic freedom relates to teachers. It is defined by Arthur O. Lovejoy in the *Encyclopedia of the Social Sciences* as "the freedom of the teacher or research worker in higher institutions of learning to investigate and discuss the problems of his science and to express his conclusions, whether through publication or in the instruction of students, without interference from political or ecclesiastical authority, or from the administrative officials of the institution in which he is employed, unless his methods are found by qualified bodies of his own profession to be clearly incompetent or contrary to professional ethics."

Interference, historically and contemporaneously, has come most massively in descending order of emphasis from (1) the clergy in their role as promoters of mythic thinking and opponents of evidential thinking, (2) politicians, often acting in concert with clergy, (3) representatives of diverse economic groups, mainly the wealthy in relation to private institutions but also the less wealthy, especially professional people and officious alumni in relation to public institutions and (4) various free-lance proponents of some traditionalist view felt to be threatened by the free utterance of novel propositions.

While academic freedom has historically been at direct issue mostly in specific cases, extensively studied,[13] the cases themselves serve merely to reveal a prevalent underlying general state of affairs. For faculties, knowing that what they say may be made a matter of issue and wishing like most people to pursue lives of tranquillity, usually have merely adjusted themselves to the demands of administrators for conformity to orthodox views. Faculties, furthermore, have through veiled psychological coercion been extensively deprived of the right of ordinary citizens to express themselves freely outside the classroom on matters of public concern.

In order to avoid actual tests of academic freedom most colleges exercise extreme vigilance in the hiring of young instructors and assistant professors, in most cases mainly with a view to eliminating those who show themselves as temperamentally independent-minded and possibly likely to question conventional opinions. As a result most of the newcomers are cultural conformists as far as this can be established by external scrutiny although some few, as history attests, are led by their inquiries out of conformist molds and may in time become iconoclasts. Temperamental non-conformists find placement more difficult until they learn required staid demeanor and reserved attitudes. Cleverness, sparkling formulations at the expense of prevalent misconceptions, ability to stir classes of students out of dogmatic slumbers and send them questioning to their elders are regarded as synonymous with shallowness and are no more wanted in the vast majority of institutions than they were in Athens in the days of Socrates. In substandard colleges the high turnover rate of young instructors and assistant professors, many not even finishing a single year, stems in the main from the initiative of the administration in getting rid of all who incite the interest of students. By way of illustration, a private field report from a professor's wife at a southern state college who attends classes to extend her own knowledge concludes that the more interesting a new man is, the more quickly he is dropped, and that she has learned far more from transient new people than from the established faculty.

Gross lapses from academic freedom in the United States have usually been shown only in comparatively isolated individual cases, leaving the impression in many minds that where it is not specifically shown to be absent, academic freedom prevails. But most teachers in most jurisdictions are afraid to test their alleged academic freedom, feeling fairly sure they would court dismissal or unpleasant indirect reprisals. As the administrators of any organization know, it is not difficult to harass subordinates by a variety of apparently innocent procedures.

How the method of academic intimidation operates was shown recently, according to the New York *Times* of November 26, 1961, in connection with the formation of the Southern Association of Intelligence Agents, whose president was named as Lieutenant H. A. Poole, chief of the security division of the Georgia Bureau of Investigation. While concerned with traditional types of criminal offenders, Lieutenant Poole said, his association was also concerned about proponents of racial tolerance. The members of the association, supporters of racial segregation in public facilities, also believe that Communist infiltration in education is a problem in the South, according to Lieutenant Poole. To segregationists, communism is invariably equated with advocacy of civil rights, although Communists, wherever they have authority, do not recognize civil rights. To traditionalists in general communism is equated with all proposals of reform and planned institutional change.

"When you are dealing with educational institutions you are dealing with dynamite," said the lieutenant. "They've got this academic freedom."

Then, the *Times* report continued, "He said the best course in handling an educator with a record of Communist activity was to submit evidence to the educator's superiors. The educator could then be 'eased out' after his contract and tenure had expired, said the lieutenant."

Here was a frank statement about the method that has long been employed, more or less covertly, by many other associations, mainly religious, business, or industrial. Some of the latter have even been caught paying to have their propaganda incorporated as certified knowledge in textbooks. All power-oriented ideological groups everywhere are identical in their aim to infiltrate the educational process with their own ideologies, and look upon the same effort in others as unwarranted intrusion. It is the basic and divergent purpose of education, however, to instruct in methods of independent thinking, without partiality toward any ideology. Education, properly pursued, is non-ideological.

It has been noted, and is often stressed, that Russian academicians function under the handicap of dogma imposed by a totalitarian state, but it is rarely if ever noticed that the American academician in most schools is similarly handicapped. A difference for the American is that the imposition is not total, an advantage. But the Russian, on the other hand, has the advantage of functioning under a clear line of restraint, whereas the American must ordinarily exercise considerable ingenuity to find which restraints are enforced in each jurisdiction. Some schools will drop anyone without long-delayed tenure who touches upon anything political whatever. Whereas the Russian must be aware of only one "line," the American must often consider the "lines" of all the pressure groups, succumbing in the process to intellectual paralysis.

The blame for conditions has been directed chiefly against school administrators. For, as Lovejoy writes, "While ambitious administrative officers chiefly concerned for future endowments have not seldom imposed upon teachers in these subjects [the social sciences] an unwholesome and unbecoming timidity and subservience, there are some indications that this condition is becoming rare. Although exception must be made of certain sections of the country . . . freedom of thought and speech in universities is growing wider and less insecure." The recent Lazarsfeld-Thielens study (note 13) shows the condition is far from rare.

But administrators are themselves employees of someone else and must do as they are required or get out. Even university presidents have been discharged or forced to resign for refusing to bow to pressure. Many cases could be cited.

The university and college administrator is called upon at the highest levels to fill a difficult role, requiring all the wiles of the most adroit diplomat. At best he must protect his faculty and at the same time satisfy his employers, represented by either a board of private trustees or the educational agency of a local government division. These latter are only rarely enlightened and sensitive to the proper role of a university in a dangerous world. The easiest way for the administrator is to defer to headstrong trustees and officials, but in doing this he comes to preside over an institution whose creative edge is dulled; most administrators, however, like others seeking relative tranquillity, clearly take this road.

Even if his job is not at stake the administrator knows his quest for funds, either private or public, will be made more difficult if propositions or observations expressed by his faculty anger influential outsiders. And any new or unfamiliar observation—outside fields such as physics and chemistry, to which society has now become accustomed—is almost sure to draw blood somewhere. The private administrator is dependent for new funds not merely upon independent wealthy donors but upon alumni, many of whom were hostile to the educational process while in school, others of whom are myth-minded, and still others of whom have acquired special economic interests seemingly endangered by the approach of new knowledge; wealthy sophisticated donors are more apt to give funds freely than many rank-and-file alumni upset by new teachings. The public college administrator must keep an eye on the legislator—state, county, or municipal—who has an even more pluralistic and usually ignorant constituency to be worried about.

Intrusions of outsiders and interference with teaching is much more frequent than commonly supposed. In the South the fundamentalist clergy ride close and vigilant herd even on the non-sectarian public colleges and universities. In the North, Catholic clergy make their wishes felt in many pliant hinterland non-sectarian schools by advising young communicants whether or not to enroll, either in the school or in certain courses. Catholic clergy even in advanced jurisdictions sometimes take it upon themselves to remonstrate with public high school teachers of history, a subject on which the Church is particularly sensitive.

Intrusion in the hinterlands also comes from business interests, particularly with respect to economics and public economic policy. In many places the teacher who does not want to be questioned with ever so patient consideration by corporation representatives or deans, as though he were an errant child, presents his subject as abstractly as possible, losing the opportunity of engaging the interest of average students. Such interviews are almost always on a cordial level, superficially, but the sinews of steel are always plainly evident underneath the velvet glove. The effect of the interviews where they are allowed is to cramp the style of the teacher.

The difficulty arises from the notion of laymen that it is the duty of teachers to lay down only conventionally approved judgments. Even if this were possible with complex subject matter, it is doubtful whether it is good educational method. Students are much more likely to react by thinking independently if they believe that what a teacher says exemplifies aberrant judgment. Some highly effective teachers use statements they do not personally believe as incitive gambits to arouse attention and discussion. A teacher enacting the role of the devil's advocate is far more likely to stimulate independent thought and extensive out-of-class checking of background than one who purveys approved judgments on display every day in hackneyed newspaper editorials. But in most parts of the country the teacher enacting this role is almost always sure to draw intrusive attention from outside, and from the administration. What most outside interests want is indoctrination, not incitement to thought, so indoctrination prevails.

Teachers have adjusted themselves to the demands made upon them and at all stages can be found in levels of performance corresponding in stratified results pretty much to that of the institutions. At the very top are to be found an inspired few. Next come what might be termed dedicated reflective teachers, a somewhat larger group. The largest group of all is probably the third, the bureaucrats, who conduct themselves routinely according to administrative demands, never extend themselves, and judiciously cut as many corners as possible in self-protection. At the bottom are the outright cynics and timeservers, long ago convinced that theirs is a hopeless role in a hopeless cause. When they succeed in getting transfers to more favorable jurisdictions, cynics and bureaucrats often rise to higher levels of performance, showing the influence of environment.

Various administrative devices exist for keeping faculties quiescent, particularly with respect to public remarks. One seemingly innocent way is to inquire mildly whether the questioned remark relates to the speaker's specialized discipline, by implication limiting the area of competence of the scholar. What, though, are the disciplinary boundaries of logic, psychology, history, literature, philosophy or, for that matter, the sciences? The man of learning, as we have noted, is properly interested not only in narrow fact-gathering theory but also in proper applications, which relate to the world.

Every discipline relates in some way to politics, economics, and public policy, a point finally discerned by ivory-tower physicists, who after the war founded the Association of Atomic Scientists to agitate in public about policy with respect to the applications of atomic energy. Every discipline could well have a similar association. The attempt to limit academicians to a narrow disciplinary approach is merely a fatuous attempt to divide the world as though it were a school. Although the learned specialist may not be more competent than others with respect to politics and public policy, there is *something* he knows that makes him more competent in a certain area than the layman. Even heads of government increasingly turn to learned men for their specialized opinions.

By practically quelling all except formally presented, laboriously buttressed, and popularly unintelligible views of professors, the American system keeps public discussion and enlightenment from enrichment and public mental stimulation, if not instruction, to a minimum. The advent of television, however, with its insatiable demand for novelty, has in recent years to some extent brought professors cautiously out into the open. What is shaping up here as a possibility for the future is a multifaceted public seminar on the world and its erratic ways.

What shows most clearly the restraints under which academicians function and brings into the open the illusions about a wide range of academic freedom is the fact that many well-certified teachings are contrary to law. An academician cannot, as a member of a tax-exempt or tax-supported institution, with impunity disobey law. The teaching of evolution is forbidden by statute in Arkansas, Mississippi, and Tennessee. Marriage between persons of different ethnic stocks, subject to the unscientific concept of "miscegenation," is forbidden in a very considerable number of states; any teacher holding that this law is groundless in nature challenges and derides the law. In many states, too, marriage is permitted for girls as young as fourteen; teachers who question the sociological wisdom of this permission are in the position of questioning the law, which is rarely tolerated outside top institutions. The sociological value of divorce or birth control cannot be asserted in some states, and sociological criticism of penal practices are in many states also taboo.

Race doctrines and laws to enforce them may not be questioned in most southern institutions. Teachers who have questioned them have been dismissed. Unscientific religious observances and taboos based on the authority of the Bible can be questioned in very few places. Even in advanced schools it is considered bad form to make a point of stressing the mythical character of biblical presentations; it is the mark of the "sound" scholar, however, to emphasize the role of the Bible in Judeo-Christian (a euphemism for Judeo-Greek) culture, but without pointing out that most of its role as far as knowledge or social improvement are concerned has been negative, an impediment.

In general, religious dogma is exempt from scrutiny in most institutions, public or private. Where it is examined at all it is rarely subjected to systematic critical analysis. Religionists, however, are permitted free and extensive academic rein to make crass misstatements about science, the scope of scientific method, and about philosophy and to recommend prayer as a way of influencing events.

It has been pointed out that while elaborate procedures exist for removing teachers under charges of wrongdoing, there are no such procedures for removing trustees and administrators. And while teachers have violated laws, subjecting themselves to removal, there are proportionately far fewer law violators among teachers than among trustees of colleges and universities, not a few of whom have turned out to be large-scale embezzlers and fraudulent operators in outside enterprises. Upon conviction, the latter merely has his resignation quietly accepted, without such fanfare as often accompanies the resignation of a teacher in only remotely similar circumstances.

Even if the university were to be made completely free academically, without various intangible and subtle restraints, it is not likely that it would play anything like a revolutionary cultural or social role.

Here we touch upon an illusion common to academicians that the Academy is a front-runner in the quest for knowledge. Historically it has never been in the forefront. The university is actually, even at its best and most liberal, a stronghold of traditionalism, venerating the past and the established, reluctantly paying some attention to the present, and closing its eyes almost entirely to the future. This emphasis it must sometime reverse, and soon. It must, in other words, ally itself with prognostics.

In the monumental *The American College,* a collaborative study sponsored by the Society for the Psychological Study of Social Issues, the editor, Professor Nevitt Sanford of Stanford University, writes that "when there is a movement toward reform in a college it is the collective faculty who usually seem to be dragging their feet. . . . College presidents, students, trustees, foundations, large donors, influential citizens, and even State Legislatures have from time to time sought progressive change only to find themselves effectively blocked by faculties."[14] But these same faculties—many members of which are as Babbittian, illiberal, intolerant, prejudiced, and bureaucratic as are broad sections of the alumni—were originally selected by each institution, so it is clearly the system and the society behind it that are to blame. But a changing society, with altered needs, must inevitably produce new types of faculties.

Sociologists David Riesman and Christopher Jencks in their contribution to the volume characterize students' college experience as a mere initiation rite and the college as "the watch-dog of the upper-middle class," to which the colleges cater by copying each other "in order to be sure of keeping their programs acceptable as certificates of respectability." Owing to this well-known orientation toward economic and status benefits, Professor Sanford remarks, they fail to educate properly "the great mass of the uncommitted, the vocationally oriented, the anti-intellectual—those who are on the road to becoming the 'alumni.'"

Self-extolled as liberal and humanist, American colleges paradoxically produce hordes of alumni unshakably committed to a narrow Chamber of Commerce scale of values. Their outlook on the world and human destiny is preponderantly in terms of commercial opportunity, a fact noticeable even in the case of many professionals such as physicians and lawyers. By the pragmatic test of their typical product, American universities and colleges are most strikingly shown to be deficient.

Originally a medieval construction, the university is a development of Plato's Academy, Aristotle's Lyceum, and the Hellenistic school at Alexandria. In the medieval period it consisted of the faculties of law, medicine, theology, and religious philosophy. During the Renaissance it resisted strongly the revival of classical learning. Once it had finally accepted the classics in its program in the form of the humanities, it resisted for a good two centuries the inclusion of developed science and technology. Physics, chemistry, and geology were nurtured outside university halls (although sometimes by university people) and it was not until the nineteenth century that the universities added them, engineering and, later, biology to the curriculum. They were similarly slow to take up the social sciences, to which university people had made contributions like those of Adam Smith under the tangential rubric of moral philosophy. The foundations of the social sciences, like those of the physical sciences, were all laid outside the university. Most of modern philosophy was produced outside the universities and often by non-university people.

Except very recently in physics and chemistry, most of the great breakthroughs in the quest for knowledge have taken place at the hands of free-lance inquirers, amateurs, or persons working under government auspices in special research institutes. It is a comparatively recent idea, and limited to only a few, that the university should be in the forefront of the quest for knowledge. As most of what the university purveys was developed outside university auspices the university is far more a repository, like a library, than a research institute. Ironically, too, much of what it now certifies as knowledge was rejected by the university of an earlier day.

Under the ideal of stimulating research the universities are clearly shaping for themselves a new role in a world of change, but the research they promote, it is stressed by academicians themselves, is mostly of a part-time nature, conducted by teachers in their spare time. At some time the universities, particularly in undergraduate divisions, will have to choose between teaching and developing new knowledge, perhaps establishing research institutes separate from their classrooms and staffed by postdoctoral people who do only research.[15]

CHAPTER X

THE FUTURE OF EDUCATION

With a general sketch of the educational institution now in mind we may proceed to consider what changes are inevitably in store for it. By "inevitably" is meant changes that will have to be made, whatever impulses there may be to contrary action, if a range of effects from extreme social discomfort to near-disaster is to be averted or minimized. Concededly, not every minute detail of change predicted is required to avert undesirable effects.

Ever since the first classroom was opened in the United States the educational institution has been changing—sometimes slowly, sometimes rapidly. Some changes introduced have been conscious, planned. But preceding all such consciously planned changes there have been massive unconscious changes induced by outside events.

The general issue now facing the schools is one of hyperconscious change in adjustment to all the varied cultural and social changes that have taken place in some three decades, the requirement for what MacIver calls the "dynamic assessment."[1]

What should be done? A conceivable decision to do nothing would merely insure unguided change, the change of steady deterioration, deepening confusion and spreading chaos. The dominant cultural bias and threats from the environment together require an *effective* school. But effective in what sense? Decision, when it is made, must relate to this question.

The "dynamic assessment" usually takes place, according to our theory of social change, only when crisis or an obviously impending crisis threatens. But crisis, although it may be long in developing as historians later trace it, usually bursts into view suddenly. A general crisis stemming in large part from insufficient educational preparation could not be resolved overnight. Education, we must notice, requires planning. Behind every educational program there is a theory, often unvoiced, about what sort of general future confronts the individual and his society. The educator, in mapping his program, is making a prediction, but rarely explicitly.

As part of the assessment, criticisms are now being freely made, proposals for conscious change formulated, both by educators and non-educators. American education, under the impact of critical domestic and foreign changes, is on the threshold of a root-and-branch reorganization. Criticism from within its own walls foretells the nature of many changes to come.

Factors Forcing Reorganization

Three main factors can be discerned in this pending reorganization, as follows:

1. The postwar birth rate lifted U. S. population from 132 million in 1940 to 180 million in 1960, according to the Census Bureau. For 1980 a population of somewhere between 230 million and 272½ million is officially forecast. By the year 2000 a population of 300 million is easily attainable. Although for a variety of reasons one may be sure the population curve will flatten out and dip, there is no way of knowing just where the turning point will be. These predictions assume, of course, that thermonuclear bombardment will not occur. Between 1940 and 1960 the net reproduction rate nearly doubled, bringing the population under fourteen years of age to more than fifty-two million. At every level, except in private schools and private upper-level colleges and universities where enrollment is limited, there is now overcrowding, confusion and serious dilution of educational effectiveness. Even with special incentives such as training scholarships only some 20 per cent of the needed additional teachers are in sight.

2. Just as important as this quantitative factor, if not more so, is the factor of quality. Established general levels of quality can obviously not be maintained under this inundation. Education for the average and below-average student in the remaining decades of this century is very obviously not going to be up to the level, say, of 1920-40. On the other hand, the "country club" college is clearly on the way out. But for a larger segment than ever before it is going to be better and, what is more, is going to be facilitated by hitherto lacking economic support. For the nation, as never before, is in need of more and better brainpower, specialized and generalized, to cope with its many internal and external problems. If some of these prob-

lems are not solved, and some sooner rather than later, the nation will find itself in serious straits. Either a quantitative insufficiency of specialists or qualitatively insufficient specialists could well bring tribulation, as our insufficiency of adequately trained political personnel has repeatedly shown with respect to foreign policy since 1914.

Foreign policy aside, if graduates of the engineering schools had to take examinations for licenses as doctors do, so one is informed by employers of engineers, a large segment could not qualify. Many such, although hired, are earmarked at once by their employers as destined to be no more than routine submanagers, salesmen of engineering products, maintenance supervisors and the like. All along the line except in medicine, in fact, there is incessant complaint against a substantial proportion of specialists turned out by the colleges, and complaints, too, about the conspicuous inability of many college graduates to write English correctly, speak foreign languages, be conversant with culturally pivotal ideas, spell frequently used words, do ordinary arithmetic, think logically (a conspicuous defect), and be at least abreast of common knowledge. Heads of large enterprises, even of the government at times, are unable to write their own speeches. Many can't speak extemporaneously on any subject or conduct coherent press interviews. The story is told of a professor participating recently in the oral examination of Ph.D. candidates in botany at a leading university who surprised them unpleasantly by asking each "to identify as specifically as possible an assortment of things, events, and people, including the Renaissance, the Reformation, the Monroe Doctrine, Voltaire, Plato, and the Magna Carta. Less than half could identify either Voltaire or Plato. Only six of the fifteen could identify the Renaissance and only five, the Reformation. Most amazing of all, only two could identify the Magna Carta."[2]

Such basic informational gaps, far from rare among diploma holders, indicate serious flaws in the education of these fairly typical candidates prior to their entry into a field of specialization.

3. The third general factor underlying the pending reorganization of American education is the need to supply entirely new categories of personnel for a labor force soon destined to be radically reconstituted to meet the needs of an increasingly mechanized and automated society. The process of machine industrialization has repeatedly made demands upon more and more people for complex

skills. While there has been room in the industrial system for more and more of the unskilled, transformed from farm laborers and fishermen to factory operatives, the state of development is now at a point beyond which there is going to be increasing technological discrimination *against* the unskilled. The thoroughly automated society will require that a much larger proportion of the population than in the past must have specialized skills to offer in the labor market if they are going to be employed. Such skills will place them in the middle and upper social strata. The categories of employment that are going to be severely shrunken are factory, office, and sales workers, at present accounting for nearly half the labor force. They are going to be subject to a shrinkage just as significant as that which has brought farm workers down from the vast majority to a small minority. In their place will be seen skilled service workers, perhaps most of them government employees.

The New Upper Labor Force

The demand for new vocational and professional categories and for increases in some existent categories, reflecting new divisions of labor, is bound to alter many areas of scholastic concentration in the colleges. Let us look at the broad trends:

(a) There will be a very heavy and steady increase in the number of those specializing in teaching simply in order to keep abreast of the population boom. Whether there will be more than a pro rata increase in the number of teachers will depend upon whether a substantial effort is made to improve American education as a whole in depth and in over-all effectiveness. Unless the country, by some fluke, enjoys farsighted political leadership over a long period, it is a virtual certainty that the system will not be improved as a whole in depth and effectiveness because the preponderance of public thinking, notwithstanding many sentimental assertions to the contrary, has never favored the best possible and attainable education for every child and youth. Contrary to such assertions, large sections of the people and their local leaders do not even now believe in anything more than a poultice education, acquired as cheaply as possible and sufficient merely to maintain surface appearances. The idea conveyed by some surveys that there is profound soul searching by extended strata of the people about thoroughgoing education and its future is completely erroneous. Most of what extensive worry there is about education in the United States is about the cost of maintaining a superficial minimum.

As only about 20 per cent of college graduates at present intend to enter teaching, there will not be enough teachers over the near term to handle the population overflow even on the established low level of today. Money can't hire non-existent people. The untrained, as often in the past, will infiltrate the ranks of teachers.

Before tax-conscious traditionalists ceased sabotaging improvement of education, severe crisis would have to demonstrate very clearly the need for something better. But in the nature of the case such demonstration, if it were ever clearly made, could come only after it was too late. It would be left to historians to record that the United States failed at some crucial moment under internal or external test because its education had proved to be too superficial for too many in a highly complex world. In relation to its own economic base the Russian educational system is at present far more extensive than the American.

(b) By the years 2000–25 there will be a virtually total decline in graduates specializing in business and commerce. Such divisions of the universities will very probably gradually evolve into schools of general social, political, and economic administration, requiring concentration in economics, psychology, sociology, philosophy, and related subjects. Office management will be the least part of such an administrative curriculum and gone will be courses in salesmanship, accounting, advertising and the like. So-called merchandising courses will be very altered in content or transferred to the department of performing arts if they are retained at all. How, the plain man may well ask, can anyone say with such seeming brash certainty that courses in salesmanship, accounting, and advertising will be eliminated? How can one say that many persons even now preparing for such employment will find difficulty finding jobs after graduation?

Technological innovation will be responsible for the eliminations, which are gradually occurring even now. At this time a single comedian on a television network in New York City can induce more people to buy more merchandise in an hour of effort than 10,000 traveling salesmen working three months. And television selling is now being done by dozens of people's jesters. At the same time over-the-counter salesmen are steadily being eliminated by self-service stores, which increasingly include even department stores. In many departments one merely selects goods from well-marked counters and takes them to a centrally placed cashier. The tasks of accountants are now being rapidly eliminated by data-processing and electronic computing machines. At this moment large enterprises can tell to the penny their financial position at the end of each day's business; errors in records can be spotted almost instantly by the machines. A single chief accountant aided by a few clerks to operate machines is all that is required. As to methods of persuasive advertising, they are changing too, and are becoming more and more indirect. Until recently advertising consisted largely of slogan-bearing billboards and newspaper and magazine displays. The message is now carried by an assortment of actors on television and is written by former drama-school students, out-of-pocket poets, unsuccessful impresarios and jokesmiths rather than by persons who have studied the writing and presentation of advertising copy. The continuing disappearance of many large newspapers and magazines testifies to the trend. Talent for the new sort of advertising approach is obviously not to be found in business schools but is a synthesis of vaudeville, dramaturgy, cartooning, psychology, photography, and the circus.

Except in highly specialized lines many persons still categorized as salesmen are no more than order takers for the audiences of jesters and performers who by the persuasiveness of their personalities have induced thousands to go out and buy everything from chewing gum to automobiles.

(c) In engineering there is certain to be a more than pro rata increase in numbers as well as more exactly trained people to serve an increasingly mechanized society that requires specialized high-level knowledge for its functioning. As more and more factories are automated, the staffs in many factories and production systems will consist entirely of a few engineers, technicians for repair work, and helpers. This is all that is now required to maintain many existing rubber and chemical, oil-refining, food-processing, textile, soap-manufacturing, and gas-transmission installations. The method is being extended to products with assembled moving parts, such as automobiles, furniture, and appliances. As a consequence some of the third- and fourth-grade engineering schools will be obliged to raise their standards.

(d) Foreign languages: There will be more specialization therein, with much greater emphasis on Russian and on Asiatic and African languages than in the past. This is because of the proliferation of new nations, which must be met politically and economically on terms acceptable to them, and to the extension of its activities by a systematically hostile Russian government to all parts of the world. Knowledge of native languages, furthermore, is necessary to an understanding of alien psychologies and to the promotion of cooperative activity, a point well understood by the language-conscious Russians. While English, owing to its head start, will very probably remain the dominant international language, the English-speaking and European peoples can no longer blandly expect others, now no longer subject to their rule, to learn European languages or to speak pidgin-English.

(*e*) Health professions: While there may be a pro rata decline in the number of dentists if hoped-for medical means of controlling tooth decay are discovered, and a decline in the number of pharmacists owing to the increasing number of prepared medicines, there may be expected at least a pro rata increase in doctors and nurses. However, emphasis in medicine appears bound to swing to psychiatry and neurology, owing to the world-wide increase in mental cases as societies wrench themselves from tribalism to familialism as in Africa and from familialism to individualism as in Europe and North America. These transformations, determined by economic factors and producing in many individuals profound psychic disorders, will lead to more patients, which will require more appropriate doctors. The advance of medical technology, it should be noted, alters medical specialties. Specialists in a long line of diseases are no longer present owing to the discovery of certain drugs with effective curative or preventive powers. No doubt other cures will be discovered but at the same time emerging new environmental conditions will produce new illnesses. Nurses will be trained in greater profusion than ever unless disease and accidents should be very massively reduced, if only because of the increasing army of semi-invalid aged. Just what to do with many of these is a problem agitating some observers, but unless there is some profound alteration in cultural outlook, they will at least be given attention in infirmity, a task devolving upon nurses, trained or untrained.

(*f*) Psychology: There will be a massive increase in the number of psychologists turned out by the schools, whether or not there is some great psychological breakthrough due to the increasingly insistent need for such personnel by large organizations—corporate, governmental, and educational. In the event the country decides to improve education in depth in response to actual need, there will be at least one psychologist attached to each school from the primary grades upward, with a staff of psychologists in the comprehensive high schools. The better schools already have both nurses and psychologists, the latter as yet only for learning placement. Remedial psychologists are yet to appear in the schools.

(g) There will be relative declines in the number of graduates in journalism and religion. The number of persons with advanced training in fine and applied arts and architecture should show pro rata increases in line with population growth. It might be argued that graduates in religious categories will show at least pro rata strength owing to population increase, particularly in the least cultivated strata where religious belief is strongest and propagation greatest. It may turn out for a time that this happens, but for the long pull the trend will, on the evidence, very probably be downward as it already is in many countries such as Italy. Even now the religious professions are not being well supported by an increasingly skeptical public; in order to raise money for tax-exempt churches in most communities it is necessary to resort to raffles, auctions of assorted gifts from politely badgered merchants, church suppers, games of chance, bazaars, and the like. Hardly anyone any longer contributes a tithe. If it is argued that people will need someone to whom to turn with their personal troubles the answer is plain: they will turn increasingly to psychiatrists, psychologists, psychoanalysts and sociological counselors as it is increasingly demonstrated that the systematic application of accumulating knowledge and insight is more effective than prayer and ritual. In European countries where religion is supported out of tax revenues the clergy are in a more assured position even when church attendance is low. These, the clergy, are looked upon as indispensable functionaries to celebrate life's solemn occasions such as birth, puberty, marriage, and death—the only provinces left unchallenged to them in the onrush of psychology. Clergy, however, are increasingly studying psychology and may retain some influence by its means.

(h) Scientific and technical personnel: The pressure of many problems incidental to technologically stimulated social change will bring about substantial increases in the number of persons employed in these categories. Not only at home but abroad, in less developed parts of the world with which North America and Europe have economic relations, scientifically trained persons will be needed with increasing urgency as time unfolds. And it will be the schools and the schools alone that must meet the demand—the schools of North America and Europe. As political influence in the world will increasingly depend upon the extent of development of the scientific establishments of nations, Soviet Russia may be depended upon to make a strong bid for the privilege of supplying scientific personnel to underdeveloped regions in competition with Europe and North America.

Although the present age is widely described as "scientific" and "scientific-minded," compared with the palpably looming needs for new discovery and the broad application of scientific method in the next century and a half the world has yet made very little use of science. The demand for physical scientists by industry and the military establishment now is plainly apparent to everyone; but the greatest coming demand will be for human behavioral scientists —psychologists, economists, sociologists, political scientists, penologists, psychiatrists, physicians, and experts in jurisprudence, linguistics, and cultural science (the latter sometimes cumbersomely designated as culturology). For although many problems remain for man with respect to external nature, the great problem remains man's internal nature. The overriding problem facing the United States and the world, therefore, is one of organization and management of the human enterprise under conditions of great and growing complexity.

It was the pressure of concrete problems—of warfare, navigation, metalworking, mining, disease, agriculture, and mechanized industry —that stimulated the physical sciences to maturity. And it will be the pressure of social problems that will bring the social sciences to maturity, greatly increasing the number of workers in this general area.

Owing to the relatively high degree of indeterminacy in the social sciences in comparison with the physical sciences, they are far less esteemed. But intensive work is going forward in the social sciences, unknown to the general public, along the lines of making their concepts more precise and of mathematicizing them beyond the employment of mere statistics. It was the harnessing of mathematics to the physical sciences, initially by Galileo, that gave them their greatest power. An analogous process is now under way in the social sciences, most prominently in economics but also in psychology and sociology. The intensive subjection of language to advanced logical analysis is placing the concepts and theories of all disciplines under scientific scrutiny with a view to ascertaining what is fruitful and what is merely decorative.

Contrary to popular supposition, there are no phenomena, physical or social, that are in principal insusceptible of being brought under the jurisdiction of scientific method. According to prevalent opinion, only some types of problem, mainly physical, are subject to scientific approach but others, such as those in human relations or individual emotional states, are not. But whatever is not knowledge in the scientific sense is merely uncertain common sense or rule-of-thumb lore, sustained by inadequate prescientific theory fossilized in habit and custom. Personal experience can give knowledge of limited situations but generalizing from such personal experience is risky and is, in fact, the source of much individual and group error of policy and action in the world.

Instead of arguing the point, which might detain us needlessly, we may simply look at large-scale business enterprise and some governmental divisions today, which have already stepped over the threshold into the future in their utilization of science. While the public is well aware that industry and the military division of government apply physical science to production, it is not aware that the entire range of social sciences is also employed in planning and management. Market research, for example, involving the determination of what things, models, and designs people will buy, is organized on the simple scientific principle of direct random sampling. Businessmen no longer make and stock what they have a hunch people will buy. Losses are too great with that method. They want to know exactly. The personnel of large-scale business is also increasingly selected, managed, and deployed on scientific principles. Overseeing the entire process are economists, psychologists, and sociologists. Smaller enterprises turn to management consultant firms staffed by similarly trained people.

While government as a whole is notoriously unscientific, one of the largest governmental subinstitutions, the military, is already thoroughly saturated with scientific disciplines, not only with respect to physical applications to weaponry but in applications of the social sciences to internal management. Psychological warfare, too, is now a well-established discipline. The military subinstitution of government in its present form provides us with a foretaste at least in method of what will in the coming 150 years amount to a total invasion of all institutions by science.

In contrast with the military institution, the legal institution is one of the least scientific in government, using methods that survive from the medieval period. This fact is clearly established by the late Jerome

Frank, for many years a federal judge of the Second United States Circuit Court of Appeals.[3]

If scientific method is to come to the rescue of institutions subject to disorganization and malfunctioning under the pressures of social change, it is clear that it must be the schools that produce the personnel needed to apply scientific method. Nearly all of our institutions have become problematic, yielding less than satisfactory results: the educational, the familial, the law-enforcement, the judicial, the penal, the economic, etc. What to do about them? As common sense analyses and prescriptions, one after the other, are tried and discarded because they bear only meager fruit, attention inevitably turns increasingly to science for the ascertainment of fact and for the development of adequate concepts, hypotheses, and theories under which one can proceed with some assurance of success.

Even though science is widely feared, as it is indeed although on false grounds, eventually it cannot be denied. For if the United States does not fully embrace it, others will, thus improving their general world-competitive positions. The fear of science is based on the assumption that the power it confers must necessarily be abused. This assumption underlies the fantasy-satires of Aldous Huxley in *Brave New World* and of George Orwell in 1984. A second assumption in these books is that the controls science is able to establish are invariably completely successful, overriding all non-scientific counterinfluences. Neither assumption is necessarily justified.

The possible abuse of science, already exemplified by the Hitler regime, intensifies the general problem of government. In the presence of science irrationality in government is obviously more dangerous than ever in the past. Whether government leaders will be less or more rational in the future than in the past there is, of course, no way of knowing, although the general influence of the scientific institution itself appears to favor the selection of governmental leaders with heightened rational outlooks.

(i) Concededly the future labor force will by no means include only college-trained specialists. It is difficult to see more than 25 per cent of the population subject to such effective training, contrary to the utopian expectations of some contemporary educators. But what of the non-college person? Where will he fit into the scheme of things?

It is noticeable that the trend of technology is to make more and more persons superfluous in the labor force. There are two and only two possible strategies for dealing constructively with this situation, both of which will be employed simultaneously and consciously, as they have been already to some extent unconsciously. One strategy will be to make provision for some people that takes them out of the labor force; the other will be to create more specialized divisions of labor within the labor force.

As to keeping people out of the labor force, it is noticeable that this is being done by lengthening the years of attendance in school for the young and by lowering the age of retirement for the aged. The emergence of the high school delayed entrance into the labor force of millions, meanwhile giving many valuable vocational training. Whereas at one time there was no fixed retirement age, each person working until he dropped in his tracks, it is now more or less officially sixty-five, with some retirements encouraged at sixty and sixty-two. For less skilled categories the retirement age may very well be lowered to fifty-five in the near future; skilled categories will be retained for longer periods, their experience often being invaluable. The more people it is possible to retain in advanced education, the less will be the strain on the absorptive power of the labor force, the greater will be the enrichment of society in skills.

The Lower Labor Force

It is to the universities and colleges that society must look for the higher labor-division skills, to the high schools for middle skills. Here the high school as a terminal vocational institution for the training of mechanics, machinists, and mechanical-service personnel will have a role to play. The comprehensive urban high school, at least, now falls into three divisions: (1) academic or college preparatory, (2) general vocational or manual trades skills and (3) technical-mechanical skills. It would better succeed in holding back from the labor force some of those who now drop out if it added a fourth division frankly devoted to games, hobbies, diversions, and athletics almost exclusively. While initially there would be both puritanic and academic objection to the development of such a division, it would serve social purposes beyond merely delaying entry into a glutted labor force.

For students in this category would be preparing for a specific life-work in the extracurricular handling of the increasing urban young, particularly during long summer vacations when, as now, they roam the city streets. What the future will see, and in this century, unless

greater difficulties than now foreseen are to ensue, is the establishment of summer camps and after-school centers for the urban young
between the ages of nine and eighteen. These camps and centers will
be tax-supported and will be extensions of the school systems. Moreover they must be manned by skilled people, college-trained and
school-trained. Already such camps exist for thousands, but they are
private and too costly for most families. The private camps, however,
are leading the way as private schools once did, to be followed by
public establishments. The public camps will offer pretty much what
the private camps now offer, the instilling of skills in hobbies, crafts,
games, and athletics in a healthy outdoor environment. As a national
system of summer camps will require trained personnel, one can readily see the need for making the comprehensive high school four-sided
instead of three-sided.

The society emerging in the future, its outlines increasingly clear,
will be under the regulation of a Welfare State that not only gives
support, domestic and foreign, where needed, but that must necessarily also find constructive employment outlets for multitudes, must
create entire new lines of work that can be justified in terms of social
necessity or desirability. It must do this, that is to say, unless it wishes
to maintain in idleness at a low level hordes of useless people as did
Rome after the spread of slavery, the modern counterpart of which is
automatic machinery. If not bread and circuses then useful employment and avocational opportunities must be provided by government.
It will not be provided by private enterprise, which must show a
profit for its efforts.

Possible New Occupations

The upsurge in personal-service workers of recent decades is bound
to be followed by an upsurge of highly skilled persons with services
to offer, services desirable if not irreducibly necessary to society. They
will be necessary to an evolving increasingly mechanized society of
intricate complexity.

All this hardly portends that unskilled laborers will be dispensed
with; but their numbers will diminish. The person without special,
developed skills or innate talents is going to find it increasingly difficult to find a job in a society of growing complexity and special artic-
ulation. But some of the older occupations may well find a swelling of

their ranks. There will surely be available more household workers as stores, factories, and offices no longer demand help in large numbers. Right now there is much unfilled demand for help in this category, particularly from mothers with small children on their hands that interfere with other household duties or jobs. The part-time baby sitter may well be supplanted by the resurrected full-time governess and tutor, particularly in the homes of persons in possession of the higher skills.

New occupations and new products, too, are entirely conceivable. Every invention has produced new occupations, some requiring high and special skills, some requiring little skill. The automobile industry provided possibly the greatest single gain in employment following World War I, but it is now increasingly subject to automation, as are others. Now both existing industries and new industries are subject to techniques aiming at the elimination of labor, so that manufacturers visualize relatively fewer production workers. If, however, there are to be customers for productive output, there must be employed people or people in receipt of government stipends. Rather than fall back on this extremity it may safely be predicted that society, after its first rejection, will gradually accept the new "frilly" employments, many of them intellectual, many financed by government out of taxes. And such acceptance will be a social gain.

A labor force with a much greater proportion of highly trained specialized personnel and more specialties is therefore in distinct prospect. It is difficult to see how this outcome can possibly be avoided short of maintaining an army of unemployed.

It is inescapable, then, that society in the future must train hundreds of thousands of persons for specialized services that are now available to only a few or that are simply not being offered. And as people will not or cannot individually purchase many of these services, they must inexorably be bought wholesale and paid for out of tax funds, through governmental agencies. The government, here again, is seen to be playing a central role, not private enterprise, although private enterprise should maintain a strong supporting role.

Few Scientists Today

The United States, an examination of the labor force in the Census of 1950 shows,[4] is kept in operation by a surprisingly small proportion of persons making painstaking use of cultivated higher mental processes. In a total labor force of 56¼ million only 4.9 plus million were classified as professional, technical, and kindred workers—less than 10 per cent. But this group included such clear non-intellectuals as actors, athletes, chiropractors, dancers, draftsmen, entertainers, funeral directors and embalmers, nurses, optometrists, osteopaths, pharmacists, photographers, radio operators, recreation and group workers, religious workers, sports instuctors and the like. Any one of these, it may be granted, could be an intellectual, but surely not in the line of his occupation.

The relatively small number of persons in the United States dedicated to increasing and transmitting knowledge as contrasted with professionals who apply it and professionals working in non-scientific disciplines is shown in the following tables:

SCIENTISTS (*1950 Census*)

Chemists, registered	74,433
Natural scientists	40,068
Social scientists	35,201
College presidents and faculty	124,686

The above group constituted less than ½ of 1 per cent of the labor force.

ENGINEERS AND PHYSICIANS*

Engineers	525,256
Physicians and surgeons	

MISCELLANEOUS

Clergy and religious workers	208,902
Lawyers and judges	180,461
Musicians and music teachers	153,456
Editors and reporters	89,325
Photographers	52,489
Dancers and dancing teachers	16,097
Authors, full-time	15,651

Accountants, auditors, and bookkeepers aggregated 1,097,436, but recreational and group workers amounted only to 16,046 and sports

* This group composed about 1.33 per cent of the labor force.

instructors and sports officials only 44,987. A sound mind in a sound body may indeed be the American ideal, as often claimed, but keeping track of the money engages far more workers than does physical training.

Below the professional-technical-specialist level the main categories in the labor force were as follows:

Managers and officials	5,017,465
Craftsmen, foremen, and related workers	7,777,560
Farmers and farm managers	4,306,253
Clerical and related workers	6,894,374
Sales workers	3,926,510
Operatives, mainly factory	11,146,220
Private household workers	1,407,466
Service workers	4,287,603
Farm laborers and foremen	2,399,794
Laborers, non-farm, non-mine	3,417,232

The only categories in the preceding list in which reasonably high-level mental skills are required to some extent in the line of work are in managers, officials, and farm managers. While skills suitable to routine operations are found in the other categories, they are mostly such as not to be unattainable after a little steadily applied effort. Below the managerial level most of the categories—particularly clerical, sales, operative, and laborers—will in the future be steadily reduced, pro rata, by technological innovation, particularly over the near term when adjustments are being made to new developments. And while new inventions bring into being new demands for workers—the entire development of automation and computer machines requires production, maintenance and repair workers—the net effect of automation and computer machines is to make low-skilled workers and many operatives superfluous. That is the purpose of such machines, unlike consumption items such as automobiles and electrical appliances.

The labor force as a whole, it is evident, represents what the market will support. It is also evident that if governmental support were withdrawn, the categories of scientists, chemists, and teachers would be severely shrunken.

On the evidence it seems impossible to escape the conclusion that as automation and electronic computers are increasingly installed, the only categories of employment that can absorb relatively more workers will be service workers, private household workers, and the professional-technical category. For the latter, and for the managerial class, more training and more education will be required than for the present numerically dominant categories. The only quarter to which society can turn for the many needed persons of higher skills and training is the educational institution, especially the colleges but also the high schools. I predict, then, a rising demand on the colleges for more graduates, for more exactingly trained graduates and for far fewer non-intellectuals. Society needs more scientists, engineers, physicians, and surgeons, high-level technicians, teachers, recreation and group workers, social and welfare workers, widely informed administrators and managers, nurses and other supportive and remedial personnel.

If public policy does not guide everybody it possibly can into categories of higher skill, it must support unskilled persons who have, in the state of high technology, no contribution to make other than their presence as impecunious consumers.

The Question of Finances

Contrary to widespread supposition, the federal government for 150 years has been making substantial and gradually increasing financial contributions to American education. A long series of statutes beginning early in the nineteenth century provided federal money to the states for college education—general, vocational, technical and agricultural. There exist sixty-eight land-grant colleges under the Morrill Act of 1862, including sixteen for Negroes and thirty-nine officially designated universities, all of which in 1956 enrolled 18 per cent of all college students. More recently the federal government has proved a boon to the colleges and universities by means of the Servicemen's Readjustment Act of 1944, through which it paid for tuition and books for men in the hundreds of thousands; by means of housing loans to colleges that aggregated $897,474,000 as of May 31, 1959; and by huge repeated grants for special research under military defense legislation. Many leading institutions, some of them private, now derive large percentages of annual revenue from such grants and would have to curtail general services without them.

Similar federal legislation is pending for aid to public primary and secondary schools, in the initial amount of $2,484,000,000. Instructively, this legislation in mid-1961 was bottled up in the House Rules Committee by an eight to seven vote, with the majority representing traditionalist points of view—five Republicans, two Southern Democrats and one Northern Catholic Democrat. All of the minority were Democrats. It was the Northern Democrat, normally a supporter of administration-sponsored legislation, who cast the decisive negative vote on the ground that the proposed legislation did not provide public money for private Catholic schools, about the public financing of which there is a pending constitutional question.[5]

But although Republicans and Southern Democrats, unshakable champions of tradition and inertia, oppose such federal expansion in every field, they must eventually capitulate unless they want the United States to lose relative strength in the world. Delay in itself can often turn out to be unnecessarily costly. The reason one can say that federal aid to all schools is going to increase steadily through coming decades is that other sources of income are drying up, in part because of a federal tax structure brought about by wars and huge defense expenditures, in part because the need of the schools is too great for many localities to handle. Private entrepreneurs, worried by the rising power of federal government in education could, if they were as devoted to principle as they claim, decide to take the burden upon themselves. The United States Chamber of Commerce and the National Association of Manufacturers could conceivably decide to have their members finance all education, thereby making it a 100 per cent private operation. But does anyone imagine they will do so?

In the period 1879–80 government in all divisions was the source of 7.9 per cent of funds for higher education, in 1939–40 for 36.6 per cent, in 1947–48 for 59.3 per cent, and in 1955–56 for 51.8 per cent.[6] In the latter year localities contributed 3.7 per cent, the states 30.9 per cent, and the federal government 17.1 per cent. In wartime 1943–44 the federal contribution was 35.7 per cent. Put bluntly, government on all levels now finances nearly all of primary and secondary education and half of higher education. It does not have far to go before it underwrites the whole bill, and the Catholics with their system, the largest private one in the country, are clamoring for federal assistance, a blow to votaries of private enterprise.

Fears of Federal Control

Fears are often expressed about federal aid, that it may lead to federal control. And federal control suggests to some that many an aberrant hand in a pluralistic society will very probably make itself felt in imposing handicapping regulations. There is always the likelihood that appropriations will from time to time be held up because some bucolic congressman has discovered that a professor of chemistry is an atheist. Also there is the possibility that administrative posts in a thoroughly federalized system would become a part of political patronage, as in the cases of some inferior state colleges and universities now.

As federal financing of education increases—as it will because it must—it will inevitably be necessary for the government to establish an educational administrative agency insulated from demagogic or ideological intrusion. The terms under which such an agency are established will necessarily provide such insulation. Congress has already established many special-purpose agencies that, although subject to review, are not called upon to account for every minute deviation from provincial conventionality. The states and municipalities, too, are establishing "authorities" to do specific jobs, and the private lives and personal opinions of the members of the authority are not called into question. In private affairs the establishment of "czars" with plenary powers in restricted areas is a familiar sight on the American scene—baseball "czars," a clothing-industry "czar," etc. Such a federal agency, emerging as more and more of the financing of education becomes federal, will not impose more than minimal professional standards. Under the system everyone will be answerable, as before, for acts of civic omission and commission to constituted authority, but will as educators be immune from molestation. One can say that this will be the method employed because any other would be self-defeating, would weaken education at the foundations. And under such a system education will be much freer than at present under its necessity to cater to the bewildering whims of private donors, alumni, trustees, free-lance demagogues, municipalities, counties, and states. As experience has shown, education now is subject to demagogic and ideological intrusion at many points from low to high.

France, for example, possesses a central governmental system of education much freer than that of the United States from extraneous ideological interference. The French Ministry of Education directs all public education through seventeen regional districts, although the Catholic Church is allowed to operate parochial schools. Except for the minister placed in charge by successive government administrations, the ministerial staff and the teachers compose a permanent body of professional civil servants, removable only for specific gross misconduct. Everything from primary to postgraduate schools is under this authority, financed out of taxes. Upon passing searching state examinations, primary-school students may enter tuition-free state-operated *lycées* and colleges, carrying them to the end of what is in the United States the second year of college, around the ages of nineteen or twenty. Upon passing rigorous state qualifying examinations, any graduate of the secondary schools may enter one of the regional universities or the University of Paris, tuition-free. As long as they pass examinations which by American standards are extremely exacting, they may continue to graduation; many drop out owing to inability to meet requirements. France does not have nearly as large a proportion of college-diploma holders as the United States; it does have, however, proportionately many more book readers and book buyers.

There remain the *Grandes Écoles* for graduate study in engineering, diplomacy, politics, education, science, law, foreign administration, and medicine and, finally, there is the *College de France* for postgraduate work, advanced research, and voluntary, no-credit attendance. In a total of 134 institutions of higher learning France has only a little more than 150,000 students, the cream of the crop. There is nothing ambiguous about the degrees awarded under this system.

Throughout Europe education is more or less similarly government-supported, tuition-free to the top, although the systems differ in details from country to country. Nobody suggests that the European system is inferior to the American; many argue that it is far and away superior in the development of significant talent.

Education for the Few and the Many

The size of the eventual federal commitments to education will depend to a large extent on an evolving decision by the national community: should education beyond the secondary level be provided only for the obviously talented or, as at present, for any casual upper-middle class wayfarer along the academic path? If only the talented are permitted beyond the high school level the total cost will be lower; but if the vocation-minded and the less serious, in need of further custodial care and withdrawal from the glutted labor market, are allowed to go to college the national costs will be exceedingly great. Educators predict that by 1970 the number of students in colleges and universities will have doubled over the late 1950s, this forecast assuming the continuance of present patterns of education.

Incorrigible optimists, educators at least publicly assume that students go to school to be educated. Many go, however, only because they can think of nothing better to do, and go only so long as the standard of required performance is not high. The very organization of the system to process a mass has unconsciously conspired to suit the easygoing tastes of the multitude. Whereas in Europe only the readily educable, the quick learners, are retained in the system, in the United States the system aims to cater to all comers. But the very attempt to handle a mass, as economically as possible, usually makes a pure farce of the central subject around which all other knowledge must be organized, English composition.

Future Emphasis on the Talented

Of one thing one may be absolutely sure: the talented will be provided for. Not only that, but they will long before the end of this century be sought out systematically and even fanatically in every jurisdiction at early ages, around fourteen. This will be done mainly because national survival now clearly depends upon bringing to fruition latent talents, many hitherto lost, whatever the ethnic, religious, or economic background of the student. Already, in fact, preliminary steps are being taken to seek out the very talented through the offering of National Merit Scholarships and other awards. However, only those properly prepared can be serious contenders for such scholarships, and the search will soon be moved back farther so that latent talent is better prepared at the secondary-school level. Educators recognize that much talent is now eluding the educational net at the secondary-school level, failing to achieve proper development in inadequate local schools and environments.

It has been proposed that special regional secondary schools be established for the very able. In the course of time, possibly within fifty years, they will be established. Protest was provoked among some educators by this proposal on the ground that it would foster an elite, a group that imagined itself superior to the common run of humanity. This elite exists in any case, and has always existed; and the excellent are seldom in doubt about their excellence. The only question is whether the elite is to embrace all those naturally eligible. Basic objections to the formal designation of an elite is not that it is really undemocratic but that the non-elite does not wish to acknowledge its deficiencies. Yet, while decrying the formal recognition of an elite, the American public ambivalently worships stars, experts, big shots, champions, and heroes—the elite!

But if the country objects to such schools for the very able, and readily educable, it has the remedy in its power in the form of better teachers and more teachers per pupil in existing local schools. As educators know, remarkable results can be obtained with many unlikely, culturally submerged pupils if they are handled in small groups and given the opportunity for stimulants such as sight-seeing trips, outside lectures, visits to cultural centers, contact with inspiring personalities, use of a wide variety of special equipment and the like.

But while the United States could once have afforded the expense of a maximum full-scale effort in education, which it has never made, it is highly questionable whether it can afford it while maintaining a record peacetime defense establishment at 85 per cent or more of the national budget, making provision for large-scale necessary foreign aid, providing subsidies for many sectors of the private economy that would never, unaided, be able to retain their present patterns of organization, and operating a profligate consumer-goods economy. Something will have to be slighted in this bill of particulars, and on the basis of evidence from the past it is not difficult to see that it will be adequate education for the masses.

The Quest of Educators

What educators now avowedly seek as college material is the upper 25 per cent of young people as determined by the General Education Test administered to nearly ten million men during World War II. A score of 100 represented the average. Approximately 50 per cent of all who took the test scored between 86 and 114. The pattern of grading was based on earlier inquiries of psychologists into the national distribution of intelligence. Approximately 25 per cent of those tested scored 115 or higher and of all college graduates who took the examination more than 81 per cent scored 115 or higher, suggesting that by present standards four out of five persons completing four years of college have the capacity suggested by the test score of 115 or higher. The test score closely corresponds to an IQ of 110, used as the basis of admission to many colleges and universities.[7]

Noting that about 20 per cent of young people (not all qualified) now at least enter college, educational researchers have found in a special study that out of 476,000 persons in 1950 who were eighteen years old and who would score 115 or higher in the army test, only 40 per cent went to college and of those who went only about half remained to graduate. In the upper 10 per cent of persons of intellectual promise, who would score 125 or higher on the army test, only about 45 per cent now go to college and nearly two thirds of these graduate. In the upper 2 per cent only about 56 per cent go to college and about three quarters of them graduate.[8]

There is evident, then, a tremendous precollege and in-college leakage of qualified persons, which many educators feel must be stopped if the national talent hunt is to be fully successful. Below the college level, it is competently estimated, of the upper 500,000 young people of intellectual promise under age eighteen, no fewer than 100,000 never finish high school.[9] The waste of talent suggested by all these statistics is nationally more damaging than past waste of natural resources.

The avowed aim of educators is to enroll in college at least 400,000 of such youth and, beyond that, all of them. It is recognized, furthermore, that "our colleges and universities now enroll many students who fall below the general level of intelligence indicated by the army test score of 115," most of whom drop out by the end of the second year.[10]

In their concern about this theoretical upper 25 per cent, educators show which way the wind of planning is blowing. Psychologists know, however, that all of this group is by no means subject to the full educational process owing to individual psychological blockage or anti-intellectual subcultural bias. It is usually an assumption of the educator that everyone with ability will seize any opportunity to get an education; but this is often unwarranted. Many individuals rank other things higher than education—marriage, economic self-sufficiency, travel, adventure, desire to sever childhood family ties and the like. Again, many high IQs have been justifiably disillusioned by their experience with the present educational process, which they have found less than inspiring. What is generally unsaid about present education is that *most* existing schools and *most* teachers are probably boring in inverse proportion to the intelligence level of the student. Many superior students, informally referred to by educators themselves as "captive audiences," grimly put up with deficient teaching personalities and programs all along the line in order to get diplomas and thus please their families or meet job requirements.

It would take a great deal of costly special work to put some of this high IQ material back on the educational track, and it is doubtful that the country would ever consent to shoulder the full cost. It seems certain, then, that educators, however laudable their aim, are not going to put all of this upper 25 per cent through college unless there should be some as yet unforeshadowed breakthrough in psychological technique. A genius is not only in the upper ½ of 1 per cent of the IQ level for the population as a whole but is held on his course by a multiplicity of non-intellectual factors, mostly hidden and as yet only dimly suspected. The person in this upper layer who actually performs up to the theoretical level is relatively rare. He is usually found coasting along effortlessly among less endowed mortals.

But even talking about a college education for 25 per cent of youth, whether that youth is of the upper IQ level or not, presupposes a purely quantitative costly expansion of our educational system to keep up with the increase of population. For if 25 per cent of youth go to college, it follows that there must be prior expansion and refinement on the secondary level.

Confusion About Education

There is much confusion about the means and ends of education, both on the part of educational spokesmen and public. The fundamental purpose of any education, as the best minds see it, was stated in the preceding chapter. But the confusion on the part of educators is evident in the acrimonious debate about different methods of education—the essentialists, the general educationists or humanists, the progressives, and the life adjusters. An education that did not contain essentials or that provided no clues for an adjustment to living would be absurd; and one that did not study and reflect on man and his works or was not centered on the needs and capacities of the student would be equally absurd. Each theory contains only part of the truth.

Heightened quality in American education as a whole is not likely unless there is a decision, costly to implement, to raise standards all along the line. In the light of case-hardened American belief that education can and should be cheap, it is not likely there will be such a decision for several decades. Effective education is invariably expensive, although expensive education is not always effective. But for students capable of scholastic achievement, standards are going to be much higher and many more such students are going to be publicly financed in their studies.

The Stimulus of Overpopulation

The population boom, by overloading the existing system with children and youth, dilutes the effectiveness of the general operation. However, more applicants for admission to the prestige-bearing major-league universities and better colleges, for whom there is only limited accommodation, will in time enable these institutions to raise their standards. Economic competition among American colleges and universities for students, either private or tax-supported, has led to slack standards, for students seeking easy ways to obtain a degree tended to favor less rigorous schools. Even the best schools were insensibly affected by this state of affairs under a version of Gresham's law that bad money drives good money out of circulation. Schools and students engaged in a polite mutual deception, the school certifying an education that was thin enough to suit the status-minded student and the student being the means through which the school gained its financial support. The standards of the economic market place prevailed: the customer was always right. How far such standards invaded the Groves of Academe is shown in reports of widespread cheating in examinations by students in leading colleges and universities.

Now, with more applicants for admission than they can handle, the major schools can safely and increasingly impose their own academic terms. Many are already doing so and further tightening of requirements for entrance and retention will unquestionably be made. In the past a variety of vague or ambiguous concepts such as character roundedness, compatibility, social position, variety of interests and the like were taken into consideration to justify acceptance. Ability to pay was always an important consideration. Increasingly, ability to do the work on a high level will be the sole standard of entrance in all schools of prestige.

If the upper universities can, as a few now do, impose more severe standards for admission, rejecting the poorer performers, they will affect the college-preparatory secondary schools. And applicants who fail to meet college requirements will either be forced to make up preparatory deficiencies or fail to gain entrance to all except unambiguously inferior schools.

Differences Among Colleges

A difference among colleges and universities is that some require applicants to take entrance examinations relating to subject matter studied in secondary school (mathematics, science, and language), some require what are known as scholastic aptitude tests, and some ask the student to show no more than a high school diploma. Among these last some require academic standing in the upper tenth, quarter, or third of the high school class; some impose no such requirement. Some even accept without tests or high school diploma. Even some of the best state universities are required by law to accept any holder of a home-state high school diploma, which for the good institutions means only that they have an extremely swollen first-year class; a large proportion of these entrants fail in the first year.

To accommodate the great number wishing to go to college but unable or unwilling to meet stringent academic and financial requirements, there has emerged the junior or community college, in various ways professing to meet the requirements of the first two years in college. Whereas in 1920 there were only 52 junior or community colleges, there are now nearly 600, holding nearly 20 per cent of all college students. There will be more if the American public wishes to underwrite their cost. In most of the junior colleges (and many four-year colleges) ordinarily exacting studies such as mathematics and science are covered for most by general survey courses, involving little strain on the attention or acumen, no personal grappling with problems, no precision of workmanship.

The desire of many, then, either for middle-skill vocational instruction or for superficial treatment of subject matter with a diploma as a reward is being met. But there is a vast difference in the two kinds of education, one grappling with fundamentals and the other toying with superficialities. There has always been a split between the intellectually tough and the intellectually tender, but in the present circumstances of the world the split is becoming more and more recognizable.

As any readily chartered institution may issue the bachelor of arts and bachelor of science degrees, various educators publicly lament the substandard qualifications they often represent. Some, as we have noted, express similar doubts about the M.A. and Ph.D. But even a bachelor's degree from a topflight school is no longer, in itself, taken as an indication of much. The practice is increasingly, as in England, to inquire whether the degree was awarded with any distinction, such as *cum laude*. In England a university degree, unless it is taken with honors, is conceded slight weight, and is no passport for exacting employments. Many American schools, however, already pointedly award the bachelor's degree in specific specialties such as law (LL.B.), divinity (B.D.), business administration (B.B.A.), education (B.S.Ed.), engineering (B.E.), fine arts (B.F.A.), library science (B.L.S.) and social sciences (B.S.S.).

The Purpose of the University

Some critics within the universities themselves contend that the university itself does not know what its purposes are. Are those purposes to teach, to propagandize for certain values, or to conduct research? It could conceivably do all, but many of its researchers are indifferent teachers, some of its teachers have no flair for research, and some can neither propagandize, teach effectively, nor conduct research.

As promotion is based largely on published work, it seems that research is favored. For *successful* published work brings renown to the universities. But as much published work represents no discernible step forward, sheer bulk, it appears, is accepted as better than nothing.

Persons whose promotion depends on publication tend, it is held, to slight teaching. The better schools of Europe and America have often been able to make a strong showing in specialties without being conspicuous for their inspired teachers in part because many of their students are highly motivated autodidacts. They excel because they are aggressive students, not because they are well taught. There is need, however, for effective teaching in the universities, even of the self-starters, many of whom need to be made acquainted with unfamiliar fields—science majors with the humanities, humanities majors with mathematics and the sciences. Most of all, perhaps, the practical-minded need to be shown the value of theory.

Caplow and McGee, authors of *The Academic Market-Place*, propose, in addition to the research ranks of professors and associate professors, teaching ranks with equal pay designated lecturers and associate lecturers. If these later did research warranting the change, they could be shifted to the professorial rank. There is almost sure to be such a division, however it is designated. But a further division, by whatever title known, will almost surely be that of examiner and associate examiner. The duty of these latter would be not to conduct research, not to lecture, but to be accessible for consultation and to determine whether extended reading assignments had been fulfilled in advanced courses of history, social science, philosophy, and literature. It is a great weakness in the contemporary university to fail to ascertain *precisely* that such reading has been done.

The university of the immediate future, at any rate, will hopefully be stripped of much of its present excess baggage, and be streamlined. It will do a much more effective job of teaching, will be more searching in many of its reading and writing requirements, and may well add postdoctoral research institutes to more efficiently organized graduate schools.

Plans have matured at some universities to bring the average level of professors' salaries up to $30,000, thus obviating outside income-supplementing activities. Some few professors in specialties for which there is outside competitive market demand now approach or equal this level. Professors of medicine, physics, and chemistry often command university salaries at least approaching what they could earn ex-Academe. But, insensibly, the universities and colleges all along have been in competition with the external market for vital personalities, who refuse to put up with the sort of direct and implied petty censorship to which their conduct and opinions are subject at most institutions.

It must be admitted, however, that in schools of inferior rank there is no prospect of increased freedom from outside meddling. These schools are all under the shadow of various "party lines," some of which express no more than conventional sentimentality. But in the major institutions free thinking and free expression will be encouraged in the face of continuing pressure of foreign and internal influences toward social disorganization. For only free minds, functioning freely and boldly, can find defensive solutions for grave problems. Academic trained seals will be useless. In the long run countries with free faculties will vastly outdistance countries such as Russia and China if these latter retain their rigidly restricted faculties.

Financing for Students

Working one's way through college has long been one of the most hallowed and most hypocritical items in the American mythical self-image. For all it has signified since the country ceased being a nation of poor farmers is that the student with parents unwilling or unable to finance him in college, whatever his talents, was thrown back on his own meager finances to develop socially useful talents. But society itself has suffered in the process, for the education so gained was either inferior because of diminished opportunity for study or was so long delayed as to be of doubtful utility. If menial work while in college were character-building, as it is often asserted, why is it not required at the national military academies, the medical schools, and scientific institutes?

The standard college program requires fifteen class hours per week for fifteen weeks or so per semester. In theory, there is supposed to be a minimal two hours of outside work for each class hour, a theoretical forty-five hours a week if the program is adhered to (which it is not by the overwhelming majority). But no serious student who has put forty-five hours faithfully into college work is in a position to do paid extracurricular work. The work program, at least for serious students, will therefore be increasingly discarded.

Very probably before A.D. 2000 total subsidization of select students will occur: the better students, no matter what their economic status, will have all their expenses paid—tuition, books, and room and board, as now at the national military academies. Payments will be made by the government on the basis of the social need for developed talents. As matters now stand, many of the talented young are expected to live fairly impoverished lives while engaging in difficult studies, meanwhile observing that the average layman is feathering his own nest without preparing himself at all for difficult and socially useful tasks. In Europe and Soviet Russia college tuition costs are paid for by the government. There are no tuition charges. The United States in time will embrace the same system.

Higher Education of Women

Another innovation under pressure of need will be the education and job placement of a much larger number of women, particularly on the highest-trained levels. The intelligence factor is distributed among women in the same ratio as among men. Although women now comprise close to one third of the labor force, they are not found in anything approaching this proportion in the higher professional and managerial employments. With encouragement, far more than at present could be developed into chemists, physicists, biologists, psychologists, social scientists, physicians and surgeons, engineers and the like. They will be, it can be predicted, owing to simple social need here and abroad. The readily educable woman is probably the greatest untapped resource of the United States, and in this area Russia is far in advance. Women, it is true, are no longer barred from high-level employment; but as a matter of public policy they are not encouraged to seek such employment. Many, therefore, function farther down in the labor force, their greater talents wasted.

Adult Education

The most novel line of development in education, however, has not yet been touched upon. It will be seen in adult education, now in its infancy.

There are, broadly, two kinds of activity known as adult education. One is concerned with hobbies, crafts, and games and the other with more serious systematized matters of class study. It is with the second variety that we are concerned.

Adult education of the serious kind, long ago ventured by various free-lance educators in this country and Europe, was pioneered on a systematically organized basis in this country by The New School for

Social Research of New York in 1919 under the leadership of John Dewey, Thorstein Veblen, Charles Beard, Horace Kallen and others. It has grown under New School auspices and has been developed as well to impressive proportions by the leading universities of New York City, Los Angeles and, to a lesser extent, Chicago. These three cities are at present the main centers of serious adult education in the country, but it is almost certain that other metropolitan centers will before long join the procession.[11]

Far from being a substitute for a conventional college education, adult education is a supplement to whatever education the student has experienced. Some half of its participants, more or less, are college graduates, but it is by no means a graduate division. While given different emphases by different schools, it is both vocational and cultural, mainly the latter. It enables mature persons to study at college level whatever they feel interested in, whatever they feel is lacking in their own background. Many turn to it to make up gaps in their general college education. Others turn to it for technical job skills. Usually it is not taken for academic credit and it does not offer a degree. It is in the main resorted to for the very best of all reasons for seeking education: out of sheer interest. The students are, in general, more sincerely interested than the average college student.

For decades in the United States, Commencement Day speakers have informed their audiences, quite literally, that on the basis of what they have studied more or less sketchily they must now prepare to make a beginning in lifelong learning; all the college has done is to show them a few tricks and vistas and give them encouragement and a push into the world. As their reactions show, few of the students believe this; for most it is Termination Day, and here and there unregenerate souls have openly vowed never to open a book again voluntarily.

But tens of thousands, whether or not they have finished high school or college, have discovered by their experience in the world after leaving school that there were wide handicapping gaps in their knowledge. Ph.D.s in some specialty have been dissatisfied with their ability to write, to understand poetry or philosophy. Some with exclusively humanist background have developed a desire to know more about science or mathematics, to study it at first hand. Scientists and physicians have acquired an interest in certain languages, perhaps Latin, Greek or Sanskrit, or in classic literature. Again, persons with a good general education have found it vocationally useful to acquire familiarity with certain technologies.

These have turned in increasing numbers to university-level courses in adult education where they have been available, free of undergraduate atmosphere. And one may confidently expect this number to grow as more and more people discover the inadequacy of their educational background—political, economic, anthropological or whatever—in a world of seemingly bewildering change. The number of persons in adult education, both as teachers and as students, will increase precisely because there are more people who have gone forward far enough in the formal educational process to want to go farther and because new industrial procedures are providing more and more leisure. As many persons have discovered, the investment of leisure time solely in hobbies and diversions can become enervating. The enrichment of the mind in unfamiliar fields has turned out to be a supplementary procedure for many.

But even in advanced specialties some form of adult education is used. Post-doctoral research has for long been an activity in some fields and is not referred to here. But in many specialties established persons return to school for "refresher" courses in order to bring them up to the latest practice. This is true with especial reference to physicians and surgeons, who often commute from outlying areas to attend classes, clinics, and seminars in medical schools and institutes that are demonstrating new techniques. Teachers in subjects to which there has been a substantial addition—physics, mathematics, biology and the like—also attend such courses. Because in some fields there is a rapid rate of "obsolescence," some universities have even proposed establishing regional seminars for alumni who wish to become acquainted with significant new developments in certain fields. Such seminars, if established, would be another form of adult education.

Well within the time span of 150 years it will be seen that the educated people, perhaps 25 per cent of adults, will be those still going to school. Government officials, for example, will be given leaves of absence to attend university courses in subjects germane to their official capacities. Military officers are now required to update their education from time to time in higher schools.

What about developing their knowledge through reading, through consulting learned periodicals, and through attending meetings of professional associations? No doubt many will do this, but a professional association, while enabling a specialist to deepen knowledge, provides no aid in entering an unfamiliar field. As to reading, the busy person established in the world does not have sufficient available time to read broadly and finds it an aid to attend lectures and seminars into which much special reading has been compressed. Furthermore, contact with intellectually alert people is a stimulus of great value and a change of pace from ordinary routine. Man's greatest adventure is doubtless the adventure of the mind. Again, many persons use their eyes intensively in their daily work and find they are unable to read much after hours but are greatly accommodated if they can attend lectures, seminars, and demonstrations.

The answer, then, to the need for broadening and deepening knowledge among the educated holding key posts in a progressively complex society appears to be found in life-long formalized adult education, pursued mainly on one or two evenings of the week but also pursued full-time in special compressed courses on advanced levels for high-level personnel. Even now a number of the leading corporations of the country maintain special non-vocational schools for executives with a view to deepening their general insights, and some corporations have made arrangements with leading universities to give their people general cultural courses.

The requirement of an increasingly complex world, in other words, is for more knowledge, more widely diffused, more sagaciously applied.

But all this innovation in education is not, so far as can be seen, leading to a general lifting of the cultural level in fulfillment of the vision of the eighteenth-century liberals. Psychological insight has advanced now to a point where by its means one is able to conclude that the population is genetically stratified in developmental potentialities. While much can be done to improve each stratum and while certain members of apparently low strata can by appropriate environmental changes and stimuli be disclosed as possessing unsuspected potentialities for self-development, it is evident that many if not most are constitutionally limited in how far they can develop intellectually.

There are many facets to human development other than intellectual, and although the school has a role to play in developing such facets, it is questionable that it will ever have the major role unless it is to supplant the home and other institutions. The grandiose plans of some educators visualize the school as responsible for everything about the individual's development. But in this, unless all other social agencies are to be superseded, educators have clearly overreached themselves.

The main function of the school has been, and will continue to be, to develop intellect as a tool for modifying the behavior of self, others, and the environment. Everything else the school does is subsidiary and contributory.

It is conceivable, of course, that the school will be given the responsibility for doing more than developing intellect and special skills, that it will be made responsible for the total development of the personality and converted into the center of community life as the Church was in the Middle Ages. In the case of the comprehensive high school of some small towns and suburbs one sees such a tendency. After-hours parties, dances, plays, movies, concerts, debates, adult classes, political rallies, individual recreations and athletic events are centered there for the entire community. But the strong trend toward an integrated total urban development appears to rule out the prospect for such a general development unless it is to take place within urban neighborhoods. While there is great and growing need for neighborhood community centers around which community life can be organized, the evidence is as yet far from indicating positively that it will be located in the high schools.

Education and Future Dominant Personalities

The trained personnel for managing an increasingly complex society, making use of more and more complicated mechanisms until the society as a whole resembles a machine, must clearly be drawn from the upper 25 per cent of the population in developmental potential that educators consider most likely to profit from a college education. And it is from this upper 25 per cent, preferentially endowed by heredity and social conditioning, that the socially dominant functional types of the evolving future will inescapably be drawn. Some 40 per cent more of the population might profit from a thorough secondary-school education.

Henry A. Wallace, former Vice-President of the United States, once described the twentieth century as "the century of the common man." True or not, it is almost certain that the twenty-first century—and beyond—will be the century dominated by the highly cultivated, educated man. It will be the era of the savant, unless large-scale warfare should, by precipitating social atavism, bring back to power the men of muscle and self-centered scheming.

Every age contains a mixture of types; but each age also has dominant types—dominant in influence, dominant in occupation of the social foreground. Until the European Renaissance societies were invariably dominated by the muscular, the natively shrewd, or by those of mixed muscularity and shrewdness. The man of learning was seldom more than decorative and there was, indeed, little positive learning of applicable utility. Most of what passed for learning was literary or little more than philosophical rationalization for existing states of affairs. Cumulatively, however, generations of such rationalization developed, through criticism and test, the methods of intelligent inquiry whose change-inducing preliminary fruits we see strewn about us today. With Galileo, da Vinci, Machiavelli, and Vesalius the methods of evidential thinking began their slow conquest over mythological methods.

The invention of new weapons, such as the crossbow and firearms, gradually dethroned the man of muscle, upon whose land seizures with sword and spear the noble families of Europe were founded. The men of shrewdness—the commercial entrepreneur, the banker, the promoter, the explorer-adventurer, the lawyer, and the politician —rose to dominance with the emergence of modern cities. Although here and there, as in Francis Bacon and Leibnitz, the man of worldly shrewdness was also a creative man of learning, for the most part the positive knowledge possessed by shrewd competitors has been meager up to the present.

Subordinate to the man of muscle, the learned man also remained largely subordinate to the man of shrewdness, who pre-empted public honors. But even now this situation is swiftly changing. Although in many areas of government and economic affairs the man of learning is still present only as an adviser or agent, in an increasing number of areas he is in complete charge. Not only is this true of many small companies that are successfully developing or applying one or more scientific principles, the boards of directors and officers consisting entirely of Ph.D.s, but it is also true of many large-scale, long-established business enterprises where a sprinkling of officers and directors hold graduate degrees. At least the bachelor's degree, for whatever it is worth, is now held by nearly everyone on the management level of the largest corporations. Those holding graduate degrees, both in government and in economic enterprises, may be expected to increase steadily until in two or three generations such holders will be the rule.

There is already intense competition among the largest enterprises, including the national government, for the top-ranking graduate students of such schools as the Massachusetts Institute of Technology, the California Institute of Technology, the Harvard Graduate School of Business Administration and similar institutions. Not only will this competition intensify, but other schools will emulate the frontier curricula of the leading schools, many graduates of which are adepts in such esoteric subjects as mathematical sociology of conflict (game theory), econometrics, operations research, cybernetics, dynamic programing, probability theory, statistical decision functions and decision processes, stochastic processes, and logistic or mathematical logic. Important applications for these exist in business, industry, diplomacy, law enforcement, and military planning.

Considering the accumulating evidence all around, my prediction is that the man of learning, whether he holds the Ph.D. or not, is going to displace the man of mere shrewdness all along the line in governmental and economic affairs just as the man of shrewdness displaced the muscular wielder of sword, mace, and spear. The so-called self-made man of affairs, unless he is an autodidact in applicable subjects, is doomed in the developed societies.

The change forecast here, as in the case of other predicted changes, will definitely not take place through some sort of farsighted public resolution—in this case to bring about a modernized version of Plato's rule by philosophers. It will take place by reason of the sheer necessities of a complex situation and of competition internal and foreign. Just as one would not think of placing a muscle man or a merely shrewd operator, a promoter, in charge of a laboratory or a scientific installation today, so in the course of a very few generations social requirements will not permit such persons even to present themselves for responsible positions in government or in the management of economic enterprises on which social well-being depends. The merely shrewd, sketchily tutored operator will be as extinct as the man in armor, and for approximately the same reason: the competitive ineffectiveness of his methods in a context deploying entirely new and complex tools and institutions.

It would be mistaken to interpret this as forecasting that the man of thought is going to replace the man of intuitive action, an ancient dream. All men, in fact, are men of thought and action; the difference among them lies in the adequacy of their thought and action to the surrounding situation. Both the man of muscle and of shrewdness was also a man of thought, and of effective thought within respective historic contexts. The point is that the context is changing very rapidly. One type of man is already obsolete, the other is becoming obsolete. It would be a complete misinterpretation of my meaning to conclude that the man of learning will be without either effectiveness or native shrewdness. He may have more of each than his predecessors. The point is that the man of learning, also aggressive like his predecessors (for the acquisition of learning requires aggressiveness in itself), pre-eminently applies learning rather than physical power or shrewdness. It is this that gives him greater leverage, greater power. He uses different tools—test tubes, retorts, cyclotrons, centrifuges, electron microscopes and the like rather than swords, castles, warehouses, manned factories, ships, money, and ledgers. That the so-called man of thought is capable of world-shaking external as well as concentrated internal action is well illustrated by the way Einstein took the initiative in advising President Roosevelt that the atom bomb was scientifically feasible and that Hitler in his allusions to an ultimate weapon might well have German scientists working on it. This untypical instance apart, what conventional representative of the man of action, such as Cecil Rhodes, Carnegie, Theodore Roosevelt, Rockefeller, Lindbergh, or Ford, has had a particle of the formative influence on the world since, say, 1800, that Dalton, Darwin, Marx, Comte, Pasteur, Keynes, Freud, or Einstein have had?

The disorder and disorganization that ensue in the modern context when a willful, merely shrewd and only randomly tutored man of action takes charge was illustrated with unusual spectacularity by the attempt in this century of various dictators such as Hitler, Mussolini, Tojo, and lesser counterparts to halt powerful long-term trends forced into being by technological advance. The same sort of eventual disorganization is seen in smaller situations where headstrong shrewd men endeavor by the audacity or pertinacity of their uninformed action to buck deep-running trends. A number of American corporations in recent decades have been brought to an impasse or to ruin by the efforts of old-style intuitive men of action to hold their own against competitors who based their actions on policies devised by highly educated specialists. Intuition, hunch, guesswork, and the repetition of traditional tactics can rarely hold their own against new theories developed on the basis of a subtle analysis of carefully gathered relevant facts. In brief, the electronic computer is mightier than the crystal ball.

As the highly educated class increases in numbers and prestige it will, inevitably, gradually impose its values more and more on society. At present its power is politically limited by its limited numbers, and it must with its knowledge largely implement the value systems established by past generations of shrewd operators. But increasingly the educated class, notably the scientists, is becoming restive as it is drawn out of its laboratories and libraries into the world of affairs. Many, for example, question the wisdom of harnessing atomic power to the war-making potential, in turn harnessed to nationalistic rivalries. Many, in fact, hold that the very ancient military institution has been made absolutely obsolete by nuclear physics. Again, outstanding Nobel laureates increasingly cry out alarms about what schemes of values are to be implemented by imminent discoveries in biology and psychology. Are populations to be converted into docile sheep for the benefit of the shrewd? Is it, many of them ask, the primary purpose of new discoveries in medicine to generate profits or to be available for all at minimal cost?

Will the values of this rising group be accepted by the population as a whole? There is little reason to suppose they will not be accepted in view of its demonstrated ability to do things more efficiently, whether it is to elevate man or degrade him.

Just what the values of the coming new class will be one may ascertain by reading the periodicals of the various learned and scientific societies. They are definitely at variance with the basic values of the market place and of international politics. And fears that the dominant educated class will consist of one-sided specialists, either narrow-minded scientists or overgeneralized humanists, neither comprehending the other, may be discounted in view of the lively prospect that formal education for the educated will be virtually a lifetime affair.

By the middle of the twenty-first century, if not before, the world will therefore definitely be entering the era of the savant, and of the savant as master rather than as servant. This will clearly be a new era in which the older controlling values will be discarded, to be replaced by new ones. Many of these, it may be said, have been at least argued for down through the centuries by solitary intellectuals but have not yet been implemented.

Karl Marx visualized the business class, very much in the ascendent in the England of his day, as being displaced by the new and growing class of factory workers. These workers, as he saw it, would simply take over the government, either by vote or by a quick revolution in which they held overwhelming power, and arrange matters to suit themselves. They would, as he visualized it, abolish all titles to private productive property. Not only has this not happened in any country, not even in Russia, but as the chain of events strongly forecasts, it is not likely to happen anywhere. What happened in Russia is that a small extremist group of Marxist doctrinaires, amid chaos produced by disastrous war, established themselves in a backward agricultural country, with few factory workers, over tens of millions of illiterate, politically supine peasants. The pattern was repeated in China and could well emerge in India.

Instead of factory workers constituting the dominant new class as Marx envisaged, the dominant new class will clearly be, as here forecast, the scientifically educated, not only in the United States and United Europe but also in Soviet Russia and eventually in China and India. The factory worker, on whom Marx placed such great store, with the advent of automated production is clearly scheduled to be greatly shrunken in numbers and of very little political influence in Russia, Europe, or the United States.

Must class stratification be continued? What of the ancient egalitarian dream? Marx foresaw the emergence of an egalitarian, classless society but this, as I evaluate the evidence, is not in sight. Barring the advent of as yet merely imagined scientific discoveries, how is the lower third of the population in developmental potential—the feeble-minded, the mentally retarded, the sub-par IQ—to be brought up even to an average level? Unless science intervenes successfully, this lower third, plus those rendered emotionally immature by childhood mal-conditioning, appears to be with us permanently as a neurological proletariat. But such, usually neglected or grossly exploited in the past, will be better cared for than ever in the future, partly owing to the greater means for their support in auto-mechanized production, partly owing to the far greater number of persons in service (including supportive) occupations, and partly owing to the ascendency of the humanistic values of the educated class.

Will not the new class, like the medieval nobility and the post-medieval commercial classes, behave with similar egocentricity, manipulating the credulous and the weak in its own special interest? Such an outcome is highly doubtful in view of the values necessarily cultivated by the educated. For one thing, the position of the new dominant class will not depend on ownership of land or capital, although this class may well become the dominant owner of such private property as remains. The power of the new class will rest on functional position in complex organizations—in government, industry, education, research, support and sustenance, etc. It cannot be transmitted by inheritance, like ownership of land or capital, but must recruit its new generations from the most capable. Its egocentricity must necessarily be more circumscribed.

The ownership of private property, however, may well be widely distributed so as to include members of the lower- or middle-class echelons. But such ownership will be much more closely regulated than now in consonance with the broadened jurisdiction of government. And it will be capability rather than property that confers power.

This new educated class is emerging in Russia as well as the West. As the members of these educated groups do not harbor antipathy or contempt for their opposite numbers in other countries, as do the embattled commissars and free entrepreneurs, it seems likely that, barring a general war, they will be the means, if there are any, by which conflicting nationalisms will eventually be harmonized. For the cultural workers entertain feelings of mutual respect for and reciprocal interest in each other, whatever their nationality.

The emergence of trained intelligence under the stimulus of intensive education in Russia and its satellite countries is bound to produce profound modifications with each succeeding generation within the Soviet-bloc countries. Already there is a growing clamor among Soviet-bloc scientists for more intellectual freedom, an absolute requirement for fully effective intellectual work. And intellectual freedom cannot be severed from general civil freedom. Soviet-bloc scientists increasingly object to superintendence by "philosophers," by which euphemism they designate official Marxist theoreticians.

Clouded by the bare possibility of atomic warfare, the prospect here visualized is also clouded by the continuance of the arms race, which spells enormous waste both for the Soviet and non-Soviet worlds in that the arms can never rationally be used. For if they are used in general warfare civilization will be destroyed, perhaps for all time, and if they are not used the respective efforts in producing arms is merely wasted.

Termination of the arms race would, without any doubt, greatly accelerate the development here forecast. For then scientists, released from preoccupation with weaponry and attendant organization, would be required to deal with the many problems besetting societies reorganizing on a full peacetime basis. Heavy construction, badly needed in all industrial countries with their burgeoning populations, would unquestionably replace for a long time to come the manufacture of the elaborate weapons systems as the central task of the economic systems.

The reconstitution of the labor force through the agency of education along the lines herein forecast may be expected gradually, very slowly, to be duplicated in the undeveloped countries as and if they mature. Of almost insurmountable handicap in coming abreast of the West in the new pattern of development, however, are the huge peasant populations of India and China. How they can be converted into the sort of finely articulated labor force necessary to assure parity with the West in development is indeed extremely problematic. All evidence indicates that in the span of 150 years they cannot do more than make a beginning. Even as these countries set themselves the task of overtaking the West in its present position, the West is preparing itself for a new ambitious technological trajectory.

But may not the ever-present anti-intellectual and know-nothing elements of the West, under demagogic leadership, successfully act to block the gradual take-over by the coming new class? Although possible, such action is hardly likely in view of the inescapable fact that any country preventing the development or rise of this new class would be automatically relegating itself to the approximate position that Spain took vis-à-vis its onetime European peers. It is practically inconceivable, on cultural grounds alone, that either the United States or United Europe would choose a way that almost certainly led to second- or even third-class status in the world, merely to satisfy diehard traditionalists.

It is evident that the task of producing this socially necessary new class falls squarely on the upper third of the educational system, the universities and colleges. These institutions, it is equally made evident by their leisurely efforts at change, are not yet fully aware of the crucial role they must necessarily play in producing an entirely new, mentally different governing class. But in consequence of the role they are slowly being coerced into playing by technological development, the universities and colleges 150 years hence will be as different from those of the present as the present universities and colleges are different from their predecessors of 1800; and the universities and colleges fifty years hence will be as different from those of the present as the present institutions are different from their predecessors of 1910. The future universities and colleges will, in brief, be intellectually far more rigorous, will be shorn of "snap" courses and bureaucratic faculties. The students, instead of being drawn predominantly from the upper middle class without consideration of intellectual ability, will consist of the most able intellectually from all class strata. The high IQs of the poorer classes will be detected in the primary and secondary schools, will be singled out and will be financed through college on an all-expenses-paid basis.

In general, the aim will be to bring the universities abreast of the best in Europe in terms of product and, if possible, to surpass the European schools in the production of scientists, professionals, technicians, engineers, teachers, designers, journalists, inventors and administrators. Upon the proper training of these will depend the fate of the nation in a technologized world.

CHAPTER XI

A MISCELLANY OF PROSPECTS

Briefer, more summary treatments of a variety of prospects are undertaken in this chapter in the interest of covering a great deal of remaining ground. No doubt the more extended treatment given to earlier topics could be profitably re-employed, or even employed more fully, but only at the cost of unduly prolonging the exposition. The method and conceptions that have controlled to this point underlie the remaining predictions.

Marriage and the Family

Social and cultural change, as we have observed, relate to accumulating unguided pressures that eventually require guidance in one direction or another. Whatever the guidance or lack of it, there are inescapable consequences, gratifying or ungratifying. The social institution that has since the very beginning of the Industrial Revolution experienced most pressure and most change—so much as now to be virtually unrecognizable, a wraith of its former self—is that of marriage and the family. The family as an institution is in fact near the point of complete extinction.

Until the Industrial Revolution the family was the central institution of society—its basic unit of economic production, the principal ground of what little formal education and individual correction there was, the chief center of amusement and recreation, the hospital, the nursing and retirement home for the ailing and the aged, and the smallest unit of local government. Whatever insight it lacked into more cosmic matters was supplied to it by religion. It has been stripped of all these inner functions by technological advance and is increasingly losing residual functions such as food processing and pre-school care of children. Once extended to include at least three generations and various degrees of collateral relationship usually working and living together, often under a single roof, it is now reduced to what sociologists call a purely nuclear form: young parents and dependent children. At the age of eighteen the children tend to relocate either at college or in jobs, leaving a post-mature couple looking forward to retirement from life in more or less straitened circumstances. We see, then, that today's family is not only nuclear but is largely temporary, lacking in continuity.

The nuclear family, most of its onetime basic functions now performed more efficiently by outside agencies, is the plaything of outside events over which it has no control. And gone is the sense of solidarity peculiar to the extended family. Prior to the Industrial Revolution the family was usually sure, barring natural calamities, of its bare livelihood; under advanced technology it is always under threat of unemployment or unsettling income variation owing to technological improvement or economic imbalance. Additionally, illness or injury of the breadwinners often threatens loss or contraction of livelihood, and with it loss of ready access to agencies of education, amusement, recreation and medical care. In order to avail itself of services it once generated for itself, now greatly improved in quality, the modern family requires more purchasing power than ever before. But the terms of competition for it are completely out of its control, regulated as they are by a market.

The high divorce rate, now involving about one in every three American marriages, is only a partial index to the difficulty of modern marriage, shorn of most practical functions. An undetermined additional number of couples become emotionally estranged, problems to each other and to children, without seeking divorce. Marriages invariably endure solely on grounds of expediency, duty, or affection. But whereas expediency, a sense of duty, and the law (in about that order) kept the preindustrial family together, the main supports of modern marriage are affection and compatibility, a sense of duty, and expediency—a reversal of order. Affection, it is well recognized, is unstable, varying as personalities develop and conditions change. The sense of duty has waned for many with the decline of community solidarity under the cult of economic individualism. And with few concrete needs being met that cannot be satisfied elsewhere, expediency has come to play little role of support. Divorcing couples, their affection turned to hate or indifference, find it more expedient to go their separate ways.

The failure of marriage is socially serious only when there are dependent children—of divorced or emotionally estranged parents, or of parents overwhelmed by illness, economic vicissitudes, or their own emotional immaturity and lack of responsible behavior. The prevalence of divorce where there are no children merely represents the indirect achievement of what Bertrand Russell and Judge Ben B. Lindsey recommended as "companionate marriage."

Where children are present, unfavorable conditions—ignorance, poverty, below-average intelligence, overcrowding, unemployment, family illness, and parental psychological immaturity (a prime cause of failure in the middle and upper classes)—produce a variety of serious social problems, mainly concentrated in the preponderant urban sectors. Among them are juvenile delinquency (now reaching what experts call "dangerous proportions"), physical and mental illness of children, crime and narcotics addiction among the young, and the development of a hard core of future destructive adult personalities who will be lifelong social problems as prison inmates and wards of hospitals and asylums.

To deal with the problem of neglected and disoriented children, government will greatly extend present measures. It will act first to prevent socially undesirable results, and second to cope far more effectively than at present with such results when they make themselves apparent. At the end of 1961 no fewer than 3½ million dependent children were receiving governmental financial assistance in the United States.

But before considering the looming necessary public measures that will be taken, let us consider briefly the argument that the family, far from wilting, is flourishing. The evidence cited is the sharp rise in birth rate, some of it extramarital. The postwar rise in the American birth rate, reversing a trend under way since 1810, under examination is traceable not to a strengthening of the family but almost entirely to economic factors and certain governmental policies. Some psychoanalysts, bemused by theory without supporting fact, during World War II hypothesized that the upturn in birth rate was induced by the desire of young men facing death in battle to achieve some posterity through progeny. An unconscious desire, it was known only to the analysts. Overlooked was the hard fact that other wars had not produced similar effects. But principally overlooked was the solid fact that the government, in its first military service laws, initially exempted married men (thereby stimulating marriages), then fathers of families (now stimulating the birth rate) and, finally, when it had to call fathers, provided unprecedentedly generous family allowances, depending on number of children. At the end of the war veterans' benefits included long-term low-cost mortgage loans, stimulating and reinforcing family formation. Married veterans attending college, with or without children, received differential benefits. To all of this was added the New Deal supportive features such as unemployment and old-age insurance, home relief, and a booming inflationary economy with many job openings. Furthermore, low wages and long hours, which had for decades prevailed under the economics of scarcity, were replaced by higher wages, shorter hours, and pension and health benefits under the pressure of legislatively strengthened labor unions.

On this firm economic base the birth rate soared. It became the style to have larger families.

Although the economic measures were not solely responsible, they contributed the means. Underlying the entire phenomenon, apart from the attraction of novelty, was probably a groping attempt by a generation reared in boom and depression between two wars to achieve some sense of stability. Family life was the symbol of such stability. But unfortunately for man's emotional well-being, the traditional family cannot be reconstituted merely by having children in a precariously affluent society. The traditional family supported itself, even the children taking a hand; the modern family must often be supported. It is wholly a responsibility, often resting on individually incapable shoulders.

These remarks in passing, before coming to what must be done in the situation, are ventured to bring out differences in the Asian and the American population booms. Asia traditionally procreates to the biological maximum, depending largely on disease, epidemic, and famine to hold down population; the population increase in Asia, as we have noted, is the result of better public-health measures, not of the willful seeking of more children. As Americans are well aware, the size of families can readily be limited by birth-control techniques. The present population boom in the United States will end or taper off probably within thirty years of its inception, around 1970 when the population will be 200 million, by reason of inner family dynamics. For the children produced by the boom, to a great extent sought for extrinsic reasons rather than for themselves, will view their own family prospects as adults in terms of their childhood experience which, on the whole, will not have been favorable. At the end of 1961, for example, one in every ten New York City children under the age of eighteen was on the public-assistance rolls. Children in New York and elsewhere are coping with a variety of family difficulties.

How can one, however, possibly conclude that the postwar baby crop did not represent, on the whole, an outburst of true familialism and a valuation of children for their intrinsic selves? The value a community places on its children is reflected by the provisions made for them—in schools and school programs, playgrounds, recreation centers and the like. Not only are these held by experts inadequate throughout most of the country, but there is highly vociferous popular demand that present minimal home relief measures be terminated. School district after school district has voted down bond issues, opposes play and recreation facilities on grounds of cost, while the taxpayers themselves resort to huge drafts of installment credit for expensive consumer appliances. When it comes to providing for children, economy is the watchword. If the generation of 1915–40 was "The Lost Generation," then the generation of 1940–65 is "The Generation of Pawns." On the basis of its own childhood experience, participating in parental anguish over taxes, installment payments, unemployment and the threat thereof, job displacement, and the threat of war, this generation will be less than eager to reproduce itself no matter what its economic base may be. It is therefore my prediction that the birth rate will fall and will, in fact, resume its pre-1940 trend. The United States will not become overpopulated like China, India, and Japan.

Returning now to specific governmental measures in support of the family, these will be entirely federal although carried out perhaps through local government agencies. Most localities are unable even now to shoulder this burden.

As to measures of preventing social catastrophes, government and leading agencies of society will increasingly stress the seriousness and difficulties of marriage under modern conditions with a view to deterring poor marital risks. Public policy will, despite religious barriers, everywhere favor the practice of birth control and probably abortion as well, especially for the immature and irresponsible. When these latter nevertheless begin to breed, legally or illegally, it is probable that they will be barred, under court order, from having additional children under penalty of being surgically sterilized.

Marriage in preindustrial society was indispensably part of a way of life, alone making possible economic as well as much other necessary activity. It was strongly supported by organized religion and endorsed by all conservatives for the stability it produced. Many children in the presence of a high death rate were a guarantee that society would survive. Although the religious and conservatives tenaciously value marriage, they are now not a little confused because the modern family, far from insuring stability, is itself an unstabilizing factor forcing many changes distasteful to traditionalists.

Although still underwritten by religion and conservatism, the principal external impetus for modern marriage, often entered into by bored and unprepared couples, comes from the commercialized romanticism of films and cheap fiction. There marriage is depicted as a panacea, promising to dissolve all difficulties in sexual gratification. Joined with this cue is the democratic idea that every individual, no matter how unsuited for responsibility, is entitled to a mate and children. As the promised gratification turns out to be less than expected and difficulties intrude from a world of change, many families present themselves, overtly or covertly, as social problems.

Modern marriage, commercially presented as a blissful haven, turns out more often than not to be a joint exercise by two unprepared people in solving an endless series of novel problems. Many find their resilience and resourcefulness limited and at some point break down under the strain.

In directly coping with the many difficulties of modern marriage in overcrowded industrial society the national government, perhaps working through agencies of local government, will gradually be forced to adopt, ultimately, the following minimal middle-of-the-road measures:

1. Applicants for marriage licenses will be required to read, prior to the issuance of licenses, manuals dealing with common marital difficulties—economic, residential, ethnic, religious, and psychological. Minimal age for marriage will be raised at least to eighteen, perhaps to twenty. High schools and colleges will increasingly develop courses in marriage and child rearing, already installed in some, but the emphasis will increasingly be on social and psychological difficulties. There will be especial warning conveyed against producing children that are unwanted.

2. With each child born, an educated social worker, part of the reorganized work force predicted in the previous chapter, will call at the home, whatever its economic level, there to obtain some impres-

sion of the environment, consult with the mother and leave literature on child care—for the modern mother, unlike her counterpart of the preindustrial family, knows next to nothing about her job and is usually without sound advisers. She must usually rely either on books or the usually unreliable "folk" advice.

3. School psychologists (also part of the revised work force) beginning in kindergarten will observe the children and will make mandatory reports to emergency centers on those with behavior symptoms indicating subnormal home conditions. Where improvement of such conditions appears doubtful even with public assistance, the children will be removed, placed under approved and supervised foster care or taken to high-quality residential centers in charge of trained personnel (also part of the new work force released by automation).

4. Indoor and outdoor recreation centers will be established in all urban neighborhoods, manned by trained personnel, and schools, now substandard in most districts, will be greatly improved both physically and in programs and personnel. There will also be established, as indicated earlier, public summer camps for all children aged nine to eighteen.

5. Adolescents unable to do further schoolwork and unable to find suitable jobs will be trained under government auspices for suitable jobs. If none is available they will be enrolled in special government work groups concerned with soil and forest conservation and like tasks.

6. When parents are unable to pay for necessary remedial medical care, physical or psychological, children will be cared for by the doctors of government agencies. In this respect children of the lower economic classes will obtain as good and as frequent service as the children of the upper classes.

7. Children with special aptitudes of promising social or cultural utility will be singled out in the late elementary grades for special attention in order to develop their talents. They may be invited to attend special high schools with enriched and advanced programs. They will attend college tuition-free, with supplementary expenses paid. They will not, as now, be prematurely put to work for family support. When this is needed it will be supplied out of public funds. Not only this, but some of these youths will be publicly financed for travel and study abroad with a view to enriching their knowledge of languages and distant cultures.

Between measures of prevention and of dealing with difficulties as they show themselves, the number of social behavior problems bedeviling urban industrial society will be sharply reduced.

One reason this program in its entirety, and even with many embellishments one cannot foresee, will be adopted for the United States, despite uninformed opposition, is that it is the cheapest as well as the most effective way of coping with the manifold problems. The situation will be made more difficult by the rise of automated technology. The problems, far from receding, are going to become more prominent. The alternative to these improvements is to implement an expensive police state. To a greatly expanded constabulary must be added many jails and detention centers. And to the direct cost of repression brought to bear against the unfortunate and miserable there will be the indirect cost of much crime and emergency care and the loss to society of many constructive talents.

The United States is presently in an intermediate, tentative stage, with vestiges of repression and neglect still prevalent but becoming more responsive to some of the new techniques. Private agencies, which originally attempted to meet these needs of industrial society, proved wholly inadequate although many did good work in limited areas. The massiveness and social threat of the general problem of the family gradually brought government on the scene, against the anguished protests of traditionalists convinced that the entire difficulty is merely a manifestation of original sin, not to be met by "coddling."

The process of externalizing the family and its functions that began with the Industrial Revolution will be completed in the next 150 years. For the quantity and the quality of the children it turns out into a complex, easily disordered society will be a public rather than a private matter.

Social reinforcement of the family, furthermore, will have the further effect of greatly reducing the number of private assaults on society, especially in the form of white-collar crime. Fraud and violation of trust, both by public officials and private figures, are probably preponderantly carried out by men seeking to guarantee the economic future of their families. They can see what happens to families when the support of the breadwinner is removed by disease, accident, and economic and political change: at best, meager, minimal assistance. When public family reinforcement becomes universal and widespread, the conditions of an economic jungle no longer present, many of the motivations for family protection by means of illegal behavior will be removed.

There is no serious possibility of dangerous overpopulation in either Europe or Anglo-America for the simple reason that in those jurisdictions population increase may be rather easily controlled—by personal decision, by the removal of tax exemptions for children, by the imposition of taxes on what are considered excess children. Sterner measures would hardly be necessary. In the Orient, governments afraid of losing popularity by requiring birth control or abortion can simply rely on famine, pleading helplessness in the face of conditions. Before succumbing to famine, however, superstitious populations can overcome their many food taboos—against the eating of cattle in India, against milk products in China. A good many of people's troubles, it is worth noticing, are self-induced, deriving from a stubborn ignorance that flouts what is to any educated person right reason. Many victims are in cultural pits of their own making, which does not make them any the less of a threat to others.

The Future of the City

The American city, as I predicted earlier, will in the coming period fall completely under the jurisdiction of the national government, like European cities which are in every way better managed. Already federal aid to cities, bypassing state governments, and the proposed Department of Urban Affairs represent tentative steps in this direction.

Other trends point in the same direction.

American cities are under mayoral-council, commission, or city-manager forms of government, with the latter innovation increasing rapidly. Eventually all cities, including the giant or extended city, will be under the manager form, with the manager either chosen by or approved by the national government.

An extensive and growing literature reveals two broad complaints against the contemporary American city: (1) more often than not managed by incompetents and tricksters, it is inefficient, graft-ridden, and scandal-infested, and (2) it has come to bristle with such a complexity of local problems that affect national life at so many points that it is often beyond the control of even well-intentioned and well-informed local management. It needs more money for support, more skill in management.

The seventeen largest cities, with populations of 500,000 and more, retain the inefficient, graft-ridden mayor-council government of divided, often conflicting powers. The electoral victors under this system invariably hold power by demagogic appeals to a heterogeneous majority and the permission of a long array of minor (sometimes major) law violations. The organized underworld is an ever-present influence. Low standards of community life prevail except in a few showcase areas—the central business district, a few upper socioeconomic neighborhoods. Much of the city is a slum or bordering upon slum conditions except where heroic measures, with federal aid, have recently made a slight dent in appearances.

Significantly, the upper socioeconomic suburbs of the large cities, where the level of education is higher, usually have come to install city managers.

The reason American cities started out with the defective mayor-council system is that all local governments in the United States—state, county, and municipal—established themselves as imitations of the venerated tripartite federal system without consideration of a difference in problems. The system of checks and balances, therefore, obtains throughout American government down to its lowest level except where it has been abandoned in this century for good reason. The result is that necessary local action is often stymied.

Political scientists almost to a man testify to the lower cost and greater efficiency of the city-manager scheme. The commission form, consisting of five independently elected commissioners who are department heads, is less effective because of rivalry among the commissioners for public favor, with consequent disorder within the government as commissioners form coalitions against each other on matters of common municipal concern. The mayor-council form is almost unanimously considered to be the least satisfactory. Characterized by inefficiency and impropriety, it is also beset by political jockeying, disharmony, and general confusion.

The objection to county government is similar to that against the mayor-council form and in some states, such as Connecticut, it has been eliminated entirely; in others only severely limited by state action. County governments often overlap and duplicate city governments, sometimes on a large scale as in Chicago and Cook County.

In the resultant confusion the cost to taxpayers and the inefficiency is considerable.

Functions in county governments are usually scattered among a number of officials and boards, with no integration or central direction. Persons in charge have as often as not been inexpert and inept, and not seldom corrupt. Many states, led by New York, Ohio, Minnesota, Massachusetts, and Iowa, now provide by law for state audit, inspection, and supervision of county financial affairs and in some states for the right to send in examiners. "Sticky fingers" among county as well as municipal officials has long been a common phenomenon. Services paid for by the taxpayers—as for the proper maintenance of jails, roads, hospitals, and poor farms—have not been fully delivered.

Various states now require uniform county systems of accounting and budgeting, and more than half require periodical financial reports. A few states require state approval before a county may float a bond issue. All of this has wrought improvement but political scientists discern the need for much larger appropriations for inspectorial work. For when the inspectors are away the local Machiavellis begin to play —with public money.

Localism and regionalism in government are defended by impassioned oratory about home rule and states' rights but, by the pragmatic test, the high-sounding principles enunciated invariably conceal some bit of impropriety in the home sector—such as the wholesale denial of constitutional rights to Negroes and of educational and social support to impoverished white rustics in the South, and the perpetration of a variety of financial malpractices in other local jurisdictions. Two factors will in the foreseeable future deal the death blows to the cult of American localism (which portrays the national government as an inimical, alien power): (1) the technology-inspired rising educational level and (2) the overwhelming complexity and diversity of local problems that even well-intentioned local government is now unable to cope with. Increasing federal aid to cities, eloquently argued for by urban representatives in Congress, unmistakably indicates the trend of affairs.

Physically the trend, with about 75 per cent of the population now urbanized, is toward a few supercities, or megalopolises. These already exist in effect although not integrated in management. The first of these, urbanized all the way, extends from north of Boston, some observers placing it at Portland, to Norfolk. In depth it has a varying range of ten to twenty-five miles. There is the outline of a similar supercity extending along the Pacific coast from San Diego to a point north of San Francisco. Ultimately it appears destined to range north to Vancouver. A third supercity is clearly taking form around and throughout the area of the Great Lakes, embracing a region from Milwaukee and Chicago to Buffalo or Rochester on a west-east line and from Columbus to Toronto on a southerly-northerly line. Many factors, among them inland ocean waterways, practically guarantee the rapid upthrust of this supercity. The fourth supercity, already definitely outlined, will be distributed along the Gulf Coast of Texas, Louisiana, Alabama, and Florida. What the names will be of these huge complexes, each with the administration coordinated from single centers, is anybody's guess; but they might well be named Atlantic City, Pacific City, Great Lakes City, and Gulf City. All should be solidly established within 150 years.

A few large American cities are now in process of reconstruction, with heavy federal aid, from the centers outward. This reconstruction is taking place by areas, with tall reinforced concrete structures arranged around central plazas. The general model is found in Rockefeller Center, New York. The vertical or skyscraper type of expansion is practically guaranteed by the concentrations of expanding population. For residential use these will be apartment buildings, many cooperatively owned, housing from hundreds to thousands of families.

Neighborhoods will consist of clusters of apartment buildings into which schools, hospitals, and churches may in time be incorporated without external distinguishing marks. Buildings will also include otherwise indistinguishable recreation centers and theaters.

Individual dwellings in suburban areas will increasingly be replaced by so-called garden or quadrangular apartments or attached, floor-through duplex and triplex homes. The individual detached single-family dwelling will slowly tend to disappear, although it may well persist in outlying areas and in distant recreation regions.

There will be no lack of access to the outdoors in these buildings, all of which will be air-conditioned. Many will have individual terraces, and roofs and abutments will provide recreational space. Depending on economic level, they will contain swimming pools indoors and some will no doubt have rooftop outdoor pools. Shrubbery will festoon roofs and terraces in a modern version of the hanging gardens of Babylon.

Theoretical objection to this type of construction, already taking place in New York and a few other cities, will hardly prevail, for the task will be to provide for multitudes. Nor need the effect be monotonous. Variations of line and exterior materials will no doubt be seen, and variations of color. New York already has blue, green, and yellow tile-sheathed buildings of this type. The city of the future can be as colorful as were Athens or Rome, where the buildings were painted. As to policing vast interior labyrinths, this will be a problem to be solved.

As cities are gradually reconstructed and their government improved, there will be a gradual return of the middle classes who fled to the outlying areas to create what is known as "suburban sprawl." The suburbs themselves, now beset by problems similar to those of the cities, will in twenty-five to fifty years begin to deteriorate physically owing to poor construction, will be taken over by the lower economic classes prior to replacement with modern multiple dwellings as forecast. For the city, properly operated, is a more convenient place in which to live than either the country or the suburbs. Its superiority is the reason for its creation.

It was largely municipal mismanagement and local powerlessness that induced the middle classes to flee as soon as they could afford to move. Unable to make headway against entrenched officialdom, worn out from coping with unsolved traffic problems, inferior and often disorderly schools, outmoded and insufficient dwellings, air pollution, substandard public transportation, insufficient supervised recreational space for children, inadequate police protection, overcrowding, outrageous rents and local taxes, the middle classes simply packed off to new suburbs where they had a more effective voice in controlling the environment. Usually they then found themselves under the city manager or commission forms of local government.

The influx of impoverished elements of lower culture—Negroes, Puerto Ricans, Mexicans, uneducated poor whites from the South into New York, Philadelphia, Pittsburgh, Detroit, Chicago, Los Angeles and elsewhere—supplied added motivation for relocating, not because of intrinsic objection to them as people or because of their strange ways but because of their often alarming, belligerent behavior. The newcomers felt resentful of the better-situated old residents, and showed it in many ways. They often became police problems. Even where older residents understood and sympathized with their difficulties they could do nothing, as they were powerless against entrenched local forces to prevent overcrowding, rent gouging, wage exploitation. Only federal power could do that.

In time, as with refugees from Europe, these new internal refugees will be assimilated and integrated, will become part of the middle class. That, thus far, has been American history.

Transportation in the coming supercity will be of the mass variety —rapid-transit trains, buses, and taxicabs. The outlook for private automobile operation is extremely doubtful and the present trend toward smaller private passenger cars no doubt presages a gradual reduction in per capita car ownership in the United States. The automobile has undoubtedly been a convenience (highly qualified, to be sure) and a great aid in integrating so large a region as the United States. But beyond its aspects of convenience it was also taken up for reasons of novelty, as a fascinating new toy. It also came to be a social status symbol of economic success. But now, with its availability to all, it has lost most of its value as a claim to status. Furthermore, its convenience is overbalanced in urban use by its inconvenience. In cities it is no longer a form of rapid transit. To this inconvenience may be added the difficulty of finding parking or garaging space, high insurance rates, higher and higher costs of operation, the increasing prevalence of serious accidents. Since its introduction into the United States the death toll from automobile accidents greatly exceeds a million, more than were killed in all United States wars. The injured each year number about one million, the dead some 40,000.

In place of private passenger-car ownership, which will strongly tend to decline per capita, there will be a great increase in private car-rental service for trips outside cities. For distant trips the airplane will be resorted to increasingly, with cars rented for local transportation where mass transport facilities are lacking.

That the large automobile manufacturers anticipate this trend is evidenced by their diversification into the manufacture of other products ranging from pocket radios and electric toasters to Diesel locomotives. The big automobile companies are becoming general manufacturers of the entire line of consumer appliances. Not much space in the city of the future, then, will be occupied by garages.

The future supercity, finally, will have no air-pollution problem, thanks to the installation of preventive devices on buildings and vehicles; will be without slums; will possess more open ground space devoted to supervised recreation areas; will have tree-lined streets (small trees, wide streets); will have no jerry-built structures; will be quite clean, almost noiseless, devoid of billboards and unsightly signs, well-supplied with self-service stores, restaurants, hospitals, clinics, libraries, and social-service centers. Manufacturing and storage will be relegated to its fringes, away from apartment houses, office buildings, and hotels.

It will not, however, be a paradise. It will be replete with problems, human and organizational. But they will be coped with rationally, out of sheer necessity, on the basis of enhanced knowledge and insight.

The Future of Recreation

Recreation as an institution has slowly flowered with the rise of civilization and was well established in the ancient Greek world. Usually restricted to the upper classes with their monopoly on leisure, recreation made itself increasingly indispensable in the life of the common man with the rise of industrialization and urbanization. But for him it largely centered around the tavern, vaudeville theater, and sports arena. On the fringes were dance halls, penny arcades, gambling houses, brothels, cheap seaside resorts, billiard parlors, and bowling alleys.

Fatigue rather than lack of opportunity probably played the major role in keeping the working masses from recreational indulgence.

As recreational activity has gradually extended itself from the top of the social pyramid downward with shortening of work hours, paid vacations, and higher real income, one may expect similar causes to induce similar effects. While automation will not produce the very short work week some labor leaders demand, it should produce longer average vacations and it should result in some shortening of average weekly work hours. Above all it will virtually eliminate fatiguing physical labor, leaving free much energy as well as some time. Some of this free time and energy, as I have pointed out, will unquestionably be put into adult higher education, itself made necessary by the complexity of modern living. However, some part of this new form of education may come to be considered recreational, pursued solely for enjoyment and relaxation.

The term recreation as used here embraces diversion and amusement as well, although it excludes dissipation and distraction. Other than this none of the other possible subtle distinctions will be drawn.

Recreation, furthermore, is broadly classifiable in various ways: juvenile and adult, individual and social, indoor and outdoor, spontaneous and organized, active and passive. In what follows, coming developments will be traced from childhood to adulthood.

At the outset it should be noticed that the institution of recreation as it develops further will absorb personnel that, if present conditions continued, would have been forced to work in factories and offices.

School children of the future will not be sent to their homes in midafternoon as at present, both because they require further attention and because the urban home is too attenuated in size and surrounding facilities to accommodate them. And often, because the mother is employed, there is nobody to receive them. School termination in midafternoon takes place because in an earlier day children were needed for household chores, mainly on farm homes; the long summer vacation similarly stems from the earlier need of children to assist with farming. Since these and other duties have been abolished by technological innovation there is nothing for most children to do.

It is part of the American self-image that it is an athletic nation of clear-eyed, stalwart young people. Yet Selective Service reports invariably find the men preponderantly flabby-muscled, overweight, and lethargic. Presidential warnings are issued from time to time, and ignored, about the low state of national physical fitness. None of it is really cause for astonishment as the nation, in fact, systematically neglects physical-fitness programs and deludes itself with a façade of athletic activity carried on by specialists.

In the schools this façade takes the form of gymnastics for two or three short periods per week—just enough to interrupt the academic program. Organized school sports are only for a selected few, the most gifted physically, an elite. Except in a few upper-class private boarding schools there is no compulsory program of intramural sports for all. If academic programs were organized the way school sports are, there would be a few squads of the intellectually most adept, on whom the teachers would concentrate. The rest of the school would be organized in cheering sections, as spectators, but not allowed to participate themselves.

As far as the children are concerned, the basic issue on use of afternoons is not the inadequacy of the modern home or poor muscle development, although these are involved in the problem. The basic issue relates to the great importance of play for learning and personality development. Knowing little of play, and approving it less, most Americans confuse it with dissipation and distraction.

Despite disclaimers that may be heard, the American cultural attitude toward play is still that of a puritanic American school of 1784 that expressed its policy as follows:

"We prohibit play in the strongest terms. . . . The students shall rise at five o'clock in the morning, summer and winter. . . . The students shall be indulged with nothing which the world calls *play*. Let this rule be observed with the strictest nicety; for those who play when they are young will play when they are old."[1]

Play has been discerned as having various functions—as a refresher from labor, as an outlet for surplus energies, as a stimulant to growth, as an emotional cathartic, as psychological compensation, as a release of aggressive drives.[2]

But play is far more than an adjunct to man's well-being and growth. It is, in fact, integral to his nature. This theme has been developed by the Dutch historian Huizinga in a now classic work wherein he shows the civilizing influence of play and its role in the development of the higher cultural forms: law, knowledge, literature, mythopoiesis, philosophy, and art.[3] Early mathematics and science, for example, were entered upon by amateurs in the spirit of play, not with utilitarian ends in view. In light of what we now know of the cultural importance of play it is hardly an accident that the extremely playful Greek civilization should have been so superlatively creative. Playful periods of history are the most creative, as witness the Renaissance. Unplayful periods, imbued with grim purposes, are the least creative, as witness Europe between the fall of Rome and the dawn of the Renaissance.

Play, then, is vital, elevating, and a powerful support for individual and group creativity, as a large and growing literature now attests. But the prevalent American idea of play for the young is to give children a ball and send them to the nearest street or park (if there is one; a vacant lot will serve). What is ordinarily self-defeating about this procedure is that they lack guidance and instruction. Even if, by dint of much effort, they manage to get some game going, they perform improperly and develop habits that frustrate them in developing self-satisfying ability and physical development. Instead of producing desired release of spirit and capabilities, most of the unguided play and sports activity of the American young convinces them that they are incapable, fit only to be spectators.

Under the coming program, all this will be done. The school plus recreation day will extend on a compulsory basis from 8:30 or 9 A.M. to 6 P.M. Saturdays will probably be devoted for the most part to a compulsory recreational-sports program, indoors in inclement weather. Sundays will no doubt be free. Evenings will be reserved for family life and studies, which will be approached with keener and more appreciative minds after a satisfactory late afternoon.

Non-urban summer activity will also be available to the young, either on a family basis or by groups in public camps. Most of the impetus for the establishment of the present rather extensive network of children's private summer camps has come from the unsatisfactory nature of the transitional industrial city. Parents who pay up to $750 per child for two months of camp wish to keep their children from aimlessly running loose on city streets when school closes. But as many campers also come from suburban areas without acute city drawbacks, it is apparent that there are other motivations. One of these is the knowledge that the summer is now a vacuum for most children, to be filled by television or movies. Balanced against this sterile prospect is the knowledge that a good camp experience teaches self-reliance, fortifies confidence by developing new skills. The entire experience is both educational and recreational, fostering initiative and showing that there is always something for a resourceful person to do.

But with the city reconstructed along the lines forecast, offering many new facilities for summer activity, there is no need to look forward to a wholesale exodus of children from the city in the summer. Larger numbers than at present, however, will no doubt avail themselves of the opportunity to go to camp. And such camps, it is evident, will make their own demands for skilled personnel to conduct operations. Children who pass the summer with parents, either in or out of the city, will obviously occupy a separate category.

Already some of these aspects of the future are visible on a token or partial basis. Private boarding schools now have daily compulsory athletics and games programs for late afternoons and Saturdays, exempting only those with medical excuses. Will the automated society, with its need to find functional outlets for the labor force as well as for youngsters adrift, confine such opportunities, as at present, only to a selected few? I predict that it will not; the private schools will be widely emulated in this respect as they have been in respect to academic programs. Indoor recreation centers, supplied mainly by private agencies, are already available here and there in the form of slum-district settlement houses and the far too few YMCA centers. Private voluntarism has done effective work in this sphere but only on a restricted or pilot basis. The number of such facilities will be increased by one or two thousand times within 100 years, paid for out of public funds. Only public support can spread the benefits and increase the effective demand for personnel. Only a few suburban communities now have fairly adequate recreational programs, partly utilizing school facilities. Such programs will be gradually extended throughout urban areas all over the nation. Europe will follow suit.

In the preceding chapter it was pointed out that educators aim to train no more than the upper 25 per cent in intelligence for the emerging new society, which leaves out a vast multitude. But intelligence as measured with respect to intellectual ability which is what primarily interests most educators is measured almost entirely by aptitude in the manipulation of symbol systems—numbers, language, and special systems of notation (as in music). Psychologists, however, already recognize other kinds of intelligence.

One kind of non-intellectual intelligence is the intelligence of the body itself. To believe there is no such thing is to ignore the coordinated, fantastically clever functioning of an almost infinitely complex chemical organism. And there are, obviously, gradations of such intelligence, as some bodies, especially in the hands (as of artists and craftsmen), are capable of far more complicated coordinations than others. Anyone who has had the opportunity to watch a first-class ballet performance, and has appreciated it, must be aware of the existence of this kind of intelligence. There is far more to it than capering through a prescribed routine. Anybody couldn't do it. And many could not do it even if they had been carefully trained.

Another kind of latent intelligence shows itself in dealings with people and is perhaps best described by the single word empathy. There is also, manifestly, esthetic intelligence.

People in their culturally biased use of language conceal from themselves the existence of these various forms of intelligence. Whereas they refer to such a phenomenon as intellectual acumen, highly valued in a complex culture, when the body, personality, or feeling is concerned they say it is bodily dexterity, social aptitude, or esthetic sensitivity—all of which are rated lower, at least by narrow-minded academicians. But the intimate relation of the mind to the body, now stressed in psychosomatic medicine, strongly suggests that there is a close interrelationship among all these forms of intelligence. When one is neglected, the others become attenuated.

It is these non-intellectual forms of intelligence that must be developed by the community for the visualized necessary further development of the labor force, and particularly on behalf of the forecast social-service and recreation programs. As matters now stand, society allows them largely to go to waste or to make out as best they can.

Most opportunities for adult recreation appear almost certain to develop on a commercial basis, in contrast with the expansion of public facilities for children. This will be necessary in order to provide greater selectivity. The commercial possibilities in the field of recreation, passive and active, in-city and ex-city, therefore appear to be virtually without limit—limited, in fact, only by the extent of the adult population and its disposable leisure time.

Let us first consider out-of-city recreational activities. With vacation periods of at least a month per year not only made possible but entirely likely, it is manifestly possible for people with the modern means of transportation to travel widely, at home and abroad. Some persons will prefer to center their vacation activities in family houses, owned or rented; some will utilize resorts, hotels, and inns. In the northerly zones people may prefer to take all or part of their vacation period in the winter, as some now do, seeking either winter-resort areas or subtropical regions.

For those seeking winter vacations in the south, the Caribbean and Mediterranean areas will be widely sought, not only by persons from the northern but also from the southern hemispheres. The single city of Miami Beach, Florida, already attracts about 1½ million visitors annually, and resort areas in Puerto Rico and the Virgin Islands draw others. Parts of the west coast of Florida are already well developed as resort areas. The southwestern region of the United States, including Arizona, New Mexico, and California, serves a double purpose in that it also attracts elderly retired people seeking year-round warmth and sunshine.

Both the Caribbean and Mediterranean regions, although already well established as vacation areas, are clearly due in an age of rapid travel for a tremendous expansion. New developments will not necessarily be modeled upon either Miami Beach or the Riviera. Rather there will be great variety in the type of facilities offered, from small single dwellings to large caravansaries. Marinas will dot both areas, airplane fields will be standard equipment, and seasonal patrons will number in the tens of millions.

National and state parks already exist for tourists and nearby residents and it has already been proposed that the national park system be enlarged in order to take redundant land out of agriculture and conserve the soil.

Specific recreational activities at winter and summer resorts and in family homes will no doubt run the entire range of presently developed indoor and outdoors sports and social activities, but there seems a strong likelihood that there will continue to be a strong emphasis on water activities, on and below the surface. Boating especially, already popular, appears almost certain to enjoy wider popularity than ever. Motorboats and sailboats will be mass-produced in larger quantities than ever before. The per capita ownership of boats will increase as per capita ownership of automobiles falls.

Both the United States and Europe, in their lakes, rivers, and extensive coasts, offer as yet unrealized opportunities for boating.

Intercontinental travel, too, will be increased far beyond present levels. Many persons, by concentrating their vacation periods repeatedly in certain distant centers, will become as familiar with them as with their home cities. World cruise ships will be vastly multiplied beyond present numbers, with ports of call and stopovers all over the world. In the process there will be intermingling of peoples and cultures on a scale never before known.

For all of this adult recreational activity, easily embracing more than half the adult population, there will obviously be required a vast increase in equipment, facilities and personnel. The demand here for the latter will have the effect of absorbing more elements of the labor force that would in earlier times have been employed in factories and offices.

Certain anticipated perspectives that have been raised in previous years will probably not be realized. More than two decades ago it was thought by some observers that a great age of private airplane operation would open up, duplicating the automobile age. This era of widespread private-plane operation does not, as I estimate the prospect, seem likely to come about—partly because the air corridors are already overcrowded with mass-transport carriers, partly owing to the great cost, and partly because specialized skills are required for operation. Technological innovations may alter the factors involved, but at the moment anything like mass airplane operation does not seem likely.

It is far from being the case that all technological possibilities are pressed into service in all possible spheres. The development of the submarine, for example, has not led to submarine pleasure cruising, the values of which appear doubtful. In principle at least people could charter a submarine now for a cruise under the North Pole. Why would they want to do so? On similar grounds it appears virtually certain that there will be no pleasure excursions into space—trips to the moon, Mars, or Venus and other variants of science fiction. As to the very distant future, that is another matter. . . . Nor does rocket travel seem very likely, either for business or pleasure. Even if it should be possible to travel from New York to New Delhi by rocket in twenty or thirty minutes, what motivation would anyone have for making a trip in such a short time? If it is argued that a medical emergency might require the transport of a doctor over such a distance in a brief time, it is evident that medical technology will be so widely dispersed as not to require such spectacular trips. To be sure, if rockets can be produced, launched, and landed more cheaply and safely than slower jet airplanes, the rocket may ultimately win out. But not, by present signs, within 150 years.

A distinct innovation in recreational activity that is very likely to be seen in the next 150 years is the envelopment of parts of the under-developed regions in Western forms of recreation by means of public-recreation scholarships. Such will be offered in order that equipment, facilities and group activities may be observed as part of cultural exchange programs. Whatever pleases the visitors will later be emulated at home. Japan imported baseball from the United States and a large part of the Western world has similarly learned special wrestling techniques from the Japanese.

No attempt has been made here, it is evident, to evaluate the various forms of recreation touched upon. What is recreation to one man may be a chore, distraction, or waste of time to another. More strenuous and elaborate—and expensive—activities are required by others. In the lives of some persons of great creativity there has obviously taken place a very fortunate fusion of recreation with work.

In general, everything that was once available only to the upper 1 per cent of income receivers and is now available largely to the upper

10 per cent will be available, if desired, to more than half the adult population and to nearly all children.

The Future of Religion

Turning to another quarter of human interest, what is the future of religion amid the developments predicted?

We are in the period, forecast by Condorcet, of the decline of the religions of the Orient, including Christianity and Judaism. Claims to religious revival, obliquely admitting there has been a decline, turn out on examination to be extremely doubtful. They turn on efforts at regrouping by sects and on tentative, often disappointed re-exploration of childhood faith.

The slow decay of the Catholic religion is seen by turning to its center: Italy. There church membership is reported to have sunk to 20 per cent of the adult population, mainly women and southern peasants. Very nearly half the population is militantly anti-Church and supports the Communist and Socialist parties without fully understanding their basic programs. The anti-clericalism of these parties is one of their prime attractions. Although the outward forms of the Catholic religion are maintained in Spain and Portugal, with state aid, the same potential hostility lies just below the surface among large masses as was shown during the civil war in Spain. Anti-clericalism continues strong in France.

The economic center of Catholicism today is in the United States. And here, although the Church no doubt holds a great part of its membership on a *pro forma* basis, there is some overt falling away and much behavioral deviation from Church doctrines. Educated Catholics with small families obviously practice effective birth control.

Protestantism in itself represents a decline of organized religion, dividing itself into more than 200 sects and tending toward the achievement of individual religious outlook, if any. Within Judaism, amongst its three divisions of Orthodox, Conservative, and Reform, there is the same centrifugal tendency.

Church attendance, as statisticians recognize, is no infallible index of religious zeal. Many persons attend religious services, it is known, simply on grounds of expediency—for economic, social, sociable, and political reasons. Not wishing to incur the animosity of true believers, notoriously inimical toward non-believers as history attests, many simply go through the forms of religious belief as protective strategy. What the clergy have to say carries little or no weight with them. The actual number of certifiable religious believers, then, is unquestionably far less than statistics on church attendance and membership indicate.

Different life experiences under diversified modern conditions induce different attitudes toward religion. Among American Catholics the attitude toward the Catholic Church, for example, is very different from the attitude of Italians, Spaniards, Portuguese, French and Latin Americans. To many if not most of these latter the Church is identified with the upholders of traditionalism—landowners and nobility—who not only wrested every farthing they could from their workers but for long successfully opposed industrialization (as in Italy), popular education, the development of science, and the introduction of necessary modern social services. To such the Church, along with its historical allies, is an enemy and it is doubtful that by altering its attitudes the Church will bring many back to the fold. In the United States, however, the Church is identified with immigrants and their descendants, for whom it acted as a helpful political and economic intercessor and guarantor. It did not oppose popular education but now, in a new setting, it established its own school system in rivalry with the emerging public system.

Whereas in Italy and much of Europe the Church is historically associated with denial of individual opportunity and with preaching submission to a harsh social system under which a few obtained undue advantages at the expense of the many, in the United States it is pragmatically identified in the minds of its members as the open door to economic and political opportunity. The reasons for such hold as the Catholic Church retains in the United States, then, are secular rather than religious.

But indifference to religion, both within and outside the churches, is the deepening hallmark of the modern attitude toward religion, both in Europe and the United States.

The broad reason for this is to be found in the slow rise of popular education and the deepening of knowledge along rational lines. Widespread, literal, and profound religious faith is now found only where illiteracy and ignorance prevail, as in India. Increase in literacy, permitting access to information about the mythological character of religion, saps religious faith, as history shows. Man's increasing control by means of advancing knowledge over many of his problems, such as disease, removes another prop. When it is known that there is a specific cause-and-effect relationship in all disability and disease, with the precise cause yet not discovered for some, fear of an invisible and inscrutably punitive Unknown subsides. Rationalism and empiricism then become ascendant over mythologism and mysticism. Dogmatism succumbs to pragmatism.

Religion has long recommended itself even to the irreligious, however, as a means of social control, as a means of frightening the rebellious and recreant into submission. But more effective and rational methods of modifying and controlling behavior are now appearing—not only in the form of education, which relies on cultivated rationality, but of psychology and neurology, which aim at controlling and modifying irrationality by special techniques and chemicals. A tribute to the efficacy of psychology is shown in the fact that many of the clergy now study it for use in their work; psychologists do not reciprocally study theology except as a symptom of psychopathology. While the clergy still insists upon the objective efficacy of the method of prayer, it is noticeable that neither governments nor businesses rely upon it but turn instead to science and technology. If prayer had any objective effect, Soviet Russia could be prayed out of existence by the faithful of the world.

And whereas organized religion was once a social bulwark, it is now emerging, at least in the most popular cults, as a source of burdens and dangers to society. The first of these dangers is seen in its aspect of a fertility cult, stimulating the continuance of a birth rate greatly in excess of the death rate. Such stimulus is seen not only in Hinduism, Taoism, Confucianism, and Shintoism but is evident as recently as 1961 when the highest Roman Catholic authority broadcast appeals for large families. Covert or overt opposition to education by many religions and the substitution of indoctrination for education under the pretense of conducting education constitute another danger. These dangers are causing it to be rescrutinized by many who once defended it on grounds of social utility.

But the main factor in the decline of religious ardor in the future has not yet been mentioned. This factor simply consists of the opening up of the world under modern means of rapid communication and transportation so that all of the major religions are under simultaneous world scrutiny. People are no longer isolated in parochial ignorance. Although common factors can be discerned in all the religions, they are all in conflict with each other in their basic tenets. They do not, as is often sentimentally suggested, worship the same God in different ways. They worship different gods. If it is a fact that God sent an only son, begotten of a human woman, to live and teach among men and there to meet his death, as Christianity in general maintains, then it is a god different from Allah, from the god of the Jews, from the various gods of Hinduism and, indeed, from the gods of all other religions. For none of the non-Christian gods had a son named Jesus.

Not all the religions, then, can be true in their basic tenets, for they contradict each other, not only in this but in many other respects. If we agree, for the sake of argument, that Christianity alone is true, then it is evident that most of the people of the world live in religious ignorance. The question naturally arises in all reflective minds how a benign and all-powerful God could permit this. It is the mutual contradiction of each other by the religions that serves under modern conditions to press the question for all rational minds: is any one of them true?

But while such a question strikes at the heart of organized religion, it leaves natural piety unscathed. Indeed, natural piety may come to be reinforced by broadening and deepening knowledge that reveals the apparently infinite complexity of nature and of natural creatures.

Religious leaders, it is true, will struggle with all the resourcefulness at their command to retain influence over the mind of man. We see this effort, for example, in all religious programs of indoctrinating the helpless young, thereby attempting to determine their future outlook. We see it, too, in all the public warnings against assimilation and mingling with other people and in indirect efforts to prevent assimilation and mingling. Leaders of Judaism, such as Premier Ben-Gurion of Israel, warn particularly against assimilation, by which presumably they mean biological assimilation. But they cannot prevent cultural assimilation, which can only be the prelude to eventual biological assimilation.

Catholic leaders attempt to insulate their communicants by indoctrination and self-segregation, reducing interaction with non-Catholics to a minimum. As part of the effort at self-segregation, they establish in preponderantly non-Catholic countries Catholic institutions for the discharge of every conceivable social and cultural function. But the Church cannot prevent the necessary interaction of its communicants on the basic economic and political levels and on the general cultural level.

The sudden rise of John F. Kennedy, a Catholic, to the presidency of the United States may seem to throw doubt on the contention that the Catholic institutional network hinders interaction between Catholics and non-Catholics and impedes functioning by Catholics. But President Kennedy was never a segregated Catholic. Educated in public schools, the non-sectarian Choate School, and Harvard and London universities, he was in his thinking freed of clerical dominance. As I had occasion to point out a good many years ago, it was not Alfred E. Smith's specific Catholicism but his obvious submission to the clergy that mobilized overwhelming opposition against him in the election of 1928.[4] Although the United States showed in the election of 1960 that it would elect a Catholic, it can be said without qualification that it will never elect an ardent sectarian of any creed. It never has.

Although all the organized religions work to insure their own institutional survival and may, on this and other grounds, be expected to continue in operation for the next 150 years (perhaps slowly continuing to wilt as during the past 150 years), as a very long-term trend religion as we know it appears to be on the way out. Developed out of ingredients supplied by primitive animism, it appears to have passed the peak of its social and cultural contribution and now shows itself as a cultural handicap. It was with this aspect in mind that the Russian Marxists, having taken power in a society of religiously stupefied peasants, launched their anti-religious crusade. Unless China and India take similar drastic action they will never be able to lift the cultural level of their swarms of illiterate, superstitious peasants.

Despite its culturally handicapping character and all organized drives against it, some 1000 years from now, and possibly even 5000 years from now, there will no doubt be many believers in the dogmas of presently organized religion, which involve deeply irrational components. In Europe and North America today there remain, for example, millions of believers in the pseudo science of astrology and in fortunetelling. Any precipitate decline in religion therefore seems extremely unlikely.

It is, to be sure, possible that natural piety will organize around itself some new form of religion, for which there is expressed a need by some. If such a new form of religion emerged it would surely have to incorporate into itself the outlook of science. For if reality in all its complexity is the creation or instrumentality of some sort of god or godlike force, it is clear that the closest and most faithful votaries of the ways of this deity are scientists rather than traditional clergy. In the light of scientific investigation the cosmologies and cosmogonies of all the traditional religions are fantastically false. Any religion, to make itself credible for cultivated minds, would need to base itself upon the most probable truth.

Long in evolving as a patchwork from many disparate sources, the traditional religions may be expected to be long in dying as their practical role diminishes under the erosion of new techniques and insights and the emergence of new types of personalities.

CHAPTER XII

FINAL PROJECTIONS

Before facing broad concluding considerations, at least two dynamic areas, medicine and science, demand some attention.

As I observed earlier, predictions on the future course of science are virtually impossible to make because there is no way of knowing precisely what scientists will discover, either affirmatively or negatively, that will bring about any major reorientation of science. A physicist of the late nineteenth century, for example, had no basis for predicting the sudden fateful rise of quantum mechanics, and none did.

And because science as an institution is now more firmly established than ever before, with more scientists in more countries, science should be more creative than it ever was in the past. It seems certain, then, that there will be more scientific discoveries and inventions in the next 150 years than in the past 150 years.

By examining those areas in which scientists seek to verify their insights, one can ascertain at least what they would like to know, what they are currently accomplishing, and what they have a reasonably good chance of learning. Scientists endeavor to fill in lacunae in the fabric of knowledge, aiming at completeness and consistency of structure. Ideal models of scientific systems are geometry and classical mechanics, wherein complicated theorems can be rigorously deduced from a few initial minor assumptions or principles. But in trying to make his science approximate such a model, the scientist is required to work with theorems he finds embedded in nature; from these he endeavors to extract the initial basic assumptions and principles. Such theorems he seeks to solve, either not knowing the initial principles involved or knowing them only partially, are what are called scientific problems. The theories and hypotheses put forth by scientists to deal with the problems are actually bundles of trial assumptions, all subject to test and all acceptable only as long as they are not proved false. But if all the elementary principles underlying a system can be ascertained then, with the aid of mathematics and logic, one can deduce from them all possible theorems or field problems. Whether any or all sciences apart from classical mechanics will ever achieve such completeness is not, of course, known. But it is the ideal toward which scientists work. Every modest success is a step forward.

Let us, at any rate, first look at medicine, in which the general reader is probably most interested as a result of his direct experience with it, and for most of whose great achievements basic science has supplied the methods and the means.

The Outlook for Medicine

In general abstract outline medicine may be regarded as having the structure of a right circular cone or funnel standing on its point. This funnel is almost as wide as the world at the level of intake of the means of prevention, relief, and cure of disease and bodily malfunctioning, and extremely narrow at the lower level of output or application of means. Although just about everything, including holy water, feather dust, and urine, has been fed into this funnel as a recommended cure in the course of history and continues to be added by quacks and fanatics, scientific method—that is, critical rationality and controlled experiment—has gradually fitted the funnel with a series of internal sieves or filters in the form of standards and accepted procedures to hold back whatever is ineffective or harmful. A few drugs and procedures ancient in origin are still used in medicine but nearly the entire content is recent.

The healer of 1800 or even 1850 and 1900 in his outlook, conceptions, and procedures bore a much closer resemblance to a witch doctor than to the contemporary physician. For it is only very recently that systematized basic research, both into the nature of organisms and of elements and compounds, has vastly extended the range of materials, tools, and methods successfully employed by the modern practitioner.

Scientific medicine, indeed, is hardly more than seventy-five years of age and, in any case, has a much shorter history of wide employment. The medical profession, traditionalist to the core, was always adamantly opposed to any and every innovation. Until well into the latter half of the nineteenth century what was known as medicine was no more than a hit-or-miss lore, mysteriously successful for a few conditions, powerless for most others. Many of its most conscientious prescriptions, it is now known, were positively harmful—as in the free employment of cathartics, bleeding, sweating, prolonged immobility of the ailing and injured, and the chaining of the mentally ill. Until approximately 1900, as James B. Conant has observed, the physician called in on a case was usually merely a helpless witness to a cure effected spontaneously or to the death of the patient. By misplaced zeal the physician sometimes hastened death. It is only since 1900, as Conant justly remarks, that the physician has increasingly come to gain the upper hand in many areas of prevention, relief, and cure. This often awesome power he has obtained from science, and from science alone.

The growing proficiency of the physician, himself usually not a scientist, was made possible only through the elaboration and verification of scientific theory, mainly in physics and chemistry but also in biology and psychology. The single germ-theory of disease propounded by the chemist Pasteur as a result of his researches into the long-familiar but mysterious process of fermentation led to the control or abolition of scores of diseases and to the creation of the subsciences of bacteriology, immunology, epidemiology, microbiology and, eventually, virology. Vaccines and new drugs were found or developed, some of the latter synthetically by the rising science of chemistry, with which to combat minuscule invaders of the human organism. With the specific causes of many infectious diseases known, large-scale preventive measures were undertaken through the agency of government medicine: treatment of water supply, sewage disposal, drainage of pestilent swamps, enforcement of sanitary measures around food supplies and in hospitals and schools, and public vaccination. To all this was added examination of imports and incoming travelers and regulation of food and drug standards.

In diagnosis and surgery too there has been enormous progress on the basis of findings by scientists that have resulted in the creation of hundreds of special instruments, solvents, tools, and mechanisms. To X rays were added metabolic, blood, tissue, and secretion analysis by chemists. The number of mechanisms and gadgets now used by diagnosticians is in fact too great to list here but includes a large array of special lights, the electron microscope, and an assortment of measuring apparatuses.

All avenues thus far successfully explored will, no doubt, be explored more intensively with a view to detecting oversights in methods of preventing or curing still obscure disease conditions. It is a practical certainty that there will be further refinements of known methods of prevention, diagnosis, immunization, and treatment by means of chemicals, surgery, and alteration of environmental conditions. New combinations of chemicals will obviously be brought into play, resulting in greater control over disease and disability.

There is, however, a significant shift in emphasis now in process in the effort of medicine to make itself more effective, a shift that in a very few-score years will very probably induce the medical art to undergo a forward revolution far more impressive than any of its earlier revolutions.

Until the present, it is evident, most of the conditions medicine has coped with have been induced by assaults on and invasions of the human organism originating in the external environment. Bacteria and viruses have invaded. A wide range of accidents, battle wounds, and criminal injuries have torn tissues, broken bones, and injured internal organs. Against all these, recent medicine has constantly refined its techniques by drawing upon basic science.

But now medicine, in consequence of basic research going forward, mainly in biochemistry, is about to be empowered to deal in a wholesale way with organic incapacities internal and congenital in origin. It would be incorrect to suggest that medicine, mainly remedial, is not already in this area. Remedial surgery for congenital defects of limbs, heart, and internal passageways is already well established. But what has been done thus far in such procedures, although ingenious, is very slight by comparison with what very probably will be done in a relatively short period of time.

Basic research now not only under way but apparently nearing early completion bears directly on the three following broad areas of animal and plant life—heredity, maturation or growth, and senescence or the late stages of aging. Viruses and bacteria are included with humans and domestic animals in the theoretical and largely experimentally confirmed framework.

The general prospect is that hereditary potentiality can be altered and patterns of growth rearranged or modified, all in ways favorable to the individual but, let us notice, raising new problems for the group. In other words, what doctors call the "constitutional factor," hitherto fixed, is likely to become susceptible to modification.

Current research (dating in the main from 1953) in a large number of North American and European scientific institutes is so far advanced in deciphering the chemical code of heredity that an announcement of a final breakthrough is momentarily expected.

The "code" in question, believed to be universal or at the basis of all forms of life, determines the form and function of living organisms, which are complexes of chemical processes. Each base or combination of bases constitutes the code for one kind of some twenty amino acids. Life, in other words, is a series of programed chemical interreactions. The code, according to experimentally sustained theory, is contained in the nucleic acids of the initiating egg and sperm. Upon fusion of egg and sperm, cells begin to form and multiply on the basis of the pattern or "instructions" of the fertilized egg for combining amino acids into various proteins. This code or pattern is repeated in all subsequent body cells, extending through embryo, fetus, and developed organism. It is the basis of the individual constitution.

Experiments at Cambridge University have already succeeded in altering with chemicals the base sequence of nucleic acids of the genes in certain viruses that infect bacteria, thus changing the power of viral offspring to carry on the work of infection through a bacterial host.

The main work remaining at this writing is to determine what sequence of bases correspond to which particular amino acids in the code.

As the entire process has been charted in detail, taking note of the specific interaction at each point of development from fertilized egg to completed output of cell-forming proteins, it is evident that research is already well advanced.[1]

Once the entire process of directing growth is fully understood, there remains a vast amount of work to be done in discovering what chemicals, introduced in what way, can modify, accelerate, or retard growth—in other words, favorably alter the genetic programing of plants, animals microscopic and large, and humans. Judging by the gradual step-by-step, trial-and-error progress of science in the past, a full verdict on this research may well take 100 years to attain. We can predict already, however, that a central project of scientific research for the next four or five generations will concern itself with the genetico-chemical nature of life and ways of modifying it. The implications of success in this field—in its way as vast in its implications as the exploration of planetary space—are immense.

Here are a few of the foreseeable effects of a complete genetic theory:

1. If plants and animals can be genetically reprogramed there will be cheaper, more easily attained, and more abundant food supplies.

2. If the hereditary patterns of viruses and bacteria can be reprogramed (as some already have been), then they can be rendered harmless to man and beast.

3. Whether humans turn out to be subject to genetic reprograming or not, one can already forecast that preconceptional analysis of ova and spermatozoa will be required of humans by law in all civilized jurisdictions, just as many jurisdictions now require premarital blood analysis to detect the presence of certain infectious diseases. The aim of such a law would be to prevent the birth of congenital defectives.

4. If reprograming of hereditary patterns becomes possible, a different avenue of development opens. But there remains to be determined how the reprograming is to be effected. As it would evidently be difficult, awkward, or impossible to reprogram individual eggs and sperms, the only recourse would be wholesale reprograming through the gonads. Chemicals would need to be introduced that did their task precisely, without undesirable side effects. On the basis of past medical experience there is no doubt that such undesirable side effects, producing some undesired accompanying result, will at first be seen. The task will then remain of finding ways, if possible, of producing only desired effects.

Many questions remain: Can a hereditary programing naturally effected be modified by chemical means after the birth of the organism, thus affecting growth and development? Can later stages of growth or aging be retarded by appropriate chemicals? If chemical "bullets" can be developed that will favorably alter already patterned cell structures, then people requiring them can absorb them as diabetics now absorb insulin in dosages.

Assuming complete success with all the foregoing over a period of time, we are evidently faced realistically with the sort of situation Aldous Huxley depicted in *Brave New World*. In that novelistic flight the biologists took charge and proceeded to breed certain types of people, being especially concerned to produce vast numbers of functionally stratified docile menials—a biologically determined class society with an ample proletariat. Huxley's, of course, was a malicious projection of the past into a scientifically controlled future. Here it may be noticed that whereas utopias were once envisioned on the basis of optimism it has become the disillusioned fashion, as with Huxley and George Orwell, to project only monstrous utopias, vastly relished by traditionalists who believe nothing can be an improvement on traditional happenstance arrangements.

But complete success in genetic programing would unquestionably produce problems quite different from those foreseen by malicious or disillusioned imaginations. They would be problems stemming, in fact, from perfection. In his history man, it is true, has often abused his powers. He has, for example, deliberately created eunuchs. Even grosser deformities have been deliberately contrived by denying the means of self-development to slaves, Helots, serfs, peasants, and servants. The deliberate effort to keep people from attaining their potentiality is still seen, for example, in white supremacists of the American South. The culturally retarded Negro is then, as the eunuch often was, taunted for the lack of that of which he was forcefully deprived. Similarly, servants who have been taught in rigid class societies to "know their place," which did not include education, have been victims of the same sort of emasculation of man by man.

The perpetrators of the various degrees of such monstrosities from the sultans with their eunuchs to the European nobility with their serfs and servants and the white supremacists with their Negro field hands have, however, been invariably physically strong and socially dominant but mentally simple-minded and thoroughly ignorant. The new techniques under discussion, however, are under the jurisdiction of the most informed and subtle minds. They need for their application highly skilled and educated technicians. Moreover, as the application of these techniques cannot be confined to a small, conspiratorial class, they cannot be controlled in the service of narrow interests. We can therefore safely conclude that if the means are ever attained, as seems theoretically possible, for the improvement of genetic programing with inexpensive and abundant chemicals, what seems more than probable is that the effort will be made to come as close as possible to producing people with maximum mental and physical potentials.

Complete success would then require a truly revolutionary reorganization of society to accommodate only perfect biological specimens, none of which would be subject to easy ideological or physical victimization by others. But even if such a society were highly automated, there would remain certain routine and relatively uninteresting tasks to perform. Who, for example, would want to tend children, administer households or even larger enterprises, or sit on committees or in legislatures when he could work at higher mathematics, compose symphonies, investigate nature, or attend assemblies of frontier thinkers? In such a society, as yet far from sight, persons would no doubt have to be drafted in a rotation system for relatively routine tasks.

But this sort of purely imaginative prospect need detain us no longer. Short of the perfection of man, the realistic prospect is at least opened to preventing or correcting many gross defectives, thereby lifting the average capability of the population and making accident the chief hazard of man. The prospect is also in sight of producing tissues more resistive to diseases affiliated with aberrant growth, such as cancer. In brief, the scientific foundation has been laid for a science of eugenics as a consequence of which responsible parents may be spared the anguish of contemplating the fate of genetically deficient offspring.

Other prospects in view are:

1. Determining the chemical basis of thought and emotion.

2. Suggesting remedies for emerging ailments traceable to genetic predispositions.

3. Creating elementary forms of life in test tubes for the further study and understanding of life processes, the results applicable to the strengthening of man.

As to the first of these prospects, there will evidently soon be established a science of psychochemistry. Thought takes place in a framework of attention and involves perception of distinctions as well as memory. And memory is now believed by scientists to consist of information or perceptions coded according to genetic capability in giant molecules imbedded in certain brain cells. While memory and perception can be trained, innate capabilities differ according to genetic determination. Judgment, a function of thinking, consists of arriving at conclusions by means rational and emotional. The subjective process of inference, if it is correct, amounts to discerning objective implications. Although the drive to make correct inferences—intense in the logician—is itself basically emotional, the emotions, often volatile, may exaggerate or minimize what is objectively implied.

The emotions are evidently end products of chemical interactions precipitated by environmental factors. Whether there are constitutional or genetic predispositions to emotional distortion remains to be determined. What is now evident is that the chemical processes that produce what we feel as emotional effects have been conditioned or patterned by developmental experience in an environment. They underlie what show in behavior as conditioned reflexes.

It is the present strategy of psychotherapy to determine what experiences produced emotional malfunctioning and to lead the way to a review and re-evaluation of the experiences and to a removal of provocative factors from the patient's environment. Whatever the constitutional factors, they remain fixed.

But a fuller understanding of the chemistry of the emotions should in a relatively short period of time lead to the establishment of psychotherapy supplemented by chemical means. Already in the tranquilizing drugs the means are at hand, although the processes are not fully understood, of bringing anxiety states under control. When there is found the precise chemistry of an emotional disorder, then doctors may treat emotions with drugs the way they now treat many physiological ailments. The disordered soul or psyche, in other words, will be accessible to treatment by chemicals. As to this, it can certainly be predicted on the basis of historical experience that religious fanatics will surely assert themselves to block the chemists and physicians as they have so often done in the past. Whatever tears the veils of mystery is opposed by those with a vested or emotional interest in perpetuating mystery.

A better understanding of the chemistry of emotions should be of enormous beneficial influence on the rearing and education of children, tending to produce a better crop of adults. Already the purely hypothetical and observational approach of psychology, able to deal only with overt behavior and the patient's own reports on his emotional life (as in reports of dreams and their associations), has very much influenced educational methods and the rearing of children at least in the educated middle classes. When more is known of the chemistry of the emotions, genetic and conditioned, paving the way for more direct methods of correction, the results should be spectacular, especially in education.

In the meantime, the efforts of psychiatry in approaching the human psyche from the outside will unquestionably be increasingly emphasized over broader and broader segments of the population. There is the lively prospect, indeed, that the psychiatrists in their probings will some day break through and meet the biochemists in the darkest recesses of the mind.

Mechanical means of counteracting body defects, already in use, will no doubt be extended. Artificial blood vessels have already been added and mechanical substitutes for certain organs may yet appear. Transplantation of tissues and organs is made feasible by knowledge of the hereditary code.

The problem remains of distributing and applying the rapidly accumulating medical means. On this score it can be said summarily that the entire outlook of the American Medical Association in favor of keeping medicine organized as a one-man business on a profit basis will be swept into the discard. What the A.M.A. denounces as "socialized medicine" will be the inescapable outcome. How, a reader may well ask, can one be so confident on this in view of the powerful medical lobby in Congress consisting of business-minded doctors, pharmacists, pharmaceutical manufacturers, the chemical industry, and parallel corporations and financial institutions? What should first be noticed is that the chief impetus for socialized medicine comes not from the outside, but from within the medical profession itself, from research men and the superlatively skilled practitioners who want their findings and skill applied without regard to a patient's ability to pay for services offered within an outmoded system. Individual preventive medicine, for example, is completely outside the range now of most citizens, who have recourse to doctors (if at all) only at the onset of fully developed illness. Again, the accumulating medical means being made available by research scientists increases the dangers for the A.M.A. point of view. For the public, continually bombarded with news of exciting new medical advances, is made increasingly tense by its inability to obtain access to them. Doctors imbued with the A.M.A. ideology appear to many persons to function as obstacles to scientific medical care.

Since the 1930s the A.M.A. has grudgingly yielded on point after point—health insurance, industrial medicine, group practice, public medical assistance for the aged. In the future it must continue to yield as public pressure intensifies, so that its position gradually shifts. Where it succeeds in holding back the means to a more effective application of services, it increases the prospect of being suddenly overwhelmed by long-delayed adjustments effected in an atmosphere of public outrage.

Just what socialized medicine might be like one may gather by looking at one of our most completely socialized institutions—education. If education were organized as medicine largely is today, pupils would be divided into those able to pay tuition fees for profit and those who were charity cases. Except where the latter showed particularly interesting personal problems or unusual promise, they would be denied a wide range of special services available to others. In the process, cultural development would suffer as public health now suffers.[2]

The Future of the Sciences in General

Although biochemistry is at present the discipline of commanding attention in science, as nuclear physics was prior to 1940, research activity is more intense than ever throughout all the sciences.

In physics attention centers in basic research on elementary or subatomic particles, of which more than thirty have already been identified. The atom is no longer, as once commonly throught, the smallest particle in the universe. Again, matter or energy in solid states, long thought to be the basic constituent of reality, has now been supplemented by the concept of anti-matter. A whole new realm of complexity is unfolding below the level of the atom. When, as, and if all the elementary particles are identified and their interlocking behavior understood, there will remain the task of integrating them in a general theory and of determining what, if anything, brings them into existence. In this connection, many questions arise. Instead of being created and standing before us in a finished state "as is" and seeking only to be understood, is the universe really in a process of continual creation? Did this process ever have a beginning in time and will it ever have an end, or is it perpetual? At the moment it all appears reducible in understanding to nothing but motion, change, rhythm, and counterrhythm, waves and disintegrating particles—a storm of particles with some sort of inner rationale.

To the non-scientist science manifests itself only in its applications. While not lacking in interest to the scientist, the applications are of secondary *scientific* importance. For the scientist knows that one sound theory is worth tens of thousands of applications. Television, for example, to the layman a marvelous example of science in action, is to the scientist just a single application of thousands possible by reason of the underlying basic theories and verified experimental findings. In medicine the layman is interested in finding the way of mastering a single disease, such as cancer. The scientist, however, is not interested in any disease at all; he is seeking an overarching theory that may, quite incidentally to his quest, establish human control over hundreds of diseases.

In developing atomic theory, for example, physicists were never interested in producing a bomb. Although this potentiality was known to be present, so were many others. Atomic bombs were developed by governments, who induced physicists to pool their theoretical knowledge with engineers. Some physicists, in fact, were opposed. Had it been in their power, this particular application of atomic theory would never have been made.

As the deep extension of chemistry into current biology and, eventually, into psychology has already been touched upon, this aspect of scientific development need not detain us here. What we can be sure of, however, is that spectacular benefits are in store for man from current research.

There remains the area beyond individual psychology, the social area of interpersonal relations. Here, according to prevalent opinion, science is still in the proto-stage, like Galilean physics, and borders, at best, upon vaguely conceptualized philosophy. Such an opinion, however, can be entertained only by those unfamiliar with recent work in the field.

Work in the social sciences already, in truth, extends far beyond the assemblage of statistical facts and their grouping under various broad concepts. Although much work remains to be done, the social sciences are well on their way to being mathematicized under precise operational concepts. And mathematics has been the logical matrix within which all science has moved forward. Without mathematics there is little coherency, breadth, or penetration in science.

The initial mathematical breakthrough in the social sciences was brought about by John von Neumann, a German mathematician who became a refugee in the United States from the Hitler regime. Although his first publication is dated 1928, his contribution consists mainly of *Theory of Games and Economic Behavior*, written in collaboration with Oskar Morgenstern (Princeton University Press, 1944). In the somewhat misleading concept of games, social interaction in the form of competition and cooperation (or conflict and coalition) is reduced to a mathematical system. The mathematics, as it happens, is also applicable to ordinary games such as chess, checkers, poker, bridge and the like and to a wide variety of inter-personal relations. There may be games between, among and in-side corporations, governments, institutions in general and among in-dividuals. A lawsuit, a political campaign, or the preparation of a meal can be reduced to a game. There can be games played against nature, as in sailing a boat, climbing a mountain, or conducting scientific research. Putting men into space is reducible to games theory.

To date games theory has been applied most thoroughly through the creation of models of games in economics and in management or operations problems. It has important military and intelligence applications. The literature is already large and growing, consisting of primer types of introductory books and advanced specialized trea-tises.[3]

Games theory as it now stands, however, represents no more than a beginning, significant but incomplete, especially when the number of participants under scrutiny becomes very large. Its application within and among societies, however, need not wait until all in-dividuals are included. Hostile and allied governments can be scru-tinized in its framework, with moves and countermoves suggested. Internal institutions are subject to its analysis.

Further development will not only depend, as careful critics dis-cern, on the application of existing mathematics to the problem, but on the elaboration of new mathematics. Science has not only drawn mathematics into its service, but scientific problems have themselves suggested new departures in mathematics itself. Sociology will un-questionably increasingly suggest new mathematical developments.

Games theory presages not only a completely mathematicized so-ciology, but the solution of sociological problems in the most ex-peditious way by means of the high-speed computer machines.

We are brought here directly up against the sphere of mathemat-ics and modern logic, in which latter division a tremendous amount of concentrated effort is going forward in Europe and America. Since the publication in 1854 of George Boole's *Laws of Thought*, logic, particularly in its mathematical and semantic aspects, has been a revolutionized discipline with important innovations of frequent sub-sequent occurrence.

What the impending discoveries may be in logic and mathemat-ics themselves one cannot, manifestly, foretell; for to forecast them would be to know them at least to some extent. But the emergence of games theory and mathematical logic in this century clearly fore-shadows the mastery of not only a great many unsolved social prob-lems but also cultural problems.

Important elements of culture itself, the complex of men's ways of habitually doing, feeling, and thinking, are already open to logico-mathematical formulation, analysis, and critical acceptance or re-jection. Cultures change slowly, it has been noticed, mainly by incorporating additions; but almost everything ever admitted, even in man's earliest days, lingers on even though it may be completely out-moded and muted in influence—witness the retention of astrology in Western culture. Until the present, cultural change has for the most part been unconscious. The new is accepted without discarding the old. Culture, then, is like a rambling house with an attic full of out-moded and broken furniture. Many people prefer to live in the attic.

But such intense logico-mathematical analysis of the natural lan-guages as is now taking place at leading American and English uni-versities indicates that men are beginning to assert conscious mastery over culture itself, a departure far more momentous in human destiny than exploration of space is ever likely to be.

Analysis of language, it is well to observe, carries one deep into the heart of any culture. For whatever man knows, or thinks he knows, he must express in language. He cannot think, correctly or incor-rectly, without language. But language itself is an accumulation from less sophisticated ages when it was shaped by the outlook of simpler and less informed people. It is, consequently, as logical analysis shows, often vague, imprecise, ambiguous, equivocal, muddled, and misleading; it contains much unconscious primitive fantasy, assump-tions, and superstitions fossilized in words, phrases, and sentence structures. At the same time it is highly evocative emotionally.

Through the analysis of language logicians come upon its use in theology, myth, philosophy, literature, journalism, law, politics, and everyday life and uncover vast confusion. Not only are many of the words and phrases employed very slippery and emotionally super-charged, but others refer to unascertainable entities and states of affairs. Many things accepted by people as real because there are words for them turn out to be wishful fantasies or complicated con-structions that block understanding. That such fantasies and con-structions are of human concern is evident from the fact that history reports tens of millions slain in their name. Men have often fought, in fact, over a mere vocal sound without any assured point of reference. Language still contains many such fighting words that are without any clear or agreed-upon reference: liberty, progress, humanity, salvation, security, fatherland.

The point is that everything embedded in a culture is not humanly constructive, that some of it may be harmful if not employed with discretion and understanding. Logical analysis is leading to such understanding and, with it, mastery over cultural creations.

So the course of recent developments with respect to analysis of language points clearly to the possibility, and even probability, of a convergence at some unknown date of a psychology thoroughly mathematicized in chemical formulas with an equally mathematicized sociology and culturology.[4] Even short of such complete mathematicization psychology and logic will converge to produce power over the culture—the relevant fact being that most people throughout the world are uncritical puppets of their respective cultures. When, as, and if the time of full convergence arrives, certain words and phrases known to stir up harmful chemical reactions in the untutored may be barred by law from public discourse the way poisons are now barred from free public distribution. If that seems unlikely it should be noticed that coarse language is already barred by common consent and libelous and slanderous language is barred by law. But the mere fact that a widening circle of the educated knows certain language to be of doubtful objective meaning serves gradually to reduce its incitive power.

C. P. Snow rightly sees the world already split at the top between two cultures, the scientific and the literary. Although many in the scientific culture, insatiably curious, are well acquainted with the literary, the reverse is not true. Most literary people, as well as theologians and literature-oriented philosophers, have little knowledge of even elementary science or scientific principles. What they say of science is usually only a reflection of their ignorance.

A basic difference between science and literature is the way each uses language. In science language is used solely to inform, and is directed solely to the intellect. In literature language is used to stir the emotions.

What is now culturally portentous about this split is that theologians, literary philosophers, and literary artists, styling themselves "humanists," assert exclusive jurisdiction over the realm of human values and the humanization of institutions. Scientists, they contend, are cold, detached, mechanical—"soulless"—concerned only with the quantitative aspect of experience while the humanists are concerned with the qualitative. Not only do the scientists challenge this formulation but they now hold, through the language analysis of logicians, that many of the values upheld are without operative meaning (such as the aspiration for immortality) and even when they are meaningful are accompanied by no indicated effective procedure for their attainment.

While the literary humanist is unquestionably most eloquent in the statement or depiction of human predicaments, all he can offer by way of assuagement is an emotional purgative or immunization. Through our vicarious participation in suffering we may become either calloused or sensitized.

However, the cultural dominance of the literary philosopher and literary artist, as of the theologian, seems slated for a sharp decline. This decline has already been seen in the case of the theologian, is currently under way in the case of the literary or rhetorical philosopher, and is due to take place for the literary artist. All these will be supplanted, steadily and increasingly, by the scientist, the logician, and the science-minded philosopher. And with their loss of dominance there will follow a loss of prestige.

Something of the outcome sought by Plato—the banishment of the poets—will be achieved, but not by decree and not completely. Language analysis, in any case, is undercutting the poet even though most poets now write in prose rather than in verse. The verse form is now in decline.

In this process of cultural analysis the vital elements of the culture will become more and more amenable to critical (that is, scientific) control. Men will become less and less the creatures of the culture, moved by strings of those dead for hundreds of generations and, necessarily, unacquainted with current problems.

The Future of the Judicial Institution

An example of an institution due for radical change through the rising cultural influence of scientific method is the judicial institution. Although greatly reformed in advanced European jurisdictions— Sweden, Norway, Denmark, Switzerland, and England, all far in advance of the United States in this respect—the judicial institution is due in the next 150 years for a radical overhaul in all jurisdictions, but particularly in the United States.

This no doubt seems a strange assertion, particularly in view of the fact that domestic social propaganda stresses the fact that the American judicial process is, if not perfect, at least as close to perfection as the mind of intelligent man can bring it. Such propaganda, emanating from dominant social groups, is conveyed through the newspapers.

The judicial institution in the United States, however, is the most backward of all social institutions, the survivor with very little change of the medieval judicial institutions. The English institution of which it is a copy has, through reform, drawn far ahead of it.

The most severe critics of the prevalent judicial process are found among its leading figures, judges such as Learned Hand, Jerome Frank, Curtis Bok. Lawyers here and there join in the criticism.

The most systematic criticism has been leveled by the late Jerome Frank, for many years a judge of the United States Circuit Court of Appeals, Second District, in his *Courts on Trial* (Princeton University Press, 1949). The chief weakness of our court system in a scientific age, Judge Frank stressed, is its extremely loose and unreliable way of ascertaining the facts, which are the heart of any legal action. The next weakness lies in the assessment of the doubtfully ascertained facts by largely incompetent juries. With the law as applied by the judges, Frank finds little to criticize. But if the facts are not fully disclosed, the final decision cannot be what justice requires.[5]

Although largely ignored by organs of domestic propaganda, Frank's *Courts on Trial*, it may be predicted, is a time bomb that at the appropriate moment will help bring about a thorough reorganization of the fundamentals of the legal process.

Few if any of the methods of the courts for ascertaining truth are employed by scientists. If they were, directors of laboratories would sit on raised daises in black robes, all workers in the laboratories would rise and stand to attention when the director entered, presentations of evidence would be under oath, the persons presenting evidence would be subjected to elaborate cross-examination about their motives, personal habits and the like. If courts were science-minded, as Judge Frank points out, they would greatly simplify their procedures and would employ scientific method in a critical approach to the fact. They would use lie detectors on witnesses, would have the trial record kept on film and tape so that on judicial review the tone of voice and expression of features during trial would be known, and would have only one expert witness supplied from a public panel of certified experts instead of the two contending sets of expert witnesses some of whom at present either lie or depend upon the ambiguities of language to block understanding.

The judicial institution, however, is an example of how long an antiquated and outmoded procedure of society can endure if there is no massive, concentrated, and direct irritation that provokes change. The only fully aware victims of the judicial process are those caught directly in its medieval toils. Those it does not touch directly, the vast majority, are seldom aware of what it is doing to handicap their personal fulfillment.

Penology, ancillary to the criminal division of law, is already long overdue for change to adapt it to modern conditions. The central principle of penology, that for the violation of a rule there must be punishment, antedates even civilization. Punishment is prescribed to deter rule violation, both in the accused and in others. While it may indeed deter some, it does not deter many. For despite punishment the per capita rate of crime in the United States steadily rises.

Punishment for crime, in short, is ineffective, which is one reason it is sure to be increasingly discarded as it has already been discarded in advanced jurisdictions such as Sweden. In its place there will rise into view in the society of the immediate future effective rehabilitation. Punishment will be discarded because it has two evil results for society: it either breaks the spirit of the offender, returning to society a crippled dependent, or it heightens his destructive drive and returns to society a more dangerous person. The record of "repeaters" shows this. Few persons once imprisoned ever turn into anything describable as good citizens. If they merely fail ever again to violate the laws they are successful from the point of view of penology.

The system that will supplant penology will be similar to that now operative in Sweden. After the guilt of the accused has been determined, a board will make a binding recommendation for treatment to the court. This board will have on it a psychiatrist, a sociologist, a penologist, and perhaps one highly educated layman. It will act on the basis of psychiatric tests and sociological background. The prisoner will be segregated from society in a mental institution until he is considered rehabilitated. The sole criteria for release from custody will be ability to function acceptably in society.

The present penal system is in the stage that mental hospitals were when patients were chained to the walls, a procedure now increasingly discarded in favor of methods that obtain the quick return of most patients to a useful role in society. Until recently a person entering a mental hospital stood slight chance of ever being released.

Some of the most dangerous criminals in society at present are those who have spent a considerable portion of their life in jail.

The main reason traditionalists argue for the retention of the penal system and the old-style insane asylums in some American states is that the direct costs are low. Cheap, untrained, and often brutal personnel are used to contain the inmates. The indirect costs to a complex society in life and property, however, are very large. Social safety and true economy both argue for new procedures, which will not be long in coming once the issues are widely and clearly understood.

Cost of Readjustments and Popular Income

A question that has no doubt arisen among realists is where the higher-skilled labor force of the future is going to draw its income. This labor force, as I have predicted, will operate culturally on a much higher level than the present labor force, with perhaps as much as 25 per cent of it on a very high level. There is also the possibility, as I have noted, that external efforts at upgrading through improved and extended education, which is certain to be seen, will be supplemented by biological improvement through the advancing science of genetics.

As very little of the new labor force, owing to automation and social demands for higher services, will be employed on farms or in factories and offices but will be scattered in various routine and highly specialized service occupations, the question naturally arises: what will be the sources of their incomes?

Many current writers appear to believe that the application of automation in a widening circle will either greatly increase profits or lower the price of goods, or will do both. The presumed gain will be at the expense of the displaced worker. But with so many workers displaced, who will have the means to purchase the products of automation?

The answer to this seeming difficulty is simple. There will be little if any relative increase in profits and no lowering of product prices through automation except, perhaps, very temporarily. Not only most but nearly all of the gain from the application of automation is going to be absorbed in taxes. Most of what formerly went to unskilled workers will go into taxes. And what is absorbed in taxes will be disbursed directly or indirectly by government to most of the new service workers, especially to those on the higher levels. These in turn will purchase the products and services of automated industry, in the meantime paying some portion of their earnings in taxes.

Anti-governmental ideologists may see this solution as an indirect criticism of private enterprise. But it is hardly a question of what one thinks of private enterprise. For it is private enterprise which, with automation, is discharging employees. Displaced workers may remain unemployed or be employed by government or employed by other private employers. As the number of prospective new private jobs, even in service industries, cannot absorb all of the displaced labor force, there remains only government as the employer or supporter in idleness. No doubt during the balance of this century many displaced workers, unable to be retrained, will have to be supported. But the children and grandchildren of such displaced workers will be prepared for service employments on high, medium, and low levels.

Although many service employments will no doubt be in the private sector of the economy, particularly for those of low and medium skills, most of those on the level of higher skills will be in the public or governmental sector of the economy. This will be the case because the general public, exercising individual option, would not pay for such services just as a very large section of the present public, if it had its own choice, would not pay for teachers, police, firemen, soldiers, sewage, garbage removal and the like. Social services, it is well to note, must be compulsory and paid for out of the tax fund in order to be fully effective.

Under the new dispensation now tentatively taking form, not only will the productivity of industry be vastly increased but the productivity of the non-industrial portion of society will be increased through tremendous enlargement and refinement of skills. Specialized services now available only to a relatively few, as in medicine, education, recreation, rehabilitation, counseling and guidance, will almost surely be available to all.

That portion of the population unable to fit into service work or into any of the higher employments, if there is any such portion when the biochemists and surgeons are through, will simply have to be carried as social pensioners, paid for out of the general tax fund.

Very possibly as incomes are more nearly equalized (with the pay of top scientists rather than film stars or stockbrokers providing maximum norms), a more effective means of taxation will turn out to be

one on all goods and services. Such a tax would supplement the corporate tax on machine production.

The Tyranny of the Machines

Fear of the machines, now widely expressed, will recede as men
become adjusted to their more or less self-sufficient presence. The
fear is presently somewhat extravagantly expressed that man will in
time be dominated by the machine, made into its servitor. But no
machine has yet been devised that can do original thinking, although
some automation enthusiasts, without offering any evidence, appear
to believe they are possible.

Fear of the machine, variously rationalized, is but an expression of
deep-rooted traditionalism in another form. All the machine ever does
is to disrupt customs and established social forms, none of them
sacred, and to require new ones in their place. So voluminous is the
sentimental propaganda against the machine that people seldom stop
to notice that the machine has never been anything but man's wholly
faithful servitor. No machine has ever wrought deliberate harm unless
directed to do so by man, as in the case of a cannon or bomber plane.
No machine has ever betrayed any expectations of man unless some
ingredient or part supplied by man has proved defective or unless
supermechanical demands were made of it. No machine has ever been
analogous to a Benedict Arnold, Hitler, Stalin, Nero, Caligula or Tor-
quemada. If it is argued that no machine was ever merciful, kind, or
otherwise benign, it is also true that no machine was ever cruel. Machines are as moral or immoral as the men behind them.

Worry over the widening influx of machines comes down in every
case, ultimately, to worry over the loss of spiritually stupefying, relatively easy work tilling the soil, tending a factory machine, or serving
a variety of manipulative machines in an office. Instead of such relatively plentiful work, the new dispensation faces people with the
morally more arduous task of cultivating themselves in order to gain
livelihoods by the use of psychic rather than muscular energy. But
faced with the opportunity to be free of routine muscular tasks, to
deal creatively with many areas of life not susceptible of mechanical
intercession, many men and their leaders appear to be afraid of freedom—and perhaps rightly, for in such freedom there will be greater
personal responsibility of the kind now lacking in field, factory, and

office. When things go wrong in these quarters there is always Nature, employers, or the social system to blame rather than oneself.

A great difference between the near-looming future and the past is that in the past it was thought merely desirable that one develop the mind, if one could and if one so desired; while in the future it will be socially necessary to do so or perish collectively. The only societies that have a chance of surviving will be those that proceed with their development of potential brainpower the way industrial societies now develop their soil and mineral resources. Brainpower is the most undeveloped natural resource in the world today. Backwardness or dilatoriness in the development of this brainpower, as other societies exploit it, will be equivalent to gradual extinction.

Science versus Politics, and the Future

In the past persons seeking rapid social and cultural change have looked to politics to take the initiative. In the light of history, however, the initiative in forcing the pace of change obviously lies with science, education, and technology, in about that order. Politics can be no more than the handmaiden of change, and will be so increasingly in the future. It may, it is true, shape change to some extent. But for the most part all it can do is to formalize change that has already taken place or attempt, futilely in the long run, to block it. The limitations on the ability of politics to produce change are nowhere better shown to view than in the Soviet Union, which has given the most emphasis of any polity in history to politics as the instrument of change. After forty-five years of intense effort, largely in expanding basic industrialization and building military power, the Soviet Union has been unable to modernize either its agriculture or the popular standard of consumption. It has been unable to produce for its people a broad spectrum of civil rights, in which respect it does not rise above the Czarist level.

No attempt has been made in the course of this study to predict specific transitory situations of the future, a fact that some readers may have attributed to simple inability to do so on the theory that the future is absolutely opaque. But while it is true that political prediction cannot go so far as to name the parties and heads of government 50 and 100 years from now, it can list and weigh the probabilities relative to types of government and government leaders.

In a lull, usually following great formalized changes, the successful political leader is the one who merely attempts to hold the new *status quo* stable, without embarking on any ambitious new projects in readjustment. As the period the world is now in is obviously one of great change, political leaders of the hold-the-line type, although they may bob up here and there for brief periods, will not be successful.

Another type of political leader attempts to resist change and even to restore earlier conditions. But no restorations or political holding operations in history have ever succeeded. None has ever been more than temporary, a matter of a few decades at most. In the meantime, the underlying society has decayed. When change has finally forced its way to the surface, it has invariably been explosive and destructive. Securely entrenched traditionalism has invariably been the great guarantor of eventual explosive upheaval—as in the cases of the Holy Roman, French, Chinese, Turkish, Austrian, and Russian empires— or of slow decay as in Spain, Portugal, and pre-British India. The successors to such regimes have been regarded as the great destroyers, but the major collaborators in the work of destruction have been the traditionalists.

A third type of political leader—flexible, acutely sensitive to the currents of change around him—attempts to adapt his policy to the need for adjustment, to supply new political forms within which change can be accommodated in orderly fashion. This kind of leader is usually hated by traditionalists and the protagonists of abrupt change alike. In the next 150 years only this type of leader will have successful administrations. Mere willingness to accommodate oneself to change is not sufficient, as the example of Soviet Russia dramatically illustrates. The accommodation chosen must be effective in the context, not according to some a priori doctrine.

As there has always been cultural and social change, why is it not a fact, in the light of the above, that only political adapters have been successful? History, in fact, shows a long line of relative successes for mere standpatters. The reason is not hard to find. In the past political adapters, while useful and successful at various junctures, have not been so needed as they are at present and as they will be in the future *because the tempo of change in the past has been much slower than it is now*. We live in a time of very rapid change because the pace of change is determined by high-speed technology and the compounding basic discoveries of science. Change in the immediate future, owing to the presence of these two factors, will be greater than ever before, requiring the presence of adaptable political leaders if disorganization, internal or external in origin, is not to result.

So much change, indeed, is impending—much of it sketched in this study—that one cannot see any approximate date of future cultural and social stability. When will there be a pause of the kind often seen historically after a time of great change? When will the chain of changes set into motion by the Industrial Revolution and its many later refinements come to an end? One cannot tell, for lack of any evidence. In modern times change, instead of slackening its pace, appears always to be gathering new momentum.

Obstacles and Variant Courses of Change

General nuclear war, as I stated much earlier, would nullify all these predictions. But the possibility of general war has been ruled out of consideration because it would, assuming full use of the new weapons, nullify everything else as well.

But, short of war, various modifications of the predicted outcomes are possible.

The mere accumulation of ever more powerful armaments will alone act as a brake on many of the predicted changes, delaying their full realization. For the armaments accumulation has the effect of diverting materials, energy, and talents from figuring in many needed adjustments. This fact is very apparent in Russia, where the concentration on arms production retards the development of agriculture and the entire consumer-goods economy, including the construction of housing, schools, roads, railroads, and pipelines.

Were the armaments race brought under effective control, social and cultural adjustment in Russia, Europe, and North America would unquestionably be accelerated in directions outlined in this study.

What can one say about the future prospects of reducing and controlling armaments, about which so much is said and so little done? The problem here is basically not one of armaments, which are but the expression of existing social and cultural patterns given concrete utterance in ideologies. Armaments are the shadow, vastly magnified by science and technology, of the troubled past in the present and extending over into the future. They are a remainder of tribalism, expressed in the modern context as nationalism.

On the subject of limiting armaments until the distant day when nationalism is culturally stripped of value one can only say that some quantitative limitation is manifestly possible. That devaluation of nationalism itself is possible, however, is shown by the action of Europe in uniting under the pressure of doom threatened by the rising power of Soviet Russia.

But considering the difficulty of integrating the extremely doctrinaire social systems of Russia and China with the more flexible ones of Europe and North America and thus striking at the foundations of nationalism, it appears highly probable that the world for some indeterminate time to come must stagger along under the burden of armaments. While temporarily reinforcing traditionalism by impeding needed adjustments, huge armaments in the long run have the effect of undermining traditionalism by sapping the economic sources of its maintenance.

Public apathy, inertia, and the force of traditionalism, cultural and social, remain as further blocks to change. But apathy and inertia are always quickly dispelled by crises, the potential number of which in contemporary society is very great. And by what is practically a law of history, traditionalism in the end must always yield, either gracefully, sullenly or, eventually, by force. And just how quickly traditionalism can be discarded and bypassed under pressure has been shown by Western Europe since 1945.

The reduction of armaments, as I have noted, will permit many of the necessary readjustments to take place sooner than if the piling up of armaments continues. Another factor that would, if it came into play, accelerate readjustment would be liberalization of the Russian political system in the direction of according civil rights to the Russian people and restoring to them some autonomy of enterprise. Choking off enterprise, either by requiring it to be exclusively governmental or private, has the effect of retarding social development by promoting internal disorganization, of which there are many evidences in Soviet Russia.

To forecast positively, however, that there will or will not be nuclear warfare, reduction of armaments, or liberalization of the Russian regime is manifestly impossible. But the many factors of disorganization present within Soviet Russia plus the rising influence of science, technology, and education, argue strongly for the presumption that there must be gradual liberalization if the Soviet Union is to keep pace with Western Europe and the United States in its developmental growth. It cannot come anywhere near its potential by retaining its present prison type of society.

The Perfection of Man

We are brought, finally, to the vision of Condorcet and other eighteenth-century philosophers of the imminent perfection of man, which was to be achieved largely through the spread of literacy. This literacy, it was somewhat naïvely reasoned, would bring into the consciousness of the common man the best of thought and science. Socially applied, these products of high culture would produce only better individuals and, a fortiori, better societies. The human race would become, in all its members, a universal aristocracy.

As anyone can see, this has not happened nor is it in process of happening. On the basis of such evidence as we have available to us, moreover, we can say there is no sign of its happening in 150 or even 500 years.

The term "perfection" is in itself vague. What does it mean? If it means the best potentially attainable, the question arises: the best in what way? Presumably the most perfect man in this sense would be the one who had attained his ideal potential physically, intellectually, morally, emotionally, and culturally. Even expressed in this way we can't be sure of a stable, precise meaning. Of all these perfections, physical perfection would be the most measurable. Intellectual perfection would probably be the next most readily measured. But what norms have we for establishing moral, emotional, and cultural perfection?

But although perfection cannot be measured, hence leaving the concept scientifically worthless, one can substitute for it another term more nearly measurable. Such a term would be "functionally effective."

Although the perfection of man (whatever it may be) has not been attained since the eighteenth century, it is no doubt a fact that there are now, in absolute numbers, more functionally effective people in the world than there were then—functionally effective in social, cultural, and intellectual senses. Proportionately, however, with increased birth rates and the proliferation of hordes of the ignorant, superstitious and diseased, there are very probably fewer functionally effective persons in the world today than there were in the eighteenth century.

Disputes there well may be about functional effectiveness—what functions are most effective and how to measure them. The context has some relation to effectiveness. In some contexts a demagogue is most effective, but only in achieving a limited end. The scope of a function, however, is manifestly a part of its effectiveness, and with this factor involved statesmanship will always be more effective than demagogy.

In general, under modern conditions the most fully educated, the ones with the firmest grasp on a concentration of knowledge, are of greatest functional effectiveness. And within the circle of the educated it is the scientists, the technicians, and the educators (using this term broadly) whose functional effectiveness has the most far-reaching scope. Technicians here refers not only to persons concerned with machine technology but to all those who apply systematic knowledge in the service of man and society.

While the perfection of man may not be in sight, the raising of the general cultural level of the populace in terms of functional effectiveness is not only in sight but must take place unless man is to be overwhelmed by the cultural complexity he has created. And it will almost surely take place with increasing urgency in all of the most advanced societies—that is to say, in the fully industrialized societies. In the superstates in particular—United Europe, the United States, and Soviet Russia—the intensive cultivation of large numbers of functional effectives will be a prime order of business. Until the present, man himself has been the most uncultivated, least developed natural resource—assumed to be a given constant rather than a potential without known limits.

Efforts will no doubt be made, as they already are being made, to develop functional effectives outside the superstate, as in Asia, Africa, and South America. But there great difficulties will be encountered owing to the lack of teaching personnel and facilities. No doubt some will be trained in the superstates and brought home for service. But it is almost a certainty that outstanding talents of Asia, Africa, and South America, if their talents are to have full scope, must function where facilities are available—that is, in Europe, Russia, or the United States. The search for such talents, already keen, will intensify, and it is a virtual certainty that the culturally developed regions will draw them from the less developed regions as they now draw raw materials.

In return, no doubt, they will export lesser talents for the practical application of knowledge. But owing to the suffocating weight of mythology-burdened cultures, the prospect of raising cultural levels significantly very rapidly in Asia, Africa, and South America appears slight.

The law of uneven development, in other words, appears very likely to be as applicable to the world future with respect to producing functional effectives as it has been of the past, although both the depth and the breadth of *rational* cultural development in United Europe, North America, and Soviet Russia will very likely transcend anything hitherto envisaged. The perfection of man in general will, no doubt, for a long time to come be no more than a beckoning mirage.

For many readers Russia unquestionably appears to be the greatest unstabilizing factor in any equation concerning the future. And about Russia just about every judgment has been made within the range of possibility. But whatever else may be said about Russia, it is a stubborn fact that it is culturally, geographically, and ethnically a part of Europe. Invested with its own historical peculiarity, it nevertheless cannot be understood apart from the history of Europe. Its historical relation to Europe is profound; its historical relation to China, India, and the Middle East is comparatively superficial.

The mere fact that it is European, however, is no guarantee of its cooperative behavior. Most of the disruption of the modern world has been wrought by ambitious European powers contending for mastery, to their own undoing. But powerful forces are operating to moderate Russian intractability. A unified China obviously wants to see Russia embroiled with the rest of the West as Stalin desired to see Germany embroiled with England and France. Not only is it doubtful that Russia will accept its own medicine as mixed by Chinese political pharmacists, it is far more likely in the next century that Russia would combine with the West against a bellicose China.

The probability, then, that the predicted course of events will be significantly deflected by a rampaging Russia appears extremely remote. China will have to lift herself to the status of a world power, if lift herself she does, by her own bootstraps, without counting on the Russians to clear the way for her.

The Future of Prognostics

What future can we see for prognostics, the systematic cultivation of social and cultural prediction?

It is practically a certainty, in the first place, that it will in the course of time become a regular university discipline, replacing much of the present overemphasis upon history. The study of history is itself an oblique invocation of prognostics. For the judgments of history can be applicable, if they are to be applicable at all, only to a future. But prognostics itself will be a separate discipline, its methods continuously refined if only because of the vast stakes of huge complex societies in making the best possible judgments about the realizable future.

Governments especially will be interested in prognostics, so much so that they will gather its various workers—statisticians, mathematicians, historians, sociologists and the like—into special bureaus. The United States Government may very well in the course of time house such activity in a Department of Scientific Procedure. Applied science, as distinct from scientific research, is already an integral part of national government. Scientific laboratories, libraries, and data-processing and evaluating units already abound in the Departments of Agriculture, Commerce, Justice, Defense, Labor, Interior, and Health, Education and Welfare. Many of their sub-bureaus are wholly scientific in their personnel, equipment, and methods—the Weather Bureau, Patent Office, Coast and Geodetic Survey, Bureau of Standards, Census Bureau, Office of Business Economics, Public Health Service, Food and Drugs Commission, Geological Survey, Soil Conservation and a truly bewildering jumble of others.

It is the role of them all to make scientific conditional statements of the form "If X . . . then Y"—that is, "If X condition is present, then Y condition will be the consequence"—in their respective areas of interest. Precisely how much of the activity of the United States is based upon scientific judgment it would be difficult to say. Offhand, most people would probably say it is very little. But careful inspection would alter such a conclusion. My own view is that most of the government's long-range policies are affected in some prominent degree by scientific findings, even in areas such as penology, wherein prescientific attitudes are most prominent. Military procedures, as is evident to anyone, are thoroughly saturated with science.

It would be a very short step to coordinating much of this activity in a Department of Scientific Procedure, the duty of which would be to render factual reports to government officials on the probable future effects within certain time limits of present conditions and actions. In economics, for example, such reports are now regularly made. But it is entirely possible, as I hope I have demonstrated, to map much broader future probable prospects. A government department devoted to such an enterprise would, in concert with the universities, be able to produce much more detailed models for different periods.

The advantage in the enterprise would lie in the avoidance of unpleasant and costly surprises, perhaps the avoidance of extinction.

The future of prognostics, then, would seem to be, on the whole, rather bright.

APPENDICES

APPENDIX A

Instead of involving the reader in a long and detailed technical comparison of the nature of statements in the physical sciences and the social sciences it seems best simply to refer to Ernest Nagel's *The Structure of Science*, mentioned in the text. Not only does Professor Nagel's book carefully and admirably distinguish between the kinds of statements and the nature of the evidence for them in both broad divisions of the sciences, showing there is no difference in principle between the two, but it serves to dispel widespread misunderstanding of the nature of science itself, physical and social.

In his book, for one thing, there is adequate recognition of the current world-wide honorific status of science and the identification of science with various models drawn either from astronomy or theoretical physics. In an earlier day the model of science was geometrical. One of many polemical functions of such models is to make invidious comparisons with newer sciences, particularly the social sciences. Such comparisons have as their purpose showing the newer sciences to be incapable of making reliable statements, thereby establishing some form of obscurantism as better or at least on a par in reliability in the making of statements.

Science in its various divisions makes use of a diversity of logical strategies, each suited to the purpose in view. Far from revealing a world more real or more true than the world of daily sense impressions, as some persons seem to believe, what science does is to establish methods of inquiry with a view to solving specific problems, theoretical or practical. Those who take this instrumental view of science do not anticipate that there will ever come a time when science will have attained complete knowledge, a complete picture, about everything. Science is no more than a critical method, ever refining itself, for evaluating evidence from which we may draw more or less reliable conclusions. The deduced conclusions vary in reliability and in scope from science to science.

Other useful supplementary readings on the nature of science are to be found in Phillip Frank, *Modern Science and Its Philosophy*, Harvard University Press, Cambridge, 1950; Quentin Gibson, *The Logic of So-*

cial Enquiry, Routledge and Kegan Paul, London, 1960; Richard von Mises, *Positivism: A Study in Human Understanding*, Harvard University Press, 1951; and Karl R. Popper, *The Logic of Scientific Discovery*, Basic Books, Inc., N.Y., 1959.

APPENDIX B

Comparison of the production figures, continent by continent and counting the Soviet Union as a continent, shows Anglo-America (Canada and the United States) and non-Soviet Europe far ahead in all specifically industrial categories and also in most basic agricultural categories. In combination they leave all the rest of the world far behind—so far behind, indeed, that it must inevitably be a long time before any other continent approaches them in development. In the meantime, United Europe is moving ahead very rapidly.

Anglo-America is first in world production of the following:*

	Per Cent of World Total
Agricultural:	
Citrus fruit	40
Corn	60
Cotton	33
Cottonseed	33
Flaxseed	40
Lumber	50
Oats	45
Wood cut	25
Mineral:	
Asbestos	67
Copper	40
Iron ore	40

* The figures in these tables (fractions omitted) have been adapted from *The World's Nations: An Economic and Regional Geography*, by George F. Deasy, Phyllis R. Griess, E. Willard Miller, and Earl C. Case. J. B. Lippincott Company, Chicago, Philadelphia and New York, 1958. The concept Anglo-America is used by them to refer to Canada and the United States, excluding Hawaii and Puerto Rico. Close study of their comprehensive work will repay those seeking knowledge in greater depth of the world's actual economic position and what is geographically and regionally possible and impossible.

	Per Cent of World Total
Lead	30
Molybdenum	90
Natural gas (consumption)	80
Nickel	80
Petroleum	50
Phosphates	50
Sulphur	50
Zinc	40

Industrial Output:

	Per Cent of World Total
Aluminum	67
Electric energy	44
Motor cars	80
Paper	60
Pig iron	40
Steel	40
Synthetic rubber	75

Communications and Transport:

	Per Cent of World Total
Radios (in use)	50
Railway mileage	33
Telephones (installed)	60

Anglo-America stands second in the production of the following:

	Per Cent of World Total
Area of cultivated land	20
Cement	33
Coal	30
Cobalt	8
Coke	30
International trade	25
Potash	30
Rayon	33
Silver	33
Soybeans	44
Tobacco	22

It holds third place in the production of the following:

	Per Cent of World Total
Barley	20
Bauxite (aluminum ore)	20

Beet sugar	13
Cattle (head)	13
Fish	17
Gold	17
Newspaper circulation (daily)	25
Peanuts	5
Potatoes	5
Swine (head)	25
Wheat	25

Anglo-America is fourth in population, with 8 per cent of the world aggregate, and is fifth in land area, with 14 per cent of the land. It holds fourth or fifth place in the production of wine, graphite, mica, and tungsten. It does not produce any tropical commodities and produces only negligible amounts of olive oil, chromite, tin, and manganese—the latter essential to making steel.

The inclusion of Canada with the United States is justified on the basis of geographical contiguity, cultural similarity, close governmental and military cooperation, traditional friendliness, reciprocal cross-border investment, and tightly intermeshed trade relations. In 1953, for example, the United States took 50 per cent of Canadian exports and supplied 75 per cent of Canadian imports.

The Position of Europe

Europe, excluding Soviet Russia, is first in the production of the following:

	Per Cent of World Total
Agricultural:	
Beet sugar	63
Olive oil	90
Potatoes	60
Wheat	25
Wine	75
Mineral:	
Coal	60
Potash	67
Industrial Output:	
Cement	40

	Per Cent of World Total
Coke	40
Rayon	50
Trade and Communication:	
International trade	44
Newspaper circulation (daily)	38

Second in size of continental population with 17 per cent of world total, non-Russian Europe stands an important second in the production of the following:

	Per Cent of World Total
Agricultural:	
Barley	25
Fish	30
Flax	17
Hemp	40
Oats	33
Rye	40
Silk	5
Swine (head)	25
Wood cut	20
Mineral:	
Bauxite (aluminum ore)	20
Graphite	25
Iron ore	33
Sulphur	25
Tungsten	17
Zinc	17
Industrial Output:	
Aluminum	17
Electric energy	30
Motor cars	14
Paper	33
Pig iron	33
Steel	33
Trade and Communication:	
Radios (in use)	30
Railway mileage	25
Telephones (installed)	25

Non-Russian Europe is third in the production of the following:

	Per Cent of World Total
Agricultural:	
Citrus fruit	13
Corn	10
Lumber	17
Mineral:	
Lead	17
Silver	17

Non-Russian Europe ranks fourth in area of cultivated land, with 17 per cent of the world's total, and fourth in production of cattle (13%), sheep (14 %), asbestos (5%) and chromite (5%). It is seventh in land area, with less than 5 per cent of the world's land, or the smallest of the world's major land masses. It either produces none or only negligible amounts of rice, millet, cotton, jute, abaca, henequen, cane sugar, natural rubber, tea, coffee, cacao, dates, bananas, yerba maté, cottonseed, soybeans, peanuts, coconut products, palm oil, petroleum, copper, tin, manganese, phosphate, natural gas, gold, nickel, molybdenum, cobalt, mica, and synthetic rubber.

Third Place for Russia

Russia, which began its modernization around 1880 (not 1917, as Communist myth has it), runs a poor third to Anglo-America and non-Russian Europe in quantitative economic development, although it is slowly and steadily gaining ground. It is classifiable separately both on political, geographic, and cultural grounds.

Third in land area among the world's major land masses, third in area of cultivated land, the Soviet Union is fifth in population with only 8 per cent of the world's people. The Soviet Union, non-Russian Europe, and Anglo-America together have slightly less than 33 per cent of the world's population.

The Soviet Union stands first in the production of the following commodities:

	Per Cent of World Total
Agricultural:	
Flax fiber	80
Hemp	50
Rye	50

	Per Cent of World Total
Mineral	None
Industrial Output	None
Trade and Communication	None

The Soviet Union is second in the production of the following:

	Per Cent of World Total
Agricultural:	
Beet sugar	25
Flaxseed	25
Lumber	25
Potatoes	33
Mineral:	
Asbestos	14
Gold	30
Manganese	30
Mica	33
Nickel	14
Industrial Output:	
Synthetic rubber	20

The Soviet Union is third in the production of the following:

	Per Cent of World Total
Agricultural:	
Oats	20
Millet	11
Tobacco	10
Wood cut	20
Mineral:	
Chromite	20
Coal	20
Iron ore	17
Natural gas	5
Phosphates	11
Potash	7
Tungsten	17

Industrial Output:
Aluminum	11
Coke	14
Electric energy	11
Paper	5
Pig iron	17
Steel	17

Trade and Communication:
Radios (in use)	7

The Soviet Union holds fourth place in production of wheat (17%), barley (13%), cotton (13%), cottonseed (13%), petroleum (8%), bauxite, copper, and sulphur and is fourth in the circulation of daily newspapers. It is fifth in railway mileage, with 7 per cent of the world's total, but is negligible in international trade, the number of telephones in use, and in the production of rayon, motor cars, molybdenum, graphite, silver, tin, natural rubber, silk, corn, rice, citrus fruits, wine, olive oil, soybeans, and tea.

Although comparing favorably with some of the major European countries in some of the basic industrial categories, the Soviet Union in relation to potential development and in output of finished goods does not show up very favorably. For example, 1950 figures show electric-energy production of 170,100 million kilowatt hours compared with 201,690 million kilowatt hours for only Germany and England as of 1955. As of 1955, Soviet consumption of energy in terms of metric tons of coal per person per year was 2.02 tons compared with 5.34 tons for Norway, 4.87 for the United Kingdom, 4.15 for Sweden, 4.10 for Belgium-Luxembourg, 3.76 for Czechoslovakia, 3.45 for Germany, 2.87 for Switzerland, 2.65 for Poland, 2.44 for France, 2.43 for Denmark, 2.22 for the Netherlands, 2.2 for Austria, and 1.85 for Finland. In Europe only Finland, Hungary, Ireland, Rumania, Italy, Spain, Bulgaria, Yugoslavia, Portugal, and Greece ranked lower.

In steel the story is much the same. In 1955 the Soviet Union consumed steel at the rate of only 225 kilograms per person per year compared with 410 kilograms for Germany, 402 for Sweden, 367 for the United Kingdom, 292 for Belgium-Luxembourg, 249 for Norway, 235 for France, 235 for the Netherlands, and 229 for Switzerland. In Europe only the following nations ranked below the Soviet Union in per capita steel consumption: Denmark, Austria, Finland, Italy, Ireland, Yugoslavia, Spain, Bulgaria, Portugal, and Greece.

Germany and England together, with substantially less population, land area, and natural resources, exceed the Soviet Union in nearly all categories of industrial production, and especially in finished goods and machinery of all kinds.

The comparisons between the Soviet Union on the one hand and non-Russian Europe and Anglo-America on the other are slightly more unfavorable to the Soviet Union here than they are in actuality, owing to the fact that the production of the captive nations of Poland, Czechoslovakia, East Germany, Hungary, Bulgaria, and Rumania belongs to the Soviet Union. European production accruing to the West for its independent purposes therefore needs to be trimmed by small percentages in various commodities, mainly agricultural.

The ominous reason so few finished goods are available in the Soviet Union and the costs of its necessities are so high is that such a great proportion of its industrial production is devoted to the maintenance of an immense military establishment, evidently designed for both further foreign conquests and the internal support of the dictatorship of the Communist oligarchy against a potentially rebellious populace. No other nation requires so much internal police power as the Soviet Union.

Agrarian Asia

Asia, excluding Russian-owned Siberia, is almost exclusively a subsistence-agricultural continent, having relatively little for export. It is second in area of the world's land masses with about one fifth of all land, and is first in population, with approximately one half of the world aggregate. It stands first in area of cultivated land, with about one third of all the cultivated land in the world.

The commodities in the production of which Asia holds first world place are as follows:

	Per Cent of World Total
Agricultural:	
Abaca	100 (nearly)
Barley	30
Cattle	33†
Coconut products exports	88
Date exports	88
Fish	40
Jute	100 (nearly)

† Cattle in Asia are used mainly for draft purposes, seldom for food. Milk and milk products are rarely used for human consumption in China. Two thirds of Indian cattle are not used for anything but are allowed to roam freely as sacred objects, absurdly consuming calories needed by an excessive human population.

Millet	67
Peanuts	75
Rice	100 (nearly)
Rubber (natural)	100 (nearly)
Silk	90
Soybeans	56
Swine	27
Tea	100 (nearly)
Tobacco	33

Mineral:

Chromite	33
Graphite	40
Mica	50
Tin	60
Tungsten	40

Industrial Output	None
Trade and Communication	None

Asia is second in the world production of the following:

	Per Cent of World Total
Agricultural:	
Cane sugar	40
Corn	17
Cotton	25
Cottonseed	30
Palm oil and kernel exports	13
Sheep	20
Mineral	None
Industrial Output	None
Trade and Communication:	
Daily newspaper circulation	30

Asia is third in the world production of the following:

	Per Cent of World Total
Agricultural:	
Banana exports	8
Mineral:	
Manganese	25

	Per Cent of World Total
Petroleum	20
Sulphur	13
Industrial Output:	
Cement	10
Trade and Communication:	
Railway mileage, mostly in India and Japan	13

Asia holds fourth place in the production of citrus fruit (10%), flax-seed (13%), lumber (5%), coal (10%), electricity (7%), pig iron (5%), steel (5%), and aluminum (5%); and in number of radios in use (7%). Most of its industrial output centers in Japan which, however, has insufficient mineral resources such as coal, bauxite, iron ore, petroleum, copper, and the like. Japan employed 4.74 million factory workers in 1954 compared with 1.63 million in India in 1955 and an unknown, but probably not much greater than the latter number in China. Other Asian countries had few factory workers in the 1950s.

Latin America

Latin America, consisting of the entire land mass and islands south of the Rio Grande River, is the next most significant economic region. It stands fourth in land area, fifth in area of cultivated land, and sixth in total of world population with 7 per cent.

It ranks first in the production of henequen, a fiber used to make twine, of which it produces all, cane sugar, coffee, bananas, yerba maté (all), bauxite (50%), and silver; second in the production of cacao, citrus fruit, cattle, petroleum (20%), lead (20%), natural gas, and molybdenum; third in the production of cotton, cottonseed, flaxseed, wine, sheep, zinc (14%), graphite, and international trade; and fourth in the production of corn, tobacco, swine, cut wood, gold, and railway mileage. It ranks below Asia in daily newspaper circulation.

Backward Africa

As to minerals, Africa is first only in the production of gold, manganese (33%), and cobalt (90%). It is second in the production of copper (20%), phosphates (33%), and chromite (30%); third in the production of tin, mica, and asbestos; fourth in the production of graphite; and fifth in the production of lead, zinc, and silver. Cotton is the only major agricultural crop of which Africa has an appreciable production,

11 per cent of the world's total. It produces 13 per cent of the world's coffee and 70 per cent of its cacao. It is strong, however, in the production of diamonds and uranium.

Australia, for the most part a huge desert, is of slight world economic importance and requires no extended treatment here.

APPENDIX C

World Reserves of Coal and Iron Ore

The most widely accepted estimates of iron ore reserves, based on 1926 compilations, are in order of magnitude as follows:[1]

	Millions of Long Tons
United States	10,450
France	8,165
Brazil	7,000
United Kingdom	5,970
Canada (Newfoundland)	4,000
India	3,226
Cuba	3,159
Sweden	2,203
Soviet Union	2,057
Western Germany	1,315
Luxembourg	270
Japan	85
Belgium	70
All others	9,721

China, it is evident, is far down the line unless the recent estimates cited in the text are included.

The most widely accepted estimates of coal reserves are as follows:[2]

	Probable Total Reserves in Million Metric Tons
United States	2,040,640
China	1,100,000
Soviet Union	998,000
Non-Soviet Europe	563,283

Canada	242,400
Union of South Africa	205,682
Australia	139,000
India	20,600
Japan	16,218
Alaska	3,549
Chile	2,116
New Zealand	1,400
Manchuria	1,129

APPENDIX D

There is a massive quantity of evidence to show the ever-enlarging economic role necessarily being played by government in the modern world—necessarily because without the economic presence of government, there would be collapse in various socially necessary sectors. A small part of this evidence is as follows:

In 1952 in the United States the government—federal, state and local —had on its payrolls one out of seven employed American civilians or nearly 15 per cent, and paid $32.5 billion in annual payrolls.[1] The average annual pay of federal employees in 1950, when only one in eight were government employees, was a little better than average pay in the so-called private sector of the economy, $3,221 against $3,015.[2] In 1910 less than 5 per cent of total employment was accounted for by government.[3]

Total output of government and non-government enterprise rose 176 per cent between 1929 and 1950, with government accounting for nearly 15 per cent of gross national product in 1950, largely as a consequence of government expenditures, which rose 396 per cent in the period compared with 157 per cent for the non-government sector. During World War II government purchases of goods and services from the non-government sector of the economy increased to 46 per cent of gross national product, while during the Korean War it rose to 22 per cent.

Private entrepreneurs, it should be noted, were responsible as creditors of the Allies threatened by losses early in World War I for making the United States a party to the round of wars that is stimulating so much rapid change throughout the world. Had the Allies lost, bankers would have suffered huge losses and the United States a financial crisis. It should be evident that private entrepreneurs, in the United States as well as in Western Europe, are primarily responsible, rather than conspiratorial socialists or other dissidents, for provoking the sharp economic upthrust of governments in the Western world.[4]

What is meant here is merely that private entrepreneurs in their various operations often contrive to bring about the conditions, for themselves or others, that provoke government intervention in social defense.

A simple illustration of this from among thousands of possible cases that could be cited is the way real estate speculators built tenements for densely packed humanity, the collections of dwellings quickly degenerating into socially disorganizing slums. Government was eventually, if tardily (for government officials are as lacking in foresight as private citizens), forced to intervene in eliminating slums and substituting better-planned public housing. A more spectacular individual example of intervention was provided by President Kennedy's prevention of a steel price increase of $6 a ton early in 1962 when the steel industry was operating at only a little more than half of rated capacity. Could the steel industry sell at a higher price what it couldn't sell at a lower price? Partly as a consequence of the demands of organized labor, steel had clearly been priced out of the market. The President was severely criticized as having taken dictatorial action. But government, though dilatory, will not forever stand by and watch organized private factions make a football out of an economy unless it is a timorous government that is prepared, for the sake of catering to popular opinion, to see the society for which it is responsible slowly deteriorate.

In 1913 routine governmental expenditure in the United States aggregated $6.4 billion. It rose to $29.8 billion in 1919 as a result of World War I, sank to $9.8 billion in 1929, rose to $43.2 billion by 1945, and stood at $27.1 billion in 1952. Government used $22.3 billion of this latter sum for the purchase of domestic goods and services.[5]

Total expenditures of the federal government including military, which stood at $98.4 billion in 1945 and $65.4 billion in 1952, stood at $71.9 billion in 1958 even though direct military expenditures were then less than half the 1945 figure. Direct military expenditures in 1945 stood at $80.5 billion compared with all other expenditures of $17.9 billion; direct military expenditures in 1958 stood at $39.1 billion and all other expenditures were $32.8 billion.[6] All governmental expenditures in this non-war year were close to 20 per cent of gross national product.

At present all federal government expenditures stand at about 100 billion or some 20 per cent of gross national product.

APPENDIX E

Only the most general indication has been left in the text of the importance at present of large economic units in the American economy. This Appendix gives some of the more precise details, showing how concentrated economic ownership and operation already is in the United States.

In 1957 the fifty largest merchandising enterprises in the country reported total sales of $30.2 billion, 15 per cent of all retail sales.[1] In the same year more than 20 per cent of all retail sales, an overlapping figure, were accounted for by chain-store enterprises having eleven or more outlets.[2]

Retailing is still widely regarded as the stronghold of the small businessman. But in 1954, when the United States had 1,721,650 retail establishments with sales aggregating $169.97 billion, a mere 230,492 corporations accounted for $82.2 billion of sales or approximately 50 per cent. The other 50 per cent of sales was accounted for by 1,203,831 enterprises with individual proprietors, 275,524 establishments under partnerships, and others under cooperatives and other forms of ownership. Department-store sales in the same year amounted to $10.6 billion.[3]

The same sort of concentration of business in fewer and fewer enterprises is also seen in the case of banks. The following table shows the steadily declining number of active banks of all kinds with their steadily increasing total assets in ten-year intervals since 1910[4]:

Year	Total Banks	Total Assets (in billions of dollars)
1910	23,095	22.45
1920	30,139	52.828
1930	24,079	73.46
1940	15,017	80.21
1950	14,666	192.24
1960	14,103	259.187

Approximately 25 per cent of all bank assets were held in 1957 by 588 New York banks, which reported assets of $65.705 billion. Far more than half of all assets were held by the banks of only New York, California, Illinois, Pennsylvania, Texas, and Massachusetts![5]

But more precise figures are available to us for 1955, when the deposits of 13,498 insured banks amounted to $202.787 billion. In that year less than $9/10$ of 1 per cent of all these banks, or only 117, held 45 per cent of the deposits, amounting to $91.535 billion! Eighteen banks, or a bit more than $1/10$ of 1 per cent, held nearly 25 per cent of all deposits in insured banks![6]

The number of enterprises doing business in the United States in 1954 was 4,185,300, seeming to suggest widespread entrepreneurial activity.[7] The number of companies reporting under the Social Security law in 1956 was 3,106,074.[8] But in the same year the United States had only 885,747 *active* corporations filing income reports, representing total assets of $948.951 billion. This was only slightly more than six times the total assets of the 500 leading industrial corporations, which stood at $148.807 billion in 1959.[9]

Farms, like retail business, are still thought by many to be a stronghold of the small entrepreneur. But such an idea is a complete misconception.

In 1950 only 2.3 per cent of farms in the United States together held 42.6 per cent of all farm acreage! And if we consider only 5.7 per cent of all farms, 53.5 per cent of all farm acreage is accounted for.[10]

Since 1920 the total number of farms has been reduced sharply, standing at 4,856,000 in 1957.[11] At the same time the size of farms and the number of farms held by corporations have been increasing. Merely from 1950 to 1954 the number of farms of 1000 acres and more increased by 7.5 per cent; of farms of 500 to 999 acres by 5.2 per cent; and of farms of 260 to 499 acres by 0.9 per cent. Farms of 10 to 179 acres decreased by percentages ranging from 13 to 20 per cent in the period.[12]

Many agricultural and partly agricultural enterprises have their stocks listed on the stock exchanges—the Great Western Sugar Refining Company; Anderson, Clayton and Company; Holly Sugar Corporation; American Sumatra Tobacco Company; Kern County Land Company; etc. Most money-crop farms represent substantial investments that make individual owners rich by common standards. They are really business enterprises.

In agriculture, trade, industry, and finance, as we see, the large enterprises are steadily enlarging. In the forty years from 1919 through 1958 there were 14,164 corporate mergers, averaging 354 a year, of sufficient importance to be reported by Moody's Investors Service and Standard and Poor's Corporation. In 1958 there were 457 such mergers.[13]

Most mergers take place in the class of companies with assets exceeding $10 million. Thus in 1958 no less than 33.7 per cent of mergers were in the $10,000,000 to $49,999,999 class and 33.5 per cent were in the

$50 million and more class. Similar percentages prevailed since 1948.[14]

While the large enterprises, including government and trade unions, are gathering more and more of economic activity into their hands and while the large enterprises themselves are becoming fewer and fewer, the managers and owners of such enterprises are also becoming relatively fewer. Thus in 1959 there were, according to data from the New York Stock Exchange, 12,490,000 individual stockholders in the United States, an apparently good-sized number of persons.[15] But according to a study prepared for the Board of Governors of the Federal Reserve System, no stock at all was owned by 89 per cent of the personal spending units in the United States.[16] A spending unit was defined as consisting of all persons living in the same dwelling and belonging to the same family who pool their incomes to meet their major expenses; a spending unit, then, consists of one or more persons and includes all individuals, adult and minor, dependent and independent, single and married.

Spending units with incomes of less than $1,000, according to the Reserve Board study, were 97 per cent without stock ownership. Stock ownership, in fact, becomes significant only for those with incomes above $10,000 annually, and here the income may be largely from the stock ownership. No less than 43 per cent of the spending units in the $10,000 and up income class owned stock whereas only 20 per cent of the spending units in the $7,500 to $9,999 income class owned stock.

Stock ownership among gainfully employed persons was distributed modestly as follows: 29 per cent of professional and semiprofessional people; 21 per cent of the managerial; 20 per cent of the self-employed, and 13 per cent of clerical and sales personnel. Only 7 per cent of farmers and skilled workers and 3 per cent of unskilled and service workers owned any stock. Evidently most of the gainfully employed, even in the managerial class, do not own stock, according to this Federal Reserve study.

In any event, only 11 per cent of the spending units of the country—families and solitary dwellers—are stockholders, and this percentage accords fairly well with the figure of 12,490,000 stockholders, which comes nearly to 10 per cent of the adult population. (After 1959, owing to speculative fever, the number of stockholders rose temporarily to 17 million in 1961–62).

NOTES

CHAPTER I

1 The large number of books on early metallurgical knowledge put into circulation by the spread of printing is discussed by Cyril Stanley Smith and R. J. Forbes in "Metallurgy and Assaying," contained in *A History of Technology*, edited by Singer, Holmyard, Hall and Williams, Oxford University Press, 1957; Vol. III, pp. 27–71. The importance of printing is usually pointed out by drawing attention to the fact that it led to the dissemination of the Bible in the vernacular tongues; but although this was in various ways an influential development, of as great or even greater concrete influence was the dissemination of early technical and, later, scientific writings. All five volumes of the comprehensive *A History of Technology* just cited show the influence of printed works on modern technical and scientific development. Indeed, the rapidity and spread of technical development since 1500 compared with all of previous history is without doubt due more to the development of the single technique of printing than to anything else. "The Advent of Printing" by Michael Clapham is treated in Volume III of *A History of Technology*.

2 Sir Charles Darwin, "Forecasting the Future," in *Frontiers in Science*, ed. Edward Hutchings, Jr. (New York: Basic Books, Inc., 1958), pp. 114–16.

3 George W. Stocking and Myron W. Watkins, *Monopoly and Free Enterprise* (New York: The Twentieth Century Fund, 1951), pp. 46–47.

4 *Ibid.*, p. 47.

CHAPTER II

1 Quoted in James Harvey Robinson, *Readings in European History*, Vol. I, p. 461.

2 The edition used of Condorcet's *Sketch for a Historical Picture of the Progress of the Human Mind* is that of The Noonday Press (New York: 1955), June Barraclough, trans.

3 Alan Wood, *Bertrand Russell: The Passionate Skeptic* (New York: Simon & Schuster, 1958), *passim.*

4 Ferdinand Lundberg, "Prophets Without Honor: 1914–1934," *The American Mercury* (October 1934), pp. 158–68.

5 Karl R. Popper, *The Logic of Scientific Discovery* (New York: Basic Books, Inc., 1951), pp. 278–81. This book was first published in Vienna in 1934 as *Logik der Forschung*.

6 For an erudite examination of this point see Felix Kaufmann, *Methodology of the Social Sciences* (Oxford University Press, 1944).

CHAPTER III

[1] William Fielding Ogburn, with the assistance of S. C. Gilfillan and Jean L. Adams, "On Predicting the Future," *The Social Effects of Aviation* (Boston: Houghton Mifflin Co., 1946), pp. 32–33.

[2] *Ibid.*, p. 80.

[3] Peter Drucker, *Landmarks of Tomorrow* (New York: Harper & Bros., 1959), p. 48.

[4] Arnold J. Toynbee, *Reconsiderations* (London: Oxford University Press, 1961), p. 4. See also his extended discussions pp. 237–39 and 240, *op. cit.*

[5] New York *Times*, July 31, 1960, p. 51, col. 1.

[6] New York *Times*, September 11, 1960, p. 32, col. 1.

[7] New York *Times*, November 13, 1960, Sec. 4, p. 6, col. 1.

[8] New York *Times*, January 31, 1960, Sec. 4, p. 13.

[9] See A. L. Kroeber, *Anthropology* (New York: Harcourt, Brace & Co., 1948). See especially pp. 8–10, 357, 387, 399–400, and Chapters VII–X, XII, and XVI; and A. L. Kroeber, *The Nature of Culture* (Chicago: University of Chicago Press, 1952).

[10] Ernst Cassirer, *An Essay on Man* (Garden City, N.Y.: Doubleday & Co., 1953), p. 234. Originally published by Yale University Press, 1944.

[11] Leslie A. White, *The Science of Culture* (New York: Grove Press, 1949).

[12] On the play element in culture see A. L. Kroeber, *Anthropology, op. cit.*, p. 357, and Johan Huizinga, *Homo Ludens: A Study of the Play Element in Culture* (reprint, Boston: Beacon Press, 1955).

[13] Various such theories are discussed at length in Pitirim A. Sorokin, *Social and Cultural Dynamics* (New York: American Book Company, 1941), IV. As to cycles of particular phenomena, see Edward R. Dewey and Edwin F. Dakin, *Cycles: The Science of Prediction* (New York: Henry Holt & Co., 1949, with 1950 *Postscript*).

[14] Richard von Mises, *Positivism: A Study in Human Understanding* (Cambridge: Harvard University Press, 1951), pp. 210–11.

[15] H. G. Barnett, *Innovation: The Basis of Cultural Change* (New York: McGraw-Hill Book Co., Inc., 1953), pp. 19–20.

[16] Curtis Bok, *I Too, Nicodemus* (New York: Alfred A. Knopf, Inc., 1946), p. 320.

[17] Barnett, *op. cit.*, p. 56.

[18] An extended analysis of this phenomenon is contained in *Mass Culture: The Popular Arts in America*, writings by many contributors edited by Bernard Rosenberg and David Manning White; The Free Press, Glencoe, Ill., 1957. The term "mass culture" relates to such literature as the detective story, the Western story, and most popular romantic and titillatingly "sexy" fiction—in short, to all that is formally inauthentic or spurious in literature; the comic strip, the cartoon book, mass-media magazines with circulations in the millions and tens of millions; the motion picture, television, and radio in most of their manifestations; popular commercial songs, card playing, sensational and tabloid newspapers, the persuasive type of advertising, and organized spectator sports. The analysts find various degrees of frightening harm and some episodic benefits resulting from mass culture, elevating mass culture itself into a many-faceted social problem. But with this aspect of degree of alleged harm we are not here concerned. All one needs to note is that mass culture at a very minimum is a direct and concrete index of social and cultural apathy, out of which the populace is confusedly precipitated

from time to time by social crises. Here in the United States as this is written we are in a time of relative crisis-free tranquillity when many people believe we have attained a plateau of stability, with everything more or less as it ought to be. From the point of view of this analysis we are merely in a phase marked by illusion-based apathy, soon to be shaken. The apathy itself apparently develops from inability to cope with an overly complex and personally frustrating reality, an inability aided, abetted, and reinforced by the ready availability of mass culture. Were Karl Marx alive today he would within his terms of reference be obliged to say that mass culture rather than religion is the opium of the people.

[19] Some of the more recent encyclopedias contain articles on propaganda and its peril. There is a good, brief treatment of the propaganda problem in Horton and Leslie, *The Sociology of Social Problems* (New York: Appleton-Century-Crofts, Inc., 1955), Chapter III. See also Institute for Propaganda Analysis, *The Fine Art of Propaganda* (New York: Harcourt, Brace & Co., 1939).

[20] See Thorstein Veblen, *The Vested Interests* (New York: The Viking Press, Inc., 1933); Donald C. Blaisdell, *Government Under Pressure*, Public Affairs Pamphlet No. 67 (New York: Public Affairs Committee, Inc., 1946); Stuart Chase, *Democracy Under Pressure* (New York: The Twentieth Century Fund, 1946); Horton and Leslie, *op. cit.*, Chapter 4; and Ferdinand Lundberg, *The Treason of the People* (New York: Harper & Bros., 1954), pp. 67–77, 84–85, 129–31, 136, and 144–45.

[21] Almost every publisher of college textbooks has on his list of publications a book on social problems written by trained sociologists. Two currently more or less standard general treatises on the subject are Paul B. Horton and Gerald R. Leslie, *The Sociology of Social Problems*, Appleton-Century-Crofts, Inc., N.Y., 1955, and Mabel A. Elliott and Francis E. Merrill, *Social Disorganization*, Harper & Bros., N.Y., 1950. While some of the material in such books necessarily overlaps, the treatments usually do not; and different aspects are emphasized by different writers. For additional problems analyzed by individual writers see T. Lynn Smith (ed.), *Social Problems*, Thomas Y. Crowell Company, N.Y., 1956. Nearly all such general presentations of a variety of social problems contain extensive bibliographies of monographic studies on each separate problem. The social problems enumerated here make up only a very partial and extremely general list.

[22] Karl R. Popper, *The Poverty of Historicism* (Boston: Beacon Press, 1957).

CHAPTER IV

[1] For a recent comprehensive report on the chaotic situation in China see "The Famine-Makers: A Report on Why China Is Starving," by Valentin Chu, formerly of the Shanghai *China Press*, in *The New Leader* (New York), June 11, 1962.

[2] Harrison Brown, *The Challenge of Man's Future* (New York: Compass Books Edition, 1956), p. 117.

[3] *Ibid.*, pp. 220–21.

[4] In addition to sources cited in the text of this chapter the following sources of information were consulted: A. M. Carr-Saunders, *The Population Problem*, Clarendon Press, Oxford, 1922; A. M. Carr-Saunders, *World Population: Past Growth and Present Trends*, Oxford University Press, London, 1956; Robert C. Cook, *Human Fertility: The Modern Dilemma*, William Sloane Associates, New York, 1951; Hope T. Eldridge, *Population Policies: A Survey of Recent Developments*, International Union for the Scientific Study of Population, Washington D.C., 1954; Richard M. Fagley, *The Population Explosion and Christian Responsibility*, Oxford University Press, N.Y., 1960; Roy G. Francis, ed., *The Popu-*

lation Ahead, University of Minnesota Press, Minneapolis, 1958; Paul K. Hatt, ed., *World Population and Future Resources*, American Book Company, New York, 1952; J. O. Hertzler, *The Crisis in World Population*, University of Nebraska Press, Lincoln, 1956; Frank Lorimer *et al.*, *Culture and Human Fertility*, UNESCO, Paris, 1954; Fairfield Osborn, *The Limits of the Earth*, Little, Brown and Company, Boston, 1953; Frederick Osborn, *Population: An International Dilemma*, Population Council, New York, 1958; Karl Sax, *Standing Room Only?*, Beacon Press, Boston, 1955; Theodore W. Schultz, ed., *Food for the World*, University of Chicago Press, Chicago, 1945; and L. Dudley Stamp, *Land for Tomorrow; The Underdeveloped World*, University of Indiana Press, Bloomington, 1952.

CHAPTER V

1 These and other similar comparisons are to be found in *The World's Nations*, by Deasy, Griess, Miller, and Case (Philadelphia: J. B. Lippincott Co., Inc., 1958), pp. 630–31.
2 *Ibid.*, p. 884.
3 *Ibid.*, p. 853.
4 *Ibid.*, p. 789.

CHAPTER VI

1 *Statistical Abstract of the United States*, 1959, p. 365.
2 *Statistical Abstract of the United States*, 1958, p. 307.
3 The word "ideology" is employed here in its sense of meaning a counterfeit social philosophy designed, consciously or unconsciously, to mask a special social interest. "The particular conception of ideology is implied when the term denotes that we are skeptical of the ideas and representations advanced by our opponent. They are regarded as more or less conscious disguises of the real nature of a situation, the true recognition of which would not be in accord with his interests. These distortions range all the way from conscious lies to half-conscious and un-witting disguises; from calculated attempts to dupe others to self-deception." Karl Mannheim, *Ideology and Utopia*, Harcourt, Brace & Co., Harvest edition (n.d.). Originally published 1936. Pp. 54–55.
4 J. Frederic Dewhurst and Associates, *America's Needs and Resources* (New York: The Twentieth Century Fund, 1955), p. 487.
5 *Ibid.*, p. 305.
6 *Statistical Abstract of the United States*, 1959, p. 478.
7 *Ibid.*, p. 766.
8 *Ibid.*, p. 764.

CHAPTER VII

1 Edwin H. Sutherland, *White Collar Crime* (New York: Dryden Press, 1949). Professor Sutherland, the late chairman of the department of sociology at Indiana University, was former president of the American Sociological Association. Sutherland's *Principles of Criminology* has been a standard treatise, regularly revised, since 1924, and widely extolled by experts.
2 Although it would be interesting to report Sutherland's findings in greater detail it would be a digression from our theme: future changes in government.

But the facts as gathered by Sutherland relate to a situation government must eventually deal with and resolve. The condition is also treated in works on general criminology by Mabel A. Elliott, Ruth S. Cavan, H. E. Barnes and Negley Teeters, Walter C. Reckless and Donald R. Taft. Special treatments may be found in Marshall B. Clinard's *The Black Market* (1952) and in Donald R. Cressy's *Other People's Money* (1953), a study of embezzlement. Although well known to specialists, these books are little known by the public owing to their being ignored or only lightly mentioned in passing by the newspapers—an instance of our internal "soft" private censorship.

³ For an effective discussion of the technique of slanting and suggestion see Monroe Beardsley, *Practical Logic*, (Englewood Cliffs, N.J.: Prentice-Hall, Inc., 1956), pp. 62–93. For a highly readable popular presentation of the most common logical fallacies, abundantly exemplified in daily newspapers, see *Fallacy: The Counterfeit of Argument*, by W. Ward Fearnside and William B. Holther (Prentice-Hall, Inc., 1959). Another non-technical book that performs a similar service is *How To Think Straight*, by Robert H. Thouless (New York: Simon & Schuster, 1950). See also *Thinking To Some Purpose*, by L. Susan Stebbing (Penguin Books, 1939). For a national news medium that systematically employs the technique of slanting consult any issue of *Time Magazine*.

⁴ The wind of change was shown by a speech delivered by Newton M. Minow, new chairman of the Federal Communications Commission, to the National Association of Broadcasters, in which he caustically arraigned the television broadcasting industry for the alleged low caliber of its programs. New York *Times*, May 10, 1961, p. 1, cols. 1, 2.

CHAPTER VIII

¹ Mortimer Adler, *The Idea of Freedom* (Garden City, N.Y.: Doubleday & Co., Inc., 1958), pp. 586–87 and *passim*.

CHAPTER IX

¹ *American Universities and Colleges*, (Washington, D.C.: American Council on Education, 1960), p. 3.

² Theodore Caplow and Reece J. McGee, *The Academic Market Place*, Basic Books, N.Y., 1958, p. 39. Lesser institutions are referred to by them as "the minor league," "the bush league," and "academic Siberia," the latter a meaning-packed designation coming from two outstanding sociologists (p. 18). The bush league and academic Siberia constitute the vast majority. The universities in the major league are Brown, California Institute of Technology, Catholic, Clark, Columbia, Cornell, Duke, Harvard, Indiana, Iowa State, Johns Hopkins, Massachusetts Institute of Technology, New York, Northwestern, Ohio State, Pennsylvania State, Princeton, Purdue, Stanford, State University of Iowa, Tulane, Vanderbilt, Yale, University of California, University of Chicago, University of Illinois, University of Kansas, University of Michigan, University of Minnesota, University of Missouri, University of Nebraska, University of North Carolina, University of Pennsylvania, University of Rochester, University of Texas, University of Virginia, University of Washington, University of Wisconsin and Washington University of St. Louis. McGill University and the University of Toronto, both in Canada, are also members of the Association of American Universities.

3 In the foreword to Caplow and McGee, *op. cit.*, summarizing the central finding of its field research.

4 Statistical Abstract, *op. cit.*, p. 129.

5 James B. Conant, *The American High School Today* (New York: McGraw-Hill Book Company, 1959), p. 3.

6 Louis Joughlin, "The Present Responsibility of Free Teachers," *Bulletin* of the American Association of University Professors (June 1961), p. 155.

7 Statistical Abstract, *op. cit.*, p. 124.

8 Quoted by Caplow and McGee, *op. cit.*, p. 9, from Charles Horton Cooley, *Life and the Student: Roadside Notes on Human Nature, Society and Letters* (New York: Alfred A. Knopf, Inc., 1931).

9 *Statistical Abstract of the United States*, 1960, p. 104.

10 "The Economic Status of the Profession, 1960–61," *Bulletin* of the American Association of University Professors (June 1961), pp. 110, 114 and *passim*.

11 New York *Times*, December 26, 1960. Associated Press dispatch.

12 Paul Woodring, *A Fourth of a Nation* (New York: McGraw-Hill Book Company, Inc., 1957).

13 Richard Hofstadter and Walter P. Metzger, *Academic Freedom in the United States* (New York: Columbia University Press, 1955); Paul F. Lazarsfeld and Wagner Thielens, *The Academic Mind* (Glencoe, Ill.: The Free Press, 1958); Robert M. MacIver, *Academic Freedom in Our Time* (New York: Columbia University Press, 1955); Andrew D. White, *The Warfare of Science with Theology* (New York: George Braziller, 1955), *et al.* The Lazarsfeld-Thielens study reveals entire social-science faculties modifying their teachings in response to external demagogy.

14 Nevitt Sanford (ed.), *The American College* (New York: John Wiley & Sons, Inc., 1962).

15 This sketch of the educational institution, touching only salient points, may seem severely critical to some; but if they turn to the literature of self-criticism and self-analysis produced in recent decades by a varied group of outstanding academicians they must agree that by comparison it is a very moderate presentation. Critical analyses that ought to be consulted are Jacques Barzun, *Teacher in America*, Little, Brown & Co., Boston, 1945 and *The House of Intellect*, Harper & Bros., N.Y., 1959; Arthur E. Bestor, *Educational Wastelands* and *The Restoration of Learning*, Knopf, N.Y., 1953 and 1955; Robert M. Hutchins, *The Higher Learning in America*, Yale University Press, 1936, and *The Conflict in Education*, Harper & Bros., N.Y., 1953; Howard Mumford Jones, *One Great Society: Humane Learning in the United States*, Harcourt, Brace & Co., N.Y., 1959; Robert Ulich, *Crisis and Hope in American Education*, The Beacon Press, Boston, 1951; George Williams, *Some of My Best Friends are Professors*, Abelard-Schuman, N.Y., 1958; and Paul Woodring, *Let's Talk Sense About Our Schools* and *A Fourth of A Nation*, McGraw-Hill Book Company, N.Y., 1957. See also a classical pioneer study, Thorstein Veblen, *The Higher Learning in America*, B. W. Heubsch, N.Y., 1918. This list is by no means exhaustive nor is it intended to represent every point of view; but it reflects a considerable body of self-critical discontent within education, which alone portends change. Other analyses have been mentioned earlier. Many educators, however, are standpatters and defend current education against every critic as the best possible. If they are right everything is approximately as it should be.

CHAPTER X

1 R. M. MacIver, *Social Causation* (New York: Ginn & Co., 1942).

2 Woodring, *op. cit.*, p. 211.

3 Jerome Frank, *Courts on Trial: Myth and Reality in American Justice* (Princeton, N.J.: Princeton University Press, 1949).

4 *Statistical Abstract*, 1960, pp. 218–21.

5 New York *Times*, July 19, 1961, p. 1, col. 5.

6 *American Universities and Colleges*, 1960, *op. cit.*, p. 23.

7 *Nature and Needs of Higher Education*, The report of the Commission on Financing Higher Education under sponsorship of the American Association of Universities (New York: Columbia University Press, 1952).

8 *Ibid.*, p. 49.

9 *Ibid.*, p. 51.

10 *Ibid.*, p. 52.

11 So extensive has adult education become that the United States Office of Education in 1961 began a study of its scope. According to an estimate by this agency, there are 35 million to 40 million Americans now enrolled in some form of adult education compared with a high school enrollment of 10.9 million and a college undergraduate enrollment of 3.7 million in fall, 1961. Not all persons in adult education pursue academic studies, but an official of the Office of Education said, significantly, that adults were returning to school because "that which they have to live with didn't exist when they went to secondary school and college." It was added, "some persons, such as engineers or doctors, sometimes discover that they have a wide liberal-arts gap in their cultural backgrounds." Paul A. McGhee, dean of New York University's Division of General Education, in the same connection said, as of fall, 1961, that there would be twice as many adults in American classroom study as students in high school and college. His Division alone in 1960–61 had an adult enrollment of 19,000 in 1,334 classes, approximately double the enrollment and classes over 1950–51. This reflects a remarkable increase from an enrollment of 2,272 in 119 classes when the Division was formed in 1935–36. Dean McGhee held technological innovation responsible for the spectacular increases. New York *Times*, August 27, 1961, Sec. 1, p. 60, cols. 3–5.

CHAPTER XI

1 Cited by Karl Menninger, *Love Against Hate* (New York: Harcourt, Brace & Co., 1942), p. 167.

2 *Ibid.*, Chapter VII.

3 Johan Huizinga, *Homo Ludens: A Study of the Play Element in Culture* (Boston: The Beacon Press, 1955). Swiss edition published in 1944, author's foreword dated June, 1938. The work has been characterized by Roger Caillois as "the most important work in the philosophy of history in our century."

4 Ferdinand Lundberg, *The Treason of the People* (New York: Harper & Bros., 1954), p. 116.

CHAPTER XII

[1] The literature is already large, but condensed accounts with charts and models may be studied in the New York *Times*, February 2, 1962, and *Scientific American*, January and February, 1962. Detailed monographs are in *Growth in Living Systems*, edited by M. X. Zarrow (New York: Basic Books, Inc., 1960).

[2] Extensive analyses of medical economics and of the A.M.A. may be found in Richard Carter, *The Doctor Business* (New York: Doubleday & Co., Inc., 1957, now also available in a paper edition); Michael M. Davis, *Medical Care for Tomorrow* (New York: Harper & Bros., 1955); Alan Gregg, M.D., *Challenges to Contemporary Medicine* (New York: Columbia University Press, 1956); James Howard Means, M.D., *Doctors, People and Government* (Boston: Atlantic-Little, Brown, 1953); and James Rorty, *American Medicine Mobilizes* (New York: W. W. Norton, 1939).

[3] A thorough bibliography may be found in R. Duncan Luce and Howard Raiffa, *Games and Decisions* (New York: John Wiley & Sons, 1957).

[4] This awkward neologism is used by Leslie A. White to denote the science of culture analysis. See White, *The Science of Culture*, Grove Press, N.Y., first published, 1949. Pp. 80–86, 116, 404–12, and 415. As to the literature of logico-semantic analysis of language, it is already very large. A few introductory works are: A. J. Ayer, *Language, Truth and Logic* (Dover Publications, N.Y., 1950; revision of 1936 edition); S. I. Hayakawa, *Language in Action*, (Harcourt, Brace & Co., N.Y., 1941); A. J. Ayer (ed.), *Logical Positivism* (The Free Press, Glencoe, Ill., 1959; see the very extensive bibliography for a suggestion of the vast literature) and Bertrand Russell, *The Principles of Mathematics*, Cambridge University Press, 1903, 2nd ed. For a representative spectrum of exemplary essays in the logical analysis of language see A. G. N. Flew (ed.), *Logic and Language*, First and Second Series, (Blackwell, Oxford, 1951 and 1953) and A. G. N. Flew and A. MacIntyre, *New Essays in Philosophical Theology*, Macmillan, N.Y., 1955).

[5] With his daughter Barbara, Judge Frank before his death also wrote *Not Guilty* (Garden City, N.Y.: Doubleday & Co., Inc., 1957), relating a large number of cases of innocent persons convicted and executed on the basis of a fictional structure presented as fact and, owing to the insufficiency of method employed, believed to be fact. Judge Curtis Bok of Pennsylvania similarly deals with miscarriages of justice under present methods in *Problems in Criminal Law* (Lincoln, Neb.: University of Nebraska Press, 1955), and *I Too, Nicodemus* and *Star Wormwood* (New York: Alfred A. Knopf, Inc., 1946 and 1959 respectively).

APPENDIX C

[1] Erich W. Zimmermann, *World Resources and Industries* (New York: Harper & Bros., 1951), p. 627.

[2] *Ibid.*, p. 466.

APPENDIX D

[1] J. Frederic Dewhurst and Associates, *America's Needs and Resources* (New York: The Twentieth Century Fund, 1955), p. 577.

2 *Ibid.*, p. 618.

3 *Ibid.*, p. 577.

4 See Harry Elmer Barnes, *Genesis of the World War* (New York: Alfred A. Knopf, Inc., 1926); Sidney B. Fay, *The Origins of the World War* (New York: Macmillan Co., 1930); and C. Hartley Grattan, *Why We Fought* (New York: The Vanguard Press, 1929).

5 Dewhurst *et al.*, *op. cit.*, p. 578.

6 Statistical Abstract, 1959, p. 364.

APPENDIX E

1 Statistical Abstract, 1959, p. 487.

2 *Ibid.*, p. 833.

3 *Ibid.*, pp. 835, 940.

4 *Ibid.*, p. 437.

5 *Ibid.*, p. 439.

6 *Ibid.*, p. 442.

7 *Ibid.*, p. 486.

8 *Ibid.*, p. 488.

9 *Ibid.*, p. 489.

10 *Ibid.*, p. 619.

11 *Ibid.*, p. 613.

12 *Ibid.*

13 *Ibid.*, p. 500.

14 *Ibid.*, p. 501.

15 *Ibid.*, p. 470.

16 *Ibid.*, p. 471.

INDEX